CW00688067

The Literature of the Irish in Britain

Also by Liam Harte:

CONTEMPORARY IRISH FICTION: THEMES, TROPES, THEORIES (co-edited with Michael Parker)
IRELAND BEYOND BOUNDARIES: MAPPING IRISH STUDIES IN THE TWENTY-FIRST CENTURY (co-edited with Yvonne Whelan)
MODERN IRISH AUTOBIOGRAPHY: SELF, NATION AND SOCIETY

The Literature of the Irish in Britain

Autobiography and Memoir, 1725–2001

Liam Harte

Lecturer in Irish and Modern Literature, University of Manchester, UK

© Liam Harte 2009

All rights reserved. No reproduction, copy or transmission of this publication may be made without written permission.

No portion of this publication may be reproduced, copied or transmitted save with written permission or in accordance with the provisions of the Copyright, Designs and Patents Act 1988, or under the terms of any licence permitting limited copying issued by the Copyright Licensing Agency, Saffron House, 6-10 Kirby Street, London EC1N 8TS.

Any person who does any unauthorized act in relation to this publication may be liable to criminal prosecution and civil claims for damages.

The author has asserted his right to be identified as the authors of this work in accordance with the Copyright, Designs and Patents Act 1988.

First published 2009 by
PALGRAVE MACMILLAN

Palgrave Macmillan in the UK is an imprint of Macmillan Publishers Limited, registered in England, company number 785998, of Houndmills, Basingstoke, Hampshire RG21 6XS.

Palgrave Macmillan in the US is a division of St Martin's Press LLC, 175 Fifth Avenue, New York, NY 10010.

Palgrave Macmillan is the global academic imprint of the above companies and has companies and representatives throughout the world.

Palgrave® and Macmillan® are registered trademarks in the United States, the United Kingdom, Europe and other countries.

ISBN-13: 978–1–4039–4987–5   hardback
ISBN-10: 1–4039–4987–5   hardback

This book is printed on paper suitable for recycling and made from fully managed and sustained forest sources. Logging, pulping and manufacturing processes are expected to conform to the environmental regulations of the country of origin.

A catalogue record for this book is available from the British Library.

Library of Congress Cataloging-in-Publication Data

Harte, Liam.
  The literature of the Irish in Britain : autobiography and memoir, 1725–2001 / Liam Harte.
    p. cm.
  Includes bibliographical references and index.
  ISBN 978–1–4039–4987–5 (alk. paper)   1. English literature–Irish authors.   2. Irish—Great Britain—
    Literary collections.   3. Irish—Great Britain—Biography.
  4. Authors, Irish—Biography.   5. Self in literature.   6. Ireland—
    Literary collections.   I. Title.
  PR8835.H37 2009
  820.8'089162041—dc22

                                                                    2008041047

10   9   8   7   6   5   4   3   2   1
18   17   16   15   14   13   12   11   10   09

Printed and bound in Great Britain by
CPI Antony Rowe, Chippenham and Eastbourne

For my parents, with love

Contents

Acknowledgements

I have been gathering material for this book intermittently for over a decade, during which time I have accumulated many personal and institutional debts. I wish to thank all of those who suggested sources, supplied me with copies of material and provided various kinds of assistance and advice, including: John Burnett (formerly Brunel University), Mervyn Busteed (formerly University of Manchester), Sean Campbell (Anglia Ruskin University), Bernard Canavan (London), Ultan Cowley (Wexford), Patricia Craig (London), Nessan Danaher (Soar Valley College, Leicester), Enda Delaney (University of Edinburgh), Mary Doran (British Library), Patrick Duffy (NUI Maynooth), Roy Foster (Hertford College, Oxford), Thérèse Gorry (Gorry Gallery, Dublin), Breda Gray (University of Limerick), Ruth-Ann Harris (Boston College), Heather Holmes (Edinburgh), Denise Horan (*Mayo News*), Maria Luddy (University of Warwick), Piaras Mac Éinrí (University College Cork), Don MacRaild (University of Ulster), Elizabeth Malcolm (University of Melbourne), Louise Miskell (University of Wales, Swansea), Martin Mitchell (University of Aberdeen), Patrick Maume (Queen's University Belfast), George O'Brien (Georgetown University), Bernard O'Donoghue (Wadham College, Oxford), Paul O'Leary (Univesity of Wales, Aberystwyth), Patrick O'Sullivan (University of Bradford), Lance Pettitt (Leeds Metropolitan University), David Pierce (York St John College), Brendan Rooney (National Gallery of Ireland), James Ryan (Dublin) and Bronwen Walter (Anglia Ruskin University).

I owe a debt of gratitude to the librarians and archivists at the following repositories for helping me to locate material: Bodleian Library, Oxford; Bolton Central Library; British Library, London; The John Rylands Library, Manchester; Mitchell Library, Glasgow; National Library of Ireland, Dublin; Public Record Office of Northern Ireland, Belfast; Trinity College Dublin Library; University of Ulster Library at Magee; Working Class Movement Library, Salford; and St Mary's University College Library, Twickenham, where the research for this book began. I should also like to thank the Bridgeman Art Library for granting permission to reproduce the Ford Madox Brown painting on the cover. The coolly evasive gaze of Brown's shawled subject, cornflower in hand, never fails to detain and absorb me.

Invitations to speak at university conferences and colloquia in Aberdeen, Belfast, Cork, Galway and Montreal stimulated me to sharpen my thinking on the autobiography of the Irish in Britain, as did the responses from fellow speakers and audience members. I would like here to record my gratitude to those who kindly invited me to such events, namely, Oonagh Walsh, Enda Delaney, Dermot Keogh, Louis de Paor and Michael Kenneally.

Warmest thanks are due to Dairmaid Ferriter, Roy Foster, Maria Luddy, John McAuliffe, Bernard O'Donoghue, Murray Pittock and Stephen Regan, each of whom generously took time out from their own writing and research to read and comment on my manuscript. Kevin Kenny was equally unselfish in interrupting his sabbatical to offer his thoughts on an earlier draft of my Introduction. I am deeply grateful to all eight fellow scholars for their invaluable criticisms, insights and suggestions. The text was much improved by their astute and exacting comments, though none of them is responsible for its shortcomings.

I wish to acknowledge the generous financial support of the Arts and Humanities Research Council (AHRC), without which this project would have taken even longer to complete. I am also grateful to the Academy for Irish Cultural Heritages at the University of Ulster for providing me with a subvention to cover permissions costs, and I thank Helen Litton for her excellent work in preparing the index.

The dedication expresses my debt of gratitude to my parents, Tommie and Frankie, to whom I owe more than I can easily say. Last but never least, I wish to thank Yvonne Whelan for her sustaining love, wise counsel and tireless encouragement during the making of this book.

L.H.

The author and publisher wish to thank the following for kindly granting permission to print extracts in this volume:

Elizabeth Bowen, from *Pictures and Conversations* (London: Allen Lane, 1975). Reprinted by permission of Curtis Brown Ltd, London on behalf of the Estate of Elizabeth Bowen. © Elizabeth Bowen 1975.

John Boyle, from *Galloway Street: Growing Up Irish in Scotland* (London: Doubleday, 2001). Reprinted by permission of the Random House Group, Ltd.

J. S. Collis, from *An Irishman's England* (London: Cassell, 1937). Reprinted by permission of A. P. Watt Ltd on behalf of Michael Holroyd.

Elaine Crowley, from *Technical Virgins* (Dublin: Lilliput Press, 1998). Reprinted by permission of The Lilliput Press on behalf of Elaine Crowley.

Peter Donnelly, from *The Yellow Rock* (London: Eyre & Spottiswoode, 1950). Reprinted by permission of Sue Knighton and Jo Slade.

Alice Foley, from *A Bolton Childhood* (Manchester: Manchester University Extra-Mural Department, 1973). Reprinted by permission of the Centre for Continuing Education, University of Manchester.

Dónal Foley, from *Three Villages: An Autobiography* (Dublin: Egotist Press, 1977). Reprinted by permission of Pat Foley.

Patrick Gallagher, from *My Story* (Dungloe: Templecrone Co-operative Society, 1945, revised edn). Reprinted by permission of the Random House Group, Ltd.

Bob Geldof, from *Is That It?* (London: Sidgwick & Jackson, 1986). Reprinted by permission of Pan Macmillan and Hixdell Ltd c/o O. J. Kilkenny & Company Ltd. © Bob Geldof, 1986.

John Healy, from *The Grass Arena: An Autobiography* (London: Faber & Faber, 1988. New edn, London: Penguin, 2008). Reprinted by permission of MBA Literary Agents Ltd on behalf of John Healy.

Desmond Hogan, from *The Edge of the City: A Scrapbook 1976–91* (London: Faber & Faber, 1993). Reprinted by permission of The Lilliput Press on behalf of Desmond Hogan.

John B. Keane, from *Self-Portrait* (Dublin: Mercier Press, 1964). Reprinted by permission of The Mercier Press.

Dónall Mac Amhlaigh, from *An Irish Navvy: The Diary of an Exile* (London: Routledge and Kegan Paul, 1964). © Dónall Mac Amhlaigh, 1964. Reproduced by permission of Taylor & Francis Books UK.

Patrick MacGill, from *Children of the Dead End: The Autobiography of a Navvy* (London: Herbert Jenkins, 1914). Reprinted by permission of Birlinn Limited.

Matt McGinn, from *McGinn of the Calton: The Life and Works of Matt McGinn 1928–1977* (Glasgow: Glasgow District Libraries, 1987). Reprinted by permission of Janette McGinn.

Michael MacGowan, from *The Hard Road to Klondike* (London: Routledge & Kegan Paul, 1962. © Michael MacGowan, 1962. Reproduced by permission of Taylor & Francis Books UK.

Louis MacNeice, from *The Strings Are False: An Unfinished Autobiography* (London: Faber & Faber, 1965). Reprinted by permission of David Higham Associates Ltd.

Bill Naughton, from *Saintly Billy: A Catholic Boyhood* (Oxford: Oxford University Press, 1988). © Bill Naughton, 1988. Reprinted by permission of Oxford University Press.

Sean O'Casey, from *Rose and Crown* (London: Macmillan, 1952). Reprinted by permission of the O'Casey Estate.

George O'Brien, from *Out of Our Minds* (Belfast: Blackstaff Press, 1994). Reprinted by permission of George O'Brien.

Richard Power, from *Apple on the Treetop* (Dublin: Poolbeg, 1980). © Richard Power, 1980. Reprinted by permission of A. M. Heath & Co. Ltd.

Nesca Robb, from *An Ulsterwoman in England, 1924–1941* (Cambridge: Cambridge University Press, 1942). Reprinted by permission of Cambridge University Press.

Michael Stapleton, from *The Threshold* (London: Hutchinson, 1958). Reprinted by permission of The Random House Group, Ltd.

William Trevor, from *Excursions in the Real World* (London: Hutchinson, 1993). © William Trevor, 1993. Reprinted by permission of PFD on behalf of William Trevor.

John Walsh, *The Falling Angels: An Irish Romance* (London: Flamingo, 1999). © John Walsh, 1999. Reprinted by permission of HarperCollins Publishers Ltd and David Godwin Associates.

Every effort has been made to trace and acknowledge copyright holders prior to publication. In cases where this has not been possible, the author and publisher will, if notified, be pleased to amend the acknowledgements in any future edition.

Ireland, Britain and the Channel Islands, showing principal locations
referred to in the text

Introduction: Migration and Autobiographical Authorship

The subject of this volume is a hitherto unexplored body of literature written over a period of more than three centuries: the autobiographies and
memoirs of writers of Irish birth or background who lived and worked in
Britain, whether permanently or temporarily, between 1700 and the present
day. As a written corpus it is fragmentary, eclectic, amorphous, uneven and
obscure. A high proportion of its contents belong to the realms of the out-of-
print and the difficult-to-access, and an unknown number of works remains
unpublished. The spectrum of literary styles, themes, settings and subjectiv-
ities disclosed by these autobiographies is truly kaleidoscopic; to say that it
ranges from the self-justifying memoirs of middle-class Victorian politicians
to the self-effacing testaments of barely literate itinerant navvies does scant
justice to its capacious and capricious nature. Stylish, highly crafted autobiographies by canonical authors such as W. B. Yeats and Elizabeth Bowen
rub up against rough-textured, episodic narratives penned by humble figures
such as Jane Jowitt or Robert Crowe, about whom nothing is known except
for what they reveal in their solitary publications. Differences in aesthetic
value, deriving from disparities in literary ability, ambition and accomplishment, must therefore be acknowledged; imagination, insight, eloquence and
design give power to some works and not to others. In many respects, this
is a literature of outsiderness and exclusion, not only because of the writers'
exilic status and the themes of struggle and alienation their work encodes,
but also because of the sizeable number of plebeian worker-writers encom-
passed by this tradition. The fact that few such writers had the literary skill
to use autobiography as an art form means that critics and canon-shapers
have traditionally dismissed their work as having little aesthetic merit. At
best, 'underclass' authors are condescended to for their literary naïvety and
sequestered under a minor or marginal rubric; at worst, they are excluded
completely from Irish critical surveys and anthologies. In common with the
editor of a recent anthology of travel literature, therefore, I find myself working in an annexe of Irish writing where there is 'no canon against which to
establish an anti-canon, no agreed list of authors against whom one might
respond, and few rules'.[1]

---

[1] Glenn Hooper (ed.), *The Tourist's Gaze: Travellers to Ireland 1800–2000* (Cork: Cork
University Press, 2001), pp. xxvii–xxviii. The most striking recent example of the
critical occlusion of Irish migrant writing is the two-volume *Cambridge History of Irish
Literature* (Cambridge: Cambridge University Press, 2006), ed. Margaret Kelleher and

Nor do the challenges and deficiencies end there. The absence of a reliable bibliographical guide to this literary territory means that the researcher is effectively reading in the dark, with all the excitement and anxiety that entails.[2] Thus, any pleasure that might be derived from uncovering a buried literary gem is soon eclipsed by visions of others lying undisturbed in archives and library storerooms. The prospect of publication merely heightens such anxieties, so that even as I haul my findings into the light, I am troubled by the fact that I cannot offer definitive answers to such fundamental questions as who the earliest Irish migrant autobiographer was, or how many such writers there have been, let alone state with any confidence who their actual or intended audience was. I am not even sure that it is appropriate to label this largely forgotten substratum a 'tradition', since few of the autobiographers under discussion display an awareness of literary lineage or cultural continuity *as migrant writers*. The under-representation of many categories of migrant is a further concern. Hopes of uncovering a hidden body of work by, say, Irish Protestant labourers in nineteenth-century Scotland or working-class women writers in post-war London evaporated as the gapped nature of this literary seam became clear. As it is, male autobiographers significantly outnumber their female counterparts, leaving one to regret the fact that so few Irish nurses left accounts of their migrant experiences, and bemoan the paucity of memoirs by domestic servants, despite their ubiquity in Victorian Britain. Such silences are instructive, of course. Remarks by one domestic servant hint at the material impediments that must have hampered many of her kind: 'My present employers are kind, and I am happy at last; but my readers will understand the writing of my book is second to my work, and the duties attached to my position. If I could have given my whole attention to my story it might have been better.'[3] While working-class male migrants

---

Philip O'Leary, which, for all its excellent coverage and commentary, conspicuously fails to devote a chapter to the literature of the Irish diaspora or any part thereof.

[2] Of the many bibliographical sources I consulted in the course of my research, the following proved most useful: John Burnett, David Mayall and David Vincent (eds), *The Autobiography of the Working Class: An Annotated Critical Bibliography*, 3 vols (Brighton: Harvester, 1984–89); Nan Hackett, *XIX Century British Working-Class Autobiographies: An Annotated Bibliography* (New York: AMS, 1985); Maureen Hartigan and Mary J. Hickman (eds), *The History of the Irish in Britain: A Bibliography* (London: Irish in Britain History Centre, 1986); William Matthews, *British Autobiographies: An Annotated Bibliography of British Autobiographies Published or Written Before 1951* (Berkeley and Los Angeles: University of California Press, 1955). Bernard Canavan's 'Storytellers and writers: Irish identity in emigrant labourers' autobiographies, 1870–1970', in Patrick O'Sullivan (ed.), *The Irish World Wide: The Creative Migrant* (Leicester: Leicester University Press, 1994), pp. 154–69 provided a number of valuable early leads.

[3] Maureen Hamish, *Adventures of an Irish Girl at Home and Abroad* (Dublin: J. K. Mitchell, 1906), pp. 189–90.

express similar complaints about the social, economic and ideological constraints upon their creativity, the following vignette from the autobiography
of Frances Power Cobbe, in which she recalls the circumstances in which she
completed her first book in 1855, underlines the gender-specific dimensions
of the struggle to write:

> At last the proofs were corrected, the Notes verified, and the time had
> come when the Preface must be written! How was I to find a quiet hour
> to compose it? Like most women I was bound hand and foot by a fine
> web of little duties and attentions, which men never feel or brush aside
> remorselessly [...]; and it was a serious question for me when I could find
> leisure and solitude. Luckily, just on the critical day, my father was seized
> with a fancy to go to the play, and, equally luckily, I had so bad a cold
> that it was out of the question that I should, as usual, accompany him.
> Accordingly I had an evening all alone, and wrote fast and hard the pages
> which I shall presently quote, finishing the last sentence of my *Preface* as
> I heard my father's knock at the hall-door.[4]

As an exercise in 'tradition-building', then, mine is a decidedly tentative
one, hedged about with caveats and qualifications. While every anthological
initiative is necessarily selective and representative, this one makes no claim
to comprehensiveness. As the first recuperative survey of a sprawling and
deceptive literary terrain, this volume seeks to open up a largely untrodden
landscape for further exploration; as such, it is more an indication of, and
inspiration to, work still to be done than an act of schematic representation.
By assembling extracts from the works of 63 autobiographers, each shaped
by a specific history, it is not my intention to impose a specious sense of
affiliation and solidarity upon them. The radical contextual differences that
divide them relate not only to transformations in the pattern, volume and
character of Irish emigration to Britain across three centuries, but also to the
changing ratios of power between the two countries, to the development
of autobiography as an art form, and to shifting conceptions of subjectivity
and its multiple determinants. Nor do I wish to overstate the extent to which
these migrants' writings can be subsumed into a discrete subgenre – they are
much too diverse for that. I am, moreover, keenly aware that the designa-
tion 'migrant writer' limits many of these authors' individual achievements,
and that each of these autobiographies might be configured under alternative rubrics to produce different readings. What, then, is the purpose of this
book?

---

[4] Frances Power Cobbe, *The Life of Frances Power Cobbe by Herself* (London: Richard
Bentley, 1894), vol. 1, p. 113.

Certainly, the desire to make visible that which has been rendered absent, as a means of widening the parameters of discussible Irish writing, is one of its primary stimuli. When I began researching this topic, I was struck by the frequency with which the Irish in Britain were characterised as an unliterary people who cleaved more to the spade than the pen. More striking still was the fact that many British-based Irish writers seemed themselves to be in thrall to this characterisation. For example, long-time émigré Dónall Mac Amhlaigh, chronicler of the astringencies endured by many of those forced to emigrate during the devitalised 1950s, observed shortly before his death in 1989: 'When we consider that an estimated million plus Irish people came to Britain to make a living since the founding of the Irish Free State in the early 1920s it is surprising to say the least that the experience of this emigration has not found more expression in literature.'[5] A few years later, the then London-based novelist Joseph O'Connor characterised this deficiency in starker terms:

> Emigration is as Irish as Cathleen Ni Houlihan's harp, yet it is only since the sixties and the generation of Edna O'Brien that Irish writers have written about the subject at first hand. That seems staggering, I know, but I think it is true. It has been taken as read that Exile is an important theme in Irish writing, like The Big House and The Catholic Church. But if it is, it's an inconsistent and entirely intermittent preoccupation. Where are the first-person texts of Irish emigrant life in the latter part of the last century and the earlier part of this? With one or two exceptions – Robert Tressel's [sic] *Ragged Trousered Philanthropists*, say, and the bleak spare poems of Patrick Magill [sic] – they're not there. At the heart of the Irish emigrant experience there is a caution, a refusal to speak, a fear of the word.[6]

The continuing durability of this perception is reflected in a remark by a contributor to a recent special issue of the *Irish Studies Review* devoted to 'Irishness in Britain': 'Irish writers in Britain have tended, on the whole, not to write about their experiences there, gaining inspiration instead, in a Joycean way, from their memories of Ireland before they left.'[7]

This critical anthology is intended to give nuance to such over-easy generalisations by providing a more comprehensive account of the unjustly neglected autobiographical writings of the Irish in Britain than has hitherto been available. While it is true that the great majority of such migrants left no

---

[5] Dónall Mac Amhlaigh, 'Documenting the fifties', *Irish Studies in Britain*, no. 14 (Spring/Summer 1989), p. 7.

[6] Joseph O'Connor, 'Introduction', in Dermot Bolger (ed.), *Ireland in Exile* (Dublin: New Island, 1993), p. 16.

[7] Tony Murray, 'Curious streets: Diaspora, displacement and transgression in Desmond Hogan's London Irish narratives', *Irish Studies Review*, vol. 14, no. 2 (2006), p. 239.

written traces, the work of those who did deserves to be recognised as more than a mere repository of historical or biographical information. That is to say, these autobiographical narratives do more than penetrate the silence that surrounds the undifferentiated mass of Irish emigrants. The best are powerful acts of imagination in their own terms, meditations on how journeys 'across the water' breed strange and unexpected dichotomies, produce new patterns of seeing, living and remembering, prompt different stories about who we are and where we belong. Even the middling, formulaic works, with their peculiarly vivid reflections of personality and experience, deserve better than to be airily consigned to the midden of literary history. In offering us intimate glimpses of interior worlds, these variegated acts of self-portraiture help us to understand better the role the migrant imagination and its witness have played in shaping those fluid, contrapuntal concepts – home, place, belonging – that are themselves cognates of that most labile and vexing of abstractions: Irishness.

This book is also intended as a contribution to the ongoing project of purging any lingering traces of the myth of homogeneity that clings to that diffuse entity 'the Irish in Britain', and the related task of dispelling assumptions that the experience of immigrants was the same throughout England, Scotland and Wales. Autobiography, as many scholars have argued, is uniquely poised to capture the complex, multi-dimensional nature of historical reality, particularly the interplay of the cognitive and affective aspects of experience, as well as the intimate dynamics of self-making and remaking, even though the writing self remains elusive. To the extent that the extracts assembled here convey a striking multiplicity of self-positionings, involvements, beliefs, loyalties, anxieties and affections, they corroborate Antonio Gramsci's contention that autobiography 'has a great historical value in that it shows life in action and not just as written laws or dominant moral principles say it should be'.[8] In these pages we hear the autobiographical voices of labourers and intellectuals, tailors and weavers, nurses and navvies, vagabonds and novelists, prisoners and politicians, journalists and domestic servants, street preachers and chimney sweeps. Some write from a position of almost complete assimilation; others, from a defiantly non-integrated perspective. Individually, they document the specific disposition of one life: the peculiarities of manner, mood and perspective, the daily minutiae of lived social relations. Cumulatively, they depict a highly complex and variable ethnic group, differentiated along the lines of gender, geography, religion, education, occupation, social class and political outlook. Although certain patterns of behaviour and response recur, there is no single, unifying migrant experience to be distilled from these works, nor is there a singular mode in which the

---

[8] Antonio Gramsci, 'Justification of Autobiography (i)', in David Forgacs and Geoffrey Nowell-Smith (eds), *Selections from Cultural Writings* (London: Lawrence & Wishart, 1985), p. 132.

'story' of Irish migration to Britain has been narrated. True, there are many accounts of the pain of terminally sundered families, the unrequited nostalgia of homesick newcomers, and the small solidarities that sustained them in exile; but so too are there upbeat testaments to the exhilaration and empowerment of emigration and the personal hopes and triumphs it can engender. Far from constituting a litany of lachrymose jeremiads, therefore, these richly various testimonies confound dogmatic equations of Irish exile with suffering and victimhood by illuminating the multiple ways of being Irish in Britain. As such, they provide an entrée into what Kevin Kenny has identified as a prime subject for historical inquiry: 'how the diasporic sensibilities of a given migrant people vary according to the places where they reside'.[9] Further, by debunking the stereotype of the expatriate Irish as 'earth-shovelling, hod-carrying automata drowning their sorrows and boosting their joys in pints of porter and noggins of whiskey'[10] in their ethnic urban enclaves, these autobiographies valuably remind us that 'diaspora is constituted as much in *difference and division* as it is in *commonality and solidarity'*.[11]

It must be acknowledged, however, that these works embody the perspectives of an *extra*-ordinary, even idiosyncratic, literate minority of migrants – those who were privileged, fortunate or determined enough to break silence. By the mere fact of putting pen to paper, they stood outside the milieux they described, sometimes exposing themselves to guilt and opprobrium in the process. Patrick MacGill pithily evokes the kinds of psychic tensions that could occur when a navvy swapped his pick for a pencil:

> My success as a writer discomfited me a little even. I at first felt that I was committing some sin against my mates. I was working on a shift which they did not understand; and men look with suspicion upon things beyond their comprehension. A man may make money at a fight, a gaming table or at a shift, but the man who made money with a dirty pencil and a piece of dirty paper was an individual who had no place in my mates' scheme of things.[12]

Dónall Mac Amhlaigh was more forcefully inhibited by the muscular materialism of Irish migrant culture in 1950s England. Although he had written two

---

[9] Kevin Kenny, 'Diaspora and Comparison: The Global Irish as a Case Study', *Journal of American History*, vol. 90, no. 1 (June 2003), p. 162.

[10] Liam Greenslade, 'The Blackbird Calls in Grief: Colonialism, Health and Identity Among Irish Immigrants in Britain', in Jim Mac Laughlin (ed.), *Location and Dislocation in Contemporary Irish Society: Emigration and Irish Identities* (Cork: Cork University Press, 2001), p. 36.

[11] Floya Anthias, 'Evaluating "Diaspora": Beyond Ethnicity?', *Sociology*, vol. 32, no. 3 (1998), p. 564. Original emphasis.

[12] Patrick McGill, *Children of the Dead End: The Autobiography of a Navvy* (London: Herbert Jenkins, 1914), p. 228.

unpublished novels before leaving Ireland, the anti-intellectual ethos of the world he entered made him turn from fiction to furtive diary-keeping during his first decade in England: 'You admired men who could work long hours and earn big money, and it seemed to me that writing and all that related to it was a complete waste of time; it was the stamp of a ne'er do well, a man who had no worthwhile qualities, an idler or a dreamer.'[13] The atypicality of such anomalous witnesses must therefore temper any attempt to make general inferences about the migrant community-at-large from particular texts, even when writers purport to 'speak for' the silent masses.[14] Although singular stories are freighted with shared resonances and implications, personal biography cannot be scaled up into collective history any more than the history of a social or ethnic group can be reduced to the sum of individual experiences. We must remember, too, the myriad purposes that autobiographical statement serves in the lives of these authors. Beneath a shared refusal to let a life's journey pass into obscurity, as if it had no meaning, lie a plethora of tangled individual motivations. Some migrants write out of a primary desire to bear witness, others to correct misconceptions, others still to testify to a life dedicated to self-betterment. A good number of the works discussed here originate in didactic intent. Maureen Hamish, for example, explains that her memoir is 'designed to show the vicissitudes through which Irish women in domestic service have to pass in their efforts to "make their fortune" across the water'.[15] For a feminist philanthropist such as Frances Power Cobbe, on the other hand, life-writing functions as a form of political discourse, her autobiography being 'the true and complete history of a woman's existence *as seen from within*'.[16] Yeats and Sean O'Casey, conversely, privilege self-dramatisation over the production of a reliable record. Such diverse conceptions and uses of autobiography discourage the application of hard and fast theories to this body of writing and demand instead that we attend to textual and contextual specificities. The unique windows these autobiographies open on to the variety and ambivalence of historical experience are seldom as transparent as they might appear.

History, textuality, referentiality

At one important level, then, this anthology seeks to illustrate the multi-layered social realities and changing self-consciousness of Irish migrants in

---

[13] Nigel Gray (ed.), *Writers Talking* (London: Caliban Books, 1989), p. 175.

[14] Roy Foster adds a further note of caution: 'One of the dangers of using "exile" expressions is that we may be generalizing from the aggressively articulate voice of a minority – those who did not emigrate successfully. Listening hard, other voices come through, which strike a new note.' *Paddy and Mr Punch: Connections in Irish and English History* (London: Penguin, 1995), p. 289.

[15] Hamish, *Adventures of an Irish Girl at Home and Abroad*, unpaginated preface.

[16] Cobbe, *The Life of Frances Power Cobbe by Herself*, vol. 1, p. iv. Original emphasis.

Britain over a period of three centuries, as represented in their autobiographical writings. Saying so, however, implies a view of autobiography as documentary rather than textual or cultural practice, yet this volume is not conceived as a straightforward documentary history of the Irish in Britain in the manner of its closest relative, Roger Swift's authoritative and wide-ranging *Irish Migrants in Britain, 1815–1914* (2002). It is not my intention simply to use literary 'evidence' to produce an annotated account of Irish migration, as if these texts were unambiguous vehicles of signification. Nor do I propose to allow autobiographies 'to speak for themselves',[17] since to do so would be to disregard the materiality of language and ignore the fact that they are crafted literary artefacts. Yet neither do I wish to adopt a wholly textual interpretive framework that would undervalue the testimonial dimension of these narratives and the specificities of the 'real', lived experiences that they reconstruct. This is because I regard much of this material as a form of resistance writing through which culturally disempowered and displaced subjects seek to become known autobiographical agents taking charge of their own representation – a case of the written-off attempting to write themselves back into social and cultural history, if you will. Since the process of claiming textual authority is central to this approach, it is important not to allow 'experience' to dissolve into the ether of textuality. But how can one retain a critical, theorised belief in the notion of texts 'reflecting' or 'giving voice' to lived history while simultaneously accepting the validity of compelling poststructuralist arguments about the discursively mediated character of all knowledge of the past? To ponder this conundrum is to enter a highly contested critical terrain where scholars dispute the status of autobiographical 'truth' within the disciplines of both literature and history, and proffer widely divergent interpretations of the relationship between material lives, textual narratives and discursive regimes. It may help to consider briefly some of the key interpretive issues at stake here, especially the problematic relation of life writing to factual truth, as a means of clarifying the critical methodology that informs this volume.

As the earlier-quoted statement by Gramsci implies, much of the cultural and historical value of autobiography lies in its documentary veracity. Certainly, many social historians of an empirical or positivist stripe have traditionally placed a high premium on the testimonial value of working-class autobiographies in particular, the great strength of which, according to John Burnett, is that they embody the subjective, 'unmediated' perspectives of 'ordinary' people.[18] Similar claims have been made for many of the works anthologised here. Joseph Keating's *My Struggle for Life* (1916), for example,

---

[17] Roger Swift (ed.), *Irish Migrants in Britain, 1815–1914: A Documentary History* (Cork: Cork University Press, 2002), p. xxiii.

[18] See Burnett's introduction to his *Destiny Obscure: Autobiographies of Childhood, Education and Family from the 1820s to the 1920s* (London: Routledge, 1994).

has been lauded as 'an unrivalled historical source about the culture and social habits of the Irish in nineteenth-century Britain',[19] a verdict that echoes the plaudits heaped upon MacGill's *Children of the Dead End* (1914) and Mac Amhlaigh's *An Irish Navvy* (1964) for their historical exactitude. In his analysis of post-war migration to Britain, the historian Joe Lee pointedly invokes the superior power of such texts to furnish a more extensive account than the documented historical record of what it felt like to live in – and to leave – mid-twentieth-century Ireland:

> It is to the writers the historian must turn, as usual, for the larger truth. It is they, some themselves emigrants, who best convey the fetid atmosphere of the forties and fifties, the sense of pervasive, brooding hopelessness at home, the emptiness, the uncomprehending remorse, the heartbreak and heroism of many caught in the web of the 'experience of abandonment' as families were sundered and communities withered.[20]

To poststructuralist historians and literary critics, however, the practice of reading autobiography referentially in terms of a putatively objective historical reality constitutes an act of gross theoretical naïvety. As they see it, narrative is constitutive rather than constative, performative rather than descriptive. Such views, it must be said, are not entirely the product of the famed 'linguistic turn' of the late 1960s and 1970s. In 1956 Georges Gusdorf, the father of modern autobiography studies, argued in his seminal essay, 'Conditions and Limits of Autobiography', that since an autobiography 'cannot be a pure and simple record of existence', its significance 'should be sought beyond truth and falsity, as those are conceived by simple common sense. It is unquestionably a document about life, and the historian has a perfect right to check out its testimony and verify its accuracy. But it is also a work of art, and the literary devotee, for his part, will be aware of its stylistic harmony and the beauty of its images.'[21] Contemporary critics such as Sidonie Smith have since reformulated Gusdorf's arguments in more theoretically nuanced terms:

> The autobiographer is the self-historian, autobiography representation. Purporting to reflect upon or recreate the past through the processes of memory, autobiography is always, multiply, storytelling: memory leaves

---

[19] Paul O'Leary, 'Introduction' to *My Struggle for Life* by Joseph Keating (Dublin: University College Dublin Press, 2005), p. xii.

[20] J. J. Lee, *Ireland 1912–1985. Politics and Society* (Cambridge: Cambridge University Press, 1989), p. 384.

[21] George Gusdorf, 'Conditions and Limits of Autobiography', trans. James Olney, in James Olney (ed.), *Autobiography: Essays Theoretical and Critical* (Princeton: Princeton University Press, 1980), pp. 42–3.

only a trace of an earlier experience that we adjust into story; experience itself is mediated by the way we describe and interpret it to others and ourselves; cultural tropes and metaphors which structure autobiographical narrative are themselves fictive; and narrative is driven by its own fictive conventions about beginnings, middles, and ends.[22]

Smith's measured remarks underline the point that since all autobiographical narratives are necessarily linguistically mediated, it follows that clear demarcation lines cannot be drawn between the factual and the fictive aspects of life writing, any more than they can between its documentary and aesthetic aspects. Her thesis is given a further twist by the critic Frank Kermode, author of a lucidly self-reflexive memoir, *Not Entitled* (1996), who opines: 'My belief is that honest truth, insofar as this suggests absolute fidelity to historical fact, is inaccessible; the minute you begin to write it you try to write it well, and writing well is an activity which has no simple relation to truth. For memory cannot do the necessary work independently of fantasy.'[23] Four decades earlier, Jim Phelan was troubled by a similar self-representational conundrum:

> For a teller of tales, a fiction-spinner, such as I have been for most of my life, even before I was a writer, any attempt at a straightforward factual narrative is very difficult indeed. It is so easy, and the temptation is so great, to round off a passage or tidy up an episode, to make a neat story instead of the succession of inconsequentialities which a life-story usually is. Add the fact that I have always tended to dramatise my own existence, as also that I would much rather forget a great many things which have happened to me, and it will be plain that the ordinary difficulties of autobiography are for me multiplied.[24]

To judge from the observations of such practitioners and theorists, then, autobiography is properly conceptualised as an act of language, memory, imagination, even fantasy, but not history. It is a subjective rather than an empirical form, in which the materials of the past are shaped to serve the needs of the present. Autobiographical truth and historical fact are not coterminous, are not one and the same. We change ourselves by narrating ourselves and we narrate ourselves in dialogue with others, whether in

---

[22] Sidonie Smith, 'Construing Truths in Lying Mouths: Truthtelling in Women's Autobiography', *Studies in the Literary Imagination*, vol. 23, no. 2 (1990), p. 145.

[23] Frank Kermode, quoted in Claire Armitstead, 'My Life as a Story', *The Guardian Review*, 27 January 2001, p. 5.

[24] Jim Phelan, *The Name's Phelan: The First Part of the Autobiography of Jim Phelan* (London: Sidgwick & Jackson, 1948), p. vii.

spoken or written forms, such that every autobiography sustains an intricate interplay of factual and fictive elements. Further, self-representation is always governed by prevailing narrative conventions and culturally sanctioned models of identity, the determinative power of which should not be underestimated. Some theorists, indeed, go so far as to dismiss all appeals to extra-textual realities on the basis that language, having no instrumental capacity, can only ever constitute social meaning. Hence Jerome Bruner's claim that an autobiography 'is not and cannot be a way of simply signifying or referring to a "life as lived." I take the view that there is no such thing as a "life as lived" to be referred to. On this view, a life is created or constructed by the act of autobiography. It is a way of construing experience – and of reconstruing and reconstruing it until our breath or pen fails us.'[25] Perhaps it is such ultra-textualist critiques of referentiality that Roy Foster had in mind when he complained that 'The conventions of magical realism and post-structuralist flannel have had a decisive effect on the genre of autobiography: while this can be presented as a liberation from the tyranny of the ascertainable fact, it makes for some confusion as far as the reader is concerned.'[26] Foster has a point here, for despite the poststructuralist attention to discourse as ideological form, many readers still expect referential rather than symbolic truth from autobiographers, if only because, as Rita Felski explains, life writing

> makes claims to historical veracity as the account of part or all of the life of a real individual written by that individual. That this claim can be undermined by exposing the distortions inherent in the writing process or problematizing the very notion of what constitutes 'truth' does not negate the fact that the intention of honest self-depiction is a determining feature of the 'autobiographical contract' which is familiar to every reader.[27]

Although Felski's observation lacks nuance – not every autobiographer enters into this contract in good faith, and some mischievously set out to mislead – it is nevertheless true that until the advent of modernism, most autobiographers had confidence in the representational powers of language to capture a historically verifiable past. Nineteenth-century British working-class autobiographers in particular made special claims to truthfulness, their

---

[25] Jerome Bruner, 'The Autobiographical Process', in Robert Folkenflik (ed.), *The Culture of Autobiography* (California: Stanford University Press, 1993), p. 38.

[26] R. F. Foster, *The Irish Story: Telling Tales and Making it Up in Ireland* (London: Allen Lane, 2001), p. 166.

[27] Rita Felski, *Beyond Feminist Aesthetics: Feminist Literature and Social Change* (Cambridge: Harvard University Press, 1989), p. 90. Cited in Smith, 'Construing Truths in Lying Mouths', p. 147.

narratives being motivated by an amalgam of didactic, political and pragmatic concerns, as Nan Hackett explains: 'Working-class autobiographers
justified their excursion into a literary genre by claiming they wrote social history [...]. They knew that their viewpoints and even the events in which they
had participated would otherwise go unrecorded, and they therefore added
meticulously detailed historical narratives, frequently backed up with quotation from other sources.'[28] The same is broadly true of most working-class
Irish migrants in nineteenth- and twentieth-century Britain, many of whose
autobiographies originate in a sincere desire to leave an accurate historical
record and demand to be read as social history. The testimonial impulse is particularly pronounced in the work of socialist autobiographers such as MacGill
and Mac Amhlaigh, who wished to break free from the cultural and intellectual constraints of working-class life, and in autobiographies rooted in the
Irish oral tradition, the style of which often enhances their claim to authenticity. Reading works such as Patrick Gallagher's *My Story* (1945) and Michael
MacGowan's *The Hard Road to Klondike* (1962), it is difficult not to be seduced
by the manifest sincerity of the lore-bearing vernacular voice and the autobiographical compact between writer and reader, so seamless is the illusion
of identification between the 'I' that writes and the 'I' that appears on the
page. The visceral rawness of John Healy's *The Grass Arena* (1988) elicits a
similar response: 'What we have here is description of the highest order, the
eschewing of all levels of morality and psychology in favour of an ethic and
aesthetic of accuracy – the determination to record what one human being
has observed and experienced.'[29] Yet it would be as naïve to assume that autobiographical candour cannot co-exist with literary artifice as to believe that
a life-story is a wholly reliable account of a person's past. Take Tom Barclay's
Memoirs and Medleys (1934), for example. This engrossing work strikes the
same emotional chord of sincere disclosure as the memoirs of Gallagher and
MacGowan, yet it is composed out of an altogether more astute awareness of
autobiography as studied self-revelation, about which the narrator himself
comes clean in Chapter 6:

> Let no one who may happen to see these things I write imagine that I
> am telling the whole truth and nothing but the truth about myself. I'm
> omitting to turn my worse side towards you, and why not? If I stripped my
> body in a public square I should be arrested and punished, and shall I do
> something as bad if not worse – strip my poor soul naked before you? No;
> I'm no realist: what would be the good of confessing my short-comings,

---

[28] Nan Hackett, 'A Different Form of "Self": Narrative Style in British Nineteenth-
Century Working-Class Autobiography', *Biography*, vol. 12, no. 3 (1989),
p. 211.
[29] Colin MacCabe, 'Introduction' to *The Grass Arena: An Autobiography* by John Healy
(London: Faber & Faber, 1988), p. ix.

and mean and selfish actions? I hate to think about them myself, and why should I create a similar hatred of them in the minds of others? I prefer to be thought better of: isn't that natural?[30]

Barclay's candid admission serves to remind us that however much a memoirist presents him- or herself as honest witness, the text must ultimately be read as a complex narrative *re*presentation of self and experience in which reality and identity are constructed through the act of autobiographical narration.

The critical methodology employed in this anthology, then, is an interdisciplinary one that sets out to read migrant autobiography as both social history and cultural product, the expressive dimensions of these texts being crucial to their interpretation of experience. My starting premise is that, as a slippery, contrary genre in which fact and fiction are intimately and indissolubly intertwined, autobiography necessarily reflects, generates and transforms social reality. This is the core paradox of the form; as Paul John Eakin eloquently puts it, 'autobiography is nothing if not a referential art; it is also and always a kind of fiction'.[31] Insofar as I offer a critical précis of each autobiography and its significance in my headnotes, therefore, I try to combine information on writers' background and the material circumstances of their self-narration with analysis of their modes of telling and self-representational strategies. This literary-historical approach also informs my arrangement of extracts according to the period to which they refer rather than to the dates of their composition or publication. This format is designed to do double service by allowing readers to trace both the correspondences between autobiography, history and memory, and the ways in which these migrant writers participate in and contest culturally prevalent representations of Irishness and the Irish in Britain at particular times and places.

The assertion of autobiographical agency seems to me to assume special potency at the point where the realms of the aesthetic and the political intersect and overlap. Clearly, the self-portraits presented in this anthology exist within the wider historical context of the quarrelsome hierarchical relationship between Britain and Ireland that began in the twelfth century. The colonialist discourse that was this relationship's leitmotif, coupled with the long-lived culture of anti-Irishness in Britain, meant that moving there, whether by choice or necessity, was the most problematic and politically charged of all acts of Irish relocation. The passing of the Act of Union in 1800 did little initially to alter hostile British public discourse on Ireland, despite the fact that 'during the period of the Union, the Irish were internal migrants rather

---

[30] Tom Barclay, *Memoirs and Medleys: The Autobiography of a Bottle-Washer* (Leicester: Edgar Backus, 1934), p. 103.

[31] Paul John Eakin, *Touching the World: Reference in Autobiography* (Princeton: Princeton University Press, 1992), p. 31.

than immigrants *per se* (though they were often perceived as such)'.[32] On the contrary, ancient prejudices were reaffirmed by the arrival of large numbers of unskilled Catholic migrants in the expanding industrial towns and cities of early nineteenth-century Britain.[33] While the Irish were not the only 'foreigners' to be vilified, their conspicuous presence in unprecedented numbers provoked a deep-seated form of native antipathy based on a tangled weave of political, religious and socio-economic factors.[34] Fears that these indigent outsiders would undercut the wages of unskilled workers and corrupt their morals fed off popular associations of the Irish with poverty, violence, disease and Catholicism, the inveterate bugbear of the Protestant state. The pronounced influx of famine-stricken refugees in the late 1840s re-inflamed cultural antagonisms and lent weight to compelling middle-class analyses of the socially disastrous consequences of Irish immigration, such as those advanced by James Phillips Kay and Thomas Carlyle.[35] Nativist prejudices hardened further in response to the spread of Fenianism among Irish migrant communities in England and Scotland during the 1860s, a trend which reinforced perceptions of the Irish as a parasitic, criminal nuisance.[36] Little wonder, then, that pejorative stereotypes of this despised outgroup flourished

---

[32] Swift (ed.), *Irish Migrants in Britain*, p. 8. Those who have migrated from Northern Ireland to England, Scotland and Wales since 1921 are also officially classed as internal migrants by the British government.

[33] These numbers are notoriously difficult to calibrate for the period prior to 1841, when the first census to take account of Irish-born people in Britain recorded 289,404 in England and Wales, with a further 126,321 in Scotland. The total Irish-born population had grown to 806,000 by 1861, falling 40 years later to 632,000. By 1921 the figure had shrunk to 524,000. British-born children of Irish immigrants were not recorded in any of these census returns. See David Fitzpatrick, '"A peculiar tramping people": The Irish in Britain, 1801–70', in W. E. Vaughan (ed.), *A New History of Ireland, Volume 5: Ireland Under the Union, I (1801–70)* (Oxford: Clarendon Press, 1989), pp. 623–60; and Donald M. MacRaild, *Irish Migrants in Modern Britain, 1750–1922* (Basingstoke: Macmillan, 1999), pp. 42–74.

[34] These factors are analysed in detail in MacRaild, *Irish Migrants in Modern Britain*. See also Alan O'Day, 'Varieties of anti-Irish behaviour in Britain, 1846–1922', in Panikos Panayi (ed.), *Racial Violence in Britain, 1840–1950* (Leicester: Leicester University Press, 1993), pp. 26–43.

[35] Kay's pamphlet, *The Moral and Physical Condition of the Working Classes Employed in the Cotton Manufacture in Manchester*, was published in 1832, Carlyle's *Chartism* in 1839. For analysis, see Mary Poovey, 'Curing the "Social Body" in 1832: James Phillips Kay and the Irish in Manchester', *Gender & History*, vol. 5, no. 2 (Summer 1993), pp. 196–211; and Roger Swift, 'Thomas Carlyle, *Chartism*, and the Irish in Early Victorian England', *Victorian Literature and Culture*, vol. 29, no. 1 (2001), pp. 67–83.

[36] See Roger Swift, 'Heroes or Villains?: The Irish, Crime and Disorder in Victorian England', *Albion*, vol. 29, no. 3 (1998), pp. 399–421. Swift begins: 'During the Victorian period the link between Irish immigration, crime, and disorder in England was widely regarded by contemporary observers as axiomatic' (p. 399).

in the popular press, borrowing authority from pseudo-scientific theories that positioned Anglo-Saxons (sober, rational, industrious, manly, Protestant) and Celts (bibulous, superstitious, imaginative, feminine, Catholic) at opposite ends of a loaded racial spectrum. As Donald MacRaild succinctly puts it, 'when the Victorians looked for a scapegoat, they saw an Irish migrant'.[37]

As MacRaild and others are quick to acknowledge, however, the cultural reception of the immigrant Irish in nineteenth-century Britain was never as schematic as this synopsis suggests. Not only did attitudes vary according to local conditions and the class of migrant involved – the respective testimonies of Justin McCarthy and Owen Peter Mangan, for example, reveal the contrasting fortunes of a middle-class newcomer in Victorian London and a peasant sojourner in Victorian Preston – they also disclosed sympathetic as well as hostile elements, albeit a sympathy often rooted in a chauvinistic imperial discourse of 'progress' and underpinned by highly asymmetrical relations of power. Thus, the more lurid tones of Carlyle's splenetic portrait of the 'miserable Irish' languishing in their 'rags and laughing savagery'[38] are airbrushed out of Matthew Arnold's more ideologically nuanced, but no less racialist, characterisation of the ineffectual Celts as 'undisciplinable, anarchical, and turbulent by nature'.[39] Indeed, a trenchant scholarly debate about the nature, extent and significance of anti-Irish antipathy in Victorian Britain has flared since the late 1960s, fuelled by polarised responses to the vexed question of whether such prejudice owed more to race, class, religion or 'national character'. It is not my purpose to dissect this debate here; interested readers might begin by consulting MacRaild's useful overview and analysis.[40] My point, rather, is that whereas British observers' impressions of the immigrant Irish, especially the Catholic poor, have been loudly articulated, from Thomas Dekker's minatory image of Irish vagrants 'swarm[ing] like Crickets to the crevice of a Brew-house'[41] in the 1630s to J. B. Priestley's hectoring vision of a prospective mass Irish repatriation in the 1930s – 'what a grand clearance there will be in all the Western ports, from the Clyde to Cardiff, what a fine exit of ignorance and dirt and drunkenness and disease'[42] – the perspectives of the migrants themselves have been much harder to hear. How have they represented their lived realities and imagined

---

[37] MacRaild, *Irish Migrants in Modern Britain*, p. 187.

[38] Thomas Carlyle, *Chartism* (London, 1839), p. 182. Cited in Swift, 'Thomas Carlyle, *Chartism*, and the Irish in Early Victorian England', p. 72.

[39] Matthew Arnold, *On The Study of Celtic Literature* (London: Smith, Elder and Co., 1867), p. 109.

[40] MacRaild, *Irish Migrants in Modern Britain*, pp. 160–2. See also ch. 6, 'A Culture of Anti-Irishness'.

[41] Thomas Dekker, *The Second Part of The Honest Whore* (London: Elizabeth All-de, for Nathaniel Butter, 1630), p. 2.

[42] J. B. Priestley, *An English Journey* (London: William Heinemann in association with Victor Gollancz, 1934), p. 248.

their place in the wider web of political and cultural relations between Ireland and Britain? How did they make narrative sense of the rifts and contradictions of uprooting and regrounding in different temporal and social contexts? What is the relationship between leaving home and imagining home in their autobiographies? And what impact did writers' negotiation of newness and difference, prejudice and alienation have on their articulation of personal, cultural and national identity? My objective in this anthology is to make a dissonant medley of responses to such questions audible and distinct.

Themes, motifs, representations

The extract from the earliest migrant self-portrait to be included here, Mary Davys's *The Merry Wanderer* (1725), powerfully illustrates the fact that, even in the early eighteenth century, to identify oneself as Irish in Britain was to engage with centuries-old systems of representation and stigmatisation.[43] Within hours of her arrival in England, Davys has her identity questioned and is compelled to authorise herself in the face of hostile stereotypes that fix her as a threatening, though inferior, alien. What follows, however, is a subtle table-turning manoeuvre in which this newcomer nimbly marshals the discourses of race, sexuality and national identity to counter her interlocutor's construction of her as a degenerative Other. Davy's satiric representation of her transformation from mere bestiality into enlightened self-possession at the coercive hands of the English deftly ironises the colonial antitheses, thereby fashioning a caustic riposte to the discursive tradition of Irish barbarism perpetuated by Edmund Spenser and his contemporaries. Moreover, her teasing remark to her interrogator that 'ever since I have been just such another as you' serves to highlight the similarity of the English and the Irish, the subliminal awareness of which so distressed the colonial mind.[44] Davys's mockery of colonialist stereotypes is complicated, however, by the dualities emerging from her status as a Protestant Anglo-Irish female migrant. English colonial discourse was, after all, primarily directed at the native Catholic Irish, so in order to challenge it Davys must pretend to be one of them,

---

[43] The spectre of generic indeterminacy haunts Davys's text, as it does the work of many eighteenth-century memoirists, whose writings inhabit the blurred boundary between autobiography and fiction. I have taken my lead from those scholars who persuasively read *The Merry Wanderer* as autobiography, notably Siobhán Kilfeather (her article subtitle notwithstanding) in 'Beyond the Pale: Sexual Identity and National Identity in Early Irish Fiction', *Critical Matrix*, vol. 2, no. 4 (1986), pp. 1–31.

[44] See Declan Kiberd, *Inventing Ireland: The Literature of the Modern Nation* (London: Jonathan Cape, 1995), p. 11. Eudoxus's remark to Irenius in Spenser's *A View of the Present State of Ireland* – 'Lord, how quickly doth that country alter men's natures!' – encapsulates the coloniser's anxieties about Ireland's potential to corrupt.

must falsely present herself as an exemplar of newly-converted Irish civility. In so doing she effectively colludes in colonial condescension, as when she characterises the Irish language as 'a gaping inarticulate Noise'.[45] This act of cultural double-cross is made all the more treacherous by her recent crossing of geo-political boundaries. Fresh from the borderlands of the Tudor state – the English Pale in Ireland – this already mediated subject finds the troubling incongruities of her composite identity shifting beneath her parodic performance of colonialist prejudice. But whereas this feisty migrant's tale shows her having the last laugh, many of those who followed in her wake appear much less sure-footed when menaced by the spectre of intolerance and hostility.

Several autobiographers suggest that anti-Irish feeling, whether originating in national, religious or racial bias, could act as a barrier to employment and social advancement for skilled and unskilled migrants alike. While the fact of its occurrence is not to be wondered at, the spectrum of narrative responses to prejudice reveals interesting patterns. Far from labouring their experiences of discrimination or wrapping themselves in the cloak of victimhood, several writers barely register their experiences of such, while others record racial and religious slurs in a light ink. For Laetitia Pilkington, a vulnerable, penniless divorcée in 1740s London, having to endure taunts of 'Irish Papist Bitch' and 'Irish Whore' as she was being brusquely carted off to Marshalsea Prison was the least of her concerns. A century later, another 'poor poetess', Jane Jowitt, mentions that anti-Irish bias thwarted her attempts to find employment in Liverpool in the early 1800s but makes little of it. The weaver William Hammond is equally dispassionate in reporting that he was not long in 1840s Glasgow when he found that 'some of the baser sort made me understand that it was not an advantage to have been born in Ireland',[46] and the doughty Owen Peter Mangan phlegmatically tells how public revulsion at the 1867 Fenian outrages forced him to sell his grocery store in Preston and emigrate to Philadelphia. James Mullin is somewhat more reflective in detailing his experience of 'polite rejection' as a recently qualified doctor in 1880s England. His attempts to purchase a medical practice in Luton quickly foundered when it emerged that he was an Irish Catholic. The vendor's response was candid:

'Well, then,' said he, 'it is useless for us to go any farther into the business; for the patients there might tolerate you if you were an Irishman only, and not a Roman Catholic; or they might tolerate you if you were a Roman

---

[45] Mary Davys, *The Works of Mrs Davys*, vol. 1 (London: H. Woodfall, 1725), p. 163.
[46] William Hammond, *Recollections of William Hammond, A Glasgow Hand-Loom Weaver* (Glasgow: 'Citizen' Press, 1904), p. 20.

Catholic only and not an Irishman, but I'm afraid they would never stand a combination of both.'[47]

Mullin rationalises his treatment by linking it to the 'wave of racial and religious prejudice sweeping over England' in the wake of the Phoenix Park murders of 1882: 'With unreasoning force of virtuous indignation good people were so carried off their heads that they judged everybody belonging to the country and creed of the murderers to be more or less responsible for their crime.'[48] In clarifying how easily the political could become the personal, Mullin cogently encapsulates the vulnerability of generations of Irish migrants in Britain to local antagonisms ignited by flashpoints in Anglo-Irish political relations.

Other writers dramatise occasions when latent prejudices are triggered by certain modes of behaviour and cultural practices associated with Irishness. Among the most memorable is Kevin FitzGerald's account of his dressing-down by the principal of his English agricultural college following his involvement in a student revolt over food in the summer of 1921, at a time when 'Ireland was ablaze'.[49] The principal's opening words take on a retrospective political and racial colouration for the author, the subtexts of which he pointedly decodes:

> 'FitzGerald,' he began, 'you are Irish, I think.' I had not yet grasped that this is the typically British beginning to particular forms of insult. 'You are Irish, I think' is a useful all-round opening for 'You are dirty; dishonest; seem to have acquired some unpleasant habits; are a Catholic, militant Protestant, red revolutionary', or anything else which the speaker dislikes. When I answered the Principal that, yes, I was Irish, he went on: 'You are also, I gather, a dangerous Bolshevik.'[50]

Trainee nurse Annie Smithson attributes her matron's insistence that she remove her spray of shamrock on St Patrick's Day in 1898 to a similar strain of bigotry. Smithson's indignant reaction to having her public display of identity curtailed can be read as the flipside of Sean O'Casey's scornful refusal to conform to English stereotypes of the rough-hewn Irish genius on his arrival in 1920s London: 'Once, when a photographer handed him a huge, green, cardboard shamrock, telling him to fix it in his coat, and look gay, Sean let loose on him; and James Fagan, going white, heard for the first time the savage and profane vernacular of the Dublin navvy.'[51] O'Casey's public,

---

[47] James Mullin, *The Story of a Toiler's Life* (Dublin and London: Maunsel & Roberts, 1921), p. 157.

[48] Ibid., pp. 157–8.

[49] Kevin FitzGerald, *With O'Leary in the Grave* (Salisbury: Michael Russell, 1986), p. 98.

[50] Ibid., pp. 104–5.

[51] Sean O'Casey, *Rose and Crown* (London: Macmillan, 1952), p. 5.

autobiographical posture is designed to symbolise his renunciation of nation-alist cliché; Smithson's, to indicate her retrospective desire to accentuate her incipient nationalism. Yet both serve as cogent historical examples of how migrants' cultural identities are contested and negotiated through everyday practices, encounters and experiences.

The quotidian spaces of home, school and work are also integral to the nar-ration of subjectivity in the autobiographies of second- and third-generation Irish writers, of which there is a small but significant cluster. Several of these works dramatise the social and psychological effects of living at the exposed confluence of the hegemonic domains of Irishness and Britishness in specific contexts, from the slums of mid-Victorian Leicester to middle-class suburban London in the 1960s. The cultural inferiority complexes triggered by the mockery of Irish traits, accents and idioms is a recurring motif in autobiographical accounts of second-generation Catholic child-hoods, though they are not the exclusive preserve of this constituency. The multiple and partial identifications produced by such abrasive experiences are mapped with varying degrees of introspection and analysis. Although some, such as Seán MacStiofáin, emphatically state that 'in spite of having been born and brought up in England, I never considered myself anything but Irish',[52] most second-generation memoirists speak out of an awareness of cultural hyphenation that is subversive of exclusivist definitions of Irishness and Englishness/Britishness. One of the most interesting aspects of these hybridised middlemen's self-portraits is the way expressions of belonging oscillate between different modes of articulation. Whereas Joseph Keating coolly disaggregates the constituent parts of his Welsh and Irish heritage, Pat O'Mara voices a deeply contradictory set of affiliations, the legacy of a child-hood caught in the crossfire of the forces of hibernicisation and anglicisation: 'The best I can say is that what I derived from my elementary English-Irish schooling was an intense love for the British Empire and an equally intense hatred for England as opposed to Ireland.'[53] School is also the site where, in the autobiographies of Bill Naughton and John Walsh, family-nurtured forms of diasporic Irishness are warped by wider social pressures to 'become' English. Despite significant class differences, both authors evince a seemingly atavistic desire to have their identities authenticated in the parental home-land, in the vain hope that cross-cultural perplexities might be resolved by a decisive act of self-emplacement. The 'romance' of roots exerts a particularly potent hold over Walsh's imagination, delaying his discovery that there is no one, true self to be accessed in Ireland, only a range of different identities

---

[52] Seán MacStiofáin, *Memoirs of a Revolutionary* (London: Gordon Cremonesi, 1975), p. 18.

[53] Pat O'Mara, *The Autobiography of a Liverpool Irish Slummy* (London: Martin Hopkin-son, 1934), p. 75.

to be performatively tested. And yet no matter how recessive and unfathomable home becomes, the homing desire itself cannot be wholly tamed or contained.

Walsh is one of several writers in this anthology who exemplify the extent to which the 'ex-isled' self is forever prone to reading 'here' in relation to 'there'. It is a truism that migration, whether coerced or freely chosen, typically entails the loss of a familiar, sustaining community and demands a fresh orientation towards a new and often discomfiting world of chance and change. Yet the past is never entirely left behind, even by those who devoutly desire it, any more than the present is seamlessly embraced, once and for all. George O'Brien's reflections on the ironies that attended his flight from 1960s Lismore express a hard-won knowledge: 'For me, the fresh start, the clean sheet, the new leaf. Name, rank, serial number, and nothing but. Being someone else was all I could think of. I had no idea that fleeing only kept alive what was left behind.'[54] One of the most salient tropes of these autobiographies, therefore, is that of the Janus-faced migrant whose existence is marked by a continual fluctuation between cultures, histories, realities. Although Elizabeth Hamilton eloquently encapsulates the adaptability of the lightly moored – 'For those whose roots are less deep or whose loyalty is divided it is easier to settle afresh – so that a strange land begins soon to lose its strangeness'[55] – it is the dualistic perspectives of the reluctantly uprooted that predominate. For some, such as Mac Amhlaigh, the cultural losses of migration repeatedly outweigh any material gains when the new country is mapped on to the old. Others find that the pleasures of detachment continually sabotage the desire to partake. For the likes of James Mullin and John Stewart Collis, an initial fascination with cultural difference modulates into gradations of outsider-insiderness, each version of which is inflected by the author's background and socio-economic situation, including the conditions under which they left Ireland. Thus, Bill Naughton utilises a nationalist rhetoric of emigration as British-induced banishment when recalling his childhood removal from Ballyhaunis to Bolton in 1914:

> There was a feeling that as a family we had not emigrated from Ireland but had been transported, and we were in bondage, living a harsh degraded life, alien in every way to our natures, our one hope being that the entire land of Ireland would one day be free from the British yoke, rid of all the soldiery and police, and that we could all go back and live there like lords.[56]

---

54 George O'Brien, *Out of Our Minds* (Belfast: Blackstaff Press, 1994), p. 14.

55 Elizabeth Hamilton, *An Irish Childhood* (London: Chatto & Windus, 1963), p. 77.

56 Bill Naughton, *Saintly Billy: A Catholic Boyhood* (Oxford: Oxford University Press, 1988), pp. 85–6.

Such figurative bonds mutate into actual manacles in the piquant jail journal of Darrell Figgis, who arrived in Stafford as a republican prisoner in 1916. Having lived and worked in London as a young man, Figgis was no stranger to England, yet his angle of vision was radically tilted by the circumstances of his return: 'I could not more strangely have been led captive among the mountains of the moon, so icy was this world and such leagues apart from that which I had known. Everything was coloured by that relation. One looked on England with new eyes, and old thoughts became startling new discoveries.'[57] That such heightened sensitivity to place could be a powerful spur to creativity is borne out by Elizabeth Bowen who, in recalling her early impressions of England, considers the extent to which migration incubated her imagination by compelling her to read and decipher differently. Clearly, the new country did not erase the old, but it did supply a perspective from which to explore the 'semi-resemblances' between the two that are so germane to her literary vision: 'As it was, where we *were* stood out in absolute contrast to where we came from. Gone was the changing blue of mountains: instead, bleached blond in summer, the bald downs showed exciting great gashes of white chalk. Everything, including the geological formation, struck me as having been recently put together.'[58]

Bowen, of course, was speaking from a position of peculiar privilege compared to the 'ragged, penniless army' that deserted independent Ireland during and after the Second World War, 'with nothing but their health and strength to hurry them on their way'.[59] For the memoirists among them, the desolate strangeness of English landscapes became a figurative mirror for their numbing anomie and acute sense of betrayal by a state that raised them on a diet of newly-minted patriotism, liberally spiced with anglophobia. Reflected there too was the guilt many felt at having betrayed that state in turn. The experience of enforced emigration left an especially bitter aftertaste in the mouths of John B. Keane, Dónal Foley and Dónall Mac Amhlaigh, all three of whom emerge as unintegrated migrants *par excellence* in their self-portraits. For them, real life was in Ireland; it, and they, could not exist fully anywhere else. Forever feeling themselves to be 'visitors' in 'godless' England, they rage against the indifference of Irish political and media elites towards the plight of post-war economic migrants, Mac Amhlaigh reserving special scorn for 'a miserable Government that won't do their best to keep these people at home'.[60] The sense of hiatus, of perpetual waiting, that afflicts these demoralised and humiliated migrants brings them into emotional as

---

[57] Darrell Figgis, *A Chronicle of Jails* (Dublin: Talbot Press, 1917), p. 66.
[58] Elizabeth Bowen, *Pictures and Conversations* (London: Allen Lane, 1975), pp. 24–5. Original emphasis.
[59] Dónal Foley, *Three Villages: An Autobiography* (Dublin: Egotist Press, 1977), p. 51.
[60] Dónall Mac Amhlaigh, *An Irish Navvy: The Diary of an Exile* (London: Routledge & Kegan Paul, 1964), p. 94.

well as physical proximity with post-war Britain's officially 'displaced persons', the Poles who lived in resettlement camps scattered throughout the country. Keane's observation of the bewildered Polish men with whom he lodged in Northampton leads him to the baneful conclusion that 'A man without a country is as confused as a dog without a tail. He knows he has lost something but he can't put his finger on it. He also knows that no other tail will replace the one he has lost. In other words he doesn't belong to a particular denomination any more.'[61]

Not every tailless dog is deracinated, however. In the autobiographies of Elaine Crowley, Bob Geldof and George O'Brien emigration is variously imagined as a longed-for escape from drudgery and obligation, a gateway to opportunity, and an invigorating test of self-sufficiency. Here, a buoyant openness to change supplants broodings on 'the scattering of the Gael and the poor state they're in'.[62] For the teenage Geldof, Dublin was a stifling backwater, a 'rat trap' from which escape was imperative: 'All of my life the mail-boat had been an object of almost mystic power. It was the instrument of my release – England was irrelevant. If China had been next door to Ireland, I'd have gone there.'[63] Such a dehistoricised representation of England as not-Ireland transforms it into a place where nothing is insurmountable, not even the traditional scourge of the immigrant Irish: 'Curiously, when I was first confronted by racism in England, I was not in the least offended. "No dogs, no Irish," said the bedsit sign. Fine. It didn't even depress me. But I didn't have to live with the constant grind of it.'[64] These are the sentiments of a narrator who, despite being green (sometimes literally so, as in the extract selected here), is determined not to succumb to the embittered destinies of so many of his predecessors. All kinds of perils and possibilities lie ahead, but the spirit of excitement and curiosity will not be cowed. For this migrant at least, there is nothing to lose.

The personal dimension

'A scholar's work is often as much a self-portrait as a writer's',[65] claims Frank O'Connor, and so it is that the compilation of this anthology has never been an entirely intellectual exercise for me. Insofar as my own background and experience bear upon this project, I grew up in an area of east Mayo that

---

[61] John B. Keane, *Self-Portrait* (Dublin: Mercier Press, 1964), p. 43.

[62] Mac Amhlaigh, *An Irish Navvy*, p. 100.

[63] Bob Geldof with Paul Vallely, *Is That It?* (London: Sidgwick and Jackson, 1986), p. 63.

[64] Ibid., p. 45.

[65] Frank O'Connor, *My Father's Son* (Syracuse: Syracuse University Press, 1999), p. 96.

has been an emigrant nursery for centuries.[66] The unpropitious rushy acres of Meeltrane, Shanvaghera and Aghamore meant that seasonal journeys to the hayfields of Yorkshire and Lincolnshire were familiar milestones on the paths to manhood for generations of small farmers' sons. Daughters went too, to work in offices, factories, family homes, hospitals, hotels, pubs and restaurants from Portsmouth to Aberdeen.[67] When, precisely, my own ancestors first took 'the boat to England' I cannot be sure, though the family habit was already established by the time my paternal grandfather was born in 1889. As a young man, Willie Harte laboured in a Normanton colliery prior to the First World War, and after his marriage back in Mayo in 1918 spent successive seasons working for a farmer in Holbeach Marsh in Lincolnshire. By the time that poor health forced him to stay at home for good in 1941, the eldest of his eight children was preparing to leave. In time, all but one (who died) would emigrate to England, with four marrying and settling there permanently.

In June 1948 my own father travelled from Kiltimagh to Halifax on an agricultural passport for what was to be the first of his ten seasons as a 'July barber', as migratory harvesters were colloquially known. Despite many privations, he quickly adapted to an improvised life of suitcases and train stations, becoming, in a way, more grounded in Yorkshire than in Mayo, although Meeltrane was always home. England etched itself on his consciousness with the intensity of a newsreel. Life in Ireland afterwards seemed smudged by a penumbra of anticlimax. Even now, my father is seldom more animated than when drawing from his well of migrant memories, the water from which seeped into my own childhood imagination, leaching it with exotic place-names – Mytholmroyd, Skipton, Hebden Bridge – and outlandish tales of hiring fairs and doss-houses. When, in the 1990s, my own educational journey took me to the affluent suburbs of south-west London to teach in a university classroom, it wasn't long before I found myself holidaying in the Yorkshire dales, paying remote homage to what I imagined to be the brave sadness of my migrant forefathers. Lines from Eavan Boland's 'The Emigrant Irish' came to me then: 'They would have thrived on our necessities. / What they survived we could not even live.'[68] Since then, I too have become a serial border-crosser, my comings and goings randomly charted in the travel

---

[66] On the culture of seasonal migration and its social impact in late nineteenth-century Mayo, see Gerard Moran, '"A Passage to Britain": Seasonal Migration and Social Change in the West of Ireland, 1870–1890', *Saothar*, vol. 13 (1988), pp. 22–31.

[67] For a discussion of the geographical patterns of settlement and fluctuating gender ratios within the Irish migrant population in nineteenth- and twentieth-century Britain, see Bronwen Walter, *Outsiders Inside: Whiteness, place and Irish women* (London: Routledge, 2001), ch. 4.

[68] Eavan Boland, 'The Emigrant Irish', *Collected Poems* (Manchester: Carcanet Press, 1995), p. 129.

cards and ticket stubs that serve as my rudimentary bookmarks. The chasm that separates my casual, cosseted journeys from the arduous crossings of my forebears – and those of many of the writers anthologised here – is, of course, unbridgeable. Yet in hearing their stories and in reading their autobiographies, moments of imaginative connection occur – moments that are often as much about *dis*identification as identification – which allow me to see myself as part of a wider narrative of migration and the making of cultural memory, if that's not putting it too grandly. So if O'Connor is right, my selection of these variously constituted selves may itself bear vestigial traces of self-portraiture.

Editorial Note

The great majority of extracts are taken from the first English language editions of primary texts. Full bibliographical details of each text are supplied in the headnotes, including details of works originally published in Irish. Information on later editions, including those currently in print, is given in the List of Primary Works. Alterations to excerpted material have been kept to a minimum throughout. In the case of manuscript sources, I have endeavoured to transcribe extracts as faithfully as possible, though the obscurity of some minor hand-written emendations presented occasional editorial difficulties. In general, however, I have resisted the temptation to correct or modernise spelling and punctuation – even when an author uses different spellings of the same word in an extract – in the belief that idiosyncrasies of vocabulary, grammar and syntax can reveal much about a writer and his or her milieu.

I have selected reasonably lengthy passages from each primary source in order to preserve a degree of narrative continuity and enable readers to get a sense of the distinctive voice and texture of individual works. Square-bracketed ellipses indicate omitted material. In choosing extracts I have favoured not only those sequences that possess intrinsic interest in subject matter and style, but also those that register aspects of, or reflections upon, the experience of being Irish in Britain in some pronounced and substantial form. While this has led to some difficult editorial choices, I have tried to blend accounts of experiences and views that are instructive or illustrative in their typicality with those that do not tell the expected story or that qualify received generalisations. Unless otherwise indicated, quotations in the headnotes are taken from the autobiographies under discussion; the decision not to reference such quotations stems from the need to keep footnotes to manageable proportions. In compiling my headnotes and annotations I have turned to many secondary sources for guidance, but none more frequently than the online edition of the *Oxford Dictionary of National Biography*, which has been an immensely valuable resource.

The process of researching and assembling this anthology has made me an avid reader of other anthologists' work, and I have certainly found ideas and inspiration in a number of excellent scholarly compilations, including, in addition to those cited in my Introduction: David Fitzpatrick's *Oceans of Consolation: Personal Accounts of Irish Migration to Australia* (1994); Maria Luddy's *Women in Ireland, 1800–1918: A Documentary History* (1995); Brian Maidment's *The Poorhouse Fugitives: Self-Taught Poets and Poetry in Victorian Britain* (1987); David Pierce's *Irish Writing in the Twentieth Century: A Reader*

(2000); Stephen Regan's *Irish Writing: An Anthology of Irish Literature in English 1789–1939* (2004); and the five volumes that comprise *The Field Day Anthology of Irish Writing* (1991, 2002). A more exemplary set of models would be hard to imagine.

1

Mary Davys, *The Merry Wanderer*

From: *The Works of Mrs Davys: Consisting of plays, novels, poems, and familiar letters. Several of which never before publish'd. In two volumes* (London: H. Woodfall, 1725). Vol. 1, viii, 280pp.; pp. 161–3.

Mary Davys (1674–1732) is one of those enigmatic writers about whom nothing is known, not even her maiden name, prior to her marriage to Peter Davys, a Dublin Church of Ireland clergyman and schoolmaster who was a friend and correspondent of Jonathan Swift. Even her place of birth cannot be definitely identified. Although Siobhán Kilfeather describes her as 'the first known Irish woman writing in English to explore national and sexual identities',[1] Martha Bowden draws attention to the significant contradiction between Davys's suggestion in *The Fugitive; Or, The Country Ramble* (1705) that she was born in England and her unequivocal claim to Irish birth in *The Merry Wanderer* (1725), a reworking of *The Fugitive* in which she records her travels through provincial England and Wales.[2] We do know that Davys was widowed in Dublin in 1698, shortly after which she settled in York, where she began her writing career. The commercial success of her social comedy, *The Northern Heiress; Or, The Humours of York* (1715), marked a career turning-point, not only in being the first publication to bear her name, but also by providing her with the financial and psychological resources to continue writing into her fifties, at a time when there was much social opprobrium attached to the category of professional woman writer. The income Davys derived from the play's London production also enabled her to open a coffee-house in Cambridge, where she spent the rest of her life and where she was buried in the Church of the Holy Sepulchre on 3 July 1732. The fact that her clothes were posthumously valued at less than five pounds suggests that she died in penury.[3] If, then, we accept Davys as an Anglo-Irish writer, she is almost certainly the first of her kind to dramatise the potent cultural encounter between Irish immigrant and English

---

[1] Kilfeather, 'Beyond the Pale', pp. 14–15.

[2] Martha F. Bowden, 'Mary Davys: Self-presentation and the woman writer's reputation in the early eighteenth century', *Women's Writing*, vol. 3, no. 1 (1996), pp. 17–33.

[3] Martha F. Bowden, 'Silences, Contradictions, and the Urge to Fiction: Reflections on Writing about Mary Davys', *Studies in the Literary Imagination*, vol. 36, no. 2 (Fall 2003), p. 139.

native, as evidenced by the opening section of *The Merry Wanderer*, extracted here. Her encounter with an Englishman named Hodge, who is curious to see some of the 'wild Irish' in the flesh, sets the scene for a witty canard in which Davys exploits anti-Irish stereotypes in order to gull her credulous inquisitor with consummate brio.

As Ignorance is the Mother of Devotion, and Necessity of Invention; so may Travelling be properly enough call'd the Mother of Observation: And tho' the petty Journeys I have taken, will hardly intitle me to the Name of a Traveller, because I have never been in *France* for new Fashions, nor at *Rome* for Religion, or a Song; yet I hope *England* is not so barren of Diversion, but one may pick up some things in it worthy of Note. To tell the Reader I was born in *Ireland* is to bespeak a general Dislike to all I write, and he will, likely, be surprized, if every Paragraph does not end with a Bull: but a Potato's a fine light Root, and makes the Eater brisk and alert; while Beef and Pudding, that gross heavy Food, dulls a Man's Brain as bad as too much Sleep. And I am going to say a bold Word in defence of my own Country; The very brightest Genius in the King's Dominion[4] drew his first Breath in that Nation: and so much for the Honour of *Ireland*, of which I am just going to take a final Leave. When I had made a Stride from *Ringsend* to *Hollyhead* in *Wales*, a Gentleman in the Ship advised every body to take the Provisions they had aboard with them ashore; for he told us a smoaky House and no Food would be our best Entertainment, and so we found it. But a few Hours remov'd us from thence, and after sixty very bad Miles riding, we got into *England*; and while we were at Supper in a very good Inn, we heard a great Noise, and the People very merry: at last one of the Maids came grinning in, and told us there was a Man without, who heard there was some of the wild *Irish* there, and offer'd her a Shilling to help him to the sight, for he had never seen any of them in his Life. She happening to have a little more Wit than he, came in with the Jest, to see how far we would encourage it; for my part, I was mightily pleas'd with the fancy, and bid the Wench earn the Shilling, and bring him in. Now, *said I to my Company*, does this Fellow fancy we have Horns and Hoofs, and imagine Humanity alters as oft as his own dull Fancy? Pray let us humour his opinion, and see how far it will go. The rest consented, and the Man (half afraid to come near the Monsters) enter'd with Eyes staring, and Ears and Mouth wide open, big with Expectation of seeing and hearing something

---

[4] The genius in question was probably Swift, whose patronage Davys unsuccessfully courted through public appeals and private begging letters, though her allusion to him here seems to be motivated as much by a desire to vindicate her nation and class as to promote herself. Margaret Anne Doody's observation is apposite in this context: 'Praise of Swift was praise of the national literary identity. [...] Swift redeems a group at apparent disadvantage; he proves the potential excellence of those traditionally judged by (imposed and alien) authority to be dull and inferior' ('Swift Among the Women', *The Yearbook of English Studies*, vol. 18 (1988), p. 70).

very extraordinary. Come Friend, *said I*, you have, I hear, a mind to see some of the wild *Irish*. Yes, Forsooth, *said he*, an yo pleasen, but pray yo where are they? Why, *said I*, I am one of them. Noa, noa, *said he*, yo looken laik one of us; but those Foke, that I mean, are Foke wi' long Tails, that have no Clothes on, but are cover'd laik my brown Caw a whom with their own Hair. Come, *said I*, sit you down, and I'll tell you all; when I was three Years old I was just such a thing as you speak of, and going one day a little farther than I should have done, I was catch'd in a Net with some other Vermin, which the *English* had set on purpose for us; and when they had me, they cut off my Tail, and scalded me like a Pig, till all my Hair came off; and ever since I have been such another as you. Well, Forsooth, *said he*, yo tellen me Wonders, but pray yo, cou'd yo speak? Speak, *said I*, no I could only make a gaping inarticulate Noise, as the rest of my Fellow-Beasts did, and went upon my hands as well as Feet, in imitation of them; but for any other Knowledge, I had it not till I got into *English* hands. Well, *said poor Hodge*, yo may bless the Day that ever yo met with that same Net: By'r Lady, I have often head of the wild *Irish*, but never saw any of 'em before. One Word more, Forsooth, and I have done: Could you not let a Body see the Mark of that same Tail of yours, where it was cutten off? No, Friend, *said I*, that may not be so very decent; I find you are a Man of much Curiosity, but must beg you would take my Word for once without ocular Demonstration. Mercy on me, *said the Fellow*, what's that? Why that, *return'd I*, is, without staying any longer, to make haste home, and tell your Wife and Neighbours what you have heard and seen. By my Troth and so I will, *said he*, but first methinks I have a good mind to give you a Share of a Mug of Beer. No thank you, *said I*, we never drink in *Ireland*, but on *Easter* Sunday Morning, and then we all get drunk and dance with the Sun. By the Makins, *said he*, you're merry Foke, and so good by to ye. Thus we got rid of our inquisitive Companion, who left us as full of Mirth, as he was of Wonder and Folly.

2

Laetitia Pilkington, *Memoirs of Mrs Laetitia Pilkington, Wife to the Reverend Mr Matthew Pilkington, Written by Herself*

(Dublin: Printed for the Author, 1748). Vol. 2, xvi, 299pp.; pp. 220–32.

As the daughter of an eminent obstetrician of Dutch descent and his well-connected Anglo-Irish wife, Laetitia van Lewen (*c*.1709–1750) had a privileged upbringing in early eighteenth-century Dublin. Indeed, when in May 1725 she married the ambitious but poor young clergyman and poet, Matthew Pilkington, some thought the match to be beneath her. By 1730 the couple were part of the literary circle of Jonathan Swift, whose patronage helped Matthew to become chaplain to the lord mayor of London. When his wife visited him there in 1733 she discovered his philandering, and so began the marital difficulties that culminated in the couple's acrimonious and very public divorce in 1738. Disgraced by allegations of adultery and denounced by Swift as 'the most profligate whore in either kingdom',[1] Pilkington fled Dublin in late 1739 for London, where she remained for the next eight years, eking out a precarious living as a hack writer, while seeking, through her own writings, to capitalise upon the sexual notoriety that attached to her. In London she attracted the patronage of the novelist Samuel Richardson and the playwright Colley Cibber, whom she entertained with her witty repartee and revealing sidelights on Swift's character and manners. It was Cibber who encouraged her to write her memoirs, which were published in three volumes between 1748 and 1754, and comprise a rich mixture of reportage, gossip, satire, invective, verse, self-interrogation and self-vindication, all bound together by an engaging conversational style. As A. C. Elias notes, 'Writing her *Memoirs* when she did, Mrs. Pilkington was largely free to suit herself. Even the word *memoirs* was nebulous at the time, carrying no clear idea beyond that of factual recollections centering on a particular person or group.'[2]

Often cited as a foundational text of the 'scandalous memoir' subgenre, in which 'fallen' women voiced their grievances in print, Pilkington's *Memoirs* reveal a woman's struggle to authorise herself, to take charge of her self-representation and speak in

---

[1] Letter to John Barber, March 1738. Cited in A. C. Elias, Jr., 'Introduction', *Memoirs of Laetitia Pilkington*, ed. A. C. Elias, Jr (Athens: University of Georgia Press, 1997), p. xvi.
[2] Ibid., p. xxv.

her own defence, manipulating existing conventions to suit her purpose.[3] Note, for example, her awareness of the rhetorical value of written correspondence in buttressing the veracity of her testimony in the extract below. Of the many faces she presents, the most interesting for our purposes is her self-portrait as an impecunious divorced Irishwoman in 1740s London, separated from her children and exiled from respectability, trying to forge an independent path in a male-dominated public sphere, using wit as her chief tool and weapon. Often, her intellectual resources were tested to the limit by the exigencies of her plight, as evidenced by the following extract from Volume 2, in which Pilkington describes the circumstances that led to her nine-week incarceration in Marshalsea Prison – later the setting for Dickens's *Little Dorrit* (1857) – in the autumn of 1742 for non-payment of a £2 debt.

Early next Morning, to my no small Surprize, entered a Couple of ill-favoured Fellows, the Sight of whom struck Terror to my Soul; I demanded their Business; one of them answered, 'Get up, you *Irish* Papist Bitch, and come along with us.' The other, who had employed himself in looking over my Papers, cried, 'Ay, the *Irish* Whore, here is something about some *Roman* Father, that's the Pope, and be damn'd to you, is it?' I was for some time quite speechless, but, when I recovered Strength enough to speak, I begged of them to leave the Room, till I put on my Clothes; but my Landlady coming in at that instant, cried, 'You're damn'd modest; — don't quit the Place': The Fellows, who had more Decency than she, looked out at the Window, while I dressed myself, in which Time, my Agony was inconceivable; they called a Coach, and thrusting me into it, conveyed me to the House of an Officer of Mace[4] at *Charing-Cross*; as I happened to have a Guinea in my Pocket, I called for a Room, and a Pint of Wine, and then considered, if I had one Friend I could apply to: My dear Mr. *Cibber* was out of Town, as were likewise most of the Nobility; however, I saw young Mr. *Cibber*[5] go by the Window, and sent to him, but like all the World, when he heard my Condition, he would not come near me. My whole Debt was Forty Shillings; O, what could I do, but give my Tears Vent! which was my only Relief; and, next Day, after paying Twenty Shillings, I was conveyed to the Marshalsea Prison. I sat withinside of the Lodge for some Minutes quite stupified, till at length a Man came, and asked me, if I was a Prisoner, which, it seems, he did not before know; I told him I was, upon which he brought me into a Room, where a Parcel of Wretches seized me, and sung a long Song about Garnish,[6] and were going to pull my Clothes off, till a Servant who had

---

[3] See Lynda M. Thompson, *The 'Scandalous Memoirists': Constantia Phillips, Laetitia Pilkington and the Shame of 'Public Fame'* (Manchester: Manchester University Press, 2000).

[4] Like many debtors, Pilkington was first taken to a preliminary detention centre known as a sponging house, run by a sheriff's officer.

[5] Theophilus Cibber (1703–1758), son of Colley, who had himself recently been incarcerated in Fleet Prison for non-payment of a debt.

[6] The entrance fee which each new prisoner was required to pay.

seen me before, said, 'For God's Sake don't use Doctor *Meade's* Wife ill'; upon this, a most ugly Woman came up, and said, 'God damn you, you Bitch, do you pretend to be Doctor *Meade's* Wife? — I am his Wife'. I begged to be heard, which was granted; I told her my Name was *Meade*, and my Husband a Clergyman in *Ireland*.[7] 'Oh, that's a different Case,' said she, going off. They were kind enough to take my Word for some Drink, and a good decent Woman said, she would accept of me for a Chum,[8] as they call it. She brought me into a little dirty Apartment, where, without examining any thing, I in Despair, threw myself down on a Bed I saw there, and resolved never to rise again. Three Days and Nights past, during which Time, I never tasted Food of any sort. At length, the Companion of my Misery pressed me to take a little Refreshment, which I was persuaded to do, and seeing so many People in my own Condition, at length reconciled me to think of making myself as easy as possible; and leave myself to the Disposition of Divine Providence: One Morning a Friend came to visit me, by whom I sent a Letter to Doctor *Meade*, telling him my Distress, and amongst other Things, these Lines:

> CAN, alas! the plaintive Pray'r
> Dictated by Grief sincere,
> Hope to reach a friendly Ear;
> Will thy kind and bounteous Heart
> Sympathize while I impart
> Such Affliction, as before
> Never hapless Woman bore.

I made no doubt but I should be relieved, and waited impatiently for the Answer, which was as follows:

> *To Mrs.* MEADE, *in the Marshalsea.*
> *Ormond-street, October* 16, 1742.

MADAM,
I have so many Applications for Charity, that it is impossible for me to relieve all; those from your Country alone are very numerous. The Family of the *Meades* there, are very rich, and should take care of their needy Branches; I have, for the last Time, sent you a Guinea.
> I am,
> Your humble Servant,
> R.M.[9]

---

[7] Mrs Meade was the name Pilkington lived under in London, drawing on an ancestry of which she was proud. Her grand-uncle was Sir John Meade (1642–1707), progenitor of the Meade earls of Clanwilliam.

[8] A term for a paying room-mate. The woman in question has evidently accepted Pilkington on promise of future payment.

[9] Dr Richard Meade (1673–1754), celebrated physician and noted benefactor.

I kept the Original of this by me, with a Resolution, when I should these unlucky Deeds relate, not to omit it. This was soon gone, I had many to satisfy: I then wrote to *Henry Furnese*, Esq.,[10] who in a polite manner sent me a Guinea, which doubled the Obligation;

> *For, oh! believe me, 'tis a dreadful Task*
> *To generous Minds, to be compell'd to ask;*
> *More dreadful still to have a Suit deny'd,*
> *Or take a niggard Alms, giv'n with Contempt and Pride.*

I was by this supported till my dear Mr. *Cibber* came to Town, who was no sooner acquainted with my Misfortune than he sent me a Guinea all changed into Sixpences, lest it should tempt some one to pick my Pocket; this was an Instance of singular Humanity; but he has often said, when he did good to People in Distress, it was only to ease his own Mind, which would otherwise have been on the Rack; Oh, Heavens! what innate Goodness must dwell in that Breast? [...]

As I have frequently observed to my Readers, that I was glad to run away from such a disagreeable Theme as my Misfortunes, I hope for their Pardon, though I am obliged to return to them again, and give them an Account even of so dismal a Place as a Jail.

Our Head-Turnkey happened to have been a Servant to Alderman *Barber*; and, like *Joseph*, I found Favour in the Sight of my Keeper, as he had seen me in better Days.

> *For, Certes, I had look'd on better Days,*
> *And had with holy Bell been knoll'd to Church,*
> *And sat at good Men's Feasts, and wip'd the Eye*
> *Of Drops, which sacred Pity had engender'd.*

This Man took great Compassion on me, and as on every *Friday*, which is Court-day, the Prisoners are all locked up in their respective Apartments, lest, when the Gates are thrown open for the Admission of the Judge and Lawyers, any of them should make their Escape: I was always indulged in the Liberty of hearing the Trials, which, as a Court of Judicature was a Scene I had never before beheld, greatly amused me.

And, indeed, I quickly perceived Sir *Richard Steel* was not mistaken, when he said the first, second, and third Excellence of a Lawyer was Tautology.[11]

---

[10] Henry Furnese (*c*.1690–1756), MP for New Romney and close friend of Colley Cibber.

[11] A reference to sentiments expressed by a character in *The Funeral* (1701), a comic drama written by the Dublin-born writer and politician Sir Richard Steele (1672–1729).

Yet this was but a transitory Relaxation, once in a Week; the Horror of my Condition return'd with redoubled Violence the Moment I heard the Key turn for my Confinement.

If Mr. *Pilkington* should alledge, that I have been severe on him in my Writings, let him but consider the Extremity that he drove a worthy Gentleman's Daughter to, nurtured in Ease and Plenty; and if he does not acquit me, I am sure the rest of the World will.

Well, we had a Sort of a Chappel belonging to the Jail, where Doctor *Friend*,[12] a Clergyman, Brother to Doctor *Friend*, the Physician, obliged us with Divine Service every Sunday: This Gentleman was himself a Prisoner in the King's Bench, and, after all the Grandeur he had once lived in, was now so low reduced as even to be beholden to such an unfortunate Creature as I for Sixpence; which, unfortunate as I was, I could not refuse to so fine an Orator, a Gentleman! and, by all Accounts, only undone by boundless Generosity and Hospitality.

The first Day I heard him preach I was charmed with his Elocution, but the rest of the Congregation, mad and drunk, bade him hold his Tongue; — he indeed, like *Orpheus*, played to Wolves and Bears; nor were they half so obliging to him, as the Storms were to *Arion*; neither could he, though uttering dulcet and harmonious Sounds, make the rude Crowd grow civil with his Song.

This fine Gentleman I often invited to my lonely Mansion; — he was not a little surprized to hear my mournful Story; — and, indeed, it somewhat alleviated my Sorrow to find such a Companion: — Poor Gentleman! Death has released him; I am sure, I should have done it, had the Almighty given me a Power equal to my Inclination to serve him.

However, I may praise God that I was, under him, the happy Instrument of Good to Numbers of my wretched Fellow-creatures, since by one pathetic Memorial I wrote for them, the sorrowful Sighing of the Prisoners[13] reached the Hearts of the Legislative Powers, and obtained an Act of Grace for them.[14]

But, as it was now near *Christmas*, and the Act was not to take Place till the *June* following, I used my utmost Endeavours to procure my own Liberty; for, oh! what anxious Moments must have passed between that dreadful Interval of Time? On a second Application to Mr. *Cibber*, he used all his Power with the Great for me, and, as he had been used to move their Passions,

---

[12] Reverend William Freind (1669–1745), brother of the famous physician John Freind (1675–1728).

[13] An allusion to 'O let the sorrowful sighing of the prisoners come before thee' from the *Book of Common Prayer*.

[14] Parliament regularly passed temporary Acts for the Relief of Insolvent Debtors. One such Act received the royal assent in March 1743, shortly after Pilkington was released from prison.

did it effectually on my Behalf, insomuch that no less than sixteen Dukes contributed a Guinea a-piece towards my Enlargement.

When I read over these Words, *Discharge from your Custody the Body of*, &c., as I was by nine Weeks Confinement, Sickness, and Fasting, rendered quite weak, the joyful Surprize made me faint away several Times and, indeed, my kind Benefactor had like to have frustrated his own generous Design of preserving me.

However, after all Debts, Extortions, and Dues were paid, I had just thirteen Shillings left, with which Sum I was once more permitted to breathe the open Air — and go where I pleased.

3

John Binns, *Recollections of the Life of John Binns: twenty-nine years in Europe and fifty-three in the United States*

(Philadelphia: Parry & Macmillan, 1854). 349pp.; pp. 63–8.

John Binns (1772–1860) was one of a number of expatriate Irishmen who played a key role in the development of a popular brand of militant radicalism in 1790s England, influenced by the heady experience of the French Revolution and the insurrectionary politics of Tom Paine. He was born in Dublin to a prosperous ironmonger who drowned when his son was just two years old. In 1794 Binns moved to London with his elder brother Benjamin and quickly became involved in radical politics, joining the London Corresponding Society (LCS) within months of his arrival in the capital. In October 1795 he chaired an open-air meeting at Copenhagen Fields to protest against two anti-sedition bills and a few months later travelled to Portsmouth as an LCS delegate, activities to which he alludes in the following excerpt from his autobiography, which chronicles the circumstances that have 'carried me into crowds, given me strange companions, made me a fugitive from thief-takers, and the inhabitant of many prisons, from the Bastile to the Tower of London'. Binns's arrest in Birmingham in 1796 led to the first of several periods of incarceration as a result of government purges. The LCS's professed solidarity with the United Irishmen brought him into close association with other English-based Irish republicans, notably Arthur O'Connor and Father James Coigley, with whom he was tried for treason in 1798. Although Binns escaped conviction on this occasion, he was subsequently imprisoned without charge for almost two years in Gloucester jail, after which he emigrated to the United States in 1801. He settled in Philadelphia, where he established a popular newspaper, the *Democratic Press*, and served as an alderman from 1822 to 1844. In his short introduction to his *Recollections* Binns reveals that it was first suggested that he write his memoirs shortly after his arrival in America, and that he subsequently preserved 'letters and papers as have presented themselves containing matter to assist my recollection'. His stated autobiographical objective, therefore, is the 'full and frank disclosure of facts', cleansed of all 'unkindly feelings' towards the living and the dead.

On the thirty-first of October, 1795, four days after the meeting near Copenhagen House, a royal proclamation 'by and with the advice of the Privy Council,' was issued, stating that, immediately before the opening of the present session of Parliament, a great number of persons were collected

in the fields in the neighborhood of the metropolis; and divers inflammatory speeches were delivered, &c. &c., and forbidding any such seditious and
unlawful assemblies. Two bills were submitted to Parliament by the ministers, one 'for the preservation of his Majesty's person and Government, and
against treasonable and seditious practices and attempts,' and the other 'for
more effectually preventing seditious meetings and assemblies.' These bills,
after an unusually-general violent and protracted opposition, passed both
houses of Parliament, received the royal assent, and became laws.

Every effort was made by the societies associated to obtain a reform in
Parliament, by innumerable public meetings; by the municipal corporations
throughout the kingdom; and by the Whig party in and out of Parliament,
to modify or prevent the passage of those bills. They were, however, in defi-
ance of all opposition, passed, by large majorities in both houses. Among
the provisions in those laws, was one prohibiting any meeting for political purposes of more than fifty persons at one time and place, unless the
meeting was called by the sheriffs or other legally constituted authorities.
On the passage of these bills into laws, the London Corresponding Society
sent circulars to all the societies with which they were in correspondence,
and to influential friends in the large towns in England, detailing a plan by
which meetings in favor of Parliamentary reform might be held, without sub-
jecting those who assembled to the pains and penalties of the law. Finding
that these communications did not produce the effects desired, the society
resolved to send delegates to some of the large towns in England, to awaken
public spirit, and organize societies for parliamentary reform. I was the first
delegate appointed, and Portsmouth the place selected as the town to which
I should go. Portsmouth was then, and I believe is now, the principal naval
station and dock-yard establishment, and the most strongly fortified town
in England. Why it was selected as the first place to send a delegate, I do
not recollect ever to have heard. I went, attended to the duties assigned me,
visited the dock-yards, naval depots, and some of the largest ships afloat and
on the stocks, naval and mercantile. Owing to contrary winds, a large fleet
of West India merchant ships, more than two hundred and fifty sail, waiting
for convoy, were then assembled in the port. I saw this fleet, under convoy of
several ships of the line, frigates, and sloops of war leave the station under a
favorable breeze. It was a most imposing and beautiful sight. It was so considered even by the people of Portsmouth, who crowded the piers and wharves
to view the departure of the fleet and convoy.

While on this mission I visited Portchester Castle. It was a short distance
from Portsmouth, and at that time the principal depot for French prisoners
of war. Two of the principal shopkeepers of Portsmouth accompanied me.
On application for admission at the castle gate, we were told by the sentinel
and officer on guard, that we could not be admitted without an order from
the governor. One of the gentlemen who accompanied me said, 'Why, that is
something new.' 'Yes,' said the officer, 'it is in consequence of some delegate

from London, who has been sent to Portsmouth to set fire to the dock-yards and liberate the prisoners. You must have an order from the governor before you can be admitted.' We went to the governor, and obtained the order without difficulty.

On our entrance, we found the prisoners, some thousands of them, in the large yards of the prison. They were thinly clad; their clothing was in poor condition. It was then the month of March, and the weather was cold. They were confined in large post and rail inclosures. Every prisoner, no matter how he was clad, had on his head a cap of liberty; which was a high red woollen cap, hanging down on one side of the head with a red tassel on the top; on the side of the cap was the French national cockade, colors, red, white, and blue. In the centre of each of these inclosures (there were four of them) was a lofty pole or 'tree of liberty,' round which the prisoners, hand in hand, in concentric circles, were dancing and singing *Ca Ira*, *La Carmagnole*, *the Marseillaise Hymn*, and other popular French patriotic airs.

In the hospital for sick and wounded French prisoners, at Gosport, a fortified town on the west side of Portsmouth, I found a young French lieutenant, lying sick on a cot-bed. In addition to his sufferings from a gunshot wound, he was languishing under a low fever, and was much emaciated. His face was thin, pale, and sickly; yet it was of a peculiarly interesting character. I talked kindly with him; he seemed gratified, and freely unbosomed himself. 'When I left my native village, a conscript, the girl I love,' said he, 'placed this cockade in my cap; for the first time she saluted me, and said: "Jean, never return, or return victorious." We embraced and parted. Since my capture, I have always worn this cockade next my heart.' As he spoke, a faint smile irradiated his wan and languid countenance, and his eye brightened and dimmed at the scenes brought before him. 'Thus,' thought I, 'the French armies are filled, and their enthusiasm, as much as their bravery, conducts them to victory.' We have no record of a more devoted national enthusiasm, or a more total overthrow of all enemies, foreign and domestic. There is no such page in human history as that on which are recorded the events of the French Revolution of 1789. It is the brightest, and yet the bloodiest, page in the annals of man; it is, to this hour, the page of deepest interest; it is, even yet, read and talked of, by all the world, and in all its tongues.

After I had been about a week at Portsmouth, I was surprised by a visit from two members of the Executive Committee of the London Corresponding Society. They informed me they had been sent to direct my immediate return, in consequence of information, on which they could depend, that orders had been given to have me impressed and sent on board one of the receiving-ships. On consultation, it was thought best that I should fulfil the engagements I had made for that evening, and depart for London the next day. This was accordingly done.

Soon after my return to London, the society appointed me a delegate to the town of Birmingham, to be accompanied by John Gale Jones,[1] as my colleague. We were very cordially welcomed by the friends of reform in Birmingham, and were in the prosperous discharge of our duties, when, on the evening of the 11th of March, 1796, we were both arrested, at different hotels, and taken to the town-prison called 'The Dungeon,' on a charge of having delivered seditious and inflammatory lectures. In a few days we were liberated, giving bail to appear at the next Court of Quarter Sessions at Warwick. While in this prison, our rooms were enlivened by the company of very many friends of much respectability, ladies and gentlemen.

I cannot prevail upon myself to leave this dungeon, which was anything but a dungeon to me, without noting that the keeper was civil and obliging; his wife, a kind, motherly, well-behaved, well-dressed woman, and their two daughters, from seventeen to nineteen years of age, pretty, amiable, and educated. My time passed so agreeably that I visited the keeper's family several times after my liberation.

The 'Dungeon' was a lock-up house for prisoners arrested in Birmingham, previously to their being bailed out, committed for trial, or sent to Warwick jail. A portion of it was well furnished, and occupied by the keeper and his family. Into their apartments I was conducted. The wife of the keeper, her daughters, and a female relation were taking tea when I was introduced. I was politely invited to join them, and accepted the invitation. The freedom of the tea-table, in a few minutes, put us perfectly at ease. The young ladies sang and played on a spinet, which was an inferior kind of musical stringed instrument then in use, which has long since been superseded by the harpsichord, and that by the piano-forte. As I could neither play nor sing, I told stories, spouted speeches, and made myself as agreeable as I could. At length a tall, fat old man, with a lantern and a candle lighted in it in one hand, and a formidable bunch of large keys in the other, advanced slowly into the room, and in the most unharmonious tone of voice, and in the most ungracious manner, loudly announced, 'It's time to lock up.' I was in high spirits, threw myself into an attitude, and in high tragedy-style said to the old man: 'Lead me to my straw, 'tis not the first time I have lodged hard to do the state a service.' Poor old man! he started and stared as though there was an insurrection in the prison. Finding, however, that I had made my bow to the ladies, and was following him with all due humility, he walked up stairs. After unlocking divers locks and padlocks, and pushing back sundry bars and bolts, we entered a bedroom, furnished somewhat in the Elizabethan style, having a very large, high four-post bedstead, with heavy, dark-colored

---

[1] John Gale Jones (1769–1838), radical agitator, with whom Binns ran a debating room in London in the mid-1790s. Jones was later found guilty of seditious libel at Birmingham, whereas Binns was acquitted of the same charge.

moreen hangings, two large arm-chairs, covered with the same material, a basin-stand, water jugs, basin, &c. He left with me a lighted candle, which, in about fifteen minutes, he returned and carried away. In the mean time I had carefully examined the closely iron-barred windows and doors, and satisfied myself that, however urgent might be the necessity, from fire or any other cause, to escape would be impossible. These examinations and considerations did not much alarm me, but when alone I shed many and bitter tears in the knowledge of the affliction and feelings of disgrace which my arrest and imprisonment would bring upon my relations. I felt this the more keenly, because I had abundant cause to be assured how very dear I was to them, to the young and to the old, to the male and to the female members. It is, at this time – it has been all my life, and in all situations – a source of joy and gratification that I had cause to believe that I was more generally and tenderly loved than any of the junior members of the family. In a short time, however, in the twenty-third year of my age, I was fast asleep in a prison.

4
John O'Neill, 'Fifty Years' Experience of an Irish Shoemaker in London'

St Crispin: A Magazine for the Leather Trades, May 1869 – February 1870; weekly serialisation. Extract taken from issue of 8 May 1869, pp. 240–1.

John O'Neill[1] (1777–1858) was born in Waterford and served his apprenticeship as a cobbler in Carrick-on-Suir before moving to Liverpool and then London, where he spent the rest of his life. When he died in Drury Lane in 1858, he was remembered as 'a Laureate of the Temperance Movement' who 'was always in the shade and on the brink of poverty'.[2] He was also said to be the author of eight plays, only one of which was published, and several volumes of prose and verse, including a number of temperance poems that brought him some notice in the 1840s. His 28-chapter autobiography, which was posthumously serialised in a magazine for shoemakers, chronicles the vicissitudes of his professional and domestic life in London from his arrival in 1808 until the 1850s. Curiously, there is an almost total absence of detail about the author's earlier life in Waterford and Liverpool. This self-improving work is woven around two main narrative strands: O'Neill's trials and triumphs as a shoemaker and his faltering attempts to establish himself as a writer, literature being for him 'the chief consolation of life in every extremity'. In addition to illuminating the material and economic forces that operated within the metropolitan working-class community during the early 1800s, O'Neill's autobiography also reveals the extent of the occupational and social networks that sustained Irish migrants in Georgian London. As the father of a large impoverished family – his first wife bore him at least 11 children – O'Neill was prone to many physical and psychological privations. Starvation and pauperism were seldom far from his mind, and he was frequently out of work. As he succinctly puts it

---

[1] The text contains no consistent spelling of the author's surname. 'John O'Neill' appears as the heading on each of the weekly instalments, yet the name appears variously as 'O'Neil', 'O'Neile', 'Neil' and 'Neill' in the narrative proper. This inconsistency may be a product of editorial carelessness, as the autobiography was serialised over a decade after the author's death.

[2] Details of O'Neill's life are given in 'Biographies of Noted Shoemakers' in the *St Crispin* edition of 20 February 1869, p. 100.

in Chapter 11, following another sacking: 'I had, as it was the common saying among the craft of that day, "three outs for the one in" – out of cash, out of credit, out of work, and in debt.' The opening chapter, published on 8 May 1869, is reproduced here. In it, O'Neil describes his attempts to locate his father on first arriving in the capital.

On the 20th of September 1808, at about three o'clock in the afternoon, I arrived at Hyde Park Corner – that date is made memorable by the destruction of Covent Garden Theatre by fire, which took place on that night. Though for many years the first desire of my heart was to visit London, the great market for genius, and I had been flattered into a belief that I had some of that commodity to dispose of; now, on my so far attaining the goal of my wishes, I felt no way elated. The loss of my papers, on which my hopes mainly depended, threw a gloom over my prospects, at least for the present, so that my reflections were far from being of a cheering nature; not so my companion, he was a man of no learning, no acquirements, no ideas above the seat, and the mere enjoyment of animal existence; but he was sober, industrious, strictly honest, generous and obliging.

Besides the loss of my papers, there were many other things to check the satisfaction I expected to feel on my entering the vast metropolis. My mind began to sink under the fear that I knew the world only by books, and had viewed things that accorded with my wishes through the deceptive prism of hope, which had before so often deceived me without teaching me wisdom. I also had a father to seek, whom I had no recollection of ever seeing, and the doubts of finding him a man with whom I could associate kindly on the relationship nature demanded, raised a feeling of uneasiness within me, that I strove to check in vain. He had been separated from his family for above thirty years and, to his own acknowledgment, often had the means in his power to assist them, but never sent a single shilling to keep them from want, or prevent them from becoming the associates of the worst dregs of society. The thoughts, too, of my own wife and children, who were now left, as he had left us, added to the distress of my mind, and helped to dissipate the castles I had built and so fondly dwelt in for years.

In this mood I passed along Piccadilly, regardless of the objects around me, merely enquiring my way to Long Alley, Moorfields, the address given in the last letter that was sent home by my father, and it was astounding news, when told that we had nearly four miles to travel eastward before we reached that locality; but, fatigued and foot sore as we were, we resolved to reach it before we rested, fully assured then we would have no difficulty in finding him. An old Irishman, who heard me ask a tall, well-dressed man, who stood at a window where some curiosities were exposed for sale, offered his services to be our guide to the place we were enquiring for; we thanked him, saying we were very low in pocket, and unable to pay him for his trouble; he said he had been a stranger in London himself, and always felt for his poor countrymen so situated.

'I don't live very far from Moorfields,' said he, 'and I know Long Alley well; it is all in my way home, so I will show you the way, so far as I am going at least, and then will put you on the right track.'

He told us the reason he spoke to us was because the man of whom we made the enquiry was a crimp,[3] belonging to the East India Company's service, a jew rascal, who would sell his own brother for a few shillings and was ever on the look out for strangers, who continually became his victims. Our volunteer guide was an agreeable, chatty man, who knew the ways of the town well, from an experience of many years; he would not leave us until he brought us to the house the billet directed us to; but the people who now occupied the house were newcomers, and knew very little of the neighbourhood. We enquired at every house in Long Alley with a like success, and at length were obliged to give it up for the night, almost dead with fatigue and disheartened by disappointment. We found it as difficult to procure a lodging, our beaten-down condition being against us, and only for the untiring kindness of our old fellow countryman, who was a native of Clonmel, we might have passed the night in the air, or become the inmates of a watch-house.[4]

'As I stayed with you so so long,' said he, 'I will not leave you until I see you comfortably housed for the night,' which he did in the neighbourhood of Saffron Hill, where, after partaking of some refreshment with us, which we all stood in need of, he departed, wishing us a sound night's rest and better success in our next day's search, luxuries we were very anxious to enjoy.

It was late in the morning when we arose. The one general theme that was in everyone's mouth was the great conflagration that had taken place in the night. We did not know what to do, or where to turn for the information we wanted; I asked several working men that I thought looked like shoemakers, as I went along, but nobody knew anything of the person I enquired for; at last I asked a man who said, with a good-humoured smile on his countenance, if the person I was enquiring after was an Irishman. 'If so,' he continued, 'your surest way to find him would be to go to St. Giles's, for,' he said, 'they all hang together, like a swarm of bees.' 'Where is St. Giles's?', I asked. 'Oh, just at the top of the street, here,' said he, and he went away laughing. Whether he spoke in jest or in earnest, I know not, but I followed his advice, and was not disappointed on reaching the 'Holy Land', as St. Giles's was then emphatically called.[5]

---

[3] An agent whose business was to entrap men for service, especially by duping or coercing them.

[4] A building used as a station for town watchmen and for the overnight detention of disorderly persons brought in by the watchmen.

[5] St Giles in the Fields was home to one of the highest concentrations of Irish-born migrants in early nineteenth-century London, a fact that contributed to its notoriety for poverty, disease and squalor.

I asked at every cobbler's stall I saw in my way for a shoemaker of the name of Tom Neill, but he was not known in the locality; no way daunted, I now resolved to ask at every shoemaker's shop that came in my way, and the first I fixed my eye on was a corner shop, near St. Giles's Church; this I entered, and made the same enquiry. A young man, who stood at the cutting-board, said he did not know the man I enquired for.

'Is he an Irishman?' said he; I answered in the affirmative. 'Then,' said he, 'I can direct you to Paddy Brian, and there is not an Irish shoemaker in London but he is acquainted with,' and in a most obliging way he gave me the direction in writing; it run thus: 'Paddy Brian, at Adam Patrick's, Horse and Groom, King Street,' which, said he, 'anybody will show you.'

Adam Patrick was a crack don and prize man in the ladies' branch, and his house was one of the noted rendezvous of the craft. The landlord directed me to Paddy Brian's domicile, in a narrow arched passage adjoining the house. As I groped up the stairs, which were very dark, a rough, hoarse voice called out, 'Who comes here?' I said a friend. 'Who do you want?' Paddy Brian, I replied; 'Well here I am,' and he came almost tumbling down a'top of me, roaring out, all in one breath, 'Who are you? Where did you come from? What do you want of Paddy Brian?' I said I was the son of Tom Neill, and I was informed that he could tell me where I could find him.

'That I cannot, my boy,' said he, 'though I know old Tom better than he knows himself; but I have not seen him these three weeks, and then he was about changing his lodgings after a glorious fuddle; but, my boys,' he continued, 'come in here and wet your whistles, for you must have had a long dry walk.'

We followed him into the Horse and Groom, where he placed a measure of gin and a pot of beer before us, saying, as he blew the froth from the top of the pot, and took a swig to christen it, 'Now, my boys, sit and enjoy yourselves until I return, and then I will send you to where you will find old Tom,' and off he went with a man they called Metre Healy, who, they said, had been burned out in Hart Street, at the great fire on the previous night.

The tap-room was crowded with shopmates, the most of whom were acquainted with my father, and we were pressed to drink on every side. It was on the eve of a great working match between two don closers,[6] of the names of Ben Ralph and Joe Mew, and the partisans of the different men were noisy in their praise; there were many wagers laid on the result.

In about an hour Paddy Brian returned, bearing in his hand a large cabbage leaf, in which he had rolled up some fine pork chops, which he asked the landlord to get cooked; but not being able to get them done, he forced them on us, saying we could get them cooked at our next resting place. He then

---

[6] Skilled cobblers whose job it was to join together the uppers of boots and shoes.

gave me a direction to old Matthew Brian, who, he said, was a particular friend of old Tom's, and always knew where to find him. Matthew Brian lived in Rosemary Lane, or Rag Fair, close to the Tower of London.

Matthew Brian was a native of Carrick, but had been settled in Waterford for many years, where he was noted as the best channel and men's pump[7] man in the city; his son settled in Carrick much about the time time that I did, and was my shopmate and one of my chief companions while he remained in the town; he went to reside in Cork soon after the rebellion of '98, where he was murdered in a trade row, at the time of a strike for wages, he having gone to work contrary to the wishes of the general body of the trade; his corpse was found in the river, under the north bridge, the day after the deed was perpetrated.

---

[7] A light low-heeled shoe.

5
Michael Fagg, *The Life and Adventures of a Limb of the Law*

(London: A. Hancock, 1836). 280pp.; pp. 122–8.

The legal memoirs of Michael Fagg, which may be pseudonymous, reveal that he was born in Cork city in 1793.[1] The author deters the reader from trying to trace 'a long pedigree of illustrious ancestors', since 'most probably they were, what their name indicates, a fagging and industrious class of people'. Fagg explains that he began his legal apprenticeship in Kenmare, where his uncle was an attorney. In 1822 he qualified as a lawyer in London and later became a bencher at Lincoln's Inn. Most of the narrative is taken up with descriptions of his 'fagging peregrinations' around London and ends with his marriage in 1834 to his Irish sweetheart, Emily Pelham. Chapter 14, reproduced below, describes the swindling of Fagg and his friend, a Mr Wheeler, in 'a disorderly house' on their arrival in Bristol in 1815. Although the duping of the naïve newcomer is one of the archetypes of immigrant writing, there are relatively few accounts of such incidents in the autobiographies of the Irish in Britain. The massive influx of Famine refugees during the 1840s encouraged organised forms of targeted exploitation in many British cities, especially in ports such as Bristol and Liverpool. A reporter for *The Morning Chronicle* observed in July 1850: 'As soon as a party of emigrants arrive in Liverpool they are beset by a tribe of people, both male and female, who are known by the name of "mancatcher", and "runner". The business of these people is, in common parlance, to "fleece" the emigrant, and to draw from his pocket, by fair means or foul, as much cash as he can be persuaded, inveigled, or bullied into parting with.'[2] An oblique pictorial analogue of Fagg's tale may be seen in Erskine Nichol's painting, *An Irish Emigrant Landing at Liverpool* (1871), which shows the eponymous traveller being assailed by two young ruffians on the dockside, while an anxious-looking young woman receives directions from a swarthy male figure in the background.

We landed in Bristol after a quick passage of forty hours; here we continued for a few days, visiting every place worthy of notice in that city, and

---

[1] William Matthews claims Fagg wrote pseudonymously, but offers no evidence to support this claim. See his *British Autobiographies*, p. 97.
[2] Cited in Swift (ed.), *Irish Migrants in Britain*, p. 22.

although it was then a common observation that the women of Bristol were so very ordinary that it was the practice, in order to induce a man to marry one of them, to confer the freedom of the city on him immediately after the ceremony was concluded, yet I confess I cannot concur in the justness of this remark, having, during my short stay there, seen several of the fair sex whose personal appearance gave it a direct negative. On the day previous to that fixed for our departure to the capital, I met a female of most prepossessing appearance in the street, who had really all the external appearance of a lady; she was leading a child by the hand, and surveyed me with a scrutinizing eye as I passed her; I turned round to look after her, supposing I was not unknown to her, when she instantly seemed to recognize me, and manifested a disposition to cultivate my acquaintance. Upon intimating to Wheeler that I had some intention of introducing myself to her, he stoutly opposed it, under the supposition that she was the wife of some respectable citizen who was mistaken with regard to my person, and that my reception would be far from agreeable when she discovered her error. My friend's remarks were not sufficient to deter me from my purpose, and I exchanged his company for that of the female, with whom I very soon fell into conversation, under the pretext that I had seen her elsewhere; she declared that she was labouring under a similar impression. After we had mutually undeceived each other in this respect, our discourse was interrupted by my fair companion stopping at the door of a house of tolerable appearance, which I supposed to be her residence, and was about to retire highly gratified with the few moments we had spent in each other's society; but Miss Henman (that being her name as I afterwards learnt) with a most bewitching smile, which it was impossible to resist, invited me in. Previous to complying, I waited for Wheeler to come up, who lagged behind, being doubtful as to the kind of reception I should meet with; as soon as he came up I made him acquainted with the invitation I had received, when to my surprise he at once declined to avail himself of it; however, after some importunity on the part of the lady and myself he was prevailed upon. We accordingly entered a room on the first floor very handsomely furnished, and had not been long seated before Miss Henman, under some trifling excuse, retired and shortly after returned, ushering in a tall, thin-faced damsel of her acquaintance, who she stated lived on the second floor, and who was consigned to the care of my friend, under the name of Miss Clarke; we had not enjoyed the society of our new acquaintances very long, before one of them let slip some hints that she was not much an admirer of dry conversation, and suggested that a little of the juice of the grape would enliven the various subjects we were descanting upon. This appeal to our generosity was sure to be responded to, and in a trice the bottle was introduced; as the glass passed round, we became more and more animated and enamoured of each other. The ladies perceiving by our accent that we were recent importations from the Emerald Isle, took both myself and my friend on the weak side, and launched

forth into a lofty panegyric upon Irishmen in general, whom they designated as being gallant, open-minded, and generous in the extreme; this
eulogium on the national character of our countrymen made us far from
being dissatisfied with our companions; on the contrary, Wheeler, who was
more enthusiastic in encouraging these hyperbole compliments than myself,
quaffed an additional glass to each flattering expression, until he began to
manifest symptoms of inebriation; when he dozed off, and gradually fell into
a profound sleep, I endeavoured to rally him, but without effect. During the
oblivion of my friend I exerted myself to supply the chasms in the conversation, till it was necessary that the bottle should be replenished; this was soon
done, and the circling glass inspired us with vivacity for a short time longer;
but our spirits gradually evaporated, and the conversation was interrupted
by frequent yawnings and symptoms of drowsiness in my companions; for
my own part, I was fast following the example of my friend, when I imagined
I heard the ladies whispering together; this aroused me a little, and caused
me for the first time to be rather suspicious of the company we had got into,
and, as a matter of precaution, I took an opportunity, when I thought they
were not observing me, of slipping nine sovereigns, which remained from
Mr. Millard's gift, into one of my stockings. In this fancied security, I yielded
to the stupor that oppressed me and was soon in a profound sleep.

In this state of utter insensibility myself and Wheeler continued until we
were aroused by the landlady, who entered the room and desired to know if
we intended to take up our quarters there for one night? This interrogatory
was responded to by a few yawns and expressions of dissatisfaction at being
so unceremoniously disturbed. Having been thus aroused, we looked around
for our fair companions; but the landlady, anticipating what was passing on
our minds, gave us to understand that they had left an hour or two previously,
having given especial directions that our slumbers should not on any account
be broken in upon; and, in answer to our further enquiries, she informed us
that she knew nothing more about them than that they occasionally frequented her house. A word to the wise, they say, is enough; and no doubt
was left upon our minds as to the real character of the house into which we
had been inveigled. Upon making this discovery, in a hurried manner we
proceeded to examine if our money was secure; scarcely had my companion
thrust his hands into his pockets, than he changed colour, and exclaimed
with a rueful countenance, 'Blood and 'ounds, Fagg, my money is all gone,
I am ruined forever.' This sudden exclamation by no means astounded me,
but instinctively applying my hand to my leg, I found it quite bare; I looked
around with much concern for my stocking, and soon espied it on the carpet,
turned inside out, and emptied of its contents. My grief at making this discovery may be readily imagined; but mine was nothing compared to that of my
friend, who for a while appeared inconsolable for his loss, which amounted
to fifty pounds, notwithstanding that I did all that possibly lay in my power
to assuage his sorrow. The landlady, who happened to be present at this

scene, appeared to enjoy the joke, which considerably added to our mortification, and I verily believe, had not her sex protected her, Wheeler would
have taken summary vengeance upon her; he, however, threatened to have
her taken before the magistrate, and punished as an accessary before the
fact, and as the keeper of a disorderly house. This language was far from
being palatable to the mistress, who hallooed out as loud as she could bawl
for Jack and Jerry when, almost in an instant, two stout, ill-looking fellows
made their appearance and, without deigning to inquire into the cause of
our contention, ejected myself and my companion into the street without
much ceremony.

After considerable discussion it was agreed that we should put up with
our loss rather than run the risk of an exposure. On the way to our lodgings
mutual recriminations passed between us, my friend attributing his loss solely
to me, while I pleaded, *Nemo omnibus horis sapit;*[3] the truth of which, Wheeler
observed, we had truly experienced.

Having now arrived at the tavern, I repaired to my portmanteau, which
I unlocked, and found the twenty pounds secure which I had received from
my parents on starting, half of which I tendered to my friend, who seemed
penetrated with this act of generosity, but declined to accept it, saying he
should for the present appoint me his banker. After a short interval Wheeler
retired to his bedroom, as I imagined for the night, but had not been long
absent before he returned in a very different temper from what he had been
in but a few minutes previously, and began to dance in a most extravagant
manner, as if he had taken leave of his senses, and it was sometime before he
could be brought to a proper equilibrium; on inquiring into the cause of this
sudden change of temperament, my friend informed me that he was fifty
pounds better off than he had any idea of, his mother having presented him
with a bank note for that sum to meet any casual expenses that might arise,
which he had not recollected until that instant, and which he produced; this
unexpected piece of good news administered no less pleasure to him than it
did to me, who was unconsciously the cause of his loss as well as my own.

After venting forth innumerable imprecations on the frail pair by whom
we had been duped, we mutually agreed that we had had enough of Bristol,
and retired to rest at a late hour with a resolution to depart the next morning
by the first coach.

---

[3] 'No one is wise at all times'.

6

James Dawson Burn, *The Autobiography of a Beggar Boy*

(London: William Tweedie, 1855). 200pp.; pp. 46–50.

James Dawson Burn's (*c*.1806–1889) beginnings were a mystery even to himself. He was born out of wedlock in Ulster to parents of Scottish ancestry, but exactly where or when he couldn't be sure: 'Where or how I came into the world I have no very definite idea.' After his parents parted his mother migrated to Dumfries, where she married a Catholic Irishman named William McNamee, an alcoholic ex-soldier who took young James with him on his begging and peddling expeditions around Northumberland and the Scottish lowlands. His travels with his profligate step-father were the prelude to his own years of vagrancy as a beggar and casual labourer in northern England and southern Scotland in the period after 1816. Burn's desire for self-betterment eventually led to his becoming apprenticed to a Hexham hatmaker in the 1820s, after which he settled to the trade in Glasgow in the early 1830s. There he become involved in trade union and radical politics, including Chartism, and played a leading role in the establishment of the Oddfellows movement, on which subject he published a book in 1845. After leaving Glasgow in 1850 Burn fell back into the grip of poverty and it was during this time that he wrote his picaresque autobiography, over the course of a year, while travelling from Aberdeen to London. Burn later spent three years plying his trade in New York in the early 1860s, after which he worked as an inspector for the Great Eastern Railway from 1871 until his retirement in 1881.

  The Autobiography of a Beggar Boy is a remarkable literary achievement by a self-taught vagabond who was unable to read until his twenties. Written in the form of a series of letters to the author's son, it is at once an enthralling account of the self-contained subcultures of nomadic begging and peddling, written from within; a perceptive chronicle of a rapidly industrialising Victorian society; a highly literate evocation of an illegitimate artisan's perilous relationship to the world he inhabits; and an acutely self-reflexive record of one man's quest for self-realisation and self-improvement. Throughout, Burn presents himself as a working-class atom without agency, his struggle to achieve social respectability being continually thwarted by the vagaries of economic forces and by his lack of a stable sense of who he is and where he belongs. Central to his sense of himself as 'an unclaimed particle of animation – a thing that belonged to nobody' was his abandonment by his natural father in infancy, the unresolved emotional repercussions of which surface strongly in Chapter 3 of his autobiography, from which the following extract is taken. Burn here records the short period he spent in 1815–16 living with and working for his father, a corduroy weaver named McBurney, then based in Killyleagh, County Down. Dismayed by his father's harsh treatment of him, the aggrieved son executes his own act of desertion, symbolically renaming himself in the process. Although he was knowingly consigning himself to years of penury, Burn later credits the birth of his self-initiative and autonomy to this decisive act of filial rebellion: 'Had I remained in Ireland, I think my natural energy of mind would have been crushed, and I might have remained a ragged outcast during my life. My conduct of leaving under the circumstances gave early proof of my determination of character.'

In the middle of April, 1816, my father took me with him to assist some neighbouring farmer in making his turf. It seems to be a regular practice in that part of the country for the neighbours to assist each other in getting in their winter's fuel; this operation always takes place in the early part of the season, in order that the turf may be thoroughly dried through the course of summer. Two little circumstances occurred to me upon this occasion, which would not be worth notice but for the after consequences of one of them. The one was having enjoyed a good dinner, and the other having my right foot severely wounded on the instep, by the tramp of a horse. I have already observed, that my feet were in a very bad condition in consequence of being always exposed to the weather, my new wound was therefore, a very unacceptable addition to my catalogue of sorrows.

As the season advanced, my yearnings for liberty increased, and my resolves began to assume something like a tangible form. One day in the early part of May, I was sent to the moss for a bag of turf; this was after I had done winding bobbins for the day; the wound on my foot was extremely painful, and what made it more so, I had no commiseration shown me, and no one seemed to care whether I felt pain or pleasure, so long as I could perform my tasks. I had got to the moss, had filled my bag and got my load resting on the highway; this was the direct road from Killaleagh to Belfast. After standing reflecting with the mouth of the bag in my hand for a few minutes, my final resolve was made; I tumbled the turf out on the road, put the bag under my arm, and turned my face towards Belfast, and my back to a friendless home. I had no such feeling as Jacob experienced when he left his father's house; my mind was made up that whatever might be my lot in life, no consideration should induce me to return. From the moment I made up my mind, I threw myself boldly upon the world, and for ever broke asunder every tie that connected me to the name I bore. I had neither staff, nor scrip, nor money in my pocket. I commenced the world with the old turf-bag. It was my only patrimony. In order that I might sever the only remaining link that bound me to my family, I tore two syllables from my name; and thus I wandered forth into the wide world a fugitive from kindred and from home. I had no fear but one, and that was of being followed, and taken back. I travelled sixteen Irish miles that afternoon. The excited state of my feelings kept down the pain I otherwise must have suffered from the wounded foot. That night I found an asylum in a cow-house in a suburb of Belfast, and the next morning I was off by day-light for Donaghadee. My reason for going there was that it was the port I landed at when first coming to Ireland. On my way I called at a farm-house and begged a little food. I reached Donaghadee about ten o'clock in the morning, and found that the packet was not to sail till late in the evening. For fear I should be discovered, I hid myself among the rocks on the sea-shore until the sailing of the vessel. When that time arrived (which I thought would never come), I stowed myself in the forecastle until the vessel was a good way out to sea. I cannot express the joy I felt when I found myself safe. The captain badgered me when he found I could not pay my fare, but this was soon over. We arrived in Portpatrick harbour, about two o'clock in the morning, where I had the honour of another good blowing up from the boatmen who put me ashore – that, too, passed by without giving me any trouble. I thus landed in Scotland a penniless wanderer, but with a mind full to overflowing, with real joy at my escape from bondage. No officious porter importuned me to carry my luggage; nor did any cringing lodging-house keeper invite me to accept of his hospitality. After looking about me for a few minutes, I observed a gentleman's travelling carriage standing before the head inn; with a light heart I took up my quarters in this comfortable abode, where I slept soundly until I was unceremoniously pulled out by a servant in livery about half-past six in the morning.

You may be curious to learn what were my future plans and prospects when I had got thus far. To tell the truth, I had no definite idea of what was to come of me, only that I was determined to fly to England. All my happiest childish associations were centred in the valley of North Tyne, in Northumberland, and I was, therefore, continually attracted in that direction. The distance from Portpatrick to Bellingham, which I looked upon as my destination, would be about 150 miles. The distance gave me no trouble – indeed, if it had been 1000 miles it would have been all the same to me. I took the road for Dumfries, and travelled about twenty miles the first day. I begged my way with as good a grace as possible; all I required was food and lodgings, and I had very little trouble in obtaining either the one or the other. The day after I landed, I went into a farm-house on the wayside to solicit a little food. The good woman observing my *bag*, naturally imagined I was one of a family, and kindly gave me a quantity of *raw potatoes*, which I could not refuse. These potatoes gave me no small trouble, as I could not make up my mind to throw them away, so I carried them to the end of my second day's journey, and gave them to an old woman in Ferry Town of Cree, for liberty to lie before her fire all night. Poor old creature! she gave me share of her porridge in the morning, seasoned with sage advice. Next day being Sunday, I took my time on the way, and travelled until nine o'clock in the evening. Seeing a farm-house a little off the road, I went and asked for lodgings. At the time I called the inmates were engaged in family worship, as soon as they had finished I was inundated with a shower of questions, to which I had to reply by a volley of answers. The gudeman *thoucht* I had run *awa'* frae me place, 'saying it was an *unca* like thing to see a *laddie* like me *stravaging* about the *kintra* on the Sabbath-day; he was *shere* I belanged to somebody, and it was a pity, for I was a weel-faured callant, he wad warrant I was hungry.' After this he ordered the gudewife to gie me some *sipper*; I had, therefore, an excellent supper of sowans[1] with milk, and bread and cheese. After my repast, the good farmer made me up a bed in the barn, with the winnowing sheet for a cover. In the morning I had a good breakfast, and before leaving, the good man gave me a world of advice. Up to this time I had been so elated with my escape that I had not had time to feel the wound on my foot; but the novelty was now beginning to wear away, and my foot began to assert its right to attention as a useful member of the body corporate, and to make me feel smartly for my neglect of it. A great part of the instep was festered, and the pain became so great that my whole limb was affected. I had, therefore, to limp along, and nurse it as I best could.

On the morning of the day I arrived in Dumfries, and just as I was leaving a farm-house where I had lodged all night, in the neighbourhood of Castle Douglas, I fell in with a man who was driving a herd of cattle to Dumfries market, which was held on the following day. Seeing that I was going in the same direction, he invited me to assist him in driving the *nowt,* and *whan* we *gat te* the *town* he *wad gie* me a *sax pence te me sel'*! I was certainly in a bad condition for such a task; the money, however, was a tempting inducement, so I accepted his offer. It would be impossible for me to give you anything like an adequate idea of my sufferings in performing the duty of a dog over eighteen miles of a partially fenced road. When we arrived in Dumfries I was fairly exhausted, and like to faint from sheer pain. To mend the matter, the heartless savage discharged me without a farthing of recompense. The monster excused himself by saying he had *nae bawbees.* There I was; hungry, lame, broken down with fatigue, and without a place to lay my head. The toll-keeper, at the entrance of the town, who had witnessed the brutal conduct of the drover, and heard my statement, tried to shame the wretch into a sense of his duty, but he was just one of those animals, in the form of a man, who could afford to put up with any amount of abuse if he could save anything by it.

The toll-keeper being a man who could feel for the sufferings of others, kindly invited me into his house, where he not only supplied me with a hearty meal of victuals, but he also got his wife to wash and dress my wounded foot. This man was a good Samaritan indeed. On leaving him

---

[1] A kind of porridge made from oatmeal, which is steeped in water until sour and then allowed to ferment.

I endeavoured to express my grateful sense of his kindness in the best manner I could.

I had some idea that there was a person living in Dumfries with whom my step-father had been on terms of intimacy; I therefore sought this man's residence, in order that I might obtain a night's lodging. After making inquiry, however, I found that he had left his country by authority! So I had to seek quarters elsewhere, and after some little time I got a lair in a hay-loft belonging to one of the inns.

7

Jane Jowitt, *Memoirs of Jane Jowitt, the Poor Poetess, Aged 74 Years, Written by Herself*

(Sheffield: J. Pearce, 1844). 54pp.; pp. 29–38.

Jane Jowitt was born in Dublin in 1770 into an Anglo-Irish family of some wealth and social standing. However, her barrister father's philandering with an actress, whom he subsequently married after his first wife's death, led him to become 'very wild and dissipated in his conduct', which in turn led to his being imprisoned in Marshalsea for debt. On coming of age, Jowitt used an inheritance bequeathed by her grandmother to acquire a Dublin seaside residence, part of which she let to lodgers during the summer months, until the adverse effects of the 1798 rebellion forced her to sell up and seek her fortune in England. When prejudice thwarted her attempts to find employment as an 'upper servant' in Liverpool – 'every place I went to I was objected to on account of my country' – she went to London and from there to Dover, where she met and married a Catholic Irish soldier in the British army. By the early 1810s Jowitt had settled in Sheffield and was prospering until her husband's illness and death left her once more in debt. It was now that she sought to exploit her literary talents, first as a professional letter-writer and then as a poet, writing memorial verses on commission. One such poem is included in the following extract from her short autobiography, in which she tells of her struggles to overcome personal and professional impediments to respectability.

The late surgeon Thompson, who used to call on me as a medical friend, strongly advised me to leave Sheffield, and said he thought the air of Doncaster would suit my constitution. I accordingly went, and found the families most liberal and kind, and have been about fifteen years among them. I came frequently to Sheffield, and was sadly afflicted by the death of the Rev. Thos. Cotterill,[1] the beloved pastor of St. Paul's, who died of brain and typhus fever; upon which occasion, I wrote the following lines: (it was my first attempt at

---

[1] Reverend Thomas Cotterill (1779–1823), compiler of *Selection of Psalms and Hymns, adapted to the Festivals of the Church of England* (1810), was Perpetual Curate of St Paul's, Sheffield from 1817 until his death.

writing poetry, and though poorly done, the verses gave general satisfaction to all Mr. Cotterill's friends, and proved advantageous to me.)

Lines on the Death of the Rev. T. Cotterill

Alas! I hear the solemn bell,
It tells the death of one we all knew well,
The Pastor, husband, father, friend,
Who to the poor, so oft did lend.

Oh happy Saint how glorious is thy change,
While we are left in this sad world to range,
His tender offspring shed most bitter tears,
His widow'd wife may mourn and weep for years.

O'er his blest clay the willows bend
For widows', orphans', and the strangers' friend;
To yonder realms, his soul has fled away
We trust, to mansions of eternal day.

I had so poor an opinion of my poetry, that I was afraid to put it in print, but it pleased some of the best families in Sheffield, who have been kind to me ever since. The many sermons I have heard him preach, made a powerful impression on my mind; I became more serious and saw I was a guilty sinner. Poor Mrs. Cotterill sent for me to her house and presented me with a guinea, and a gown, and was ever after a friend to me; she is gone for some years to her eternal rest, and is buried with her beloved husband in St. Paul's.

The news of my composing this scrap of poetry spreading abroad, ladies and gentlemen frequently called upon me to purchase the lines. An artful old man who frequently passed through Chapel walk, had his eye constantly on my house; the front door being usually open in fine weather, he could see me writing or selling some of my poetry, and had an idea that it would be a good job to get me for a wife; he had not the courage to speak to me on the subject, but sent a person who lived near me, and as he was above twelve years older than myself, I had not the least idea that he was for making love to me; I allowed him to come in and sit down, and he began by telling me that he had worked twenty years for Messrs. Smith, Holt, & Co. at a silver platers' manufactory, in Arundel-street: that he had fourteen shilling per week and a pension, and thought we might live very comfortable; I told him I would enquire into his character before I made any reply. I accidentally met Mr. Dams, who married Mr. Smith's sister, I told him about the offer made to me by an old man whom I saw every Sunday at Church, and that I believed he worked for Smith, Holt, & Co. He advised me to accept the offer, that he and Mrs. Dams had known him for above twenty years, that he was honest and industrious, and he thought with what I earned myself, we might live comfortable. In consequence of hearing this, I gave my consent, and we were married in Sheffield. I left Chapel walk, and got a better and cheaper house in the neighbourhood of St. Paul's. For about six months he behaved well, but soon returned to his former habit of drinking, which so offended his employers that they immediately discharged him; he now had nothing to take to, and I had the mortification of having to bear with his drunkenness and abusive language, and blows whenever I refused him money; however I told him he might live on his pension, or go into the workhouse, and that I could not lead such a life. He brought in a broker, sold all my furniture and drank the money. I was now left in a state of destitution, and knew not what to do. When he found he could get nothing more from me, he threw himself on the parish, and gave up his pension papers to the overseers. However, it pleased the Almighty to withdraw him from this world, and I trust he will pardon his misdeeds.

I still had to struggle for a living for myself, the overseers refused to give me any outdoor relief, and I was in a destitute situation, however, I appeared before Mr. Hugh Parker,[2] who decided that I should receive 1s. 6d. per week. As I had this trifle to pay my lodging, I determined upon writing a little more poetry. Soon after, the beloved wife of the present Earl Fitzwilliam[3] died very suddenly, leaving ten children to mourn the loss of a most amiable mother. Upon which occasion I wrote the following lines [...].

These lines gave general satisfaction, and I sold above eight hundred of them to the tenantry. I went to Mrs. Haugh's boarding school at Doncaster, and sold them to all the nobility and gentry about the neighbourhood, and soon was taken great notice of, got many presents of clothing &c. so that I soon made a decent appearance and lived well. [...]. I never had courage to send these pieces to Wentworth House,[4] or I am almost sure that I should have received some recompence.

I went to York about a week before the Musical Festival, the City was getting so very full and lodgings were very scarce and dear; I was very sorry that I took this journey, and thought it best to return to Doncaster. I had paid for some printing and was quite bare of cash when I went out, but I managed to sell a few of my verses on the road, and paid for two nights lodgings and thought I would go on Monday morning and trust to divine providence. I got about half way on the road to Thorpe Arch; when I was accosted by a poor old Irishman who asked me for charity, he seemed in great distress, he was lame and almost naked, and the tears were trickling down his aged cheeks;

---

[2] Doncaster-based Justice of the Peace.

[3] Whig politician and landowner Charles William Wentworth Fitzwilliam (1786–1857) was an advocate of parliamentary reform and an outspoken opponent of the Corn Laws. His wife Mary, who bore him ten children, died in premature labour in 1830.

[4] The country seat of the Fitzwilliam family in the West Riding of Yorkshire.

I felt hurt that I had it not in my power to relieve him; I told my situation, that I had been disappointed in the sale of my little books, but advised him to call at some of the Farm houses; he said if he had a crust to take in his hand he would ask them for a little milk, I immediately recollected I had a dry crust in the bottom of my basket, I took it out and gave it to the poor man, and he appeared so delighted that I knew he was in great want; he immediately prayed most fervently for God to bless me and send me every thing needful, for he was sure I had a feeling heart, and desired me to call on Mr. Carrol at Boston, who he said was a good Irish gentleman; and then went forward on the road and I heard the old man praying for me as he walked on; I immediately thought, that perhaps the prayer of this poor man would be heard and that I would have some good luck; my hopes were realized, for I got in the course of the day about thirty shillings for my scraps of Poetry, and after that I determined to relieve any poor creature I met according to my means; how sinful it is to waste any kind of food that is clean and wholesome, when my poor dry crust seemed of such value to the Irishman that was starving.

The death of Lady Charlotte Lane Fox, next occurred, I went to the house of George Lane Fox, Esquire, of Bramham,[5] this gentleman, whose mind is possessed of a large share of benevolence and tenderness towards the poor, received me in the most courteous manner, bought a large number of my verses and desired me to call at his house whenever I had any new pieces; paid me in a most generous manner, and has been a kind of benefactor to me many times since; I had good success in the neighbourhood, and I really thought I received those blessings on account of the old crust.

---

[5] George Lane Fox (*c*.1793–1848) of Bramham Park, Yorkshire, MP for Beverley.

8

J. E., 'Life of an Irish Tailor, Written by Himself'

The Commonwealth, 18 April 1857, p. 2.

J. E., who identifies himself only by his initials throughout his condensed autobiography, was born in County Antrim in 1816, the youngest of a family of seven. Orphaned at a young age, he spent some time in care before being apprenticed in 1828 to a country tailor, with whom he spent seven years. At the end of his apprenticeship he moved to Belfast and thence to Liverpool, where he joined the Tailors' Club. The following extract, sub-headed 'Journeymanship – Belfast and Liverpool', covers the unhappy period he spent working in the north of England in the late 1830s, after which he returned to Ireland, where he eventually found employment as a caretaker and watchman in an unnamed northern town. In many respects, his is a classic economic migrant's tale that tells of discriminatory employment practices, workplace rivalries and the vicissitudes of being on the tramp. Yet there is a didactic as well as a documentary dimension to the text, which was published in a Glasgow newspaper devoted to the moral and intellectual improvement of the working class.[1] The tailor is much exercised by the evils of alcohol, tobacco and gambling and, having succumbed to the temptations of all three at various times in his life, concludes his life-story on a morally improving note by extolling the benefits of temperance. The fact that he ultimately defines the meaning of his life in moral rather than social or political terms means that his narrative is closer in tone and purpose to seventeenth- and eighteenth-century puritan autobiography than to the more secular memoirs of nineteenth-century political radicals such as James Dawson Burn and Robert Crowe.

I engaged in Belfast as a club apprentice at eight shillings per week. My new master had a good small trade. His staff consisted of a journeyman, an apprentice, and a daughter – a waistcoat maker – who could join in obscene conversation with the journeyman without a blush. I wrought here

---

[1] *The Commonwealth* frontispiece bore a legend from Benjamin Franklin: 'A Bible and a Newspaper in every house, and a good school in every district, all studied and appreciated as they merit, are the principal support of virtue, morality, and civil liberty.'

sometime, but as I did not get my pay too regular, nor enough of it, and as my master was always wishing me to believe I could do nothing right, I left. I wrought a few weeks elsewhere, at higher wages; but trade became slack, and the season being far advanced, I accepted the offer of a friend who kept a ready-made clothing store, and wrought to him for a few months during the winter. I saw this was no way to improve in business, so in the spring I set off to Liverpool, having received a letter of recommendation to the manager of a large tailoring establishment there.

I forthwith got a call to work, having first joined the Tailors' Club; but my shopmates said I had got an irregular call, and were for striking, unless I paid 18s. of a fine. The rules of society did not prohibit a young hand entering free, but jealousy at a stranger obtaining a special call prompted them to give an unanimous verdict against me. Policy dictated that I should pay the fine. Shortly after I commenced to work, the twenty men on the board would make the greenhand pay his footing.[2] Five shillings was demanded; with some difficulty I put them off with the half, to which each added his mite,[3] and a quantity of ale was sent for. This appeared to be a common practice. Here I was paid according to the job, and could earn a pound a week; others could earn more, as good jobs seldom came my road. I found these club men, who designated themselves 'honourable,' but aped the name; for when an extra hand was wanted, a special call would be given to a friend, and no notice taken of it or fine imposed. And some of those who were loudest in denouncing men for working in shops unconnected with the society, could, if work was slack, take a job home out of said shops. Besides, they were most profuse with the porter and ale to the foreman cutter and sewer, so that they not only got the best paying jobs in our shop, but were the seldomest idle.

For weeks and months after I commenced working in this shop I was the butt of their ridicule and scorn; every mean and vile epithet was too good for me. There was one person in particular who took the lead in this affair; and one day he so enraged the stranger that he challenged him to a fight; but the sneaking fellow cowed before a justly-incensed man, and there and then I gave him an admonition, which he remembered till the day I left the shop. On another occasion, one of these bullies, with whom I was joined in making a coat, gave me the lie several times in the most contemptuous manner. The quiet man, in an unmistakable tone, told him, that if he dared repeat the words he would make him repent it. The boaster sang dumb, and from this time forth I had peace.

I had now passed the ordeal, and was recognized as an equal. The general subjects of conversation on the board were women, politics, and the diversions of the day. Obscene language of the grossest kind was used, not

---

[2] The fee required for admittance to the trade.
[3] A modest contribution, specifically, half a farthing.

only without remorse, but with the greatest delight. To a man they were red-hot communists. Only give them the reins of government, and they would legislate and rule for the people's good. There were, as it were, honourable exceptions, but the majority of them were inebriates; and though they could earn 25s. per week, they were in debt, their families and themselves badly clothed, and filthy in their persons. From Saturday night till Tuesday was generally spent in drinking; and when they returned to work, their breath was odious, their heads ached, their stomachs were disordered; they were all wrong, and doses of seidlitz powders[4] and gin were alternately sent for, to recruit their jaded bodies. When they became convalescent, then the talk went on about the fine house, first-rate ale, the jovial company, the theatre, &c, &c. 'They gloried in their shame.' And these are the men who were the pets, and got the best jobs. As to their religious opinions, there was a sort of Protestantism, a large mixture of Romanism, and a sprinkling of avowed infidelity.

At the end of every fortnight each member had to attend to hand in his subscription towards the funds of the society. For the benefit of the innkeeper, a pint of ale was paid for each member – let that member drink it or not. What at first was repugnant to me, by and by became apparently harmless, then I relished it, and finally I fell from my innocence, not, 'tis true, to be a sot, but to love a glass of ale and the company of a tavern. Let young men beware of these clubs, particularly when their place of rendezvous is a tavern. [...]

After working eighteen months in this shop, there came a dullness in trade, and several of us were turned off. We entered our names on the slate of 'the house of call,' that when an employer wanted hands he could send for them, for these club men say it is dishonourable to go to look for work. Three times a day the call was given, and if the man at the head of the slate was absent, the call was given to the next, and so on. Lest one should miss his turn, many sat the greater part of the day in the club-room, drinking, smoking, and card-playing, and to beguile a tedious hour, I tried my hand also. For three months I got about a fortnight's work; my board money of 10s. 6d. per week was running on; I had a few sovereigns saved, but now they were all gone, and what was I to do?

I lifted my *card*, which stated that 'J. E. was a member of the honourable tailors' society,' and which gained a bed only in a strange town. After pawning my spare clothes for a few shillings to help me on the way, a Paisley man and I set off on the tramp. Manchester, Preston and Birmingham were the only towns we could get work in; during a tramp of some ten weeks we got about sixteen days' work. In going up from Chesterfield to Birmingham, we were so pressed for want of food that we made free to some potatoes growing in a

---

[4] A laxative consisting of sodium bicarbonate, sodium potassium tartrate and tartaric acid mixed in solution.

field, and tried to eat them raw. A person whom I had seen in Belfast assisted us in Birmingham, and got us a few days' work, but in an irregular shop. We were afraid of being found out, so we left the town, as we couldn't get work in a regular shop, and not a job could we get till we returned to Liverpool. On the last days tramp from Bolton to Liverpool, we felt the gnawings of hunger keenly – not having eaten anything from the previous morning in Manchester. When within five miles of Liverpool, my companion found 4s. 6d. on the road, which caused a thrill of joy to go through our hearts, and enabled us to get a hearty meal in the first convenient house, which we ate with thankful hearts, and got into Liverpool safe and well.

On arriving there each took his own road. I got a bed in new lodgings. On the following day I got no work, and being *minus* of cash to procure a bed, I went to a shed at the docks, and put over the night as best I could – where there appeared to be several as forlorn and penniless as myself. On the third day I mustered courage to go to my usual lodgings, and was kindly received. I could get no tailoring to do, so I took a day's work as a labourer in a cotton store at the quay at 3s. My hands were greatly blistered at night, turning the machine which hoists the bales of cotton. There were three other men at this turning machine, and I imagined they looked upon me as an intruder, and left the onus of the turning to the stranger.

I had tried everywhere for work. I paid to get my name down in a shipping office for a steward of a vessel, and even spoke to several captains, but to no effect. At length I got some clothes to make for a clerk, a fellow lodger, with the price of which I paid my fare to Dublin, and landed in Kingstown with threepence in my pocket. I bought one pennyworth of bread at Kingstown, on the strength of which I walked into Dublin, a distance of seven miles. I got a bed on my card in Dublin.

9

Robert Crowe, *The Reminiscences of Robert Crowe, the Octogenerian Tailor*

(New York: n.p., n.d. [1902]). 32pp.; pp. 7–11.

Robert Crowe was born in 1823 into a poor Dublin Catholic family, 'no silver spoon being in my mouth when I came into the world', as he puts it in his short *Reminiscences*. At the age of 14 he emigrated to London to be apprenticed as a tailor to his elder brother, arriving in the week of King William IV's death. In 1843 he joined a juvenile temperance society and soon became a public advocate of the cause, acquiring 'a name throughout London as a youthful orator'. The same year marked the beginning of Crowe's involvement in two of the great political movements of the 1840s, the campaign for the Repeal of the Union and the agitation for the People's Charter. Crowe's Chartist activities led to his arrest, trial and imprisonment in 1848, the details of which are recalled in the following extract from his episodic autobiography, which consists of 48 very short chapters, described as 'the gathered fragments of a checkered life'. In 1854 Crowe emigrated to the United States and spent some time working as a tailor in Georgia, where, he claims, 'the slime of slavery was everywhere apparent'. Forced to leave Athens because of his abolitionist views, he settled in New York, where he played a prominent part in trade union organisation and labour agitation over the next 40 years. He composed his *Reminiscences* in 1901, aged 78, at the behest of Miss Helen Burns, principal of the non-denominational Cooper Settlement in New York, whose generosity the author acknowledges in his dedicatory preface.

Before I reached my nineteenth year (1843) my spare time was divided between three public movements – the temperance movement under Father Mathew,[1] the repeal movement under Daniel O'Connell[2] and the Chartist

---

[1] Father Theobald Mathew (1790–1856), Capuchin friar and temperance campaigner. He led a major temperance crusade in England during the summer of 1843.
[2] Daniel O'Connell's (1775–1847) campaign for the repeal of the Union sought to bring about the re-establishment of the Irish parliament. In 1844 he was honoured with banquets and public demonstrations of support in London, Liverpool and Birmingham.

or English movement under Fergus O'Connor.[3] In the bewildering whirl of excitement in which I lived during these years, I seemed almost wholly to forget myself. Night brought with it long journeys to meetings and late hours, though the day brought back the monotony of the sweater's den.

In the Irish or repeal movement came those monster meetings of 1843 and 1844, which so alarmed the English government as to cause the hurried dispatch of over a hundred thousand troops to Ireland. An amusing incident occurred in one of those meetings, which in this connection deserves a place as illustrating the ready wit with which Daniel O'Connell was gifted. The Government employed a well-known stenographer named Hughes to attend these meetings and make correct reports of all speeches for future use. When O'Connell arose to address the meeting, he turned in the direction where Mr Hughes was sitting, and shouted in that rich Irish brogue for which he was distinguished:

'Mr Hughes, are you ready to proceed?'

'Mr Hughes answered: "I am, Mr O'Connell."'

Then O'Connell commenced one of his most remarkable speeches, which lasted over two hours. In English? Oh, no; in pure Irish, all of which the peasantry could understand. Poor Hughes dropped his note-book and stared into vacancy. The speech to him was so much Greek.

Parallel with the repeal movement in Ireland was the Chartist movement in England, which commenced in 1838 under the leadership of Fergus O'Connor. The platform consisted of the following six propositions or points:

1. Universal suffrage.
2. Vote by ballot.
3. Annual parliaments.
4. Payment of members.
5. No property qualifications.
6. Equality of electoral districts.

In the year following its organization the movement assumed vast proportions, owing mainly to the prevailing distress. Disturbances broke out in Wales, headed by Frost, Williams and Jones, which the Government quickly suppressed.[4] The prosecution of the leaders followed, and they were sentenced to be 'hanged, drawn and quartered,' but the sentence was afterward

---

[3] Cork-born Feargus O'Connor (*c*.1796–1855), charismatic leader of the Chartist movement. Prior to his involvement with English popular radicalism, O'Connor was a member of O'Connell's repeal party during the early 1830s, but left the party in 1835 as a result of political differences.

[4] John Frost (1784–1877), William Jones (1809–1873) and Zephaniah Williams (*c*.1795–1874) led the Chartist rising in Newport in November 1839. It was the last large-scale armed uprising on British soil.

commuted to transportation for life. In the Chartist movement I took an active part up to the period of my prosecution in 1848. The movement did not develop its full power until about 1846, when that blighting, withering curse fell on the Irish people in the failure of the only food of her population. I think it was the *Times* of London that declared the only cure for Irish agitation was to sink the whole island twenty-four hours in the water. The famine of 1846–7 was not a bad substitute. This brings me nearer to the most stormy and momentous period of my life [...].

[O]ur agitation, both in England and Ireland, rose to fever heat. The Young Irelanders[5] were in a fierce conflict with the adherents of O'Connell, repudiating his 'peace at any price' doctrine. On all sides, especially in the north of England, men were arming; bold and defiant utterances were heard on every hand. A convention was called and a day fixed for the presentation of the national petition praying for the enactment of the People's Charter. The day, the 10th of April 1848, memorable in the history of the time, was selected for the occasion. A petition containing 3,500,000 signatures was prepared, and the procession which accompanied the same to the place of meeting (Kennington Common) was certainly the largest and most imposing I ever participated in.

During all this time were the authorities idle? Oh, no. Police spies were scattered among the people. Government buildings, such as the Mint, the Bank of England, the Mansion House, and others were barricaded. Troops were poured into London from every quarter, and the Iron Duke of Wellington[6] declared, in the House of Lords, 'he would not be answerable for the safety of the city of London if 40,000 troops were not placed at his disposal.' Anticipating a possibility of trouble, the Executive Committee who had charge of the movement issued an order on or before the morning of the procession 'that no man walking in the ranks should bear any kind of arms.' This, said the order, was intended as a peaceful demonstration, and if the Government designed a coup d'etat let them have the whole credit of it.

Such was the condition when we marched over the bridges, eight abreast, on our way to Kennington Common, but no sooner did the procession pass over than the police and soldiery took possession of the bridges, and for nearly three hours we were held as prisoners. But for the previous order of the Council a conflict would have been inevitable. At length the order was revoked, and the crowd was permitted to pass, and all went off quietly.

---

[5] Young Ireland was a pro-repeal nationalist movement whose leaders, Thomas Davis (1814–1845), Charles Gavan Duffy (1816–1903) and John Blake Dillon (1814–1866), clashed with O'Connell over strategy and tactics. The movement collapsed following an abortive rebellion of 1848, the so-called 'battle of Widow McCormack's cabbage patch'.

[6] Dublin-born Arthur Wellesley (1769–1852), the first duke of Wellington, was Tory prime minister from 1828 to 1830.

Following quickly on the heels of the above action the Government started a series of prosecutions commencing the following month (May) with a batch of five – Ernest Charles Jones,[7] a barrister and our leader; John Fussell, Sharp, Williams and Dr Vernon. [...]. The above-named prisoners were lodged in the Westminster House of Correction for the term of two years. Then came the second batch, consisting of thirty-two, of whom I had the honor to be one. [...]

The six weeks of our detention in Newgate prior to trial hung heavy on our hands, enlivened only by an occasional glance at the notorious Calcraft,[8] England's public executioner, and Chaplain Davis, the alleged 'man of God.' We used to see them while they were engaged in inspecting the gallows and conferring on the preliminaries of an execution to take place in front of the jail on the following Monday morning. [...]

At last the long looked for time arrived and I was summoned to court. [...] 'Bring the prisoner Crowe to the dock'. A few steps brought me there, and as I stood and gazed around me I asked myself the question: 'Can this be the place where criminals are tried?' Around on every side were ladies of fashion, fans in full play; the court had more the appearance of a theater – for the women outnumbered the men. Right in front of me sat the venerable Judge Baron Platt, in powdered wig; below him sat Her Majesty's Attorney-General, Sir John Jarvis, who was my chief prosecutor, surrounded by a formidable array of subordinates, and all along the tables a dazzling array of powdered wigs.

Again I asked, 'Can it be possible that in this dock where I now stand, a Jack Sheppard,[9] a Jonathan Wild,[10] a Greenacre,[11] and a long line of notable criminals have stood?' I was soon awakened to a consciousness that the scene before me was a well arranged farce by a whispered hint from my solicitor, Mr Dudgeon, to the effect that my counsel, J. Humphrey Parry, dined with Attorney-General the day before. Add to this a complacent middle-class jury – sworn to render a true verdict according to the evidence? Oh, no, but to give a verdict which would guarantee additional security to the few pounds they had deposited in bank from the greedy clutches of those would-be thieves, the Chartists, whose aim was not principle, but pilfering.

Well, the work is finished, and Chartism is crushed, and the wheels of Government roll along smoothly once more – the universal howl of the money-bag press throughout the land has settled it (at least for the present)

---

[7] Radical and writer Ernest Jones (1819–1869) was the last of the Chartist leaders. He was later a leading member of the legal team that defended the Manchester Fenians in 1867.

[8] William Calcraft (1800–1879), famous nineteenth-century hangman who held his post for 45 years and had a reputation for incompetence.

[9] Jack Sheppard (1702–1724), infamous thief and prison breaker.

[10] Jonathan Wild (1683–1725), notorious thief-taker.

[11] James Greenacre (1785–1837) gained infamy as the Edgeware Road murderer.

that the ostensible aim of the Chartists was not principle, but wholesale confiscation of property; not 'universal suffrage and vote by ballot', but, as *Punch* put it, 'universal suffering and vote by bullet'. [...]

Well, the farce is nearly gone through, but one more act remains, namely, passing sentence; another gala day in the Old Bailey, when the prisoners are placed in a row in front of the dock to receive sentence; again the court is crowded with a fashionable throng, and at the opportune time the Attorney-General rises, his pale face suffused with a cold, sardonic, sickly sneer, and conjures his lordship to 'pass a heavy sentence on the prisoner Crowe, because of the dangerously seductive and poetic character of his eloquence and its influence on the minds of his uneducated hearers'; and his lordship, who, no doubt, like another Barkis, passed the following sentence: to be confined in the Westminster House of Correction for the term of two years, with hard labor, and at the expiration of said term to give bonds myself in £100, and two additional securities (householders) at £50 each, to keep the peace with Her Majesty's subjects for the term of five years, and in addition to pay Her Majesty the sum of £10. So red did his lordship grow in the face while delivering the above that I really expected to hear his lordship add the usual declaration when consigning a culprit to the gallows, 'and may the Lord have mercy on your soul,' but his lordship omitted that part of the ceremony. [...]

In the afternoon of the day on which I was sentenced I was hurried off in a cab, accompanied by the Deputy-Governor of Newgate, to the Westminster House of Correction, where I was placed in line with about twenty other criminals, and inspected by the Governor. He was not slow to single me out.

'How long are you here for?'

'Two years, sir.'

'Have his hair cut short.'

I ventured to step a little forward, intending to ask permission to work at my trade, but he roared at me like an infuriated bull, 'Go back there. You're in too great a hurry.' So I went to the oakum room and sat with 750 prisoners daily, picking two and one-half pounds of oakum for nearly six weeks. Very soon my fingers, one by one, began to blister, so that I fell short of accomplishing the required quantity by three-quarters of a pound, and was accordingly reported. Eleven o'clock the next morning the Governor entered.

'Prisoner Crowe, stand up. What reason can you give for not finishing your work yesterday?'

Holding up my two hands, I answered: 'The state of my fingers is the only reason I can assign.'

'That is no reason in this prison. Bread and water for three days.'

The Deputy-Governor (Mr M'Crea) whom on all occasions I found to be directly the opposite of his superior, as soon as my term of punishment was up, called me out in the yard, and asked if I would like to work in the tailor shop. I answered I would. 'Well, come along,' and he placed me in charge of the officer. This made matters more agreeable for the balance of my time.

10

William Hammond, *Recollections of William Hammond, A Glasgow Hand-Loom Weaver*

With a preface by William Winthrope (Glasgow: 'Citizen' Press, 1904). 106pp.; pp. 13–15; 19–20; 29–33.

William Hammond was born around 1830 near Stewartstown in County Tyrone to a weaver and a domestic servant, both of whom were Scottish immigrants. He himself emigrated to Glasgow in the 1840s and settled as a pattern weaver in the Calton district, where he quickly became involved in secular education and trade union politics, as the following excerpt from his *Recollections* makes clear. Elsewhere in his autobiography he records his acquaintanceship with European radicals and revolutionaries who visited mid-Victorian Glasgow, including Garibaldi, Louis Blanc and Lajos Kossuth, and reveals that he was a member of a committee established to help Hungarian refugees who fled the country after the 1849 revolution. Hammond dwells only briefly on his political and trade union activities, however. Most of the book's 11 chapters are given over to detailed accounts of his walking adventures with the Bridgeton Rambling Club, of which he was the last surviving member. A prefatory note explains that Hammond's life-story was recorded and edited for publication by one Thomas Lugton, the author himself being too infirm to use a pen in his old age. The book was published under the auspices of the Glasgow Campbell Club, a society established by students of Glasgow University in honour of the poet Thomas Campbell.

Later in my Irish life I beheld some of the poverty resulting from potato disease, but the worst part of that misery I did not see. Emigration was in the air, and, like other young fellows in Tyrone, I was debating with myself where to go, how to raise money, etc. Being too young to have any dark-eyed colleen to hinder, Scotland or America were in my thoughts, when a letter arrived from a married sister in Glasgow which settled my fate. She and her husband, who was a beamer in a Bridgeton weaving mill, had made up their minds to emigrate to the United States, where a number of Calton and Bridgeton weavers were doing well and recommending others to follow. So there was no time to lose. I laid the matter before my parents, and with their consent set out for Scotland. I sailed in the old *Glowworm* paddle steamer from Belfast at noon, but owing to very stormy weather did not reach Ardrossan till one o'clock next morning. Leaving Ardrossan in an open cattle truck, which was completely filled with Irish emigrants like myself, we reached Bridge Street Station about four o'clock on a fine Sunday morning in midsummer. Some had friends in Glasgow who were expecting them, others had none, but owing to the late arrival of the boat and the early hour nobody was at the railway depot to bid us welcome. The women of our party looked a little woe-begone, and some of the children had fear written on their pretty faces. With my sister's letter in my pocket and sure of a good home, I was about the only cheerful individual in the company, and tried my best to raise their spirits. After shaking hands all round I set out for the Calton, and in a short time was seated in my brother-in-law's house to a breakfast of Lochfyne herrings, good coffee, and Glasgow baker's bread – new delicacies to me. We attended the Relief Church (now Calton U. F.) at a later hour, and in the afternoon discussed my prospects for the following day. I found that my brother-in-law had made some arrangements beforehand for me, so that next morning at six o'clock my first day's work commenced. [...]

It may be in place here to mention that it was not all smooth sailing my settlement in the Calton. Some lads, weavers like myself, helped me to better my skill at the craft, so did the old men with whom I had worked, but some of the baser sort made me understand that it was not an advantage to have been born in Ireland.

When I first came to Glasgow the old Scottish stone-throwing fights among schoolboys were still in vogue, but a desperate battle of this sort which took place at the old wooden bridge at the Farme ford, in which a Rutherglen boy was killed, put a final stop to these barbarities. [...]

Some time after coming to Glasgow I became connected with the Sunday secular schools, where the three R's were taught free of charge, but no religious instruction given. Several leading citizens were supporters of these schools. My own voluntary work in connection with them was to induce young men and boys unable to read and write to attend the classes and get a little instruction. I have gathered in men over forty years old from Glasgow Green on a Sunday to the nearest secular school. The promoters believed that education would help greatly to elevate the masses, but there was keen opposition on account of not using the Bible as a class-book, and after a good record for satisfactory work accomplished the secular schools had to succumb for lack of public support.

Looking backwards, I am obliged to confess that education will not lift a drinking man, and with all our present-day educational advantages there are still too many working people of the low class living like dogs to enable them to save every possible copper for a drink. Old fogies like myself often speculate on the state of the body politic if intoxicants were to go back to the old price, '5d. for the gill and bottle o' sma' yill.' More jails and lunatic asylums might be required.

After my experience with the secular schools, I became connected with the Calton District Hand-Loom Weavers' Trades Union. Very little money was paid into this union, its main objects being protection and education in current politics. At that time Glasgow working men were keen politicians.

I held the position of assistant secretary to our union without a break for many years. The most important part of my work was to attend the meetings of kindred societies and write down such jottings as would enable me to give a fairly correct account of their proceedings to my own union. These meetings were mostly political in character – in fact, they were Chartist meetings pure and simple.

I was an interested eye-witness of the Glasgow Chartist riot of 1848. The rioting broke out simultaneously in the Cowcaddens, Cannon Street, and Trongate. The Trongate mob, by far the largest, broke into Deacon Gilmour's bread shop in the Gallowgate, Landell's edge-tool maker's shop in the Trongate, and an adjoining jeweller's shop. The Sheriff, at the head of a body of horse soldiers, read the Riot Act on the Jail Bridge, but it had very little effect. The Sheriff kept cool, as he saw the mob was simply crazy for a fight. A fool at the head of troops that day would have raised a terrible riot – fortunately no oil was thrown on the flames, and the flames naturally fizzled out. It was a bread riot. There was great distress – some people having actually died from want. The four-pound loaf cost from 11d. to 1s. 0½d., and very inferior bread at that; lowgrade oatmeal was 3s. 6d. to 4s. 6d. per stone; potatoes, owing to disease, were scarce and dear; and Indian meal was 2s. 6d. to 3s. per stone. The Indian, or maize, meal, as it was generally called, was not the help it should have been, for the people did not know how to cook it. From having relatives in Ireland and the United States my own family were able to enjoy the maize meal – indeed, looked upon it as a luxury. We had it boiled the night before, and next morning had a little fat bacon fried from a flitch which had been sent to us from Tyrone. The cold corn porridge was then sliced on the American plan and fried in the bacon fat, and a very appetising and healthy diet we found it to be.

I shall never forget those miserable, hungry years. A Scotsman is not a snappy, aggressive being, but he becomes desperate when roused by great trouble, and the sight of hungry children wailing for food is something he cannot look upon unmoved. But times gradually grew better. The repeal of the Corn Laws, after twenty years' agitation, had a growing influence for good upon working classes.[1] Wages slowly rose, and labouring people began to enjoy little comforts and luxuries to which formerly they had been unaccustomed.

---

[1] The Corn Laws were repealed by Sir Robert Peel's government in February 1846.

11
Ellen O'Neill, *Extraordinary Confessions of a Female Pickpocket*

(Preston: J. Drummond, 1850). 11pp.; pp. 4–8.

The short but intriguing 'confessions' of 17-year-old Ellen O'Neill, described as 'a well-grown young Irishwoman', born in 1833, cannot unproblematically be characterised as autobiography, as the contexts of their narration and presentation make clear. As a member of 'a gang of criminals who have played a conspicuous part in the police history of Lancashire', O'Neill (her married name) was being held in Preston jail as a prisoner 'under sentence of transportation' when her life-story was written down. So not only did she not write her testimony herself – a young woman of her background would almost certainly have been illiterate – but her narrative voice and agency were heavily circumscribed by a troika of male authority figures: the *Daily News* journalist who transcribed her story, the editor who printed it, and the prison chaplain, Reverend John Clay,[1] who, we are told, 'had the evidence copied out under his own inspection, and who can vouch for its entire accuracy'. The motivations of these mediators are not hard to find. The title page refers to O'Neill's 'serious charge against the factory over-lookers of Manchester' and 'her revelations respecting the conduct of the female factory operatives'. The first accusation relates to corrupt practices by mill managers, the second to mill girls' involvement in prostitution. Thus, sensation and self-revelation are ultimately made to serve calculated social and moral ends, though the text also indulges Victorian appetites for first-hand accounts of criminality. The organised criminal subculture O'Neill describes would doubtless have opened up a frightening vista for respectable readers and would do nothing to alter the identification of the Irish with crime, disorder and immorality in the public mind. In view of such factors, it cannot be assumed with any certainty that O'Neill's extracted testimony is precisely her own, even though the text is prefaced by an italicised introduction and punctuated by parenthetical editorial interjections. Yet despite the constraints on her self-authorisation, this convicted transportee somehow succeeds in representing herself. Even though O'Neill is not, in a literal sense, responsible for her confession in its published form,

---

[1] Reverend John Clay (1796–1858) was an influential advocate of Victorian prison reform. He regarded crime as a moral failing on the part of the individual and believed in the remedial power of Christian instruction and example.

her individual turn of phrase gives her a beguiling textual presence and imbues the narrative with the tang of authenticity.

I was born in Stockport; my father was a pensioner, and had 1s. a day; my father and mother were both sober and industrious, but my mother would have done anything to get us meat. My father was more shy; he was a shoemaker. I went for nearly three years to a Roman Catholic school, at threepence a week. I went to the factory at ten years old, and worked there until I was twelve. Then I went to service at Mosley (three miles the other side of Manchester), at a boarding school. I staid there until I was fourteen. I then left on account of the small wages. I came home, and was sent by my father to learn to be a lad's capmaker. I was learning for three mouths, and then I came home again. When I came home, I saw that my brother Richard was dressed very fine, besides having a gold ring and a watch. My brother was not then living at home regularly, because he could not stand my father's reproaches. I used to say to my father, 'how well Richard's dressed!' and my father would say, 'But who thinks anything of it? *He's a prig.*'[2] My mother was more unhappy about it than my father, and often followed him about the town begging him to come home.

When I was just fifteen, my mother gave me threepence to go to Knott Mill Fair, and I met my brother there. He told me what to do, and I stood before him so that nobody could see his hand, while he picked a woman's pocket of 7s. 6d. and a purse. He gave me a shilling, and then told me to go home. I went into a show, and picked a woman's pocket of 1s. 6d. I trembled very much when I did it. I met the young woman again in a short time, and she was crying. I heard her say that the money was her mother's. I cried too, and would have given her the money back, but I was afraid of being took up. I dare not take the money home, so I took it to a stay-shop, and paid it (in advance) towards a pair of stays.[3] I remained at home for three months without doing anything more. At the end of that time my little brother Edward was taken up for picking pockets, and got three months (summary conviction). He had been taken up three times before; and had only been out three days. During twelve months he had only been at liberty four days. One of the witnesses against him was one of his own companions, and after he had been the means of convicting him, I leathered him just outside the court. I was taken up for the assault on this witness, and remained in the New Bailey a week. I was then bailed out by two navvies. [These two navvies who gave bail for her, the deponent describes as perfect strangers to her or her family. This kind of security is very common.] My mother met me in the street, and we were treated to some rum by a companion of my brother Richard, James O'Brien. O'Brien had £100, which he had stolen from a woman.

---

[2] Archaic slang for a petty thief.
[3] A type of corset.

My brother was then in Gloucestershire picking pockets. O'Brien gave me money to complete the purchase of my stays. I had been at Blackburn fair with another young woman, only for a day, and we got £3 between us. When I got home again from Blackburn, my mother had a letter from Richard, saying that he was put back for trial at Gloucester for pocket-picking, and wanted money to pay for a counsellor. I went by the train to Congleton; at the station I picked a woman's pocket of 15s., which paid for my place to Kidderminster. I went in a waggon from Kidderminster to Worcester, with five or six other females, and got 15s. more from them. I stopped all night at Worcester. I went in an omnibus to the Gloucester station next morning, and picked a lady's pocket (in the omnibus) of £1. 2s. I got into Gloucester on Friday night; saw my brother next morning; told him that I would try to get some money for a counsel; and went to the market, but it is a very poor market, and I only got 10s. 9d. I could not get money enough to fee my brother a counsel, and he received three months, having been recommended by the jury on account of his being so young. I then went to Derby, and then to Sheffield, where I saw O'Neill, whom I had previously known in Manchester through my brother. I went to Rotherham Statute fair, and got about £4. I saw O'Neill again, who said 'I think you have done better than any of us'; for a great many pickpockets were there. I went to 'Bam' Statute fair, about eighteen miles from Sheffield. I got nothing, for it rained, and no people came. I afterwards returned to Sheffield, and then went to Hull. I went to all those places by myself, having heard O'Neill and his companions say they were going. It was the fair, and I got between £6 and £7. I seldom kept my money, for other travellers in the lodging-houses used to say they were hard up, and borrowed it from me. O'Neill wanted me to live with him without being married, but I would not.

My brother John (eldest brother) was then in Hull, serving a month for picking pockets. I waited till he came out, and then he leathered me for coming away from home. I ran away from him and went to Leeds; there I met O'Neill again, and 'the askings'[4] were put up for us to be married. I filled up the three weeks by going to Sheffield and York, and got about £10 or £11 at both places together. We were then married at the Old Church.

Up to this time I could only pick outside pockets, but O'Neill taught me how to raise the outside dresses and pick inside pockets. I was married on the Thursday, and on the Saturday I got ten shillings in the market. On Monday my brother Edward came to Leeds. We all went out, and Edward picked a pocket of 13s., but we had been watched, and we were all took up, and got (summarily) three months.

After our liberation we went to Hull, and found Prince Albert was going to lay the foundation stone of Grimsby Dock. At Hull I got seventeen shillings.

---

[4] The banns of marriage.

We went to Grimsby, and Edward and I got thirty shillings each. From Hull we went to Newark, where we got £7; then to Redford, £4; then to Sheffield, where I was took up for thirty shillings I had just taken from a woman. This brought me six weeks, and O'Neill two months in Wakefield. I travelled (after I came out) until O'Neill came out, and got in the fortnight about £15. Then we went to Selby, and got £4 in the market. Then to Hull, and got £5 at the station. Then to Manchester, where I and my husband went to live with my father. While I lived at Manchester, I went out with O'Neill almost every day by the trains six or seven miles out of Manchester, sometimes second, sometimes first class, having very good clothes. The largest sum I ever got was £22 going from Manchester to Stockport. O'Neill did nothing but 'shade me off'. He was a great drunkard, and I had to pay from 20s. to 35s. every week to the beer-shop for him.

We carried on this way for about six months, making, on the average, about £10 a week. We lived at my father's all this time. He used to fret and cry, and tell us we should get into disgrace, but we took no heed. He was too good-natured with us. We then heard that Preston market was very throng of a Saturday, and for thirteen weeks we came over – O'Neill, Richard, and I – every Saturday. O'Neill and I went together, and Richard and O'Gar (another of the gang). At night we shared all equally, The largest sum I ever got in Preston was £17, and the smallest about £3. I used to call £4 and £3 nothing. It was owing to the wet day we went into the shop, few people being in the market – when the offence took place for which we are transported.

12
Owen Peter Mangan, 'Memoir'

Northern Irish Public Record Office, T/3258/53/1. 37pp.; pp. 20–6.

Owen Peter Mangan's unpublished memoir has been accurately described as a virtual 'case history of the forces which pushed Irish persons out of Ireland, and the energy and enterprise necessary for survival after emigration'.[1] It is also a wholly unsentimental record of a life of continual adjustment to the disorientations and depredations of displacement on both sides of the Atlantic. Mangan was born in the parish of Kilcoo, County Cavan around 1838, the youngest of a family of five boys. The early death of their father, a drover, caused the older sons to scatter and left young Owen in the care of an abusive foster mother, from whom he eventually ran away to seek his birth mother. Further childhood hazards lay in wait, however, including smallpox, famine and harsh treatment at the hands of his stepfather, Francis Mullen, to whom he alludes in the following extract from his 'Memoir', written in Massachusetts and dated 'January 3, 1912'. At the age of 12 Mangan found work in a cotton mill near Drogheda, where he learned the skills of weaving that enabled him to emigrate to Preston in 1853, following a dispute with his mother over money. It was here that he met and married a girl from Maynooth, with whom he ran a successful grocery store until Fenian activities in northern England in the late 1860s drove customers away from Irish-owned businesses. With a growing family to support, Mangan emigrated to Philadelphia in 1869. There he secured a loan to pay for the passage of his wife and children the following year. Despite irregular employment and the absence of financial support from his 'rich relations' in Philadelphia, he succeeded in making a good living and eventually settled in Lynn, Massachusetts, where he died as a result of an unsuccessful prostate operation in June 1924 in his late eighties. The typescript he left behind bears many hand-written corrections and marginal marks, some of which obscure the legibility of individual words and sentences. There is also a marked unevenness of punctuation and spelling, including the liberal, random use of parentheses.

March of 1853 a little trouble started up between Mother and I that caused me to leave home for good. Seventeenth of March, of course, is always a strict

---

[1] Ruth-Ann M. Harris, *The Nearest Place That Wasn't Ireland: Early Nineteenth-Century Irish Labour Migration* (Ames, IO: Iowa State University Press, 1994), p. 145.

holiday in Ireland, and, of course, the factory closed down. The cloth that I was weaving was paid (for) at eighteen pense a cut. Well, through being off on St. Patrick's Day, I missed a cut of each loom, which made three shillings (less) for the week. Just half of the week's pay. Mother could not see how I could loose three shillings for one day when I only earned six shillings per week. She was very angry on Saturday when I brought my pay home although I did my best to explain. My stepfather happened to be home that week. When Sunday morning came, Mother was getting breakfast ready. Mr. Mullen was dressing in his room. Mother began to complain about the three shilling shortage. She said something that made me angry and I retorted saucely back. What ever I said I do not remember, but my stepfather ran out of his room to chastize me but I hapened to be near the front door, I cleared out and slammed it after Mr. (Mullen). He never saw me again till 1860, he came over to England to see me and staid a month. At this time his boys had learned trades and they had all moved to Dublin. His old employer, Johnny Oats, had failed, and the factory was stoped. I never met Mother till 1869 when I met her in Philadelphia. That Sunday morning when I missed the wallop from my stepfather I went derict to one of my Chums' house named Andy Heeney. Andy was a big good natured fellow. And I had breakfast with him. I told them why I left home (and they said I would be back in the evening). We all went to Mass (and) after dinner Andy and I went and hunted up two more chums and we all maid up our mind we would go to England that evening.

The fare was only two shillings (and) we had all been saving up a little money with the intention of going to England sometime. And now was the time. So we started off that Sunday evening on board the Linster Lass and arrived in Liverpool on Monday morning at 5 o'clock on the 27th of March 1853. We went straight to Preston. It is about 18 miles from Liverpool. We heard of it being a cotton manufacturing town. That was what we wanted. After a few unsucful attempts to get a Job, we finely struck it rich at a Factory owned by a man named Humbers. We got only 2 looms to start with but we could earn 10 shilling and a penney per week. That was 4 more that I could earn in Ireland. I was then in my sixteenth year and must now shift for myself, in earnest. I and my chums remained there for about one year and during that time I only wrote home to Mother once, just to let her know where I was. We had a good time just the same as boys do have. Nothing of any consequence occurred till one of the boys began to keep company with a young lady and was called out to be married. When his Mother in Ireland heard of it, she came right over and stopped it, as he was under age. He was so mad he went and listed in the East India Company and that was the last of poor Andy Heeney. I never seen or heard tell of him after. Peter Curtis went to America shortly after so there was only Tom Lawless and I left out of the Inarlett. After the Boys went I got four looms and that nearly doubled my pay. We had to have helpers for four looms. Those helpers was little boys or girls who went to school a half day and worked the other. And you had to pay them one shilling per week each. Oh these were great times. I didn't know what to do with my money so I thought it was nearly time for me to look out for a girl. I did not have to wait long. I selected a nice little Irish girl from Maynooth Ireland. And we sported round for six months and we thought. So we put up the askings and got married on the 21st of October, 1856. I was then about eighteen years and three months old, and although there was a 100 on show for getting up still I had made up my mind that I would get there sometime. The wages of a working Man is so small in England that it is almost impossible to save Money. The first thing I did after Marriage was to give all my Chums the cold shoulder, and spent the first year studying in evening, particularly Arithmetic. Our first Child came along on the 20th of August, 1857. And that was the commencemett of bad times in England for the Indian Mutiney commender in the Spring of 1857 and it was of such a terable nature that business was neglected and nothing thought of only how to get souldiers to enlist for the seat of war.

War was not in my line, just then I had other work to do. In 1859 the good natured stork brought home a little girl to keep the boy company and the Indian war was over and we were all very happy till the American war broke out in 1861. Then commenced the worst times I had experienced in England. And to make matters worse I lost my little Daughter who was then near two years old. She died from whooping cough. We had no employment in Preston of any kind, outside of the cotton factories, worth speaking of, and on account of the Southern ports being blockaded we could get no cotton till they began to grow it in India. They also pushed the growth of it in Egypet, altho we always got some from Egypet and the very best, for it had long fibre.

In 1862 I joined the police force. I was sent to Saint Hellens where I remained for six months. I moved my furniture and we settled down in an out station about a half a mile of the town in a place called Thatte Heath. I did not like the place for it was in the midst (of) colliers and glass blowers. And they were a wicked class of people. At the end of six months I heard the Factory that I worked in had commenced full time so I left St. Hellens and started back to Preston and got my old job again. I went to live on Wellfield road near a new Church called St. Walberger, which was in course of erection. They put a large bell in, and I got the Job of Ringing it together with the privilage of blowing the organ at a Sallary of three pounds a year. That was not quite fifteen dollars but it was a big lot when you had it in your hand.

Mother and I were always building castles and making up our minds to get rich some day. Two weeks before Easter of 1864 I drew my three pounds as my first years sallery for Ringing the bell. We had a few pounds saved, together with my weeks pay, in all about seven pounds, and with that we made up our minds we would start a store.

I got a little lumber and commenced to put up shelves in my parlor. We bought scales and everything and everything nessary for a small grocery store, and with the ballance we went to the whole sale stores to buy in. Being that it was so near Easter, we thought nothing would go better than eggs and Bacon and Butter. We had also a nice selection of candies. When we had all our money spent the wholesale man gave us credit. So that we started up a nice little store and all the neighbors came in to trade. I followed my work in the cotton factory, and Mother tended the store during the day and I helped in the evening.

We flourished in that little store, until the landlord coveted it for his sister. So I had to move out. I went to a corner store lower down in the street and did very well for some time, till a singular event cropped up which caused me to lose my trade, and eventually to leave the street and locate elsewhere.

About this time Fenianism was at its height, both in England and in Ireland. In 1867, as every one who lived then remembers, Kelly and Dorsey[2] was arrested in Manchester for Fenianism, and while they were being taken to prison, the van was broken into by a number of men. One fired a pistol through the door and shot a policeman named Sargent Brett. He happened to be standing inside the door when the pistol shot (came) through and killed him. Quite a number of men were arrested for the act (and) all got off but three, Allen, Larkin and O'Brien. They were tried, found guilty, and were hanged in Manchester on the 23 of November 1867.

A neighbor of mine, a young man named Brennan, happened to be in Manchester at that time, and he got into the hands of the police on suspicion for participation in the murder (although) they (subsequently) found that he was inocent. The news soon spread round my neighborhood that Frank Brennan was a Fenian (and) all my English customers came in, paid their bills, and never entered my store after. My landlord gently told me that he wanted the store for himself, so I had to find another store.

I then moved up to Adelphia Street. That was nearer to the City, a little too near, for when people came so far, they would go a little farther into the center of the town. And my old customers, who were not English but who owed me considerable bills, seldom ever came near me. I still followed my work, and was independ to the store, as far as supporting my family went.

My family at this time had increased to four, with an expectation of another increase in a month. 'What am I going to do' said I. 'Bring up a family in poverty', as scores around me that I could point out. I had a good many rich relations in Philadelphia (and) it struck me that if I could get out they would help me to get a good position. So I broached the subject to mother and, after two or three days deliberation, she volunteered to let me come and try my fortune. But it was a great sacrifice on her part.

---

[2] The arrest of Colonel Thomas J. Kelly, the head of the Irish Republican Brotherhood, and Captain Timothy Deasy in Manchester on 11 September 1867 set in train the sequence of violent events which Mangan summarises here.

So we made up our mind to sell out our store and all its belongings, which we did in a short time. After all our debts were paid, we had enough left to support the family for six months and pay expenses out to this country.

Mr. Aarron Hunter, a good old friend of mine, promised to take care of my family until such time as I would send for them, for I would not think of taking them out till I had a home for them. Mr. Hunter and his wife and family lived upstairs and we lived down. Mr. Hunter and his family which consisted of one boy and a girl, were very kind. We had no relations in England w(h)atsoever. And I have always experienced through life that the strangers or non-relatives was more ready and willing to render me a service than my owen relatives.

Having settled all my business, I lost no time in procuring the passage tickets and, on the 5th of February 1869, early in the morning, I kissed my dear wife and children good by(e), and with a heavy heart I bid farewell to Preston forever.

My son John, who was then about eleven years, come with me to the depot, and my greaf in parting with him was so great that I was very near turning back. But, as if to prevent changes of purpose, the whistle blue and with one more fond embrace I was off to Liverpool. I had my passage secured on the Virginia which sailed that afternoon and in coming over, I commemorated the event by composing a song. One verse ran thus:

> On Feb. 5th we sailed, and, the weather being fine,
> All things seemed gay, our passengers, a jolly crew,
> To the English shores we bid adieu.

A chorus followed.

13
Justin McCarthy, *The Story of an Irishman*

(London: Chatto & Windus, 1904). viii, 411pp.; pp. 81–8; 91–2.

In addition to being a prominent parliamentarian, who held the vice-chairmanship of the Irish Party from 1880 until the Parnellite split of 1890, after which he led the anti-Parnellite faction until 1896, Cork-born Justin McCarthy (1830–1912) forged a distinguished literary career in Victorian England. Between his taking up employment with the *Northern Daily Times* in Liverpool in 1853 and his entry into parliament as a nationalist MP for Longford in 1879 he established himself as an influential liberal journalist, successful novelist and noted historian. He worked for the radical *Morning Star* newspaper from 1860 to 1869 and was a leader writer for the *Daily News* from 1871 to 1894. During these years he also published many novels, including *Dear Lady Disdain* (1875) and *Miss Misanthrope* (1878), and several works of non-fiction, including the hugely popular *A History of Our Own Times* (1878), which ran to several revised editions. McCarthy's prolific literary output continued after his retirement from parliament in 1900, though the onset of blindness meant that he wrote by dictation during his last decade. His award of a civil-list pension for services to literature in 1903 confirmed his stature as an eminent Victorian, while simultaneously reinforcing many Irish nationalists' jaundiced view of him as a careerist West Briton, despite his long-standing devotion to the cause of Home Rule.[1] Yet, as Paul Townend observes, it was precisely his 'peculiar brand of anglophilia and deeply held Irish patriotism' that made McCarthy an ideal 'ambassador between Parnellite nationalism and British opinion which despised that cause'.[2] McCarthy's deep affinity for London culture is certainly apparent in *The Story of an Irishman*, as evidenced by the following extract from Chapter 6, 'The Road of Imagination', in which we witness him wrestling with the disparity between the idealised metropolis of his imagination and the intrusive social realities of the actual city.

---

[1] See James H. Murphy, 'Between Drawing-Room and Barricade: The Autobiographies and Nationalist Fictions of Justin McCarthy', in Bruce Stewart (ed.), *Hearts and Minds: Irish Culture and Society under the Act of Union* (Gerrards Cross: Colin Smythe: 2002), pp. 111–20.

[2] Paul Townend, '"No Imperial Privilege": Justin McCarthy, Home Rule, and Empire', *Éire-Ireland*, vol. 42, nos. 1 and 2 (Spring/Summer 2007), pp. 208–9.

In this small seaside place on the Kentish coast of England,[3] where I have lately passed some secluded years, I can see from one of my windows a road which gently winds along a rising ground, having the blue waves at its side, and then reaching the highest level of the land is lost in the horizon. This road seems to me an emblem of that ideal road we may all be said to look upon in our moments of fanciful musing. It is the road leading to the land of imagination and of poetry, to the ideal country of our vague aspirations, to the capital city of a realm of romance for which we have all yearned at one time or another. During that early period of my life the road of imagination was always leading my fancy to London. I am not ever likely to forget my first sight of Rome, of Athens, of Constantinople, of Cairo, of Jerusalem, and I can easily recall to mind my early longings for a first sight of these immortal cities. But at the time about which I am now writing my yearnings were especially for a first sight of London.

That desire was not merely inspired by the literature of prose and poetry, which made London to me the central point of the universe. There was an element of the prosaic and the practical stimulating my wish for a first look at London. I had got into my mind that London was the only place where a young man with a love for literary work, who had already become associated with journalism, could hope to make a good living by the exercise of his intelligence and his pen. The conditions of my family were making it more and more necessary that I should strive for an engagement in the English capital. My sister had been for a long time in sinking health, and while she lived I could not think of leaving her for the sake of any hope of advancement, and I could not subject her to the risk and trouble of an enterprise in a new and distant place of settlement. But my sister died at the age of twenty, and my brother had already made up his mind to seek his fortune at the first opportunity in the United States, and there was thus no serious difficulty in the way of my making an attempt to secure an engagement in London. I resolved to get together a few pounds, and to go over to London for the purpose of trying to obtain a place on some newspaper there. The only friend I had in London was a fellow-countryman, who had been a colleague of mine for some time on *The Cork Examiner*, and who had more lately obtained a seat in the Press Gallery of the House of Commons as a reporter for one of the London daily newspapers. I knew that he would help me if he possibly could, and it was something at all events to have a friend in London who could at least put me in the right way of getting an engagement. So I made my arrangements, and in the early part of 1852 I accomplished my first expedition to the London of my dreams.

I went by steamer from Cork to Liverpool, and spent two or three days there at the house of a friend and his sister, who were then settled in the

---

[3] McCarthy moved to Westgate-on-Sea with his daughter Charlotte in 1897.

city of the Mersey; and I may say in advance that this visit proved a great event in my life, for the sister of my friend afterwards became my dearly loved and now long-lamented wife. I left Liverpool for London early one morning, travelling by what was then called a parliamentary train, that is, a train wholly composed of carriages, for which only the lowest recognised rates of fares was charged, which had to stop at all manner of stations and get itself 'shunted' in order to allow the trains with first and second class carriages to pass it on the way. I did not arrive at London until late evening was already darkening into night, and I got my first sight of the great city as we rumbled slowly along on the top of an omnibus from Euston Square to the regions of the Bank and the Mansion House. It was not certainly a very fascinating sight, but still it was a sight of London. I had already been studying London for years, and the name of every street through which or across which we passed brought to my mind some memories of what I had read in plays and poems and novels. It seemed to me, not that I was coming into an entirely strange and unknown city, but that I was revisiting streets with whose history and associations I was already quite familiar. Perhaps for that very reason the darkness of the hour was only all the better fitted for the realisation of my dreams about London. The gas lights in the streets – I need hardly say we had no electric lighting then – did not illuminate strongly enough to reveal all the prosaic characteristics of the streets and the houses, and only lent a new touch of the poetic to the regions I was then looking on for the first time. 'Darkness,' says a poet, 'shows us realms of light we never saw by day.'[4] The poet was writing only of the stars, but the darkness of that London showed me not merely the realms of gas light, not to be seen by day, but with that gas light's help some realms of the London of my imagination which might not have been seen so clearly by me if I had looked upon them for the first time under the pitiless revelations of the noonday sun.

I may dispose briefly of the practical results of my expedition to London. These practical results amounted for the time to little or nothing, but they were not without some later influence on the purposes of my visit. My friend, whom I have already mentioned, introduced me to the managers of the reporting staffs of two or three daily newspapers, and got my name put down as a candidate for a place at some vague future opportunity. Just now, however, I am more inclined to say something about my first impressions of London than to deal much with the personal incidents of my own early struggles. I spent a fortnight in London, and all the time that I had to spare from my quest after an engagement was devoted to the delightful task of see-ing everything I could see of London's sights and London's famous places. I had come too late to see that great exhibition in the Crystal Palace, the first

---

[4] 'Oh Thou! who dry'st the mourner's tear' by Tom Moore (1779–1852) ends: 'As darkness shows us realms of light/We never saw by day!'

of all those many and memorable exhibitions of industrial products which have been organised since then in so many great cities of the world, from London and Paris to St. Louis. The Crystal Palace exhibition was opened and closed in 1851, but I had at least the satisfaction of seeing the Palace itself in Hyde Park on its old site before there was any thought of its removal to its present situation. So far as its older streets and quarters were concerned, London was then in outer aspects very much the same as it is at the present day. Only in the methods of street traffic was there much difference in those older regions between the London of 1852 and the London of our own time. There were no tramways then, and there were no underground railways or 'tubes,' but we saw just as now the old-fashioned four-wheeler and the hansom cab, while the sort of vehicle described in Dickens's earlier novels, the vehicle in which the driver occupied a seat planted close to the side of that assigned to the 'fare,' had already wholly disappeared from the streets of London. There was no Thames Embankment at that time, or for many years after; and the banks of the Thames within the Metropolis itself were lined by dingy wharfs, rows of old-fashioned warehouses and tumbled-down shops, shanties, and places for the sale of drink. From Westminster Bridge to London Bridge the banks of the river were made about as unlovely and unpicturesque as could well be accomplished even by the perverted ingenuity of man. There were some peculiarities of the London streets which recalled even still the old times and habits described in many of the books I loved. The swinging signboards, the tablets illumined by the great names that make part of the history of certain houses, the narrow lanes which turned sharply and abruptly out of broad thoroughfares and seemed to bring back the living presence of mediaeval town life, these and other such evidences of London's historic antiquity were studied by me with an ever-freshening delight.

But there were other peculiarities in some of the smaller streets running out of or behind the Strand which impressed my stranger mind in a very different and less favourable manner. A reader whose recollections of London do not go back farther than the last twenty years might find it hard to believe that a civilised community could behold such sights as we might all have seen in London at the time when the great exhibition was held in Hyde Park and for long after. Certain small streets here and there seemed to have acquired the privilege of outraging public decency in the grossest fashion without any interference whatever on the part of the constituted authorities. I shall not ask too much attention from my readers to this repulsive subject, but I think it is as well, as a mere matter of historical narrative, to say something of the sights to be seen every day, which I myself saw at that time in the immediate neighbourhood of the Strand, of its thronging crowds, its numerous police, and its great churches. To many Londoners of these days it is quite possible that the names of Holywell Street and Wych Street may suggest no particularly repulsive idea. But at the time of which I am writing these two streets bordering the very centre of the Strand were such as the lowest slums of London or New York in the present day could not compare with for abomination. Most of the houses in these streets were shops for the sale of indecent books and pictures. The pictures and books – more especially the pictures – were flauntingly displayed in the windows of each shop, and were gross beyond all possible description. Then a great many of the small houses in these streets were occupied by women of the professionally immoral class, and it was the habit of these young women to stand at their doors in the open day and to invite the attention of passing men, each woman wearing no costume whatever but her chemise and her slippers. The police authorities do not seem to have given themselves the slightest concern about these exhibitions. [...]

I gave up my evenings for the most part to the theatres and to the opera-houses; saw with genuine delight some performances by Charles Mathews, the greatest of English light comedians at that time, or, as I still think, at any later time; Helen Faucit,[5] Phelps,[6] the Keeleys,[7] Buckstone,[8] and Benjamin Webster.[9] And I heard in the opera-house Grisi,[10] Alboni,[11] Mario,[12] and Lablache.[13] Macready[14] had given up the stage not long before my visit to London, but I had already seen him more than once in the theatre of my native city when he was making a starring tour in Ireland. I must say that much as I loved the drama and the opera, the greatest attractions for me were found in the streets and the parks of London itself and in the Temple Gardens. I loved to visit every spot which had some association with history and poetry and novels, with Shakespeare and Dr. Johnson and Charles Lamb, with Dickens and Thackeray. The result of my visit on the whole was to make London for me a place of even greater fascination than it had been when it was yet only the London of my dreams. I became more than ever resolved to make it if I possibly could my home and the place of my work. I remember that once when I was passing the Houses of Parliament I stopped and looked

---

[5] Helen Faucit (1814–1898), Victorian actress famed for her emotive performances.

[6] Samuel Phelps (1804–1878), actor, producer and manager of London's Haymarket Theatre.

[7] Robert Keeley (1793–1869), a popular comic actor, and his actress wife Mary Ann (1805–1899) often appeared together on the English stage during the middle decades of the nineteenth century.

[8] John Buckstone (1802–1879), actor, playwright and theatre manager.

[9] Benjamin Webster (1798–1882), prominent character actor and accomplished theatre manager.

[10] Giulia Grisi (c.1810–1869), Milan-born opera singer beloved of Victorian audiences.

[11] Marietta Alboni (1826–1894), Italian opera singer, one of the greatest contraltos of the age.

[12] Sardinian-born Giovanni Matteo de Candia (1810–1883), popularly known as Mario, was considered the most famous tenor of his age.

[13] Luigi Lablache (1795–1858), renowned Italian opera singer who once gave singing lessons to Princess (later Queen) Victoria.

[14] William Charles Macready (1793–1873), eminent actor and theatre manager who was a dominant force in nineteenth-century English theatre.

back on the towers of Westminster Palace, and I formed in my own mind the audacious ambition and hope that I might one day be privileged to enter that enclosure as a member of the House of Commons. Then I felt inclined to laugh at myself for the audacity of my youthful aspirations, and consoled myself for my revulsion of feeling by the more modest hope that I might at least at some not very distant time be privileged to have a seat in the Reporters' Gallery.

14
Jim Blake, *Jim Blake's Tour from Clonave to London*

(Dublin: M. H. Gill, 1867). vi, 24pp.; pp. 3–7.

Whereas the London to which Justin McCarthy came in 1852 was already imaginatively familiar to him from books and plays, the city Jim Blake entered 14 years later was perfectly foreign to him in every respect. Blake, a barely literate peasant from Clonave, an island in Lough Derravaragh, County Westmeath, appears as the archetypal innocent abroad in his short *Tour*, in which he chronicles his first visit to London in the closing weeks of 1866. The purpose of his visit was to sit for the Scottish artist Erskine Nicol, whose four-year sojourn as an art teacher in Dublin in the late 1840s had given him his preferred subject matter, the Irish peasant, whom he depicted in a variety of poses and predicaments, some of them comic caricatures reminiscent of the stereotypes propagated by the London illustrated press. Although based in London, Nicol returned to Ireland almost annually after 1850 and in 1862 built a studio at Clonave, which he used until poor health made long-distance travel untenable. It seems certain that Nicol first painted Blake in Clonave, and it is possible that he became the prototype for his 1860s paintings in which 'one figure in particular became a constant; the fortune-seeking former peasant, who can never hide his origins and will never fully understand cities and high finance'.[1] The fact that Blake was recognised by at least one of Nicol's London acquaintances – 'he knew me, he so often saw me in the pictures' – suggests a special affinity on the part of the artist. Nicol certainly arranged for his 'faithful servant' to come to London in late 1866, where he generously entertained and painted him at Clonave Villa, his Bayswater home.

In a short preface to the *Tour*, which Nicol illustrated, a Royal Irish Academy member known only by the initials 'A. A.' writes that while the work 'is purely natural, it abounds in humour and is racy of the soil'.[2] The writer goes on to explain that the

---

[1] Fintan Cullen, 'Erskine Nicol', in Jane Turner (ed.), *The Dictionary of Art* (Basingstoke: Macmillan, 1996), vol. 23, p. 107. While Blake's rustic naïvety is much in evidence throughout the *Tour*, there is nothing of the fortune-seeker in him.

[2] Both the catalogues of the Bodleian Library and the British Library identify the writer as Adam Anderson, but this name does not appear on the membership lists of the RIA. The fact that the initials are also those of Nicol's principal Dublin patron, Andrew Armstrong, MRIA, who delivered a speech at the opening of the artist's Clonave

text was not written with publication in mind, but 'has been printed *verbatim et liter-atim* as it was written, except in the matter of punctuation, of which the manuscript was perfectly destitute'. The preface ends on an admonitory note that underlines the honourable motives of Blake's influential benefactors: 'James Blake is a fair type of his class – the peasantry of central Ireland – who present many characteristic features, in depicting which, either by pen or brush, it is not only unnecessary, but positively false and cruel, to resort to caricature.' What follows is the narrative of an awestruck ingénue who speaks out of a state of permanent astonishment. In fact, so giddy is this traveller with wonder, trepidation and curiosity that at times he seems close to ocular overload. The sheer rawness and immediacy of Jim Blake's testimony, which is clearly more diaristic than autobiographical, supplies an intense response to the shock of the new that cannot easily be found in other first-hand accounts of Irish arrival in England.

At ½ past 7 o'clock in the morning I looked about me and saw that we were coming into Liverpool. Each side of the river was all ships and boats; all I thought running in and out about me, all sides of the river streaming lights. When she landed thair came in 2 fellows to take away my bag; they both fought to see who would have it, then a young lad came to polish my shoes. By dad, says I, this is great respect for me, an Irishman! I did not mind any of them.

This was on the morning of the 22nd. I proceeded to a gentleman of the name of Mr. Gray, at No. 2, Tower Buildings. After a little delay I met him, and received me verry kindly. He received a letter that morning from my particular friend Mr. Nicol, of London, to start me to him by the first train. He took me through Liverpool to show me some of the city. I must confess it is a great place. I saw Lord Willinton thair,[3] and the late prince albert statue, which is beautiful. The market place is grand. Surely everything I saw was new to my eye. He sent off a telegraph message to Mr. Nicol that he started me off to him. I was 8 hours sitting on a train, as often under the ground as over it. I saw nice fields, and nothing grazing thair but sheep and small cattle, only 2 or 3 cows I think; we went through about 20 stations; we met hardly any roads, and them I thought to be very narrow when compared to Ireland; a few stacks of corn, a dale of hay, some nice fields of wheat newly sowed; a dale of cannals, and thair long boats pulled by a horse on them; the houses all brick, no stone at all. I saw two mills and one wind mill. The land appeared to me to be as redd as brick clay, it had nothing to say to the irish land. I got on well to my journey end. Every 20 minutes trains passing by us, and them awful long. Every side I would look out of the train, nothing but the smoke of trains running in every direction. When I landed at a little after six o'clock, I found myself in the middle of the Great City; nothing to be seen but all the

---

studio, tempts one to think that he may have been the prefacer. For an analysis of Nicol's Westmeath paintings, see the article by Brendan Rooney in the Gorry Gallery Catalogue, 14–22 June 2001, pp. 14–17.

[3] The Wellington Memorial, sculpted by George Anderson Lawson in the early 1860s.

beautiful shops lighted with Gass. Nothing so beautiful to be seen. But still I was in great trouble to no where to go; to my great joy I saw my old friends standing on the platform, Mr. and Mrs. Nicol; they were both laughing at thair New visitor, to see him come at last; the both shook hands with me, and got me into a beautiful carriage; drove me home to their beautiful house, 24 Dawson place. I then was taken in their Dining parlour; plenty of Beef and pudding for dinner, then plenty of spirits and wine and fruite for thair Irish visitor; then served to some tea; then Mr. and Mrs. Nicol sang and played Musick till thair newly arrived visitor fell asleep, so I bid them good by and got to bedd, slept very soundly, had very pleasant dreams about home.

When I awoke on the morning of the 23rd I dressed myself; I walked out of the room, went astray through the house, walked into the studio of Mr. Nicol, was frighted to see all the old fashioned weapons thair amongst the pictures, formerly used in Ireland. I then washed myself and sat down to write home to poor Nancy and children that was wearing to hear from me; then Mr. Gray of Liverpool, and to Mr. Armstrong of Dublin, that was good friends to me on my way to London. That night Mr. Nicol took me into a cab, and drove me down to a Mr. Robinson of Long acre; he knew me, he so often saw me in the pictures. Next to Covent Garden Market; saw pears at £18 18s. a dozen; walked down Strand to Trafalgar square, up Regent street, then got tired walking, took a cab and got home. Oho dear! the beauty and riches of the shops of London surpasses all the world: it is all a stream of gass light. Mr. Nicol had to hold my hand for fear of I being trod on by the busses and cabs. But the streets are beautiful and wide, the footpaths twice as wide as in ireland. Oho dear! all the strange faces I saw that night. I saw great streams of water springing up in the air, and falling down into a beasin, still nothing higher. Thair stood beside this, on a high tower, admiral Nelson, and 2 more old warriors on horses. Beside this place stood the Royal acaddimy of arts, the Duke of Northumberland's house with lion on top of it, and his long tail standing up in the air. Coming up Regent street, I was greatly amazed, my guide shewed me several turtles enside glass, which was of an awful size, and they alive. Returned home to 24 Dawson place, and had my tea and went to bed; slept soundly; had some pleasant dreams about my people in old ireland.

On the morning of the 24th I was sitting for Mr. Nicol. Mrs Nicol came into the studio, invited me to another curiosity, the like I never seen before, a sewing machine; she was in the act of sewing; I declare it went like the wind, and the stitching most beautiful. That night Mr. Nicol took me to the Meauseum.[4] It put me in mind of heaven to see the place so beautifully lighted up, just as if the sun shone down on it: nothing to be seen but curiosity; the first he took me to was the old cover of a Missle belonging to the queen of Charles the first; gold enameld; cost £700; about the size of my own prayer book. The

---

[4] Kensington Museum.

next was a curious old fiddle, made a present of by Queen Elizabeth to the Earl of Lister;[5] a curious candle stick of Hennery the second ware, cost £700; and I saw two swords of honnor presented a great old warrior, Sir James outrim,[6] that fought out at india, all sparkling with diamonds and jewels. I saw the figure of old David, dreadful looking man, as big, I think, as 4 common men at present. I saw a bronze wolfe as big as a large calf, her tongue out, and 2 black children sucking at her paps. All the beautiful ivory carvings was splendid to see. I saw a most curious old pulpit and an old alter piece come from italy, together with most curious old vestments. We then went up stairs to see the picture gallerys, to see the drawings. The first thing caught my attention was all the old and young artists standing with their pallads and brushes just as if they were alive. Next I saw was the specie of dogs, young and old, drew by Sir Edwin Landseer;[7] next was all the old gentlemens portraits that made presents of these drawings to this beautiful picture gallery. Next I saw all the old cartoons. I saw Christ feeding the sheep, and the apostles all about him was most lovely: I saw St. peter and St. John cure the lame man. I went allong the gallerys. I saw a casket that cost £1000, and all the old crosses of old. I saw an old beautiful chrisening plate of gold, I don't know its value. I then come down stairs for home; my mind was atractted with old looking carriages from parris. I next saw the old carriage that the Lord Chancilor drove in to open the irish house of parliament; the old shoewing[8] of the wheels was greatly impaired. I saw the most rich beautiful sitdan chairs of old, used for bringing infants to be baptized. I saw all the newest fashions of roofing and slating of glass and other materials. My general impression of this place is, I think cannot be compared in Europe for riches and grandeur. Mr. Nicol and my self then come to the door, got into a most lovely cab, drove home to 24 dawson place, had tea and punch, then to bed, where I slept soundly, still dreaming of poor Clonave, and all my old neighbours.

---

[5] Robert Dudley (1532–1588), the fourteenth Earl of Leicester, was a favoured courtier of Queen Elizabeth I and one of the most powerful noblemen of her reign.

[6] Sir James Outram (1803–1863), army officer in the East India Company, who became a British hero after his capture of Lucknow in 1858. A bronze statue of him by Matthew Noble was erected on London's Victoria Embankment in 1871.

[7] Sir Edwin Landseer (1802–1873), animal painter. His famous bronze lions at the base of Nelson's Column in Trafalgar Square were unveiled in February 1867.

[8] Tyre.

15

Frances Power Cobbe, *The Life of Frances Power Cobbe by Herself*

(London: Richard Bentley, 1894). 2 vols, Vol. 2, 662pp.; pp. 390–8

Frances Power Cobbe (1822–1904), journalist, philanthropist and women's rights campaigner, was the only daughter of an Anglo-Irish Dublin family, owners of Newbridge House in Donabate, where she spent the first 36 years of her life. Her early rejection of her family's evangelical Christianity and corresponding struggle for moral and intellectual autonomy caused tensions with her autocratic father, whose small legacy left her in straitened circumstances. Freed from familial duties by his death in 1857, Cobbe moved first to Bristol, where she worked with street children, and then to London, where she wrote for *The Echo* and *The Standard* and contributed polemical articles on social, scientific and religious issues to numerous periodicals. Over the next three decades she became an outspoken feminist contributor to the debate about women's civil, legal and political rights in late nineteenth-century England. As the following extract from her autobiography shows, Cobbe's journalism was underpinned by a determination to prove herself the intellectual equal of her male colleagues and to surpass them in her attentiveness to the social and domestic plight of impoverished women. She herself remained unmarried, but lived with her companion Mary Lloyd for over 30 years. A conservative unionist in politics, Cobbe was also a vehement anti-vivisectionist, seeing a close correlation between the sufferings of animals and those of women in Victorian society. She was instrumental in the passage of the Cruelty to Animals Act (1876) and the Matrimonial Causes Act (1878). Cobbe's espousal of these causes features prominently in her two-volume autobiography, which she describes in the preface to Volume 1 as 'the true and complete history of a woman's existence *as seen from within*; a real Life, which he who reads may take as representing fairly the joys, sorrows and interests, the powers and limitations, of one of my sex and class in the era which is now drawing to a close'.

Journalism is, to my thinking, a delightful profession, full of interest, and promise of ever-extending usefulness. During the years in which I was a professional journalist, when I had occasion to go into a bank or a lawyer's office, I always pitied the clerks for their dull, monotonous, ugly work, as compared with mine. If not carried on too long or continuously – so that the brain begins to *churn* leaders sleeping or waking (a dreadful state of things into which we *may* fall) – it is pre-eminently healthy, being so full of variety and calling for so many different mental faculties one after another. Promptitude, clear and quick judgment as to what is, and is not, expedient and decorous to say; a ready memory well stored with illustrations and unworn quotations, a bright and strong style; and, if it can be attained, a playful (not saturnine) humour superadded – all these qualities and attainments are called for in writing for a daily newspaper; and the practice of them cannot fail to sharpen their edge. To be in touch with the most striking events of the whole world, and enjoy the privilege of giving your opinion on them to 50,000 or 100,000 readers within a few hours, this struck me, when I first recognised that such was my business as a leader-writer, as something for which many prophets and preachers of old would have given a house full of silver and gold. And I was to be *paid* for accepting it! It is one thing to be a 'vox clamantis in deserto,'[1] and quite another to speak in Fleet Street, and, without lifting up one's voice, to reach all at once as many men as formed the population of ancient Athens, not to say that of Jerusalem! But I must not 'magnify mine office' too fondly!

From the time of my second journey to Italy I obtained employment, as I have mentioned, as correspondent to the *Daily News* with whose Italian politics I was in sympathy. I also wrote all sorts of miscellaneous papers and descriptions for the *Spectator*, the *Reader*, the *Inquirer*, the *Academy*, and the *Examiner*. When in London I was engaged on the staff of the short-lived *Day* (1867); and much lamented its untimely eclipse, when my friend Mr. Haweis[2] unkindly 'chaffed' me by mourning over it:

> '*Sweet* Day!
> How *cool!* how bright!'

I was paid, however, handsomely for all I had written for it, and a few months later I received an invitation from Mr. Arthur Arnold (since M.P. for Salford) to join his staff on the newly-founded *Echo*.[3] It was a great experiment on the part of the proprietors, Messrs. Petter & Galpin, to start a half-penny paper. Such a thing did not then exist in England, and the ridicule it encountered, and boycotting from the news-agents who could not make enough profit on it to satisfy themselves, were very serious obstacles

---

[1] Meaning 'a voice crying out in the wilderness', from the Book of Isaiah.

[2] This may have been Reverend Hugh Haweis (1838–1901), the Anglican cleric and writer who contributed to many publications, including the *Pall Mall Gazette* and *The Echo*.

[3] Arthur Arnold (1833–1902) was the editor of this new evening newspaper from 1868 to 1875. An early supporter of Home Rule, he was Liberal MP for Salford from 1880 until 1885. He stood unsuccessfully as a Home Rule candidate in North Salford in 1886 and in North Dorset in 1892. He was knighted in 1895.

to success. Nevertheless Mr. Arnold's great tact and ability cleared the way, and before many months our circulation, I believe, was very large indeed. My share in the undertaking was soon arranged after a few interviews and experiments. It was agreed that I should go on three mornings every week at ten o'clock, to the office in Catherine Street, Strand, and there in a private room for my own use only, write a leading article on some social subject after arranging with the editor what it should be. I am proud to say that for seven years from that time till I retired I never once failed to keep my engagement. Of course I took a few weeks' holiday every year; but Mr. Arnold never expected his contributor in vain. Sometimes it was hard work for me; I had a cold, or was otherwise ill, or the snow lay thick and cabs from South Kensington were not to be had. Nevertheless I made my way to my destination punctually; and, when there, I wrote my leader, and as many 'Notes' as were allotted to me, and thus proved, I hope, once for all, that a woman may be relied on as a journalist no less than a man. I do not think, indeed, that very many masculine journalists could make the same boast of regularity as I have done. My first article appeared in the third number of the *Echo*, December 10th, 1868, and the last on, or about, March, 1875. Of course at first I found it a little difficult to write exactly what and how much was wanted, neither more nor less; but practice made this easier. I wrote, of course, on all manner of subjects, politics excepted; but chose in preference those which offered some ethical interest, or (on the other hand) an opening for a little fun! The reader may see specimens of both, *e.g.*, the papers on the great *Divorce Case*; *Lent in Belgravia*; and on *Fat People*; *Sweeping under the Mats*, &c., in *Re-echoes*, a little book compiled from a selection of my *Echo* articles which Tauchnitz[4] reproduced in his library. A few incidents in my experience in Catherine Street recur to me, and may be worth recording.

Terrible stories of misery and death were continuously cropping up in the reports of coroners' inquests, and I found that if I took these reports as they were published and wrote leading articles on them, we were almost sure next day to receive several letters begging the Editor to forward money (enclosed) to the surviving relations. It became a duty for me to satisfy myself of the veracity of these stories before setting them forth with claims for public sympathy; and in this way I came to see some of the sadder sides of poverty in London. There was one case I distinctly recall of a poor lady, daughter of a country rector, who was found (after having been missed for several days, but not sought for) lying dead, scarcely clothed, on the bare floor of a room in a miserable lodging-house in Drury Lane. I went to the house and found it a filthy coffee-house frequented by unwashed customers. The mistress, though likewise unwashed, was obviously what is termed 'respectable.' She told me

---

[4] Leipzig publishing house, which launched an inexpensive 'Library of British Authors' series in 1841.

that her unhappy lodger was a woman of forty or fifty, perfectly sober and well conducted in every way. She had been a governess in very good families, but had remained unemployed till her clothes grew shabby. She walked all day long over London for many weeks, seeking any kind of work or means of support, and selling by degrees everything she possessed for food. At last she returned to her wretched room in that house into which it was a pain for any lady to enter, and having begged a last cup of tea from her landlady, telling her she could not pay for it, she locked her door, and was heard of no more. Many days afterwards the busy landlady noticed that she had not seen her going in or out, and finding her door locked, called the police to open it. There was hardly an atom of flesh on the poor worn frame, scarcely clothes for decency, no food, no coals in the grate. '*Death from Starvation*' was the only possible verdict. When the case had been made public, relatives, obviously belonging to a very good class of society, came hastily and took away the corpse for burial in some family vault. The sight, the sounds, the fetid smells of that sordid lodging-house as endured by that lonely, dying, starving lady, will haunt me while I live.

Another incident (in January, 1869) had a happier conclusion. There was a case in the law reports one day of a woman named Susannah Palmer, who was sent to Newgate for stabbing her husband. The story was a piteous one as I verified it. Her husband was a savage who had continually beaten her; had turned her out of the house at night; brought in a bad woman in her place; and then had deserted her for months, leaving her to support herself and their children. After a time he would suddenly return, take the money she had earned out of her pocket (as he had then a legal right to do), sell up any furniture she possessed; kick and beat her again; and then again desert her. One day she was cutting bread for the children when he struck her, and the knife in her hand cut him; whereupon he gave her in charge for 'feloniously wounding'; and she was sent to jail. The common sergeant humanely observed as he passed sentence that 'Newgate would be ten times better for her than the hell in which she was compelled to live.' It was the old epitaph exemplified:

> 'Here lies the wife of Matthew Ford,
> Whose soul we hope is with the Lord;
> But if for Hell she's changed this life
> 'Tis better than being Mat. Ford's wife!'

Having obtained through John Locke[5] the well-known Member for Southwark, who had married my cousin, a special permit from the Lord Mayor,

---

[5] John Locke (1805–1880) was elected MP for Southwark in 1857 and held the seat until his death. In 1847 he married Laura Rosalie, Cobbe's first cousin.

I saw the poor, pale creature in Newgate and heard her long tale of wrong and misery. The good ordinary of the jail felt deeply with me for her; and when I had seen the people who employed her as charwoman (barbers and shoemakers in Cowcross Street) and received the best character of her, I felt justified in appealing, in the *Echo,* for help for her, and also in circulating a little pamphlet on her behalf. Eventually, when Mrs. Palmer left Newgate a few weeks later, it was to take possession, as *caretaker for the chaplain,* of nice, tidy rooms where she and her children could live in peace, and where her brutal husband could not follow her, since the place belonged legally to the chaplain. [...]

I wrote on the whole more than one thousand leading articles, and a vast number of Notes for the *Echo* during the seven years in which I worked upon its staff. The contributors who successively occupied the same columns of second leaders on my off-days were willing (as I believe Mr. Arnold desired) to adopt on the whole the general line of sentiment and principle which my articles maintained; and thus I had the comfort of thinking that, as regarded social ethics, my work had given in some measure the tone to the paper. It was *my pulpit*, with permission to make in it (what other pulpits lack so sadly!) such jokes as pleased me; and to put forward on hundreds of matters my views of what was right and honourable. We did not profess to be 'written by gentlemen for gentlemen.' The saturnine jests, the snarls and the pessimisms of the clubs were not in our way; and we did not affect to be *blasés*, or to think the whole world was going to the dogs. There were of course subjects on which a Liberal like Mr. Arnold and a Tory like myself differed widely; and then I left them untouched, for (I need scarcely say) I never wrote a line in that or any other paper not in fullest accordance with my own opinions and convictions, on any subject small or great. The work, I think, was at all events wholesome and harmless. I hope that it also did, now and then, a little good.

16

John Denvir, *The Life Story of an Old Rebel*

(Dublin: Sealy, Bryers & Walker, 1910). viii, 288pp.; pp. 117–22.

Born in Bushmills, County Antrim, where his father was working at the time, John Denvir (1834–1916) spent most of his life in Liverpool, a city he describes in his auto-biography as 'a "stony hearted stepmother" to its Irish colony [...] which it held for so long unregarded or despised in its midst'. It was here that he established a success-ful building firm and worked for the Irish nationalist cause as journalist, publisher, cultural activist and political organiser. In addition to editing the *Catholic Times*, the *United Irishman* and the *Nationalist* newspapers, Denvir published the popular *Illus-trated Irish Penny Library*, consisting of cheap volumes of history, biography, fiction and poetry. He also wrote *The Irish in Britain* (1892), the first book-length survey of the subject, and the novels *The Brandons: A Story of Irish Life in England* (1903) and *Olaf the Dane* (1908). His first experience of political activism was as a Fenian at the time of the 1867 rising, after which he gravitated towards constitutional nationalism, seeing it as a more pragmatic route to Irish self-government. In 1873 he became a founder member and first secretary of the Home Rule Confederation of Great Britain and later served as its national agent and organiser. Through this work he gained an intimate knowl-edge of Irish nationalist networks and personalities in late Victorian Britain, which he chronicles at length in his autobiography. As the record of a life devoted to the promo-tion and propagation of the cause of Irish nationalism in Britain, *The Life Story of an Old Rebel* reads as a paradigm of diasporic patriotism in which selfless devotion to the aspirations of the motherland not only betokens the emigrant's rightful membership of the 'imagined political community',[1] but also serves as a compensatory substitute for effective revolutionary action on behalf of the emergent nation. The following extract from Chapter 8 shows Denvir recalling his participation in a theatrical troupe called the Emerald Minstrels, the performances of which were clearly intended as a

---

[1] The phrase comes from Benedict Anderson's celebrated definition of the nation in his *Imagined Communities: Reflections on the Origin and Spread of Nationalism* (London: Verso, 1991), p. 6. There is a certain symbolic aptness in the fact that Denvir's first impression of Ireland was in representational form – a map on the back of one of O'Connell's Repeal cards – since the country existed for him primarily as an imaginary homeland of which he had little first-hand knowledge or experience.

counterblast to Victorian stage-Irish caricatures. In their idealised representations of Irish rural life as the locus of a wholesome patriotism, the group's musical dramas look back to the work of Thomas Davis and the Young Ireland writers of the 1840s and forward to the peasant plays of the Irish Literary Revival, which were central to that movement's recalibration of Irishness.

It has been suggested to me that it might form an interesting portion of these recollections if I were to give some account of how we came to start the 'Emerald Minstrels', and what we did while that company was in existence. I may say without hesitation that we got our inspiration from the teaching of Young Ireland and the 'Spirit of the Nation'. We called our entertainment 'Terence's Fireside; or The Irish Peasant at Home'.

We had most of us been boys in the old Copperas Hill school, then in the Young Men's Guild connected with the church, and some of us members of the choir. At the Guild meetings an Sunday nights, the chaplain, Father Nugent,[2] an Irishman, but, like most of ourselves, born out of his own country, used to delight in teaching us elocution, and encouraging us to write essays, besides putting other means of culture in our own way.

After a time he founded an educational establishment, the Catholic Institute, where, when he left Copperas Hill, many of us followed him and joined the evening classes. About this good priest I shall have more to say in this narrative, and, though he was no politician, I don't think any man ever did so much to elevate the condition of the Irish people of his native town, and make them both respectable – in the best sense – and respected, as Father Nugent.

We started the 'Emerald Minstrels' at a time when there was a lull in Irish politics; our objects being the cultivation of Irish music, poetry and the drama; Irish literature generally, Irish pastimes and customs; and, above all, Irish Nationality.

Father Nugent's training from the time we were young boys had been invaluable. We numbered ten, the most brilliant member of our body, and the one who did most in organising our entertainments, being John Francis McArdle.[3] Besides our main objects, already stated, we considered we were doing good work by elevating the tastes of our people, who had, through sheer good nature, so long tolerated an objectionable class of so-called Irish songs, as well as the still more objectionable 'Stage Irishman'.

---

[2] Father James Nugent (1822–1905), Liverpool-based social reformer, educationalist and temperance campaigner. In 1853 he established the Catholic Institute and became its first director.

[3] A journalist, playwright and actor, McArdle's credits include *Innocents Abroad* (1882), a one-act operetta, and *Puppets*, a whimsical play performed at the Criterion Theatre in London in 1893.

Some items from the programme will give an idea of our entertainment. We opened with a prologue, originally written by myself, but re-cast and very much improved by John McArdle. I may say that we two often did a considerable amount of journalistic work in that way in after years. I can just remember a little of the prologue. These were the opening lines:

> Sons of green Erin, we greet you this night!
> And you, too, her daughters – how welcome the sight!
> We come here before you, a minstrel band,
> To carol the lays of our native land.

There was one particularly daring couplet in it, the contribution of John McArdle:

> In your own Irish way give us one hearty cheer,
> Just to show us at once that you welcome us here.

Had mine been the task to speak these lines, I must inevitably have failed to get the required response, but in the mouth of the regular reciter they never once missed fire. This was Mr Barry Aylmer. He afterwards adopted the stage as a profession, and became recognised as a very fine actor, chiefly in Irish parts, as might be expected. He also travelled with a very successful entertainment of his own, and it is but a short time since he informed me that he spoke our identical 'Emerald Minstrel' prologue in New York and other cities in America, adapting it, of course, to the circumstances of the occasion. I found that during the many years which had elapsed since I had previously seen him until I met him again quite recently he had been a great traveller, not only in this country and America, but also in South Africa and Australia.

We had a number of harmonized choruses, including several of Moore's melodies, Banim's[4] 'Soggarth Aroon', 'Native Music', by Lover;[5] McCann's[6] 'O'Donnell Aboo!' and others. 'Killarney', words by Falconer,[7] music by

---

[4] John Banim (1798–1842), Kilkenny-born novelist and poet whose multi-volume *Tales by the O'Hara Family* was written in collaboration with his elder brother Michael (1796–1874). 'Soggarth Aroon' is one of his best-remembered poems.

[5] Samuel Lover (1797–1868), novelist, artist and composer. In the 1840s he wrote, performed and toured popular one-man shows called 'Irish Evenings', comprising songs, stories and recitations, which may have proved inspirational to Denvir and his colleagues.

[6] Michael Joseph McCann (1824–1883), Galway-born poet and journalist. His 'The Clan Connel War Song', popularly known as 'O'Donnell Aboo', first appeared in *The Nation* newspaper in 1843.

[7] Edmund Falconer was the pseudonym of Dublin-born actor and playwright Edmund O'Rourke (*c*.1814–1879). 'Killarney' was the most popular song from his 1871 melodrama *Eileen Oge*.

Balfe,[8] was sung by James McArdle, who had a fine tenor voice. Richard Campbell was our principal humorous singer. He used chiefly to give selections from Lover's songs, and one song written for him by John McArdle, 'Pat Delany's Christenin'.

John had an instinctive grasp of stage effect. A hint of the possibilities of an idea was enough for him. On my return from the Curragh I told him of how I had heard the militia men and soldiers singing the 'Shan Van Vocht'[9] on the road. He decided that this should be our *finale*, the climax of the first part of our minstrel entertainment.

We had a drop scene representing the Lower Lake of Killarney. When it was raised it disclosed the interior of the living room of a comfortable Irish homestead, with the large projecting open chimney, the turf fire on the hearth, and the usual pious and patriotic pictures proper to such an interior – Terence's Fireside.

Ours was a very self-contained company. Each had some special line as singer, musician, elocutionist, story teller or dancer.

John Clarke was our chief actor. He excelled in 'character parts', and when well 'made up' as an old man made a capital 'Terence' in the first part of the entertainment, besides giving a fine rendering of Lefanu's 'Shemus O'Brien'[10] between the parts.

In the miscellaneous part there was a rattling Irish jig by Joseph Ward and Barry Aylmer. The latter, being of somewhat slight figure and a good-looking youth, made a bouncing Irish colleen. These two made a point of studying from nature, not only in their dancing, but in their acting and singing, so that their performances were always true to life, without an atom of exaggeration. They were always received with great enthusiasm, particularly by the old people, who seemed transported back, as by the touch of a magic wand, to the scenes of their youth.

We finished the evening with a sketch, written by John McArdle, called 'Phil Foley's Frolics' – he was fond of alliteration. Noticing that Joseph Ward had made a special study of the comfortable old Irish *vanithee*,[11] and had many of her quaint and humorous sayings, he added to the characters a special part for him – 'Mrs Casey' – to which he did full justice. Indeed, so incessant was the laughter that followed each sally, that he and Barry Aylmer, who was the Phil Foley, sometimes found it difficult to get the words of the

---

[8] Michael Balfe (1808–70), Dublin composer whose best-known opera was *The Bohemian Girl* (1843).

[9] Political ballad about the expected arrival in Ireland of French troops to support the United Irishmen in the late 1790s. The first printed version appeared in *The Nation* in 1842.

[10] A popular ballad by Joseph Sheridan Le Fanu (1814–1873), which Samuel Lover incorporated into his 'Irish Evenings' to great acclaim.

[11] Phonetic rendering of 'bean an tí', Irish for 'the woman of the house'.

dialogue in between. We had another sketch, 'Pat Houlahan's Ghost', which used to go very well.

The first part of the entertainment, showing old Terence in the chimney corner and the others singing songs and telling stories, almost necessitated our sitting around in a semi-circular formation. This gave us much the appearance of a nigger troupe. To depart from this somewhat, we occasionally introduced a trifling plot. We made it that one of the sons of the house entered while the family were engaged in their usual avocations, having unexpectedly returned from America. Then came the affectionate family greeting, and the bringing in of the friends and neighbours, who formed a group sitting around the turf fire, making a merry night of it.

The services of the 'Emerald Minstrels' were in great demand, and were always cheerfully given for Catholic, National and charitable objects.

While our own people mostly furnished our audiences, our entertainment was appreciated by the general public. The best proof of this was that Mr Calderwood, Secretary of the Concert Hall, Lord Nelson Street, gave us several engagements for the 'Saturday Evening Concerts', in which, from time to time, Samuel Lover, Henry Russell, The English Glee and Madrigal Union, and other well-known popular entertainers, appeared. Mr Calderwood told us he was well pleased to have in the town a company like ours, upon whom he could always rely for a successful entertainment.

17

Tom Barclay, *Memoirs and Medleys: The Autobiography of a Bottle-Washer*

Edited by James K. Kelly, with a foreword by Sydney A. Gimson (Leicester: Edgar Backus, 1934). xi, 142pp.; pp. 3–9; 22–4.

Tom Barclay (1852–1933) was born in a Leicester slum to parents who fled famine-ridden Ireland in the late 1840s. Apart from brief spells in London and Ireland, he spent his entire working life as an unskilled labourer in various Leicester factories, while assiduously pursuing his personal goal of intellectual independence through self-education. His autobiography, which was written in the 1920s and edited for publication after his death, is the self-portrait of a politicised working-class autodidact, the central stand of which charts Barclay's ideological journey from pious young Catholic to freethinking secularist and socialist activist, who came to believe in 'Heaven on Earth as fervently as ever the Religionist believes in a Blessed State of Immortality'. Throughout the text Barclay promotes his particular brand of radical socialism with polemical brio, chiding rapacious capitalist and apathetic worker alike, while eulogising his hero George Bernard Shaw, with whom he occasionally corresponded. The breezy conversational intimacy of Barclay's prose style belies his sharp understanding of autobiography as calculated self-portraiture and his alertness to the transformative power of memory, as the following extract reveals. In addition to being a compelling record of proletarian activism during the Victorian socialist revival, *Memoirs and Medleys* is also a key historical source for the study of the second-generation Irish experience in nineteenth-century England. In particular, Barclay's graphic account of the forces that shaped his attitudes towards his Irish cultural heritage during his formative years has been used by scholars both to substantiate and to refute the thesis of second-generation assimilation.[1] Much of this debate centres on the following passages, which vividly encapsulate

---

[1] Whereas Lynn Lees and Graham Davis regard Barclay's youthful rejection of his Irish cultural inheritance as evidence of his assimilative desire, Sean Campbell convincingly reinterprets this as part of a complex, evolutionary process of identity formation. For a summary of the arguments, see Sean Campbell, 'Beyond "Plastic Paddy": A Re-examination of the Second-Generation Irish in England', in Donald M. MacRaild (ed.), *The Great Famine and Beyond: Irish Migrants in Britain in the Nineteenth and Twentieth Centuries* (Dublin: Irish Academic Press, 2000), pp. 266–88.

the psychological dilemmas of a second-generation Irish child caught between mutu-ally exclusive discourses of Irishness and Englishness. Barclay's account of his resultant feelings of 'cultural cringe' and his desire to mask the outward signs of his ethnic differ-ence represent one phase of a complex process of identity negotiation by a 'would-be Irishman', as he memorably styles himself.

Here in this eighteen foot square court off Burley's Lane, Leicester, St. Margaret's bells rang dismally every Sunday morning as I tried to play with duckstones for toys. I'm afraid the one door and one chamber window of the two-roomed crib we lived in were seldom opened, though not six feet from the muck hole and the unflushed privies, and air could only get in from one side of the house. How did we remain healthy? But let me not imagine that because others were born in country cottages and manses with meads that slope away in front and wind swept hills in view that therefore they lived happy ever after. Open-air exercises, a sumptuous table, purple and fine linen and a University education awaiting, yes: but in spite of all these, they will suffer disappointments, boredom, weariness – perhaps poverty – and some will murder or be murdered, while poverty-stricken *moi qui parle* may end up calm as a Buddha and in tune with the Infinite.

After the monotony and dreariness of that Burley's Lane hut, I somehow find myself in a similar two-roomed hut in a similar court in a similar slum – Abbey Street: our walls are now plastered with woodcuts from newspapers, and there are mounds of thick ice all round the gutters. Now there are five of us sleeping in one little upper room. I remember nothing of this locale but the attitudinising of kiddies in the yard doubling their fists and prattling of the great fight between Sayers and Heenan.[2] We were commanded to remain shut in, father and mother being out most of the day earning a living. Father knew no trade and to dig was not able: he collected rags and bones, rag-bag on back, without as much as a truck (or handcart): mother worked at a ragshop or marine store dealer's, or she got blocks of wood from the wood-yards, chopped them small and sold the chips in pen'norths for fire-lighting round the neighbouring streets.

'Now see that ye don't stir a foot out of this till me or yer mother comes back, or I'll tan the life out of ye, do ye hear?' Such the command, but it wasn't in juvenile flesh and blood to obey always.

The scene changes once more, and we are again still in a two-roomed pigsty-crib in a court off Woodboy Street, but all dreariness is gone, exchanged for alarms and excursions, chases and flights and mad uproar. How could anyone resist breaking out of that dirty kennel on a summer's day when the sun shone even into that court. We broke bounds and ran up and down the street like

---

[2] The champion English bare-fisted pugilist Tom Sayers (1826–1865) and the American John C. Heenan (1833–1873) took part in a famous fight at Farnborough in April 1860. The contest was declared a draw after 37 gruelling rounds.

little mad things. Why had we to stay in? Well, you see, we might get lost or run over or beaten – hounded and ill used by the Sassenach kids: as a matter of fact we were hounded and harrassed.

'Hurroo Mick!'

'Ye Awrish Paddywack.'

'Arrah, bad luck to the ships that brought ye over!'

These were the salutes of the happy English child: we were battered, threatened, elbowed, pressed back to the door of our kennel amid boos and jeers and showers of small missiles. The unkind expressions must have been borrowed from the grown-ups whose animosity was often evident enough. To tell the truth, Sassenach kids fought among themselves; street fought street and district district without the slightest cause. And after all, why expect youths (who are mentally but at the stone-age period) not to fight without cause while grown-ups, backed and abetted by college professors and ministers of Jesus Christ, fight with almost as little? I would like to know, and I wish I were anthropologist and psychologist enough to answer, is there any such reality as race-hatred? There should not be among intelligent grown-up people. My own attitude towards a foreigner of whatever colour or creed is simply one of interest – intense curiosity. And this makes me social: the only thing that might repel me, or make me cold, is denseness, want of mentality; but this repels me in men of my own nationality. [...]

Fenianism is rife about this time: I remember our parents rejoicing over the escape from prison of the Head Centre, James Stephens[3] (I think it was). Also, we were greatly excited by the news of the blowing up of Clerkenwell Prison.[4] We lamented the hanging of the Manchester Martyrs,[5] and our English neighbours danced and rejoiced. What wonder? Some priest said hell was not hot enough for the Fenians.

Whenever an English man or woman did anything disreputable, my mother was wont to remark 'Ah well, sure, what better could one expect from the breed of King Harry?' The Sassenach was regarded by us with a mixture of contempt and hatred. God had made him it is true and Jesus Christ had died to save him, but we clean forgot that, and only saw him embodied in Calvin and Cranmer, the lustful King Henry VIII, Queen Bess the Persecutor, the Orangeman's idol, William of Orange, and 'the bloody Cromwell.' There were though a few good Englishmen no doubt, like Alfred the Great,

---

[3] James Stephens (1824–1901) founded the Irish Republican Brotherhood, also known as the Fenians, in Dublin in March 1858.

[4] In December 1867 a Fenian bomb exploded at Clerkenwell Prison, killing several Londoners.

[5] William Allen, Michael Larkin and Michael O'Brien, publicly hanged in Salford in November 1867 for the murder of a policeman during the rescue of two Fenian prisoners in September of that year.

Sir Thomas Moore, and William Cobbett who wrote the history of the Protestant Reformation. My father was a Limerick man, and we were often hearing eulogies of the hero Patrick Sarsfield, and the women of Limerick who fought and repelled the English during the siege of that city. How we gloated over the way the Irish Brigade defeated the English at Fontenoy! But what filthy little wretches we children were, and how could it be otherwise? Not Papuans nor Basutos nor Fijians could I think be more degraded. And this was in the middle of the nineteenth century. O great and glorious empire! What chance to be clean was there in a house on whose only floor bags of dusty rags and putrescent bones were spilled out to be sorted? Nevertheless, we were used to this, and before going to bed we all knelt down, after a supper of Indian meal, on the bare uneven brick floor and recited the Rosary, father leading off: one Our Father to ten Hail Mary's: one of the prayers spoken fifty times by the help of a string of beads: and we arose feeling good and comforted and strengthened for the morrow's work. [...]

One day the kids from the other end of the court, or 'yard,' as we called it, attacked us under Billy, their leader, and broke a pane of glass and thrust a rod through: unable to get out, or fearful of a spanking if we did, we scuttled upstairs and threw cinders from the chamber window on Billy and his pals: they battered the door, and we retaliated as we could. My imagination went to work: Billy was King William and we were the Irish: it was the siege of Limerick being in some mysterious manner enacted over again. There it was Gael and Sassenach once more. What neighbours quarrels when father and mother came back, what fine excuses for our conduct, why shouldn't we defend ourselves? There followed weltings and wailings, but I can't blame father and mother for venting their anger: the whole crib from floor to roof showed but too horribly a state of siege.

What sort of an existence was it where a mother giving suck had to be hours away from home trying to earn something? When the kids of the yard were not molesting us, I as eldest was nurse, and often have I put my tongue into baby's mouth to be sucked in lieu of 'titty' to stop her cries. The cries used to cease for a minute, and then were resumed as the tongue gave no satisfaction. Poor cooped-up vermin-infested brats! But I am suffering much more now probably in simply remembering our state than I actually suffered then: we did not feel the dimness and squalor and foul smells – the horror of the bugs and lice and black-beetles – as I now, many years after feel them: we had no other life, no other sensations and feelings. This was life, and we knew no other to contrast it with. Does the worm wish to be a butterfly, or the mole a lark? [...]

I never went to day-school, only to Sunday-school, and for a while to night-school; but night-school was mixed – boys and girls, and we were far more interested in one another than in learning: we were beginning to rehearse the drama of sex. Dear old school-master John Mee, you were a gentleman, and if I mistake not, a real saint. How was my propensity to draw and sketch brought over from some previous generation, I wonder. I never saw father draw nor sketch, and mother never could write her own name. My brick scratching with slate splinters in infancy must have remained unnoticed, I think. Mother taught me to spell and read. She was held to be quite exceptional among her countrywomen in that she could read Dr. Gallacher's sermons in Irish.[6] This Gallacher was the bishop of Raphoe in Donegal. How she who read English with difficulty could read these sermons, though in Roman characters, with their transliteration nearly as bad as Welsh, is something I do not understand: but read them she could, and often have I seen the tears come into her eyes over the sermon on the passion of Our Lord. This she used to read on a Good Friday. 'Glory to God but you're the one!' neighbours used to exclaim. It did them good to hear a blessed sermon read in the first language they ever spoke. I don't know was her maiden name MacLin or Maglyn, for I never saw it written; her mother's people were O'Reillys. She was well acquainted with the old legends of Oisin, and Fin, and Cuchullan, and the Gobawn Sayr, and could sing and recite a goodly number of old Irish songs and poems. The old bardic legends and laments and love songs must have been transmitted orally from generation to generation for centuries: they were crooned and told round the turf fire of a winter's night. But what had I to do with all that? I was becoming English! I did not hate things Irish, but I began to feel that they must be put away; they were inferior to things English. How could it be otherwise? My pronunciation was jeered at – mimicked, corrected. I pronounced TEA 'tay' like Alexander Pope used to do instead of pronouncing it 'tee' as your present-day speaker does. Outside the house everything was English: my catechism, lessons, prayers, songs, tales, games – 'English, quite English.' Presently, I began to feel ashamed of the jeers and mockery and criticism, and tried to pronounce like the English. I had yet to learn that these same English were slangy, and ungrammatical, and continually mispronounced their own language.

---

[6] Fr. James Gallagher (*c.*1690–1751) was consecrated as Catholic bishop of Raphoe in 1725 and translated to the diocese of Kildare and Leighlin in 1737. His *Sixteen Sermons in An Easy and Familiar Stile* first appeared in 1736 and proved hugely popular with generations of Catholic Irish peasantry. Nineteenth-century editions of the work featured English translations by Fr. James Byrne.

18
William Butler Yeats, *Reveries over Childhood and Youth*

(New York: Macmillan, 1916). 131pp.; pp. 34–9.

Although widely divergent as works of literature, the autobiographies of Tom Barclay and W. B. Yeats (1865–1939) exhibit a telling congruity in their depiction of an Irish childhood in England in which racially motivated bullying, and the anti-English animus that was its converse, play a formative role. Yeats, of course, was a scion of the provincial Irish Protestant bourgeoisie, whose ancestors would have been mistrusted by Barclay's peasant forebears. Yet neither religion nor breeding could insulate young Willie from being mocked as a 'Mad Irishman' by his London schoolfellows, as the following extract from his first piece of sustained autobiographical prose, composed in 1914, attests. Yeats was still an infant when his family first moved to London in 1867 and he was to spend the next decade being ferried between Sligo, Dublin and Bedford Park in Hammersmith, where John Butler Yeats temporarily settled his cash-strapped family. In January 1877 Willie was enrolled at the Godolphin School in Hammersmith, where he remained until 1881, the year in which the family moved back to Dublin. Six years later Yeats returned to London to play an integral part in several literary and dramatic ventures, including the establishment of the landmark Irish Literary Society in January 1892. By this time, his Bedford Park residence was a hive of expatriate Irish cultural activity and the poet himself was embarked upon a path that would see him definitively transform the image and identity of Ireland and the Irish, not only in the minds of his compatriots but in the eyes of Britain and the world.

Yeats's impressionistic recollections of his early London years in *Reveries* register both the 'romantic excitement' and solitary outsiderness of the migrant artist's son, emphases that are part of the poet's overall project of retrospectively delineating his progess towards intellectual and artistic independence from his father.[1] As in all of Yeats's autobiographical writings, his dramatic self-conception as a poet fundamentally conditions his interpretation of his personal past. This means that factual detail and temporal linearity are frequently sacrificed to what Roy Foster refers to as Yeats's 'heroic

---

[1] See David G. Wright, *Yeats's Myth of Self: A Study of the Autobiographical Prose* (Dublin: Gill and Macmillan, 1987), pp. 38–9.

self-construction':[2] his aesthetic need to render the influences that moulded the inner man and weave a unified autobiographical persona from multifarious former selves. Yeats's prefatory disclaimer to *Reveries* sounds an oblique warning in this regard: 'I have changed nothing to my knowledge; and yet it must be that I have changed many things without my knowledge; for I am writing after many years and have consulted neither friend, not letter, nor old newspaper, and describe what comes oftenest into my memory.' The poet's psychological self-portrait as an unhappy, dislocated Victorian child must therefore be read as a complex amalgam of memory and imagination, forged by an inveterate self-mythologiser.

The only lessons I had ever learned were those my father taught me, for he terrified me by descriptions of my moral degradation and he humiliated me by my likeness to disagreeable people; but presently I was sent to school at Hammersmith. It was a Gothic building of yellow brick: a large hall full of desks, some small class-rooms, and a separate house for boarders, all built perhaps in 1840 or 1850. I thought it an ancient building and that it had belonged to the founder of the school, Lord Godolphin, who was romantic to me because there was a novel about him. I never read the novel, but I thought only romantic people were put in books. On one side, there was a piano factory of yellow brick, upon two sides half-finished rows of little shops and villas all yellow brick, and on the fourth side, outside the wall of our playing field, a brickfield of cinders and piles of half-burned yellow bricks. All the names and faces of my school-fellows have faded from me except one name without a face and the face and name of one friend, mainly no doubt because it was all so long ago, but partly because I only seem to remember things that have mixed themselves up with scenes that have some quality to bring them again and again before the memory. For some days, as I walked homeward along the Hammersmith Road, I told myself that whatever I most cared for had been taken away. I had found a small, green-covered book given to my father by a Dublin man of science; it gave an account of the strange sea creatures the man of science had discovered among the rocks at Howth or dredged out of Dublin Bay. It had long been my favourite book; and when I read it I believed that I was growing very wise, but now I should have no time for it nor for my own thoughts. Every moment would be taken up learning or saying lessons or walking between school and home four times a day, for I came home in the middle of the day for dinner. But presently I forgot my trouble, absorbed in two things I had never known, companionship and enmity. After my first day's lesson, a circle of boys had got around me in a playing field and asked me questions, 'who's your father?' 'what does he do?' 'how much money has he?' Presently a boy said something insulting. I had

---

[2] R. F. Foster, *W. B. Yeats: A Life. Volume 1: The Apprentice Mage* (Oxford: Oxford University Press, 1997), p. xxv. See also pp. 526–31 for a discussion of the compositional contexts of *Reveries*.

never struck anybody or been struck, and now all in a minute, without any intention upon my side, but as if I had been a doll moved by a string, I was hitting at the boys within reach and being hit. After that I was called names for being Irish, and had many fights and never, for years, got the better in any one of them; for I was delicate and had no muscles. Sometimes, however, I found means of retaliation, even of aggression. There was a boy with a big stride, much feared by little boys, and finding him alone in the playing field, I went up to him and said, 'rise upon Sugaun and sink upon Gad.' 'What does that mean?' he said. 'Rise upon hay-leg and sink upon straw', I answered, and told him that in Ireland the sergeant tied straw and hay to the ankles of a stupid recruit to show him the difference between his legs. My ears were boxed, and when I complained to my friends, they said I had brought it upon myself; and that I deserved all I got. I probably dared myself to other feats of a like sort, for I did not think English people intelligent or well-behaved unless they were artists. Everyone I knew well in Sligo despised Nationalists and Catholics, but all disliked England with a prejudice that had come down perhaps from the days of the Irish Parliament. I knew stories to the discredit of England, and took them all seriously. My mother had met some English woman who did not like Dublin because the legs of the men were too straight, and at Sligo, as everybody knew, an Englishman had once said to a car-driver, 'if you people were not so lazy, you would pull down the mountain and spread it out over the sand and that would give you acres of good fields.' At Sligo there is a wide river mouth and at ebb tide most of it is dry sand, but all Sligo knew that in some way I cannot remember it was the spreading of the tide over the sand that left the narrow channel fit for shipping. At any rate the carman had gone chuckling all over Sligo with his tale. People would tell it to prove that Englishmen were always grumbling. 'They grumble about their dinners and everything – there was an Englishman who wanted to pull down Knock-na-Rea' and so on. My mother had shown them to me kissing at railway stations, and taught me to feel disgust at their lack of reserve, and my father told how my grandfather, William Yeats, who had died before I was born, when he came home to his Rectory in County Down from an English visit, spoke of some man he had met on a coach road who 'Englishman-like' told him all his affairs. My father explained that an Englishman generally believed that his private affairs did him credit, while an Irishman, being poor and probably in debt, had no such confidence. I, however, did not believe in this explanation. My Sligo nurses, who had in all likelihood the Irish Catholic political hatred, had never spoken well of any Englishman. Once when walking in the town of Sligo I had turned to look after an English man and woman whose clothes attracted me. The man I remember had gray clothes and knee-breeches and the woman a gray dress, and my nurse had said contemptuously, 'towrows'. Perhaps before my time, there had been some English song with the burden 'tow row row', and everybody had told me that English people ate skate and even dog-fish, and I myself had only just arrived in England when I saw an old man put marmalade in his porridge. I was divided from all those boys, not merely by the anecdotes that are everywhere perhaps a chief expression of the distrust of races, but because our mental images were different. I read their boys' books and they excited me, but if I read of some English victory, I did not believe that I read of my own people. They thought of Cressy and Agincourt and the Union Jack and were all very patriotic, and I, without those memories of Limerick and the Yellow Ford that would have strengthened an Irish Catholic, thought of mountain and lake, of my grandfather and of ships. Anti-Irish feeling was running high, for the Land League had been founded and landlords had been shot, and I, who had no politics, was yet full of pride, for it is romantic to live in a dangerous country.

I daresay I thought the rough manners of a cheap school, as my grandfather Yeats had those of a chance companion, typical of all England. At any rate I had a harassed life & got many a black eye and had many outbursts of grief and rage. Once a boy, the son of a great Bohemian glass-maker, and who was older than the rest of us, and had been sent out of his country because of a love affair, beat a boy for me because we were 'both foreigners'. And a boy, who grew to be the school athlete and my chief friend, beat a great many. His are the face and name that I remember – his name was of Huguenot origin and his face like his gaunt and lithe body had something of the American Indian in colour and lineament.

19
Joseph Keating, *My Struggle for Life*

(London: Simpkin, Marshall, Hamilton & Kent, 1916). xv, 308pp.; pp. 4–10; 13–14; 268–9.

Born to Irish Catholic parents in the coalmining village of Mountain Ash in south Wales, Joseph Keating (1871–1934) worked at a variety of jobs – pit-boy, gardener, clerk, travelling salesman, newspaper reporter – before turning to writing in the late 1890s. The romantic novels *Son of Judith* (1900) and *Maurice* (1905) brought him some recognition but insufficient income to sustain his ambition to become a professional writer. To make ends meet, Keating turned to writing short stories for the British and American magazine market. Commercial success eventually came his way in 1914, when his novel *A Perfect Wife* (1913) was adapted for the West End stage as *Peggy and Her Husband*. This theatrical triumph proved to be the high point of his literary career, however, as the First World War shifted Keating's energies from literature to politics. Although he failed to win the Labour nomination for the Aberdare constituency in 1918, he succeeded in becoming a Labour councillor five years later and went on to play a prominent role in the Welsh labour movement until his death.[1]

In tracing the author's evolution from artistic awakening to imaginative self-realisation, *My Struggle for Life* conforms to the *Künstlerroman* pattern of literary memoir, making it a distant cousin of Joyce's *A Portrait of the Artist as a Young Man*, published the same year. Keating's 'zig-zag course' from the obscurity of a Rhondda coalmine to 'Grub Street, the coal-mine of literature' is rendered in rich social and psychological detail; there are some particularly evocative descriptions of coalmining and the forms of masculinity it engendered. The book is infused throughout with a muted didacticism that stems from Keating's belief that 'a child of the workers might be born with as much intellectuality, spirituality, and manhood as the child of any other sort of people'. This leads him to present his literary success as a triumph of working-class aspiration over social disadvantage, which he offers as an exemplum to others. From a historical perspective, Keating's encomiastic portrait of the behaviour and outlook of Irish 'colonists' in nineteenth-century Wales, as exemplified in the following

---

[1] For further biographical details, see Paul O'Leary's introduction to the reissued edition of *My Struggle for Life*, pp. ix–xxx.

extract, can be read as a corrective to prevailing views of the immigrant Irish as a socially malign influence.[2] His view of nationality is equally revisionary insofar as it refutes narrow-gauge Irish nationalists' emphasis on birth and residency as touchstones of belonging. Indeed, his succinct disaggregation of 'home' and nationality gestures towards a version of diasporic identity that pre-empts by several decades the kind proposed by contemporary theorists such as Avtar Brah.[3]

We lived with a little colony of Irish emigrants, a small pool formed by a trickle from the flood of emigration which had been rushing out of Ireland to every corner of the world since the famine in the middle of last century. Ironworks and mines in Wales could provide work and bread. The Irish landed at various parts of the Welsh coast; and husbands, wives and children tramped away from the ship, until the men found work. Wherever they could earn bread they settled down.

The first comers secured places near the coast. Later groups had to march farther inland amidst the valleys.

They became labourers, navvies, miners, and puddlers. They worked in the dust and darkness of 'rubbish-stalls' underground, and in the scorching blaze of steel-furnaces above. They swung pick, shovel, bar and hammer, and handled drills, blasting and hewing tunnels and cuttings through mountains and valleys. Destiny drove them from their beloved Irish homes and farms to build railways, sink pits, and carry the hod up to the tops of boiler-stacks that seemed to be taller than the hills of this country of the stranger. The exiles landed with the power to labour as the sum total of their wealth; and as they owned nothing but their poverty and their strength, they took the poorest dwelling-places as shelter for themselves and their families. [...]

I do not know the house I was born in. I think it was somewhere in a place called Nixon's Row. That was not its administrative name. I believe it had a charming Welsh name. But people with imagination like to be intimate with their surroundings; and Nixon's Row was christened by its tenants after the name of the man who built it, as they named a child after its father. I remember vaguely that we must have removed to another house. I become quite sure of our address when we lived on the Cardiff Road in a row of high, square houses, called The Barracks, a term which accurately described their appearance. Once a year the block was whitewashed. Then it looked like the gaunt ghost of a giant towering formidably over the small, drab houses opposite.

Inside and outside we had space. Huge mountains rose in front of us, and it was only necessary to cross a canal and evade the gamekeeper – an added

---

[2] See Paul O'Leary, *Immigration and Integration: The Irish in Wales, 1798–1922* (Cardiff: University of Wales Press, 2000), pp. 132–3.

[3] See Avtar Brah, *Cartographies of Diaspora: Contesting Identities* (London: Routledge, 1996), pp. 192–3.

attraction for boys – in order to have the entire broad woods and slopes for bird-nesting, nutting, poaching, or the fun of Bedlam.

At our back was a railway; beyond that, the fields of Cwmcynon Farm and the river Cynon – at that time a clear amber stream – for bathing; and beyond that again still more mountains, which, however, were not considered as desirable as the ones on our side of the valley.

Our house had three storeys, with the top floor entirely unoccupied. Up there we held boxing-matches – boxing was a most admired accomplishment in our quarter – Christy minstrel entertainments, and dramatic performances. A portable theatre, Ebley's, Johnny Noakes', or Norton's, the price of admission to which was threepence, nearly always encamped at Mountain Ash.[4] I was a grave student of the drama, and my brothers, Matt and Maurice, were enthusiasts who could not only appreciate but imitate; and all our favourite dramas 'Dred the Avenger; or Alone in the Dismal Swamp,' 'Ingomar, the Terror of the Wilderness,' 'Maria Martin; or the Murder in the Red Barn,' 'The Dumb Man of Manchester,' 'The Maid of Cefn Ydfa,' and countless others were reproduced in our 'top loft'. My mother insisted as a great joke against me that the first words I ever spoke were uttered when I stabbed our front door with a breadknife, and said in a hoarse voice: 'Die, villain, die!'

I was always hoarse as a child – from so much crying. I am told I was the most miserable child ever born. I refused to have anything to do with my mother after she weaned me, I was so much offended, and would only allow my sister Molly – Heaven pity her! – to nurse me.

Three steps led up to our door, with a low wall at each side to protect us from falling into the open areas below. The earth had been excavated to allow light to reach the windows of houses underneath ours. The street door led into our big kitchen, which was floored with stone flags. My sisters washed these flags and freshly sprinkled them with sand of a lovely red-gold tint every Saturday. The kitchen was our morning, dining, and drawing rooms. At the inner end, to the left, was a pantry spacious enough for a town house. Around the pantry walls were clean white wooden shelves, and at the back a wide, flat stone, its surface very rough. The big 'pantry-stone' had been hewn from the hillside quarry and fitted in its place without further preparation. A large pantry was necessary for the never-satisfied appetites of four boys and three girls. The shelves were kept as well-stocked as possible. My mother's pride was a full pantry. She bought her potatoes in sacks, her salt in huge bars like the beams of a ship, her butter in mountains, and her bread in continents. Ever since then, I have pitied people who are compelled to buy half-pounds of butter, quarter-pounds of tea, pinches of salt and contemptible carbuncles called cottage-loaves.

---

[4] Portable theatres were common in Wales during the late 1800s and early 1900s. The Edward Ebley Theatrical Company was among the most well-known.

We went to Mass every Sunday morning in the 'long room' of a public house called the Scroby Arms. Drink and the devil had possession of the room until midnight, and the Holy Ghost descended upon it in the peace of the Sabbath morning. The long room was at the back of the inn, with a platform at the far end, holding the altar and a piano. Songs and hornpipes had been sung and danced there a few hours previously. Flowers of great beauty decorated the altar, and a tiny red lamp burned before it. When we entered the room we blessed ourselves with the holy water which was placed in a tin can near the door, and genuflected profoundly to the altar and piano. Sunlight poured in from a side window. A few coarse benches, without backs, made seats for the first arrivals. Men and women, boys and girls, crowded in until the interior became warm and suffocating. While waiting for Mass to begin we took out our rosaries and prayed for souls in purgatory.

From a door behind the people the priest appeared, robed in richly coloured vestments, and came slowly forward with great dignity, preceded by one small altar-boy in black and white. All the stifling congregation went silently upon its knees, as the priest passed up to the altar. The murmur of musical Latin words rolled through the silence. The wonderful ceremony of the Mass began; and, instantaneously, the drink-stained long room became, as if by a miracle, a cathedral of hushed reverence and worship, from which the sacred had utterly banished the profane.

Later, the Catholics were able to secure the Workman's Hall on Sundays. Acrobatic and conjuring tricks were performed in the hall during the week. A travelling theatrical company might have been playing there the previous Saturday night, and on the stage the sacred altar was erected and the holy sacrifice of the Mass celebrated amidst exit and entrance wings, and scenery representing a castle dungeon or a forest glade. [...]

We who lived in The Barracks – which was also a generic name for the whole district – were intensely proud of the place. Its people were hard-working, honest and neighbourly. They gave generously to their church; of course, there was only one church for them – the Catholic Church. They were kind to one another. If illness or poverty happened to be in one house, nearly every other house proffered help. If one man was killed in the pits, his neighbours helped to carry his dead body from the pit to his home and from there to his last home on the hillside. Everybody's home was open to everybody else, and there was great friendship. There was not a thief in the district. Loafers and swindlers were not able to live there. Matrimony was regarded as a sacrament, and the colony had no need of divorce courts.

There was no bawdy talk in the young men's conversation. I used to feel horribly ashamed when I went amongst better-off youths and heard them speak insultingly of women. The girls of the colony were bright-eyed and pure. And I am merely repeating statistics when I say that the rate of illegitimacy there would work out at, perhaps, two in a million; and in those isolated cases, the man was blamed and not the girl. [...]

The place where a man spends the first twenty years of his life remains for ever in the centre of his heart, and is, for him, the centre of the world. That was how I had always felt about Mountain Ash. A curious element was in that fact. I was entirely Irish in every way – in blood, traditions, sympathies, training, and temperament. I regarded Ireland as my country; and not only as mine, but as God's, and its people as a race chosen, above all other nationalities, by the Almighty, to establish the ideals of spiritual perfection, moral perfection, and intellectual perfection, 'the triple tiara of the Gael,' as an enthusiast phrased it.

Now Mountain Ash was Welsh. Yet this bit of Wales, where I was born and had spent my first twenty years, was so rooted in my Irish heart that I neither would nor could think of any other place on earth as my home. It seemed to me that the feeling of nationality had nothing to do with the land of birth, but was inherited in the blood. Irish children, scattered to the ends of the earth, loved the lands in which they were born, yet still regarded Ireland as their country, though they had never seen it.

20

James Mullin, *The Story of a Toiler's Life*

(Dublin and London: Maunsel & Roberts, 1921). 235pp.; pp. 180–1; 196–9.

James Mullin (1846–1920) was born in Cookstown, County Tyrone, the only child of abjectly poor Catholic tenant farmers. Although forced to leave school at the age of 11 to be apprenticed to a carpenter and wheelwright, his passion for learning eventually led to him to Cookstown Academy and from there to Queen's College Galway, where he studied medicine with the help of scholarships and prizes. On graduation in 1880 Mullin secured a medical assistantship in Brynmawr in south Wales, but quickly swapped it for a better paid post in nearby Blaenavon, where he worked for a former Galway classmate, a fact that lends weight to the view that ethnic support networks were as important for skilled Irish immigrants as they were for their unskilled compatriots.[1] There followed a period of locum work at various locations in England and Wales, Mullin's autobiographical account of which provides glimpses of the racial and religious prejudices with which an Irish doctor had to contend in the late Victorian era. He eventually established a successful medical practice in the burgeoning town of Cardiff, where he worked with 'the regularity of an automaton moved by faultless machinery' until the onset of diabetes caused him to retire in his late fifties. Mullin's last years were devoted to 'the pursuit of travel spiced with journalism, and sometimes mingled with a renewal of professional duties as ship's surgeon' on ocean cruises to various parts of Europe, Africa and Asia.

The Story of a Toiler's Life, which Mullin completed in 1917, has been aptly described as 'a Smilesean story of self-definition through work',[2] throughout which the author sounds a consistently self-improving note. The book also charts Mullin's journey from youthful Irish separatist to integrationist Home Ruler and anti-sectarian agnostic, whose unorthodox opinions did not always endear him to fellow nationalists, as the following extract attests. Emigration revived Mullin's interest in politics, which

---

[1] See Louise Miskell, ' "The heroic Irish doctor?": Irish immigrants in the medical profession in nineteenth-century Wales', in Oonagh Walsh (ed.), *Ireland Abroad: Politics and Professions in the Nineteenth Century* (Dublin: Four Courts Press, 2003), pp. 82–94.

[2] Patrick Maume, 'James Mullin, the Poor Scholar: A Self-made Man from Carleton's Country', *Irish Studies Review*, vol. 7, no. 1 (1999), p. 29.

had lain fallow since his abandonment of Fenianism after the botched 1867 rising. Angered by the prejudicial coverage of Irish affairs in the London press, and by the anti-Irish sentiments provoked by the Phoenix Park murders of 1882, he joined the Cardiff branch of the Irish National League and was soon elected chairman, a position he held for 25 years. In this capacity he met a number of leading Irish nationalists who visited Cardiff, including Michael Davitt, whom he revered, and Charles Stewart Parnell and Patrick Pearse, both of whom he distrusted. That Mullin's Home Rule sympathies were infused with a strong measure of Gladstonian Liberalism, which later shaded into a bourgeois imperialism, is evidenced by his use of phrases such as 'our Empire' and 'our tropical possessions', and by his explicit endorsement of what he terms 'the beneficent policy of late years, which has turned all our old rebels, like myself, into a staunch supporter of the British connection'.

When I came to Cardiff the 'United Irish League', or 'National League', as it was then called, had not been introduced into the town, but was started immediately afterwards at a meeting at which I was present. Although I was a stranger and absolutely unknown to any of my own countrypeople I suppose my position as a doctor gave me some claim to recognition, and I was unanimously elected Vice-Chairman of the branch that was then organised. The Chairman was the leading Irishman of the place – a man of wonderful ability and highly popular, being endowed with the gifts that are said to distinguish our race – eloquence, humour, and geniality.

I attended the meetings for some time afterwards, and as the Chairman did not do so, I always occupied the Chair. Finding me there on one occasion he made a very flattering speech in my favour, and proposed that I should take his place as Chairman, seeing that he should be unable to attend regularly. This was agreed to, and so I became Chairman – a position which I filled for at least twenty-five years, and one that brought me into contact with many eminent Irishmen, and modified the unfavourable views of politicians that I previously held. [...]

I tried, but tried in vain, to indoctrinate my supporters with my views, which must have appeared very unorthodox in their eyes. I invariably impressed it upon them that Ireland was a Nation and not a denomination; and when it was suggested that the Catholic Bishop should be asked to one of their banquets, I proposed that the Protestant Bishop should also be asked, so that the League should act consistently with its non-sectarian programme. The study of the Past in which they were so much absorbed received from me but little respect, and I always inculcated that Life is a race in which those who would win must keep looking before them, not behind. Whatever admiration I bestowed on Ireland's Past was confined to Fionn and his pagan warriors and bards, and not to Patrick and his saints.

On being told that every Irishman who neglects to have his son taught the Irish language is a traitor to his country, I replied that every Irishman who neglects to have his son taught a trade is a traitor to his country; and that it matters little what language a man speaks if he lives a slave and dies a pauper. Though long accustomed to swallow flummery and soothing syrup, my people resented the change of diet that I recommended far less than I expected, for I never allowed any hostile outsider to traduce them to my knowledge.

In spite of my outrageous heresies our people put up with me, and I was able to inspire some few of them with the belief that if ever the League got into a tight corner I would not turn my back on it. But if I did not turn my back on the principles of the League I turned my back on my position as Chairman.

It came about in this way that a lot of young men had recently joined, and these were the products of a lop-sided education, which is the curse of so many, making them more prejudiced and intolerant than those who have no education at all. The worst of the lot was their leader, a foxy-headed firebrand of a priest, who puffed them up with the idea that they were God's chosen people; and if they wished to remain so they must carefully give the cold shoulder to their friends who were leprosied with the deadly sin of being neither Irish nor Catholic. When they were getting up a banquet for Saint Patrick's Day, our National festival, they passed a resolution in my absence that none but Irishmen should be admitted. At the next meeting I vehemently protested against this idiotic course, and pointed out that it was a direct slap in the face to the people from whom they earned their living, and amongst whom they had so many well-wishers and friends. I told them I would on no account sit at such a banquet, neither would I any longer act as Chairman to a body of men capable of making a proposal so abjectly fatuous. So I not only retired immediately, but set about getting up another banquet to which all our friends, English, Welsh, and Scottish, were invited, and that, too, irrespective of their politics or religion.

I spoke to some of our parliamentary leaders about my action and they warmly approved of it. No further attempt was ever made by any body of Irishmen in Cardiff to exclude friendly outsiders from their banquets, and though often asked I never again, except for a few weeks, took office in the National ranks. But though absent in body I was with them heart and soul, and as a private individual always did my very best for the Irish cause, and without seeking popularity obtained it. I have, indeed, always held the opinion that a man who goes in for politics, especially Irish politics, for the sake of popularity does not deserve to get it.

Small as the sphere of my political labour was, it extended beyond Cardiff, and at one time included both Newport and Merthyr, by which towns I was twice elected a member of the Executive Council, and on each occasion was opposed by Cardiff – an illustration of the old maxim that a prophet is without honour in his own country. That, however, is not to be wondered at when the prophet bears the character of a crank, as I did.

As their representative I once had a deputation from the Nationalists of a neighbouring town to learn how they should act in a quarrel they had with their priest, who set himself up to become their political dictator in opposition to their political principles. I told them the means of dealing with him were very simple, and lay entirely in their own hands: let them cut off the supplies and starve him out of the place; after all, he was their servant, not their master; they paid the piper and had a right to choose the tune. The reply was if they did so he would cut them off from all religious benefits and let them die like dogs. I then told them if they were afraid of that there was no use in asking me or anybody else what they should do: they put the whip into his hand and must blame themselves and not him if he used it upon them.

All the enemies I made and all the opposition I encountered were due to the fact that I was credited with being strongly anti-clerical. Now, this was quite true, but only in a limited sense, for my anti-clericalism went no farther than opposing clericalism in the domain of politics. I respected the cleric, be he priest or parson, so long as he confined himself to his clerical functions and administered spiritual consolation to those who stood in need of it, but when he plunged into politics I considered his influence positively pernicious on whatever side he chose to use it. Such influence makes no converts, but repels rather than attracts, and if I were a parliamentary candidate and could afford the expense I should adopt the Machiavellian policy of secretly hiring some clerical orators to support my opponent. I say this well knowing the harm that priests, animated with the very best intentions, have done to the Home Rule cause in Ireland by perpetually crowding its platforms and thereby keeping away Protestant sympathisers. In like manner I know how some Protestant ecclesiastics, both bishops and parsons, discredit the Unionist cause by their blood-curdling appeal in support of it. My aggressive attitude on this matter made me many enemies amongst my own people, but the Nationalists of Newport, Mon., were an exception. I could always reckon on their support, and was always honoured with their confidence. For many years I have been Vice-President of their branch, and often represented them at our annual conventions. I have never done so without feeling happier from the renewal of old friendships, and always felt more patriotic from the contact with the spirit that pervaded these reunions.

21
Michael MacGowan, *The Hard Road to Klondike*

With a preface by Seán Ó hEochaidh (London: Routledge & Kegan Paul, 1962). xiii, 150pp.; pp. 39–41. Translated by Valentin Iremonger from *Rotha Mór an tSaoil* (Conamara: Cló Iar-Chonnachta, 1959).

The autobiography of Michael MacGowan (Micí Mac Gabhann) (1865–1948) is one of the most celebrated works of twentieth-century Gaelic literature. Shorn of self-consciousness and animated by the living voice of a story-teller, it presents a seemingly artless account of the author's migrant experiences in late nineteenth-century Scotland and the United States. Born in Cloghaneely, County Donegal, MacGowan was hired out as a spalpeen (migrant farm labourer) at the age of nine and in 1880 crossed to Scotland, his first impressions of which are chronicled in the following extract. In 1885 he emigrated to America and spent several years working in the silver mines of Montana before setting out to join the Klondike gold rush in 1898, which epic journey is at the heart of the narrative. MacGowan returned to live in Cloghaneely in 1902, marrying and raising a large family there. In the 1940s his life story was recorded and transcribed by his son-in-law, the folklore collector Seán Ó hEochaidh, who was keen to preserve for future social historians the 'living lore which the story-teller himself had actually experienced', as he puts it in his preface. The manuscript was subsequently edited by Prionsias Ó Conluain and published as *Rotha Mór an tSaoil* ('The Great Wheel of Destiny'). A documentary film based on the book, directed by Desmond Bell, appeared in 1999.

As Ó hEochaidh's remarks suggest, MacGowan's work has been valued more for its documentary realism than its autobiographical content, a critical tendency which, as Cathal Ó Háinle explains, is directly related to the cultural and compositional contexts of Gaeltacht autobiography: 'The life of each of the authors was in a very deep sense the life of a member of a close-knit rural community rather than that of an independent individual. Furthermore, those who urged the Gaeltacht autobiographers to write their life stories undoubtedly saw them first and foremost as representatives of a particular kind of society and of a traditional way of life; and so too did their editors.'[1] Such emphasis on the memorial aspect of Gaeltacht life-writing also obscures the ways in

---

[1] Cathal Ó Háinle, 'Aspects of Autobiography in Modern Irish', in Ronald Black, William Gillies and Roibeard Ó Maolalaigh (eds), *Celtic Connections: Proceedings of*

which the production of written texts from oral accounts involved editorial decisions by interlocutors. Traces of such silent mediation are evident in the inconsistency between Ó hEochaidh's claim to have got 'the whole story' from MacGowan and his admission that 'The tale could be as long again', a paradoxical assertion that prompts questions about the temporality of the autobiographical act and the constructedness of the autobiographical self.

We got in to Glasgow quay sometime about six o'clock in the morning. The first question then was which direction should we go in – where would we be likely to get something to do. Conal was as ignorant as I was myself about this part of the business, but while we had been standing on the quay at Derry the day beforehand we got into conversation with a man from the Rosses – a fine man named Paddy O'Boyle. He was middle-aged and we knew by his clothes that he was going back to Scotland. We questioned him and he told us that he was working in the big iron works at Coatbridge. He had been there for years and was well satisfied with it. Coatbridge is in Lanarkshire about nine or ten miles east from Glasgow. The Baird Company built the Gartsherrie Iron Works there and for many a long year they were the most famous ironworks in the three kingdoms. There was nothing you could think of from nails to huge anchors that didn't come out of their enormous furnaces but if that was the case there was plenty of sweat being lost in their factories. The work was heavy and the hours long but it was better than spending half your life tramping the Lothians and down to England looking for work.

'Would we have any chance of getting a start there,' I asked O'Boyle, 'if we made our way up there?'

'Well,' he said, 'I can't give you a straight answer on that but I'm friendly with the foreman and if you come up there, I'll put in a word for you.'

As the people disembarked from the boat when we reached Glasgow, O'Boyle went off with himself and we didn't see any more of him at that time. We strolled up town and spent some time looking around. We saw biscuits on sale in a shop for a halfpenny each and one of them would do any man for a meal. We bought a couple each and stuck them in our pockets. After that, we put our heads together and decided that the best thing for us to do was to go east to Coatbridge. It was too early to start work on a farm and we thought we might pick up something that would do us until about the middle of the summer.

We asked and got directions and started on our way. Neither of us had the remotest idea about the country and, whether long or short the journey, we hadn't an inkling. One thing was giving me some worry. I used to hear the older people who had been to and from Scotland years before talking about a village they passed through on their way to the harvesting – a place called

---

the 10th International Congress of Celtic Studies (East Linton: Tuckwell Press, 1999), p. 364.

Armadale. In those days, people from our place used to wear breeches and great-coats made from home-spun bawneen[2] and no matter where they went they were recognized as being from our area. Whatever hatred the people from Armadale conceived for them, it appears that they would attack our people with bottles and stones anytime they saw them. Our men at that time had to bring their sickles over with them and they used to bind the blade with rope so that no damage would be done; but coming towards Armadale, they'd take the rope off the sickle so as to be ready to fight if the toughs of the village started attacking them. I was afraid that we might have to go by that village but, luckily enough, we didn't – it lay further on eastwards.

We didn't know that at the time, however, so we walked warily. We had a couple of pairs of old boots on us and as we weren't used to wearing them it wasn't long until our feet were hurting. Well, we sat down on the side of the road and took them off. We threw them over our shoulders and forged ahead bare-foot. Then, like the women who carried their boots going to Sunday Mass and who put them on at Colleybridge, outside Gortahork, we put ours on again outside Coatbridge. We ate the biscuits we had bought in the shop and when our repast was over we went into the town and headed for the iron-works. There was a right lot of men to be seen there and they all looked very busy. We asked for O'Boyle and a boy brought us to him. He was almost in his skin, I can tell you, loading ore as fast as he could into one of the furnaces. When I saw him there bathed in sweat, I thought to myself that even if I got a job, I'd never be able to stick it for very long.

O'Boyle recognized us immediately and he called to another man to take his place while he was talking to us. He knew well, of course, what brought us there. He brought the pair of us into a little office and told the man there that we were two young fellows looking for work – friends of his own – and said that if anything could be found for us, he'd be very grateful. The man asked us where we were from and when we told him, he said, 'you're both very young but I'll see what I can do.'

O'Boyle left us there and said that he'd see us at knocking-off time. The man in the office told us to follow him and he ordered another man to get us two barrows.

'Now,' he said, 'come along here.'

Off we went and he brought the two of us to a part of the works where there was a heap of ore as high as Errigal.[3]

'Now,' he said, 'if you want work, you can barrow that ore over to that furnace. You'll be paid ten shillings a week from Monday to Saturday. Think over it now but if you don't take it there's nothing more I can do for you.'

---

[2] Undyed knitting yarn.
[3] Donegal mountain, the highest peak in Ulster.

We looked at one another and made up our minds instantly to take the job. We took hold of the barrows. We hadn't arranged lodgings or anything else but we knew that O'Boyle wouldn't let us sleep out. When we knocked off, we met him and asked him if he had any address where we could try for lodgings. He said he had. He took us along with him and settled us with a woman from Annagry who kept lodgers. We were as well off as we could be then; we had work, a bit to eat and a bed of our own to stretch out on. I tell you, we didn't find making the bed too hard that night; and you can imagine our satisfaction as we stretched our bones in it – our first night in Scotland and our first day's pay earned as grown men making their own way.

22
Francis Fahy, 'Ireland in London – Reminiscences'

National Library of Ireland, MS 11431. 44pp.; pp. 27–31; 34–6.

Francis Fahy (1854–1935) was born in Kinvara, County Galway and moved to London in 1873 to join the civil service, for which he worked for the next 46 years. His interest in Irish expatriate culture in the capital, which was for him 'the world-city of my readings and my dreams', was awakened by the outbreak of the Land War in his native Connacht and the emigration of his parents and two siblings to London in 1879. Over the next four years, Fahy, described as 'small in stature, genial in disposition and unassuming in manner',[1] emerged as a guiding force in the first, often overlooked, wave of Irish cultural revivalism in London that had its epicentre in Southwark. In addition to organising lectures and debates on social and political topics for the local Home Rule Association, he coordinated the activities of the Southwark Junior Irish Literary Club, formed in 1881 to inculcate in second-generation Irish children an awareness of their cultural and linguistic heritage. The dearth of suitable teaching materials led Fahy to write and compile children's reciters and songbooks that were published by John Denvir, with whom he kept up a two-year correspondence. It was during this time that he wrote his most celebrated poem, 'The Ould Plaid Shawl', which was later set to music and became hugely popular. In January 1883 Fahy was instrumental in founding the Southwark Irish Literary Club, the forerunner of the Irish Literary Society established in 1892. He went on to serve as the first president of the London Gaelic League from 1896 to 1908, years that witnessed a rapid growth in membership and an expansion of the group's cultural and educational programmes. The following extract is taken from Fahy's short, detailed memoir, which was written and delivered as a lecture to the Irish Literary Society in Brunswick Square, London on 12 March 1921. As Clare Hutton points out in her excellent edition of this neglected text, Fahy's memoir offers rare insights into the nature and extent of Irish cultural revivalism in London in the years leading up to the founding of the more famous Irish Literary Society.[2] It enables us to see the mixture of pragmatism and idealism that inspired the initiatives

---

[1] Mark Ryan, *Fenian Memories* (Dublin: M. H. Gill, 1945), p. 157.

[2] See Clare Hutton (ed.), 'Francis Fahy's "Ireland in London – Reminiscences" (1921)', in Wayne K. Chapman and Warwick Gould (eds), *Yeats's Collaborations. Yeats Annual No. 15: A Special Number* (Basingstoke: Palgrave Macmillan, 2002), pp. 233–80.

of a small, indefatigable band of cultural activists, and the kinds of challenges they faced in unpropitious circumstances.

The success of the Children's Club and the lesson it brought home to us of the need for self-education led inevitably to the foundation of the Southwark Irish Literary Club in January '83 – the first Society In England founded, as its membership card states, to cultivate and spread among adults a knowledge of Irish History, language, art and literature and to serve as a medium of social and intellectual intercourse for Irish people of both sexes. The original members, about 40 in number, were the teachers and helpers, male and female, of the Children's Classes, but a little active canvassing soon brought this number up to 100. We met on successive Wednesdays, at first in the Surrey Rooms, then 2 years later in a hall or chapel hard by belonging to the Peculiar People,[3] in Bath Street, London Road, a street so dark and gloomy that one of our humorous lecturers dubbed it 'Cut-throat Lane' and hearing who our landlords were, prophesied that we should one day become absorbed in that Sect and die without benefit of doctor or clergy. I have often since then passed that street at night to find it forbidding beyond belief and to marvel at the power of youth, hope and enthusiasm to ignore and set at nought the most glaring defects and inconveniences.

I must say for our landlords they were always kindly and well-disposed towards us, although the only time they sent a representative to overlook our proceedings, we were holding a Gaelic Night, and he listened in evident bewilderment, unable to make head or tail of what was going on, and possibly reported to his principals that we must be one of those new Sects whose speciality is the speaking of unknown tongues.

Those of you who are familiar with the functions and features of the present Irish Literary Society would have recognised their germs in the programme of our Southwark Club. We had lectures by prominent Irish literary men – Edmund Downey,[4] the witty author of *Through Green Glasses* – a handsome Waterford man, and well-known London book-publisher, bubbling over with humour in conversation, but shy and nervous on a platform – John Augustus O'Shea,[5] the 'Irish Bohemian', whose fun was infectious – Dan Crilly, M.P.,[6] versed in many a byway of Irish literature. It was on Mr Crilly's night that we first made our acquaintance with W. B. Yeats, then a tall, slight, dreamy-faced young man of 23, who later lectured to us on 'Irish Fairy Lore', and really seemed from his manner and voice to have (as one of us put it) derived his knowledge of the subject from personal experience of the 'good people'. The

---

[3] A fundamentalist Wesleyan sect founded in 1838 by James Banyard (1800–63).
[4] Edmund Downey (1856–1937), novelist and publisher.
[5] John Augustus O'Shea (1839–1905), novelist and journalist who moved from Tipperary to London in 1859.
[6] Daniel Crilly (1857–1923), MP for North Mayo from 1885 to 1900.

young poet was greatly attracted by our work and gradually became one of ourselves.

It was on Yeats's night, too, we came to know Dr Todhunter,[7] whose scholarly face also beamed approval of our labours, and Katherine Tynan,[8] brought to us by her dear friend, Willie Yeats, both of whom I accompanied later, a delighted admirer, to the latter's home in the West-End.

Other memorable lecturers were J. F. Hogan,[9] author of *The Irish in Australia*; Halliday Sparling,[10] a genial Socialist, editor of the splendid little volume of *Irish Minstrelsy* in the Canterbury Classics, who lectured to us on Ireland's influence on Iceland and her literature; Mrs Sophie Bryant,[11] on 'The Celtic Races of Ireland'; and Eugene Davis,[12] the poet, on 'Irish Poetry'; Michael McDonagh[13] on 'Irish Graves in England'; Robert May of Belfast, on the 'Irish Drama', and others. Most memorable of all, was Justin MacCarthy's lecture on 'The Literature of '48', not alone for the personality of the lecturer, and the charm and grace of his delivery, as for the fact that the Chair was occupied by a man who had made history in that very period of '48, and had risen abroad to an eminence denied to him in his own land to which he had now come back after 40 years, and who was still, at the age of 71, full of hope and love for Ireland, and as young as the youngest of us in eagerness to work for her redemption – Sir Charles Gavan Duffy.[14] Among the audience that night was a stout, clean-shaven man of about 33, dressed exquisitely, who, in seconding the vote of thanks to the lecturer, praised the work of the Club and promised a copy of his mother, Lady Wilde's, *Legends of Ireland* to the Library. Oscar Wilde was then at the height of his fame, and I need not say with what curiosity we looked at and listened to him, happily ignorant of the terrible destiny hidden for him in the future.

---

[7] John Todhunter (1839–1916), Dublin-born poet and playwright, famed for the lyric 'Aghadoe'.

[8] Dublin-born Katharine Tynan (1859–1931) was the author of over 100 novels and five volumes of memoirs. She was a lifelong friend of W. B. Yeats, who proposed to her in 1891.

[9] James Francis Hogan (1855–1924), journalist, author and politician. He emigrated to Australia in 1856 and became an authority on Australian affairs. His *The Irish in Australia* appeared in 1887.

[10] Henry Halliday Sparling (1860–1924), socialist who worked as William Morris's assistant at the Kelmscott Press in the early 1890s.

[11] Sophie Bryant (1850–1922), campaigner for women's suffrage and the higher education of women.

[12] Eugene Davis (1857–97), nationalist poet and journalist.

[13] Michael McDonagh (1860–1946), Limerick-born journalist and author whose *Irish Graves in England* appeared in 1888.

[14] Duffy emigrated to Australia in 1855. He was prime minister of Victoria in 1871–72 and later served as speaker of the legislative assembly (1877–80). In 1892 he became the first president of the Irish Literary Society.

We did not, however, rely solely on those great names to fill our bill. We planted and grew the home-made article. About a dozen of us set about the study of Irish subjects, each as took his fancy, with the view of supplying lectures to Irish Clubs and League Branches, and for a number of years, these members went all over London 'spreading the light' as we called it. I do not claim that we had the root of the matter in us, but we added to our own knowledge, accustomed ourselves to speak clearly and to be able to reply readily. Our audiences were eager to be entertained and instructed, mostly they had no leisure for study themselves; criticism was rare; extravagant praise was indeed the usual reward we met with, not that we were taken by it, however. Like the ancient oracles we laughed at each other. In a skit on the various activities of the Club, one of the members wrote:

> We sent out lecturers in pairs
> What one asseverates the other swears
> We sprout such sentiments and we air such airs
> And oh, don't we chuckle when we get downstairs.
> [...]

The study of the Irish language was not neglected. Our motto was the Gaelic 'sgar an solus' (Spread the light). At the little meetings of the Catholic Young Men's Association in '79 we had Irish classes, where the teacher was only a lesson or two ahead of his pupils, and, in the Surrey Rooms in '81, a dozen years before the foundation of the Gaelic League, we held the first of a series of 'Gaelic Nights' at which all the songs, stories and sketches contributed were in Irish and by native Irish speakers. On this first night, a lecture was delivered by Mr. Thomas Flannery,[15] the well-known Irish scholar and contributor of Gaelic items to the Irish press, one of the cleverest, but most modest and approachable of learned men. Among those present were Father O'Sullivan, known to you all, and many native speakers of Irish, including Tim Mac-Sweeney and John Rogers. MacSweeney no sooner wrote in his native tongue than he exhibited a power, wit, and fluency of style incredible to those who knew his English work. Rogers, a Mayo man, revelled in old Gaelic legends, traditions and sayings. About this time the *Irish Fireside* offered a prize for the best list of Irish Christian names. Rogers and I had many a fireside chat over the matter and mutually sounded each other's knowledge, each concealing the fact that he intended to compete, and much to our amusement, my list got first place and his second. I took an absurd pride in the result especially when I learned later that the publication of the list had the effect in Ireland of replacing in many families the old Irish names for usurping Saxon ones, and

---

[15] Tomás Ó Flannghaile (1846–1916), Mayo-born poet, editor and teacher who moved with his family to Manchester as a child.

when proud fathers and mothers among my London friends came to me for suggestions for their latest arrivals, and Irish homes in my neighbourhood rang to the yells and screams of little Noras, Eileens, Cormacs and Desmonds, instead of Eliza, Sarah Ann, Tom, Dick and Harry. One of our friends called me the Name-Giver and said that, my own name being Francis Arthur, the whole thing reminded him of a bald-headed barber recommending to his customers an infallible hair-restorer.

We were a rather Happy Family over there in Southwark. Many a soiree of dance and song relieved the heaviness of our programme, many an outing into the woodlands of Kent and Surrey gave some of us our first delightful pictures of the English countryside. We made up parties to the theatre when Irish plays were on. We assembled 'in our thousands' at Irish demonstrations in Hyde Park. On Jubilee Day '87, resisting a temptation to go into mourning, a score of us hired a brake and rusticated on Box Hill. I have still a snapshot of the party in which the hard bowlers of the men, and the old time hats and dresses of the ladies are now an unfailing source of merriment. One memorable visit was to a certain Olympia Exhibition in the mid-80s, the special feature of which for us was an Irish produce Section, and of that produce, most Irish and most attractive, a group of some dozen dairymaids from Kerry, whose dark hair, blue eyes and dazzling complexions had become the talk of London. Good Heavens, the quantities of milk and butter and 'barmbrack' we consumed at their stall, and the difficulty it was to drag us away from it.[16]

---

[16] The Irish Exhibition was held at Olympia in West Kensington from 4 June to 27 October 1888. Designed to redress prejudicial English perceptions of the Irish, it presented visitors with an array of attractions, from craft demonstrations to musical and dramatic performances, all of which were intended to define an Irish identity based around industry and creativity. See Brendan Rooney, 'The Irish Exhibition at Olympia, 1888', *Irish Architectural and Decorative Studies*, vol. 1 (1998), pp. 101–19.

23

John Sweeney, *At Scotland Yard: Being the Experiences during Twenty-Seven Years' Service of John Sweeney*

Edited by Francis Richards (London: Grant Richards, 1904). ix, 358pp.; pp. 34–6; 45–50.

John Sweeney was born in 1857 to a farming family in Staigue, County Kerry. He reveals little about his early life in his autobiography, except that his family suffered eviction when he was two years old and emigrated to London in 1875. In that year he joined the London Metropolitan Police and was posted to Hammersmith. In 1884 he moved to the Criminal Investigation Department at Scotland Yard and was assigned to the Irish (later Special) Branch division, which had recently been established to counteract the growing threat of Fenian violence in the capital. In May of that year Sweeney had personal, 'nerve-shaking experience' of such violence when a bomb destroyed the Branch's offices at Scotland Yard. As a sergeant, Sweeney was also involved in curbing the frequently disruptive public clashes between Irish nationalists and unionists over Home Rule, as described in the extract below. He eventually rose to the rank of detective inspector and often acted as a bodyguard to members of the royal family and visiting foreign dignitaries. One of his 'most honourable calls of duty' came in 1900 when he was selected for the special police protection unit that accompanied Queen Victoria on her visit to Ireland. Sweeney retired from the police force in 1903 and immediately set about writing his memoirs, which comprise a detailed record of his professional activities during his long years of service.

As befits a retired detective sergeant, Sweeney is primarily concerned with factual accuracy and verisimilitude: 'I am confident that I have in no way romanced, and that nowhere have I been guilty of any misrepresentation of fact that should do harm or injustice to anyone.' Like James Mullin, he defines himself exclusively in relation to his work, about which he writes with a manifest degree of pride and satisfaction, underpinned by a rather exalted notion of the importance of his duties as a Special Branch officer. Such conceit is typical of the dozen or so memoirs published by Branch members during the period before 1914.[1] Sweeney also resembles Mullin in keeping his inner life hidden from view. It is as if the personal sphere did not exist for him,

---

[1] Bernard Porter, *Plots and Paranoia: A History of Political Espionage in Britain 1790–1988* (London: Routledge, 1992), pp. 117–18.

or that he did not attach any significance to it, or that his private self was insep-arable from his professional role. Politically, Sweeney was firmly pro-establishment; he writes as a loyal imperial subject whose respect for monarchy and the institu-tions of the state was matched by a deep disdain for political subversives of all kinds, including 'the seditious Irish, particularly the Irish-Americans'. His background and fluency in Irish made him a natural choice for the covert surveillance of Fenian and Clan-na-Gael activists, work that evidently caused him no unease. Indeed, it is clear that he had nothing but contempt for extra-parliamentary Irish agitation, whether it emanated from the militant ideology of Fenianism or the social grievances of the Land League.

Most people know that the East End, and districts such as Clerkenwell, Saffron Hill, and Soho are the refuge of Anarchists, Nihilists, Fenians, Clan-na-Gaelites, and other revolutionaries that flock to London to work out their sinister purposes; but it is less generally realised how carefully such criminals are watched by Scotland Yard. The archives of the Criminal Inves-tigation Department are crammed with details concerning individuals who, if judged merely by appearances, would seem to be the most insignificant of persons. But these records must never be allowed to be out of date, and that the Yard may have its knowledge always fresh, there exists a system of constant espionage. Fortunately for the public weal, rogues are always falling out, and so there are everywhere spies who supply the authorities with news, advice and warning. But there need to be official spies as well; and thus it is a very large part of a detective's work to 'shadow' those who are under suspicion. And this 'shadowing' is not light work. Day or night, rain or shine, the 'shadower' must follow his quarry's every movement. The detective knows that at any moment the man followed may realise him-self pursued, and turn on the pursuer with a knife or revolver; the detective does not know when relief may come. Nominally, you are not on shadow-ing duty for more than a certain time; but here is the difficulty. You may begin in Shepherd's Bush or Kennington, and find yourself obliged to follow your man to the Mile End Road or Maida Vale; you may telegraph to the Yard for your relief to meet you somewhere in the Euston Road; but before he can get there you may have had to hurry off to Finsbury. I have known three such telegrams sent in succession, and all to no purpose. The detective eats and rests when he can; and he seldom has the consolation of feeling that in this weary chase are many opportunities of distinction for himself. He must have perseverance, presence of mind, and resourcefulness; he can-not be too strong physically; and he should know his London well, that he may not let himself be decoyed into some *cul de sac* and there quietly disposed of. [...]

Besides carefully watching individuals, it was our business to keep an eye on the revolutionaries when they met together in large gatherings. They were fond of congregating together, and had also a troublesome weakness for inter-fering with the meetings of people more respectable than themselves. During the years 1886–1890 the Land Leaguers[2] and seditious people generally were particularly busy in holding gatherings of their own and in interfering with other political meetings. In the first-mentioned year I remember two Unionist meetings had interesting features. The first of these meetings was held in the Kensington Town Hall, the second in St James's Hall, Piccadilly. The former was to take place in the evening. That afternoon I happened to be in the north of London; while there I was informed that an organised attempt would be made to break up the meeting. I felt satisfied that this information was reliable and that bad work was likely to be done, so I drove swiftly to headquarters and reported to Mr Monro. He promptly sent me off to warn Superintendent Giles of the Kensington Police. The Superintendent at once told off twenty extra officers under an inspector to wait in reserve near the Town Hall, ready for any disturbance. Sure enough, the meeting had not been going on very long when a sudden and determined rush was made for the platform. The railings were torn down, the people on it were badly hustled and dragged down into the body of the hall, chairs were broken, and a free fight set going, while someone made the confusion worse by turning the gas out, so that the hall was quite dark. The police came promptly to the rescue, and several ringleaders were arrested. One or two members of Parliament who were present were assaulted; Mr Hobhouse,[3] I remember, was one of them. I was in the thick of the *melée*, as I stood near the entrance, trying to help peaceable individuals out of the building. The Commissioner afterwards thanked and rewarded me for the promptness with which I availed myself of the information I had received; otherwise it is not too much to say that if those police in reserve had not been present, several more assaults would have been committed, the hall badly damaged, and the consequences in general very serious.

The political meeting in St. James's Hall passed off in a fashion not altogether unamusing. Several Irish and Radical clubs selected their most able-bodied men to form one large gang which should attempt to break up the meeting and prevent the speakers from being given a fair hearing. As admission was only to be by ticket, in order that their representatives might get inside it was necessary for them to have tickets forged similar to the genuine ones. One particular member undertook to carry this part of the preparations through, and the secretaries of the clubs were informed by a secret memorandum that on the afternoon of the meeting, between two and three o'clock, he would be waiting at the Piccadilly end of Swallow Street to distribute these forged tickets. He himself would be carrying a paper and a

---

[2] The Irish National Land League was founded in Dublin in October 1879 by Michael Davitt to orchestrate a nationwide campaign for peasant proprietorship. With Charles Stewart Parnell as president, it quickly became a vehicle for nationalist mobilisation and attracted Fenian support.

[3] Henry Hobhouse (1854–1937), who entered parliament in 1885 as a Liberal MP for East Somerset.

walking-stick. The password for each man was to be the name of the club to which he belonged. The distribution was carried out as arranged; and I took care to be one of the people who received tickets. Previously I had warned the attendants at the hall that a disturbance was planned, and those who were concerned would seek admission by means of tickets that were not genuine. I should say that it was necessary to go up a flight of stairs in order to enter the room where the meeting was to be held. When the time came attendants scrutinised all tickets with extra care, and the bearers of the forged ones were ushered into a separate room. I of course was waiting; at the moment when the meeting was timed to begin the ticket-distributor made his appearance. 'Now, boys,' said I to the attendant, 'here's the bounder who's running the business.' He was promptly seized, 'bonneted,' and literally flung down the stairs. He did not ascend them a second time. We then had to deal with the men we had herded into that separate room. Carefully we brought them out one by one, and each man as he appeared was summarily kicked out without his friends knowing what was going on until their own turns came. It was beautifully done, the whole thing going off without a hitch. There were about fifty of these fellows, all specially selected for their strength, and had they got into the meeting there would no doubt have been trouble. As it was everything went off with perfect smoothness.

Besides sharing in the protection of legitimate gatherings, it was part of my business, with a view to the public safety, to attend meetings and watch *rendezvous* of the Clan-na-Gael[4] agents. Being an Irishman born and bred, I knew quite as much of the Irish language as did the people whom I had to watch, and so was specially selected for this work. One day we received information that a prominent Clan-na-Gael agent would be present at a meeting of the Irish Land League in the Surrey Rooms, Blackfriars Road. I was deputed to be also present. As a matter of fact the meeting turned out to be only a social gathering of the Irish-speaking people in London, for singing, reciting, and so forth; but we had been led to expect something different.[5] I went along with a colleague who knew no Irish. He found a place by the door of the building, while I sat in the third row from the platform. We had not been there long when a man who seemed to be a sort of master of the ceremonies, came up and handed me a little pamphlet, a primer of the Irish language, remarking at the same time: 'Take that and read it.' He spoke in such a way that I thought he must have some notion who I really was. I answered in Irish, 'Thank you; I'll read it; I think I can do so as well as you.' He turned very red and left me. A few minutes later the chairman got up and said: 'I call upon

---

[4] Irish-American revolutionary organisation committed to physical force republican-ism, which had links with the Fenians.

[5] It is probable that Sweeney had happened upon one of the 'Gaelic Nights' alluded to by Francis Fahy in the previous extract.

Mr Sweeney for his song, "Father O'Flynn."'[6] For a moment I did not know whether I was on my head or my heels, as people say. My brother officer took himself off at once. My relief may be imagined when another Mr Sweeney got up and gave 'Father O'Flynn' in true Irish style. Finally I was satisfied that no one seriously suspected me. I have been to hundreds of gatherings of this sort, but this one was unique in that not a word of English was spoken the whole time.

---

[6] The most famous composition of Alfred Perceval Graves (1846–1931), poet and educationalist. It was first published in *The Spectator* in 1875 and later appeared in *Songs of Old Ireland* (1882). Graves presided over the inaugural meeting of the Irish Literary Society of London in 1891 and later served as its president.

24

Walter Hampson, 'Reminiscences of "Casey"'

Forward, 28 March – 31 October 1931 (24 October excepted); weekly serialisation. Extracts taken from the issues of 11 April, 25 April and 2 May 1931.

Walter Hampson (1864–1932) was born in Dublin, where he spent the first seven years of his childhood with his mother, an itinerant fishmonger, before being taken to Stockport in Cheshire by his nomadic father, whom he had not seen since birth. Within a year he was working as an assistant chimney-sweep to his father, in contravention of the Climbing Boys Act of 1840. Hampson continued as a sweep until the age of 14, even though he hated the work and repeatedly ran away from home to escape it. In 1885 he found employment as a caretaker at Whittingham Asylum near Preston, and it was here that his 'book-worshipping period' began. His avid reading of Dickens, Thackeray, Carlyle and Huxley laid the groundwork for his later immersion in the work of Robert Blatchford and William Morris after his conversion to socialism in the 1890s. Music was Hampson's other great passion. He learned to play the violin as a child and became proficient enough to play in several orchestras in the north of England, including the Stockport Theatre Royal Orchestra. From 1905 he began to develop a reputation as a socialist propagandist through his concerts, pamphlets and articles in the Labour press, published under the pseudonym 'Casey'. According to the editor of *Forward*, the socialist weekly that serialised his memoirs, Hampson was a familiar figure on political platforms throughout pre-war Britain, where audiences appreciated his 'pawky wit' and musical virtuosity. It appears that he was also well known in Irish socialist circles, since in 1917 he was invited by the Socialist Party of Ireland to speak and perform in Dublin. During this visit Hampson was introduced to the widow of James Connolly, whom he regarded as Ireland's first socialist martyr.

In his engaging episodic autobiography, written when he was living in retirement in Stockport, Hampson recalls the varied phases of his eventful life with humour and verve, though he has little to say about his domestic life with his wife and nine children. The most compelling parts of the narrative are those in which he gives an intimate, first-hand account of the horrors he endured as a Victorian 'loo jawler', as chimney-sweeps were known in the local argot. Passages such as those excerpted below offer rare insights into the 'purgatorial punishment' to which juvenile climbers were subjected as late as the 1880s, long after legislation had prohibited this particular form of child exploitation. Indeed, Hampson candidly acknowledges the flagrant breaches of the law by property owners and claims that magistrates and policemen were among the worst offenders. Yet in recording his own miserable experiences he eschews self-pity and makes no claims to exceptional status, except in writing about them. Rather, he locates his boyhood ordeals within a broader cultural context in which children 'were held cheaply and used up like flies'.

Few writers have attempted to deal with the climber's suffering, for none but the children who have sampled the torture know it. While working one's way upwards huge blood-blisters would form on the left palm. As the blisters quickly began to form they seemed to grow until they felt as big as one's head. When the soot began to work into the bleeding flesh the agony was intense, and being forced upward, assisted by such kindly advice as 'You young 'ellhound, I'll cut your b——y liver out if you don't hurry up', developed nerves. The skin came off the knees, a slip of a few yards tore the shirt and scarred the back from buttocks to shoulder-blades. The toe nails broke, the heart beat like a trip hammer, an excruciating headache, with floating lights, comes on, and the purgatorial punishment continued up and down each chimney until one became acclimatised to the unnatural conditions.

Nowadays people who have a small cut are very careful. They dread blood-poisoning. In past days they simply placed a cobweb over a cut, or a bread poultice on a wound, and they bothered very little about the matter. Whether we had better healing flesh, or whether the food was purer is a matter for the experts.

After my first lesson I rubbed my knees, hands, and feet with neatsfoot oil,[1] a sovereign elixir at one time, and after a while I became more proficient in my calling. At eight years of age I used to go out with my father to work at four o'clock in the mornings. If 'early to bed and early to rise makes a man healthy, wealthy, and wise' I ought to be a cross between Solomon and the Haggis Khan,[2] who spent over £100,000 trying to find a Derby winner. But these proverbs seem to work out in a different manner after being tried. Most of the people who have got on seem to rise very late indeed. [...]. I think that the proverb should read 'Early to bed, early to rise, makes you unhealthy, not wealthy, but otherwise.' [...]

I have had almost every stitch of clothing burnt off me in hot boilers. In one boiler, where I had to take two wet bricks to kneel on, I tried to clean a side flue, but the lantern became so hot that I had to drop it, and work my way back quietly to save myself from suffocation. Later I returned for the lantern, but the pewter had melted and a few pieces of tin and glass were all that remained of the borrowed lantern. This was at Cheadle Mental Asylum

---

[1] A softening and preservative agent, rendered from the feet of cattle, which was used to treat scaly skin conditions in the eighteenth and nineteenth centuries.

[2] Probably a misnomer for Aga Khan III (1877–1957), influential Indian politician and leader of the Ismailis, who was a keen equine enthusiast.

in 1887. I suppose it was the right place for such unnecessary antics. A year or so later a second boiler was installed, and, instead of the boiler fires being put out five or six hours before one entered, to allow for cooling, the fires were raked out twenty-four hours before, and the job was thus made easier.

A peculiar circumstance of the early days was the number of stunted children and physically deformed people. Men walked about with one knee touching the other, and one leg shaped like the letter K. I fancy these men must have worked at the mules,[3] which, moving to and fro, necessitated reaching forward to piece the ends up. Commencing work very young, their soft bones gradually assumed a permanent twist.

Two men were one day twitting[4] each other, after a drink or so. One said, looking at his bow-legged friend: 'By gum, Joe, tha'd better hurry straight home.' 'Nay,' said Joe, 'tha' conna expect me to hurry straight home wi' a pair of legs like mine. Thy own legs are not much to brag about, they're wider than mine.' 'Never thee mind my legs, they're good enough for maesters to mek profit out of, and doan't thee forget it.'

Hard work in youth and malnutrition played havoc with people in those days. I was so puny at ten years of age that the cook at Marsland's, Woodbank Hall, would not let me enter the house to sweep the chimneys. She said I was too small, and might be smothered in them, and nobody would know how to get me out.

One of my early climbing efforts was to tackle a chimney in Wright's Court, Portwood, Stockport. I wasn't feeling very well at the time. The fire had only just been put out, and the smell of sulphur and soot didn't seem to act as a tonic. When I got part of the way up I was very sick and began crying. The old woman (her name was Mrs Bailey) was slightly deaf. However, she sensed something wrong.

'What's he doin'?' she enquired of my father. 'Oh,' said my father, 'he's only singin'.' 'Singin'! Singin'! Well it's damn queer singin' that is.'

It was. My father told the story to me ten years afterwards. Give him due credit, however, he could climb like a squirrel, and if there had been real danger he would have come up after me. However, he was not always with me, and on one occasion when the slant caved in at Longstaff's, the shoemakers, in Henry Street, Portwood, I had a narrow squeak.

In addition to his other accomplishments my father could do sleight-of-hand tricks, and was also a magnificent diver. [...] His drawback, however, was an ungovernable temper. Like the Slasher in Eugene Sue's *Mysteries of Paris*, he saw red.[5] He seldom gave you a warning, but knocked you down first, and gave the reason when he felt so disposed. His temper was like molten lava.

---

[3] An early type of spinning-machine which produced yarn on spindles.
[4] Good-humoured or teasing talk.
[5] *Les Mystères de Paris* by Eugène Sue (1804–1857) was published serially in 1842 and 1843.

I remember, after the lapse of almost sixty years, the occasion when he tried to teach me to tell the time. A lad of seven, in a state of fear and trembling, cut over the hands, head, and face with a long thin cane, was liable to make wrong answers every time he looked at the fingers on the clock. The lesson concluded by him picking me up and throwing me so high that I hit the ceiling and fell back on a couch. I could not walk for a fortnight thereafter. Incidents like this made him feel so sorry that I felt sorry for him myself. [...]

After the free childish roaming days in Dublin, this part of my life was most bitter, but child-thrashing in those days was a common practice in mines, mills, chimneys, and schools alike. 'Knock 'ell out of 'em' was the keynote. The records of Lancashire and Yorkshire show that children were of very little moment.

We used to go to Lyme Hall, the present Lord Newton's place, every three months. We used to work at night when the family was away in London. Many of the chimneys were very dangerous on account of the long slants and turns in them.

Lyme Hall stands in solitary grandeur about a couple of miles from Disley. It is situated in the midst of a huge park, where rabbits run in myriads, and large deer roam over the moorland. On the hill, half way to the Hall, rises Lyme 'Cage', a huge square tower, supposed to be the place from where ladies watched the hawking in the olden times. There is a lot of hawking today, but without the aid of a falcon. It was usually ten o'clock at night when we arrived at the Hall, with its six high pillars in front, and its dungeon-like aspect of the lower storey. We were generally admitted by the Hall porter, Bob Gosling, a big portly man. A meal was prepared for us, either in the servant's hall or in the kitchen. [...]

There were three of us to do the work at Lyme. Many of the chimneys were swept by means of the machine, whilst others needed the services of a climbing-boy. The three were my father, an old climbing-boy known as John Sutton, and myself. I was carried on John's back from room to room, put into the chimney bottom, and up I went. No small two-storied climb here, but a toilsome, tortuous reach upwards. Half-a-dozen Lyme Hall chimneys, with their long arduous ascents from kitchen or stone parlour were more trying than thrice the number of slum chimneys. I loved riding on John's back. It was a restful interval between the chimney top notes. How I appreciated it, and hoped it would continue!

Never shall I forget the scene that greeted me one summer's morn at 4 a.m. After a hard night's work we finished at the kitchen. A long toilsome climb it was to the topmost turret of the tower. Pulling off my climbing cap, I sat on the stone coping and gazed around. The sun was breaking through the silver grey clouds. The lovely moorland, upon which stood another Cage, now fallen into ruins, rose up to the famous Bow Stones. Beneath stood a huge leaden statue on the topmost part of the house front. Underneath was the ornamental lake, and in front an avenue of trees. The Cheshire plain rolled onwards to the estuary of the Dee, and the Alderley Edge Hills, tree-clothed, seemed within a stone's throw. The screaming of the peacocks, the call of the birds, the pipings and whistlings and the delightful smell of the pure bracing air of the Disley Hills showed Nature at her best and fairest.

After the long night's climbing, however, came the weary walk home. It was close upon ten miles, and this was a real purgatory. Wearing moleskin trousers, without lining – underwear was a luxury I first discovered when I was twenty – the soot stiffened the cloth. The seams were rugged and before one had proceeded a mile, the friction of the stiff moleskin seams against the thighs finally caused red weals and bleeding, and, as usual, with the soot getting in, the pain was intense. In vain did one try to escape from the torture by walking down the Buxton Road with one leg pointing east and the other leaning west. The relief was only temporary. If one complained he was foxing or soft, or else a 'flatty', in other words, no true tradesman.

Another episode, although small, caused me some worry. Some nights after going to bed – knowing that there was a heavy morning's work awaiting me – I used to have a strange dream. In the dream I went to every chimney I had to do that day, climbed it, spoke to the people, and returned home tired and ready for breakfast. I was rudely awakened out of this dream by the usual formula: 'You b—— young whelp, are yer goin' to sleep yer b—— seven senses away, or must I throw this bucket of water over you?' The awakening was very bitter, because I had dreamt that I had done my work.

25

Maureen Hamish, *Adventures of an Irish Girl at Home and Abroad*

(Dublin: J. K. Mitchell, 1906). 239pp.; pp. 25–32.

Nothing is known about Maureen Hamish other than the few biographical details she supplies in her memoir, many of which are opaque. It appears that she was born in Cookstown, County Tyrone around 1870 and that her real name was Mary Loughran. She explains that illness hampered her education to the extent that domestic service was one of the few employment opportunities open to her. In 1886 she emigrated to Scotland and found work as a servant in Grangemouth, near Falkirk, where her grandfather lived. When after six months she decided to leave this position, her mistress refused to give her a reference, thereby jeopardising her chances of future employment. However, with the help of a local parish priest she was taken 'on trial' as a kitchenmaid by a wealthy family in Melrose, although judging from her account of her duties in the extract below, her role appears to have been closer to that of a general 'maid-of-all-work'. Over the next 20 years Hamish led the peripatetic life of a domestic servant, traversing Scotland, England and Ireland in search of suitable employment, her chief criteria for which was proximity to a Catholic church. Religion, indeed, is central to the book's *raison d'être*. Hamish explains in her preface that the work is intended to illuminate the hardships that Irish domestic servants in Britain have to endure and to demonstrate that 'things are not always what they seem, and that throughout Great Britain, Roman Catholics, especially in service, have not the same facilities, nor the same freedom for the exercise of their religion as at home'. The corollary of her didactic emphasis on the perils of female emigration is an acute, self-limiting nostalgia for the family and community she left behind in Tyrone. This longing often finds expression in the sentimental verse that was her primary source of comfort during her occasional bouts of depression, loneliness and self-pity.

On a lovely day in the middle of summer I arrived at Melrose. The house I was going to was one mile from the station, and there was no one to meet me. I remember I had a very bad headache from the (to me) long journey and the great heat. I was so clever, of course, I lost my way and walked nearly two miles instead of one. When I arrived at my new quarters the first thing I did was to go to bed. There was a nice, kind cook, and she saw how ill I was.

Often I have wondered how ladies could allow a poor strange girl to find her way alone. Whatever remedies the cook prescribed cured me directly, and I was all right in a couple of hours. She seemed to like me from the first, was English, but unlike most of her class, had a knowledge of Ireland and the Irish. I could stand any amount of abuse personally, but when people began about Ireland my blood boiled. Later on I never noticed, just passed all disparaging remarks over with silent contempt.

The new household I found myself a member of was composed of many different nationalities – Scotch, English, German, and Scotch-born Irish. I was the only real Irish girl, and was treated by some of them as a kind of curiosity. Not being able to hold my tongue, I ventured to give an opinion at the table on a subject under discussion, on which I was well read, and knew those taking part in the discussion were completely ignorant. The contempt with which my remark was received nearly withered me up. Never did I risk an opinion again on any subject to the same company. On the first morning after my arrival when I was preparing the housekeeper's table for breakfast, I found a sixpence on it. I put the coin aside and when the cook came downstairs I drew her attention to it.

Afterwards I understood the peculiar look on her face as she removed the coin. It had been left in such a way that a poor ignorant girl might think it was a find. It is one of the most pernicious methods of trying a poor girl's honesty, and the person who done it borrowed a stamp from me that day and never returned it or those that followed. She was in a higher post than I, had a fairly good salary, but was either unscrupulous or careless. I will give her the benefit of the doubt and say she was careless.

On the evening of the second day my mistress summoned me to the drawing room, and put me through a very severe cross-examination about why my last mistress did not recommend me. I told her the truth, but looking back now I know she did not believe me, for after I told her she asked me if I had done anything wrong, and then if I was quite sure I had not. I felt bruised and sore, and wondered if they thought I had no feelings. I remember rising with an aching heart in the middle of the night and standing at the window wondering how it would all end. It was bad enough to be under a cloud, but to be treated not like a fool but a knave was far worse. My only comfort came to me then, and I forgot all my troubles and revelled in the delights of my verse-making once more:

> The silver moonbeams pure and bright,
>   With beauty gild each little flower,
> Relieve the darkness of the night
>   And brighten this, the midnight hour.
>
> Alone I stand; ah, me, alone –
>   Not a friend save nature near,

Far from the woods of old Tyrone,
   There's no one left my path to cheer.

Farewell, farewell, to that dear home,
   No more at eventide I'll stray,
Or through the verdant woodland roam,
   To while the happy hours away.

Farewell to father, mother, all –
   Brothers, sisters, kind and true,
How oft will this poor heart recall
   The happy hours I spent with you.

Farewell to friends and comrades dear,
   Farewell to all I left behind,
My barque on life's bright stream I steer;
   But where shall I a harbour find.

I had then the last bad fit of depression I was to suffer for some time. On the morrow the young ladies arrived from school. The family consisted of a widow, six daughters, one son, and a governess. When the young ladies came home everything was changed; they were so bright and cheerful, and I simply adored them, from a distance at first, but gradually we got acquainted, and I was consulted in all or most of their escapades. The eldest was only fifteen years old and the youngest five. I had to milk a cow morning and evening, and often there were four of them hanging round me to get a try at the milking. Now I hope now one will be shocked, but somehow they found out I set great store by kisses. That luxury was very scarce with me at that time. They would come in a coaxing way and promise me so many kisses, to let them just have one try. I always gave in, and sometimes I forgot, when revelling in the enjoyment of their presence, that stern reality, and a mountain of work was awaiting my attention. I must have been a sore trial to the cook at this time. 'Mary,' she would say to me, 'I never thought you were such a silly child.' I was up with the lark now and had a heart as light as a feather, for had I not seven beautiful creatures to love, and sometimes to play with. Some of the servants voted them as nuisance, and whatever poetical remark I made about them caused great merriment in the servant's hall. I was always treated as a kind of buffoon, and as a butt for their humour in the hall. [...]

Time wore on; the mistress had been abroad for nearly eight months. Then we got orders to prepare the nursery. The youngest little lady and her nurse were coming home and was I not joyful when they did come. I used to get charge of the little one to go for walks, to work in the garden and amuse her. It was delightful. Many a long carry she had on my back, and one day I will never forget. Nurse reprimanded her in some way; she burst into tears; all at once she smiled, and 'tween smiles and tears it was the loveliest sight one could wish for; she was like a little angel, and oh, how I worshipped her.

It was drawing near to Easter when the rest of the family returned, and I had now been in the place about ten months. The same cook came back, but the rest were all strangers; some of them did not remain long. I was eagerly looking forward to the young ladies coming from school, but there were only the young gentleman and the governess came with the mistress and, alas, my playtime with the little one was over. In early spring when a friend of the housekeeper's and I were making up her garden we planted a slip of monthly rose tree each to see if they would grow. Mine took root and his withered, and I will tell you more about mine later on.

When the little lady and her nurse came home I had a young boy to assist me with the kitchen work. He whistled like a bird the sweetest music one could wish to hear. One day the governess enquired who it was that gave such delightful music. She could hardly believe it was the little lad till she saw him at it. I often wonder what became of him or if he is still on the land of the living. The young ladies arrived, and as they were getting older, there was more company in the house. That made more work for me, and though I enjoyed the holidays to a certain extent, I was kept very busy. There were eight in family, and nine in the household, and the stablemen were boarded in the servant's hall. I mention this to show how much work one pair of hands can do if there is inclination. I had the housekeeper's room, the servant's hall, two long passages, the kitchen, scullery, larder, meat safe, dairy, kitchen yard, and my own bedroom to scrub out and keep clean. I had also all the dishes to wash, vegetables to cook, sauces to make, milk the cow, keep the dairy dishes clean, and look after the milk and cream; sometimes I churned when there was cream enough, and if the cook was busy I made the butter. My good mother had taught me to do that at home. I had also two large fires to attend to and to keep all the pots and pans in order. I have often been washing dishes, and the perspiration pouring into the dish-tub off my face. I got so thin that one evening when I went out for a walk I met the lad who planted the rose tree. He looked at me in a frightened way, and then he said: 'Losh keep me, lassie, what hae the done to ye?' 'Worked me well,' said I and passed on.

It was drawing on to August now and there were rumours of another break up. The gardener and his wife were to come into the house and no girl would be required; and oh, but I was sorry, for I have a very bad habit of attaching myself to any place I go to, and that was doubly dear on account of all the pleasant times I had there. A relative of the mistress, who was a good priest, wanted a kitchenmaid and I got the situation which was down in Hants, and had to take the long journey alone.

26
Patrick Gallagher, *My Story*

With a foreword by E. P. McDermott (Dungloe: Templecrone Co-operative Society, n.d. [1945]). Revised edn. 328pp.; pp. 79–86.

'This is a new kind of book to come out of Ireland, and it is written by a new kind of Irishman.'[1] Thus begins Peadar O'Donnell's introduction to the first edition of the autobiography of Patrick Gallagher (1871–1966), which he hails as the testimony of a pioneering social radical, 'a human document alive with an infectious gaiety and hope'. Gallagher came from the same socio-economic background as O'Donnell and Michael MacGowan and, like them, was steeped in the oral storytelling tradition of post-Famine Donegal. In 1881 he left his native Cleendra in the Rosses to work as a spalpeen in the Lagan, the farming region east of Letterkenny, and six years later crossed to Scotland, where he worked as a farm hand and miner, principally in Lanarkshire and Roxburghshire. It was in Scotland that Gallagher and his wife Sally, whom he married in 1898, first experienced the benefits of co-operativism and saw its potential to regenerate the rural Irish economy. On returning to Ireland at the turn of the century, he set about planning a co-operative venture and in 1906 founded the Templecrone Co-operative Society, which earned him the nickname 'Paddy the Cope'. His struggles to assert the principles of co-operativism against the powerful vested interests of rural merchants and shopkeepers is the subject of much of his autobiography; hence O'Donnell's admiration for it as an account of anti-capitalist regional activism.

As a migrant memoir, *My Story* is distinguished by its emotional frankness as much as its historical authenticity. In addition to capturing the social mores and resilient camaraderie of Donegal spalpeens, Gallagher records the transient intimacies that sometimes occurred between immigrants and natives, as when the wife of a Kelso farmer confided her unhappiness to him. Gallagher's attempt to express his emotional response to this encounter brings him up against the limits of written forms of self-narration and exemplifies the importance of extra-linguistic features to an oral narrator: 'I cannot put in writing how I felt when I heard of the unjust treatment that charming woman got, but if you were near me I would whisper it to you.'[2] The shaping

---

[1] Peadar O'Donnell, 'Introduction' to *My Story* by Patrick Gallagher (London: Jonathan Cape, 1939), p. 7.
[2] This sentence was added to the revised 1945 edition.

influence of oral modes on Gallagher's life story is again in evidence in the following extract from the expanded 1945 edition of the book, which is replete with the actual speech patterns and rhythms of an oral performer whose style is attuned to the ear rather than the eye. The unlettered eloquence of the speaking voice, combined with the interpolation of candid private letters, sustains the illusion of orality and enhances the affective power of this colloquial articulation of a migrant family's concerns for the fate of their child's identity under the impact of transplantation.

Our house was what was known in Scotland as a butt and ben. When you entered the hallway, the butt was to the left and the ben to the right. The same applied when you went upstairs. We were upstairs. We were in the butt, and there was a middle-aged couple in the ben. They did not agree. God save us, the language they used to each other was awful.

The first St. Patrick's night we were in the house, everyone from home came to see us, and the singing and dancing started, just the same as if we were back home in Cleendra. Johny Morroughou lilted, and my Uncle Jimmy danced a hornpipe, although he was sixty-eight years of age then. There were no girls in the house and Sally was the only woman. We all enjoyed ourselves, and Sally and I thought it was a great night.

The following evening when I came in from my work, the landlord was standing at the foot of the stairs, and he handed me a notice to leave the house within seven days.

'Mon,' he said, 'ye deceived me, I thought ye were a respectable mon, until Mr. — toul' me a while ago about the bad house ye were keeping.'

When I recovered from the shock, he was gone. The Mr. — whom he mentioned, was the man who lived next door. When I got upstairs and showed the notice to Sally she was terribly annoyed. The lodgers were as sorry as ourselves. Next day when I came home from my work, Sally was at the door waiting for me. She was smiling, and as I came towards her, she said, 'Paddy I have good news for you. I was in the Uphall village to-day, and I got a fine house on the ground floor for a shilling a week less than what we are paying here. It is not a butt and ben. The door is private. I know your walk will be a little longer, but, thank God, we will not be listening to the bad talk any longer.' I was glad, and so were the lodgers.

That night we decided to go into the new house as soon as possible, but then the question of flitting was a thorny one. We had so little furniture and all of it was second-hand. We knew when our sticks would be on the cart that there would be plenty of gossip about our wretched furniture. We therefore decided that our flitting should be a moonlight one. There was a carter at the Station Rows, I do not remember his name. He agreed to flit us at night for five shillings extra. He came to the foot of the stairs at twelve o'clock that night, and all the lodgers who were not on the night-shift gave willing hands to carry our bits of things down the stairs and put them on the cart. Little as we had, we were not able to take them all on the cart. All of us had to take as much as we could carry. Sally carried a few holy pictures. We met two men on the road, as they passed us one said to the other, 'Damn them gipsies, ye ne'er ken when ye'll meet them.' None of us spoke for some time, as we thought they might be under the influence of drink. After a while my Uncle Jimmy said, 'If I was as young as I used to be, I would not let the likes o' them call us gipsies. I think we are more like the poor people that were put out on the roadside during the Gweedore evictions.'

When we got all the things into the new house we were very tired. We did not put up any beds, just spread the clothes on the floor, made one big shakedown, and all of us, including Sally, slept in our clothes that morning.

The following St. Patrick's night, all the Cleendra boys who were in Uphall were with us. We had singing, but no dancing, and we never heard any complaints. We remained in that house while Sally and I were in Scotland.

I had a place in Portnuck Pit. I had four boys working for me and I was earning a good wage. Sally went to the Co-operative Store every Monday morning and lodged on deposit nearly every penny I gave her on the Saturday. She had six lodgers and they kept the house going. Although we had to be up each morning at 5 a.m. to be at our work at 6 a.m. we were very happy and had the best of fun. The lodgers were very good and used to help Sally with the house-work. One day when I came in from the pit, Sally was at the door as usual waiting for me, and as soon as I looked at her, her eyes filled up and I asked, 'Sally, what is wrong with you?' She put her hand into her breast and pulled out two letters, and reached them to me. God, but she gave me a fright. I was sure some one was dead at home. I began to read the first as soon as I reached the kitchen, before I took off my lamp and cap.

Dungloe, 4
4th September 1898.

Dear Sally,

Heavens, but I was delighted when I got your letter, but I would like to see Paddy now. I went to the Chapel and prayed for you, and I say the rosary every night and offer up a prayer for you both. Mother wants you to come home Sally, do come, don't refuse your mother. Paddy should come too the poor fellow is killed working. My father will give him some of the land. Sure they say you have plenty of money. Come both of you home in God's name.

We are all well at home. The crop is very good this year, thank God.

Kindest regards, from sister
Madgie.

The next letter was,

Dungloe,
4th Sept., 1898.

My dear Paddy,

I heard the good news, now you both must come home, you know you never intended to live long in Scotland, your child must be Irish not Scotch. We will all be waiting. I am going out to Cleendra to-night with the good news. I think I see your father singing and dancing. Heaven! but they will be glad.

I have no time to tell you any news, it is mail time. Come home and don't disappoint us.

Sincerely yours,
Madgie.

When I read the letters, I said, 'Sally, what are you crying for?' She said, 'Well Paddy, sure we are very happy here, and perhaps if we go home we will not be so happy. Sure we are saving money every week, and if we go home, we may have to spend it.' Then the lodgers began to come in, and when we were at our dinner, you would think there never was a tear in Sally's eyes, she was as jolly as ever. But that night neither Sally nor I slept much, Madgie's letter kept us awake.

Next day in the pit, I could not help talking to myself, and every time I talked, this is what I said, 'Your child must be Irish.' It was Saturday, after I got washed and the lodgers and I had our dinner, I said, 'Come boys, we will go out and have a drink.' As we were passing out, Sally said, 'I hope you will not be long.' We went over to Terrice's. I ordered a gallon of beer. During all the time I was afraid the boys would hear me saying, 'Your child must be Irish.' When the gallon was drunk Johnie Murchu hit the table with the measure. When old Terrice came in, Johnie said, 'The same again,' flinging down his 2/- piece. I said, 'Boys, excuse me for a wee while.' Out I went for home.

When I went into the house Sally said, 'Paddy, you are back early, are the boys not coming with you?' 'No Sally,' I said, 'You must go home, your child must be Irish.' 'Well Paddy, whatever you say,' said she, 'but won't it be a pity of the poor boys, that are working for you, do you think they would be able to get work with any other man?' I said, 'Oh Sally, I'll not go, I'll wait a wee while longer; you go home and when you are better, look out for a wee farm; I'll be still earning good money and then when I go home, I'll never come back again.' Sally put her head down in her lap, and I am sure it was ten minutes before she lifted it. She was crying when she looked up at me, and said, 'I'll not go if you don't come.'

Well for the next few days, when we were by ourselves, we were crying. When the lodgers were in, you would think neither of us ever shed a tear. Anyhow, Sally in the end agreed to go home, and leave me behind. Patrick Mulhern, a neighbour of ours at home, was going home in a few days and it was arranged that Sally would travel with him. When I told the lodgers damn but everyone of them was as sorry as myself.

The night before she left, the house was packed, everyone was jolly, but Sally and me, the boys saying, 'It's good for you going home, I wish to God we were all going.' I did not go to work the following day. I saw Sally and Mulhern off at the station. I sold out the bits of sticks, beds and delph we had. Sally took all the clothes home with her. The lodgers and I separated here and there. I went to lodge with Dan Bonar.

Shortly after Sally left for home there was a fire in Portnuck Pit. We all escaped. My workers and I had the narrowest escape, as we were working in the high workings and did not hear the explosion. The first thing we found was the after damp. We made for the bottom as quickly as we could. When we reached the bottom we were nearly finished, but we were just in time for the last going up on the cage to see us. The cage-man came back and took us up. Some of us were ill for a few days. The pit was closed down and flooded to put out the fire. It belonged to Young's Company, the same company that owned Glendevin, the first mine that I went down. After a week or so we all got work in Glendevin on a night-shift. The places were hard and I could not make much of a wage. I left and went to Tarbrax, worked there for a while, could save no money, went with the boys to the pubs and football matches. Sally wrote to me every week to come home.

One day when I came in from the mine, there was a letter for me. I opened it. It read:

Dungloe.

My Dear Paddy,

Thanks be to God, Sally is better, she has a lovely child, born last night. Your mother and father are just after landing, they are delighted. The child is going to be christened this evening, and is to be called Annie for your mother. (My mother was called Nancy, Annie is the English for Nancy.)

Lord! Paddy, I wish you were with us to-night, we will have the best of fun on your father, they are getting jolly already. Now Paddy, surely you will come home, sure your child is Irish, God bless her. Come home.

Sincerely yours,
Madgie.

A few days afterwards I had a letter from Sally, while reading it, damn but I was as bad as Sally, we both thought nobody had a child but ourselves.

She finished up with, 'She is called for your mother, surely you will come home now.'

The following week I decided to go home. All the boys from home gathered into the lodging house in Tarbrax, the night before I left. I was sorry to part with them.

When I reached Dungloe, they were expecting me. My father and mother were in. Sally was at the door with the child in her arms. Damn but I do not think there was a happier man in the world than I was then. God bless my heart, if you saw Madgie, she was crying with joy. Oh! such a night.

27
Annie M. P. Smithson, *Myself – and Others: An Autobiography*

(Dublin: Talbot Press, 1944). 293pp.; pp. 110–14; 119–21.

Annie Smithson (1873–1948) was born into a middle-class Protestant family in Sandymount, Dublin. Her mother's remarriage after her father's early death meant that she spent part of her childhood in Warrington, the home of her stepfather, where she was deeply unhappy. Although she originally aspired to a journalistic career, Smithson ended up choosing to nurse, training first in London and then in Edinburgh in the late 1890s. She spent five years nursing in County Down, a period overshadowed by an ill-fated relationship with James Manton, a married doctor. Their futureless affair prompted her to move to Glasgow in 1906, where she suffered a bout of severe depression, after which she converted to Catholicism in 1907. This decision had important later consequences for her thematic concerns as a writer, as Oonagh Walsh explains: 'For Smithson, ever after, Catholicism was firmly linked with what she felt was "real" Irishness, and her experience of conversion led her texts to become in turn vehicles for the conversion of others.'[1] Smithson's political conversion to the cause of Irish nationalism soon followed. The 1916 Rising galvanised her imagination and inspired her to write *Her Irish Heritage* (1917), which she dedicated to the memory of the dead rebels. This was the first of almost two dozen romance novels, many of them strongly nationalist in theme and tone, which won her a huge readership. Smithson's autobiography is inflected with a similar nationalist polemic. Not only does she frame her life-story within a redemptive Catholic teleology, she carefully selects incidents from her past that testify to her nationalist commitment. Chapter 10 features an account of one such incident, a contretemps Smithson had with her matron while training at London's Chelsea Hospital for Women in 1897.

What I felt most, during that first summer I spent in London, was the intense heat. I had not experienced a London summer before, and it seemed as if the

---

[1] Oonagh Walsh, ' "Her Irish Heritage": Annie M. P. Smithson and Auto/Biography', *Études Irlandaises*, vol. 23, no. 1 (1998), p. 30. Although religion and politics are central strands in Smithson's narrative, the book is less proselytising than Walsh's comments might lead one to expect.

very paving stones were scorching my feet. I can vividly remember sleeping – or trying to do so – with my head on a pillow resting on the sill of the wide open window, vainly hoping for a breath of air. It was some time before I grew accustomed to the noise of the streets which seemed to go on all night. Only for about an hour in the early morning would there be any sort of quiet, and even that would be broken by some drunken person rolling past, or by the street women who would often be screaming at one another, and using language which was as a foreign tongue to me.

Then, after a while, would come the rumbling of the country carts on their way to Covent Garden, and to me these always seemed to bring a breath of fresh air as from the cleaner places of the world than was this modern Babylon. They conjured up fields of clover, of humming bees, of old-fashioned gardens such as I had left behind at Rathfarnham. And then, sometimes, the tears would come to my eyes, and I would cry a little, lying there, sleepless in the midst of London's noise and heat.

The period of training in the Chelsea Hospital was two years, but I only remained there fifteen months. The reason for this was that I had made up my mind to become one of the nurses of the Queen Victoria's Jubilee Institute, for nursing the poor in their own homes. I had often seen these nurses in Dublin, and watched them at service in St. Patrick's Cathedral, where they had a pew reserved for their own use. I wished to return to Ireland, and thought that I should like to work amongst the poor. So, with my aunt's help, I made the necessary application, filled in certain forms, and was then informed that the Institute would give me two years' hospital training at the Royal Infirmary, Edinburgh, and that there would be a vacancy there in October 1898, and that I could enter on that date. So it was settled that I should stay in London until September, 1898, and then after a short holiday proceed to Edinburgh for my general training [...]

I was glad when the hot weather passed, and more glad still when in the autumn I was put on night duty. I had for room mate, in our lodgings across the road, a cheery little Cockney, full of fun and good humour, with whom I got on amazingly well in spite of the fact that we had not an idea in common – outside the hospital walls. But as we nurses, then as now, seldom talked anything but 'shop' when together, this did not matter much. We used to go for long bus rides in the morning before going to bed. We would go on top and get as near as possible to the driver. It was a delight to see the way he drove his horses, flourishing his whip, and in that way we got some air after our nights in the wards.

I well remember one morning when I was perched close to the driver as we drove by Hyde Park. I was alone as my friend had not come out that morning. The bus pulled up suddenly, and remained so for a few moments. Looking around – what a grand place for seeing everything was the top of one of those old buses! – I noticed that all the traffic had ceased. 'What is it?' I asked the driver. 'Is anything wrong?'

The driver smiled at me – they were genial fellows those drivers.

'It's the old Lidy – she's jest coming into the Park,' he said, and even as he spoke a carriage with the usual escort of Royalty passed through the space made by the waiting traffic, and on through the gate into the Park. I could only see a small old woman, who bowed mechanically to the watching crowds.

'I saw your Queen to-day,' I said to the little Cockney later that day when we were getting ready for bed, 'and I don't think much of her!'

'*The* Queen, I suppose you mean,' she replied. 'She is just as much your Queen as ours – isn't she?'

'She has no right to be anyway,' I said, 'we should have our own King and Queen!'

My companion laughed. 'Don't talk rubbish,' she said. 'Surely you are not going to turn Fenian – are you? You will soon find yourself in prison if you don't take care!'

At that very time, although I did not know it, Tom Clarke[2] and other Fenian prisoners were being tortured in English prisons. But I knew nothing of these things, I only knew a little about the ancient history of Ireland, and this I started to expound to my friend, who turned a deaf ear to it all, and saying she was too sleepy to listen, tucked the clothes around her and went to sleep.

But I did not sleep for a little while. It was strange – yet perhaps not so strange after all – that now, when I was in England, I should have become much more Irish in heart than when at home. [...]

The days passed, and the 17th March, 1898 came round. I was again on night duty, but on another floor, and was enjoying hospital life and feeling very happy when I came off duty that morning. In my pigeon-hole I found my box of shamrock, sent by my cousins. The dear little plant – how glad I was to see it. I kissed it as I tucked a spray in my belt and went along to the dining-room. As I was crossing the hall afterwards, on my way to our quarters across the road, Matron was at the telephone. Her lifted hand brought me to a standstill. I went in mortal dread of Matron, yet so far I had got on fairly well with her, and had only been 'on the carpet' a few times. This morning my conscience was quite clear, so I waited serenely for her to speak. Then came the bombshell.

Putting down the receiver, she turned to me.

'Do you not yet know the Rules of the Hospital?' she asked.

I stared at her, not understanding. She pointed an accusing finger at my belt.

'No flowers are allowed to be worn on duty,' she said.

---

[2] Thomas J. Clarke (1858–1916), Fenian organiser and first signatory to the 1916 Proclamation. He fought in the General Post Office and was executed in Kilmainham Jail on 3 May 1916.

Then I understood. 'This is not a flower, Matron,' I said. 'It is the shamrock – and this is St. Patrick's Day.'

'No – it is not a flower,' she replied. 'It is a weed.'

A weed! The shamrock a weed! I forgot my awe of Matron for the moment and answered back: 'It is *not* a weed – it is the shamrock.'

'I will give you exactly five minutes by my watch to remove that weed – grass – whatever it is from your belt.' She took out her watch and stood there, and I stood there, too, determined that no matter what might happen I would not remove the shamrock from my belt. Slowly the minutes passed – to me they seemed like hours – and then Matron put away her watch and looked at me.

'You will go to your room at once,' she said.

As I had been going there when she stopped me, that was no hardship, but I wondered what would be the outcome of my act of open rebellion to authority? Insubordination was a terrible crime in hospital. Probably the lay person can have no conception of how terrible and serious it is, but any nurse reading these lines will understand my anxiety. But this did not keep me long awake, and it only seemed a moment until I was being called by one of the day nurses. This happened to be my night off, and I had permission to attend the St. Patrick's Day concert in the Albert Hall. As luck would have it, I again encountered Matron as I was leaving the hospital – where I had gone for a cup of tea. This time, as I was in mufti,[3] she had to turn a blind eye to my large spray of shamrock.

For days I waited, wondering when Matron's verdict would go forth – and what it would be? But time passed and I heard no more about the affair. Some time afterwards my aunt told me that Matron had talked to her about the matter. She told her that she was inclined at first to dismiss me from the staff, but that she really could not bring herself to do it.

'She stuck to her guns so well, that I really had not the heart to send her away – I just had to admire her spirit,' she said.

'It is a dangerous thing to tell an Irishman or woman that they must not wear the shamrock,' replied my aunt. 'I should like to see the person who would tell me not to do so!'

Strange, indeed, it seemed to me that I heard no more of the affair. Stranger still, when years later I was in London, my general training finished, and I went to see my old hospital, that Matron should actually have me to tea in her own sitting-room, and as we chatted, allude laughingly to the episode.

'Oh, you Irish!' she said. 'You are dreadful people – but you make the best nurses in the world!'

---

[3] Plain, non-uniform clothes.

28

Elizabeth Bowen, *Pictures and Conversations*

With a foreword by Spencer Curtis Brown (London: Allen Lane, 1975). xlii, 193pp.; pp. 23–7.

Born into the Anglo-Irish Protestant ascendancy, Elizabeth Bowen (1899–1973) was the product of a close-knit society described by Spencer Curtis Brown in his foreword to *Pictures and Conversations* as 'English but in no way English, Irish but in no way Irish'. She spent so much of her life manoeuvring between London, Dublin and Bowen's Court, her family estate in County Cork, that her fiction has become synonymous with themes of dislocation and interstitiality. Indeed, the shaping influence of ambivalence on Bowen's work and thought has been so frequently asserted as to have become by now a critical commonplace. Roy Foster's claim that Bowen's 'real themes are dispossession, double-crossing, cruelty, betrayal'[1] is amplified and extended in excellent recent studies by Maud Ellmann and Neil Corcoran, both of whom regard 'the gift or pain or dislocation of living between Ireland and England, of being bilocated' as 'deeply intrinsic' to her entire oeuvre.[2] Like her contemporary Louis MacNeice, another Protestant Irish outsider-insider in England whom we shall encounter later in this volume, Bowen's sensibility was finely attuned to the ironies and ambiguities of doubleness and split-mindedness, qualities that also inflect her conception of 'the self-told story': 'One might say that whereas autobiography used to be based on statement, now it derives from query, being tentative rather than positive, no longer didactic but open-minded. It is mobile, exploratory.'[3] However, *Bowen's Court* (1942), which chronicles ten generations of her family history, hardly conforms to this template and is in many respects her least personal autobiographical work. *Seven Winters*, Bowen's brief childhood memoir published the same year, reveals much more about 'the interplay

---

[1] R. F. Foster, 'The Irishness of Elizabeth Bowen', in *Paddy and Mr Punch*, p. 103.

[2] Neil Corcoran, *Elizabeth Bowen: The Enforced Return* (Oxford: Oxford University Press, 2004), p. 13. See also Maud Ellmann, *Elizabeth Bowen: The Shadow Across the Page* (Edinburgh: Edinburgh University Press, 2003).

[3] Elizabeth Bowen, 'Autobiography', in *Afterthought: Pieces about Writing* (London: Longmans, Green, 1962), p. 201.

between the inner and the outer "I" ',[4] before ending abruptly on the threshold of her move to the Kent coast with her mother in 1906, after her father's nervous breakdown. In the last months of her life Bowen was again mining the seams of memory, preparing a work, posthumously published as *Pictures and Conversations*, that she envisaged as a study of 'the relationship (so far as that can be traceable, and perhaps it is most interesting when it is apparently not traceable) between living and writing'.

Possibly, it was England made me a novelist. At an early though conscious age, I was transplanted. I arrived, young, into a different mythology – in fact, into one totally alien to that of my forefathers, none of whom had resided anywhere but in Ireland for some centuries, and some of whom may never have been in England at all: the Bowens were Welsh. From now on there was to be (as for any immigrant) a cleft between my heredity and my environment – the former remaining, in my case, the more powerful. Submerged, the mythology of this 'other' land could be felt at work in the ways, manners and views of its people, round me: those, because I disliked being at a disadvantage, it became necessary to probe. It cannot be said that a child of seven was analytic; more, with a blend of characteristic guile and uncharacteristic patience I took note – which, though I had at that time no thought of my future art, is, after all, one of the main activities of the novelist. At the outset, the denizens of England and their goings-on inspired me with what a hymn epitomises as 'scornful wonder' – protective mechanism? – but I was not a disagreeable child, so any initial hostility wore off. Lacking that stimulus, my attention wandered: society not being by nature interesting, or for long interesting, to the very young, I transferred my gaze from it to its geographical setting. Thereafter, England affected me more in a scenic way than in any other – and still does. It was the lie of the land, with that cool, clear light falling upon it, which was extraordinary.

Well for me, that we pitched our camp where we did! Fortunate, I mean, that 'England' was Kent, and, above all, Kent's dramatizable coastline. Suppose, for instance, some Cousin Lilla or Cousin Isabel had siren-sung us into the Midlands, with their soporific monotony? Or, for that matter, into the West Country, with its rainy semi-resemblances to Ireland? As it was, where we *were* stood out in absolute contrast to where we came from. Gone was the changing blue of mountains: instead, bleached blond in summer, the bald downs showed exciting great gashes of white chalk. Everything, including the geological formation, struck me as having been recently put together. Trees were smaller in size, having not yet, one could imagine, had time for growth. 'Thunderbolts' – meteorites? – to be collected along the slippery dogpaths of the Warren might have rained down from the heavens the night before. And this *newness* of England, manifest in the brightness, occasionally the crudity, of its colouring, had about it something of the precarious. *Would* it last?

---

[4] Ibid., p. 202.

The edifices lining the tilted streets or gummed at differing levels above the Channel seemed engaged in just not sliding about. How much *would* this brittle fabric stand up to? My thoughts dallied with landslides, subsidences and tidal waves.

England's appearance of youth was, however, gainsaid by evidences of history. Those were all over the place. In Ireland, history – because, I suppose, of its melancholy, uneasy trend – had on the whole tended to be played down; one knew *of* it, but spoke of it little. Here, it burst from under the contemporary surface at every point, arousing enthusiasm. A success story – or, in these days one might say, a gigantic musical. Everyone figured, including the Ancient Romans. Nor had any of the stage-sets for the performance – or, indeed, any of those rigged up for performances which had not, after all, taken place, such as a Napoleonic invasion – been cleared away: east of me Dover Castle, shored up on tier-upon-tier of fortification, flew its triumphant flag; west of me, martello towers diminished into the distance, more than one of them pounded down into massive jumbles of broken masonry, not, after all, by enemy cannon-fire but by the sea, which had also breached the sea-wall, for the elements had also taken a hand. Our Military Canal was not the less seductive for boating-picnics for having as yet served no military purpose. Foundations of circumspect-looking buildings were (I heard) riddled with secret passages. The Cinque Ports' navy[5] had torn up and down the Channel harassing any marauding French; smugglers had cat-and-moused with revenue men over the marshes, into the woods. To crown all, there had been terrific marine pageantry, spectacular arrivals and departures, monarchs, brides, envoys and so on – a constant, glittering, affable come-and-go between here and France. Not a dull moment.

'History' inebriated me, and no wonder. Moreover, *here* was where it belonged: Kent-England had a proprietary hold on it. So it was this landscape, with everything it was eloquent of and comprehended, which won me (the newcomer to it) over – filling me, at the same time, with envy and the wish to partake. Not long after my eighth birthday, celebrated at Folkestone, I entered upon a long, voluptuous phase in which I saw life as a non-stop historical novel, disguised only thinly (in my day) by modern dress. I saw myself, even, in an historic light, which gave at once a momentousness and a premonition of their possible consequences to all my doings. And the same attached to anyone who attracted me. When or how I divested myself of this daydream, I do not remember – did I entirely do so ever? Becoming a writer knocked a good deal of nonsense out of my system. But always there is a residuum. (I detect in my betters, the giants of my profession, a magnificent,

---

[5] Confederation of five ports – Hastings, Romney, Hythe, Dover and Sandwich – that supplied ships to the English navy prior to the establishment of a permanent fleet in the sixteenth century.

self-exonerating silliness: would or could anybody become a novelist who was not internally silly in *some* way?) As a novelist, I cannot occupy myself with 'characters', or at any rate central ones, who lack panache, in one or another sense, who would be incapable of a major action or a major passion, or who have not at least a touch of the ambiguity, the ultimate unaccountability, the enlarging mistiness of personages 'in history'. History, as more austerely I now know it, is not romantic. But I am.

29

Alice Foley, *A Bolton Childhood*

(Manchester: Manchester University Extra-Mural Department, 1973). 92pp.; pp. 57–61.

The paucity of personal narratives by second-generation Irish women in Britain makes the autobiography of the trade unionist Alice Foley (1891–1974) a precious source for diaspora scholars, not least because it bears witness to the considerable social achievements of a female working-class activist who struggled to realise her potential against the impediments of birth, education and poverty. Born in Bolton to an illiterate Lancashire washerwoman and a 'big, intelligent but unruly' Irish labourer, Foley's domestic politicisation – her father was a Fenian sympathiser, her sister an active suffragette – meant that she was already attuned to agitation and dissent by the time she started working in the local cotton mill in 1905. The factors that led to her becoming a 'critical spokeswoman' for her fellow millworkers are sketched in the following extract from her short autobiography, in which she exposes the human costs of industrial capitalism, displaying a keen eye for social detail. Foley was appointed to a full-time trade union post in 1912 and during the following decades rose steadily through the ranks to become the first female secretary of the Bolton and District Weavers' and Winders' Association (1949–61) and president of Bolton Trades' Council (1956–57). She also had a lifelong dedication to the cause of adult education and was for many years a leading member of the Workers' Educational Association (WEA), an involvement that may well have spurred her to produce her own life-story.[1] Certainly, her eloquently descriptive autobiography reveals the centrality of autodidact culture to her evolution from 'pious little Catholic' into committed socialist, propelled by a desire 'to transform an inborn humility into some kind of achievement, however insignificant it might prove, in the all pervading glow of socialistic idealism'.[2]

Of importance also was the example of Alice's elder sister Cissy, whose political empowerment through self-education is obliquely visible throughout the text. In fact,

---

[1] Walter, *Outsiders Inside*, p. 137.
[2] Jonathan Rose says of Foley that she 'read some Morris and less Marx, but for her, a liberal education for the proletariat was not merely a means of achieving socialism: it was socialism in fact, the ultimate goal of politics'. *The Intellectual Life of the British Working Classes* (London: Yale University Press, 2001), p. 54.

the sisters' stories are so closely intertwined that *A Bolton Childhood* can be read as a relational autobiography that illuminates the opportunities for upward social mobility afforded to politicised second-generation Irish women in the early twentieth century.[3] But to read the book solely in such terms is to overlook Foley's natural skills as a writer, skills that enable her to combine a documentary description of industrial toil with a quasi-Wordsworthian evocation of nature's beauty: 'On certain frosty mornings before the break of dawn I awoke from torpor to the vision of a full moon riding majestically and aloof in the clear heavens with a host of stars and planets poised in channels of vastness.' Such mini-epiphanies, by hinting at the promise of release from grey workaday lives, bring the suffocating drudgery of the narrator's economic servitude into even sharper relief.

Immediately after entering the cotton factory in 1905 I had my first experience of a bitter industrial dispute, the great Daubhill strike, at a near-by mill. I was too young at the time to understand its cause or development, but later learned that the conflict grew out of the firm's action in applying a mechanical gadget to the looms in the form of a warp-stop motion. In return for this technical innovation management claimed a substantial reduction in wage rates and this was stoutly resisted by both the trade union and the weavers concerned. Negotiations broke down and the operatives came out on strike. Management then ordered other employees to run the idle looms, but as this failed the firm brought black-leg labour from Cornwall.

Ignorant of the nature and import of this head-on struggle, we youngsters heartily enjoyed ourselves after working hours by thronging and shoving round the factory gates. In high glee we dodged the bobbies who tried to disperse the crowd, chanting doggerel verses to the tune of a then popular song *In the shade of the old apple tree* and booing lustily if we spotted a suspected 'knobstick'.

This particularly long and exhausting dispute ended, I remember, in a compromise agreement which satisfied neither side. In retrospect, however, it could be seen as a first shot in the human struggle to retain traditional methods of production against those fierce on-coming thrusts of technocracy and automation which were to harass and bedevil the cotton industry for the next half-century.

In the preparation department we were a smaller and more homogeneous group than in the weaving shed and accepted each other in varying degrees of good will or toleration. By temperament I was rarely shocked by natural or crude vulgarity, but had a strong innate objection to being expected to snigger at dirty tales or sly innuendoes and work-mates learned to embrace me as a 'bit of an oddity'. Most of my companions were attached, loosely or otherwise, to church or chapel; some of the younger folks had been caught up in the Moody-Sankey missions of the period, and for a time became Hot

---

[3] See Walter, *Outsiders Inside*, pp. 137–43.

Gospellers.[4] In our singing sessions the strains of 'Throw out the life-line, someone is sinking today' floated in competition with the regular hum and throb of the engine.

We held to a fairly conventional, if unexplored, moral code and if anyone in the group was suspected of 'going out' with a married man she was usually due for a telling-off by her companions. Those few culprits known to be living 'tally' were accepted, but such behaviour was generally frowned upon. There were few concessions to personal vanity; smoking or the use of cosmetics were deemed 'fast'. A small cracked mirror tied round a pillar did service to reflect our pale, tired faces after ten hours toil in a hot, steamy atmosphere.

The monotonous drudgery of machine-tending was occasionally broken by our traditional 'footings' when a work-mate announced her approaching marriage. This usually took the form of mock procession down the broad-alley, the bride-to-be draped in a curtain or white sheet, followed by a squealing cluster of well-wishers, the elder ones offering ribald jokes, the younger girls giggling to hide their embarrassment. Later we were regaled with pop, pies and eccles cakes in a community mood of hearty fellowship.

I remember a fat, jolly Irish woman who gave up part of her dinner-break to try and teach we younger workers how to waltz; singing out the time, one-two-three, we in turn jogged in her plump arms, our clogs scraping and clinking on the lumpy, flagged floor.

By this time I had abandoned the traditional woollen shawl and went to work in a shabby sailor hat discarded by my sister. One day on returning unexpectedly I noticed a procession of laughing women parading round the alleys, the leader holding aloft my old hat on the top of a sweeping brush. At my approach they quickly scattered, replacing the offending head-gear on its appropriate hook. No words were spoken for, though somewhat puzzled, I sadly lacked the art of communication. During the afternoon several of my companions offered toffee or an orange and I knew it was their way of saying 'sorry, old pal, if we have offended, but for goodness sake, do come off that stilt'.

Some of the prevailing working conditions were little short of degrading; no hot water was available for washing dirty, oily hands, and each Saturday noon after laboriously cleaning clogged, fluffy machinery on hands and knees, we trudged off to the factory lodge seeking to remove excess of grime and grease in its steamy stagnancy before going home for the half-day rest.

Old sinks were receptacles for wet tea-leaves and sodden news-papers; no towels were provided and toilets were dark, smelly and inadequate. Of social

---

[4] American evangelists Dwight Moody (1837–99) and Ira Sankey (1840–1908) held missions in many British cities during the late nineteenth century. Their campaigns provoked much popular acclaim as well as controversy and opposition. The original 'hot gospeller' was the courtier and religious radical Edward Underhill (1512–1576), so-called because of his zealous Protestantism.

welfare or refinement there was no hint. If we fell sick we merely took ourselves off to the factory yard, hoping that the cooler air might revive us, but if not, our partner might see us safely home. In this capacity of 'good samaritan' she also was penalised by loss of earnings whilst absent on such an errand of mercy. But most resented of all was the lack of human dignity accorded to our status as 'hands' with appropriate check numbers, for I found nothing in the regime to touch one chord of loyalty or positive goodwill within the workers. For me the deadening monotony of machine-minding was rendered bearable only by the harsh necessity of earning a living and redeemed solely by the day-to-day fellowship of countless other toilers.

I vividly recall an incident when, as a girl of fifteen we organised a deputation to interview the head manager on some out-standing grievance. His office stood at the end of a narrow, winding passage and the tramping of clogged feet must have sounded like a disordered battalion. Our knock on the door produced a growling 'come in'. Pushed forward by my work-mates I began to stammer out the substance of our complaint, but the manager, now too bad tempered and irritable to listen or argue, let forth a volley of abuse and ended by peremptorily ordering us back to work under penalty of immediate dismissal. Cowed by this unexpected onslaught, and too nervous to stand our ground, we stumbled out of the room in disarray and, as a parting shot, the manager hurled after us 'An' I suppose next time, yo'll bi axin' mi to give yo' sofas fur t'lie on.' We later christened him 'owd sofa' but in my young heart I despised that bully 'dressed out in his little brief authority', insensible and incapable of merely decent communication.

As weeks and months passed by I became more sharply aware of the care-worn faces of my elderly workmates. They wore little neck-shawls pulled tightly round neck and shoulders and seemed to dread every gust of fresh air that might seep into the foetid atmosphere.

Trapped on a treadmill of monotony, I wondered vaguely must the years go on and on until I, too, became just such another faded figure? I increasingly rebelled against the injustice of a factory system that could not even offer a degree of security to its toilers. For the majority, especially those with ageing parents to maintain, there was constantly the ache of fear at recurrent periods of short-time working and unemployment. We had neither work guarantees nor assured wage-packets; earnings were brought round each Friday afternoon in individual tins and the money emptied into our palms. Eagerly we counted the coins, relieved if we had a good week, silently worried by a bad one.

In the main we were a decent, hard-working, good-natured community. If anyone belonging to you died, the bereaved operative was usually summoned to the watch-house by an errand boy; with all eyes turned in that direction you followed the messenger like a prisoner, but all mouths immediately got busy telegraphing the misfortune, whilst willing, sympathetic hands kept your machinery running so that earnings should not suffer.

There was one line of communication that rarely failed us; that was telling each other about our family rows, even if the story went against the teller. I recall an occasion when my partner came to work with a shocking black eye; it appeared that she had pawned her husband's best suit and had then feigned illness so he would not want to go out; her spouse had discovered the ruse and in his temper had given her a 'reight hefty thump' but no malice was left between them. Another girl used to recount how her old granny, when out of ready money and expecting the rent-man, invariably put on a clean apron and went out for a walk.

When the 1914 war clouds hovered around one weaver remarked to another 'It looks like another war.' 'What's it about this time?' enquired her partner. 'Oh, I dur'nt know; they'll blame it on God or t' King.' 'Bugger t' King, an' let God look after hisself' came the prompt reply. Yet when war did break out and lads were called up in their thousands one Catholic girl near-by framed her mouth with the request 'Let's say a Hail Mary for the boys at the Front'; ceasing shuttle-changing for a moment, with heads bent over the breast-plate and thoughts winging to Flanders' fields, we intoned 'Mother of God, pray for us sinners now and at the hour of our death.'

30
Bonar Thompson, *Hyde Park Orator*

With a preface by Sean O'Casey (London: Jarrolds, 1934). viii, 287pp.; pp. 77–9; 111–17.

Bonar Thompson (1888–1963) was born at Carnearney in County Antrim, the illegitimate child of a poor Presbyterian girl. He was raised by an elderly aunt until the age of 13, when he moved to Manchester to live with his mother and step-father. While working for the Great Central Railway he decided to become a public orator, seeing it as a satisfactory means of 'getting a living without working'. Soon 'the boy orator' was advocating revolutionary socialism from public platforms throughout Britain and supplementing his income by begging. His agitatory speeches sometimes led to his being fined for breaches of the peace and, when unable or unwilling to pay such fines, to short spells in prison. In 1916 he was arrested for evading military service and spent the rest of the First World War in a variety of work-camps. Thompson resumed his soapbox socialism in 1922 but by the late twenties had adopted an 'independent non-party attitude', having 'grown to look upon all movements as intolerably frowsy and silly'. He edited and produced a review entitled *The Black Hat* between 1930 and 1932.

By the time his autobiography appeared, Thompson was, by his own estimation, one of the best-known open-air speakers in London, dubbed 'the Prime Minister of Hyde Park' by some. The Labour politician Michael Foot remembers him as a 'one-man satirist of the universe, this world and the next'.[1] His literary charisma was evidently powerful enough to inspire at least one reader of his autobiography, the Derry-born writer Robert Greacen, to travel to London to hear 'the oratorical champ from the Glens of Antrim'. The demagogue did not disappoint: 'He cast a cold eye on politicians and propagandists of all stripes, and served up a piping-hot commentary spiced with wit and humour, a man-in-the-street's GBS.'[2] *Hyde Park Orator* is enlivened by a similar combination of declamatory energy, caustic wit and pungent opinion. Thompson's well-honed rhetorical skills and 'inborn histrionic talents' make him a

---

[1] Michael Foot, *Debts of Honour* (London: Davis Poynter, 1980), p. 118.
[2] Robert Greacen, *The Sash My Father Wore: An Autobiography* (Edinburgh: Mainstream, 1997), p. 107.

highly self-dramatising autobiographer who adroitly exploits the genre's affinity for egotism, bombast and display. Throughout, he cultivates an iconoclastic persona, provocatively pronouncing on a host of topics from war to contraception. His self-conceit is also much in evidence, as is his contempt for the very people who patronise him, as the following excerpt reveals.

As the result of a chance visit to Stevenson Square,[3] I had been brought into contact with a world of which I had previously been in total ignorance. The things I learned gave me a new outlook on life. Several of the regular speakers there fascinated me to a degree which, in the light of later experience, appears absurdly impossible. I sat at the feet of men who were the veriest ranters and gasbags. But I have always been susceptible to the sound of words. These men were dealers in words. Few of them possessed any real knowledge of anything, but they had the jargon of revolt at their tongues' ends. As the wellworn phrases fell from their lips I imagined myself to be listening to the most wonderful and original thoughts. How could I have known that it was the standardized fustian of half-baked mouthers and half-baked malcontents? It seemed new to me.

Before long I came to an important decision, and one which was to shape the course of my life. I resolved to become a speaker. To sway masses, to dominate crowds, to hear the applause – here was an easy road to fame. More than that, it was a chance to escape from poverty and hard, irksome, badly paid labour. It was the same motive as had driven the labour leaders out of the factory and the mine – the stern resolve to get away from hard manual labour at all costs. It was often said of the late Keir Hardie[4] that he was wearing himself out in the service of his class. It is certain that he would have worn himself out much sooner had he remained down the pit. The labour leaders had left the workshops to toil on the floor of the House of Commons. It was a great racket.

My object was to emulate these men. I would enter the lists as a minister of the gospel of revolt. I had a strongly ingrained exhibitive complex and a keen urge to be at the centre of the stage of human affairs. The time had come when I could no longer tolerate being treated as a cipher. At work and at my lodgings I was a nobody. I could not assert or express myself. I had no proper education, no social gifts, no powers of speech. I could not sustain an intelligent conversation. I was a dumbbell. So that in choosing to become a speaker I was seeking both to escape from hard work and to find a means of exploiting my inborn histrionic talents. Had I been able to get on the stage I should never have bothered my head about socialism. But I was too shabbily dressed, too

---

[3] Named after William Stevenson, this was a popular meeting-place and open-air forum for public speaking in late nineteenth-century Manchester.
[4] James Keir Hardie (1856–1915), Scottish-born founder of the British Labour Party.

lacking in self-confidence. I did not know to set about it. In seeking a chance to play a part in the melodrama of political life, I did the next best thing.

I realized that to sustain the role adequately I should have to train myself, to acquire a vocabulary, learn to handle the language with accuracy and point, and, if possible, with rhetorical force. I should have to conquer diffidence and develop self-confidence.

I was too well aware of my educational and intellectual limitations not to realize how hard a task I should have to equip myself properly for the new career. My nature had been stifled by a narrow and narrowing environment. I had been cramped, frustrated, and repressed. But I was set on the change.

I had difficulty with my reading, but I persisted. It was dull work wading through the socialist writers and teachers. Most of them are as dull as dull can be, and the gross sentimentality, the sickly whining and cheap moralizing, the bombastic assertion of half-truths as if they were great scientific discoveries, brought me to the verge of vomiting. But I shut my eyes to all this and tried to master the socialist theory and revolutionary dogmas I proposed to advocate. [. . .]

My arrival in the metropolis caused no interest whatever. Walking in through the Edgware Road from the north, I found myself in Hyde Park. The time was three o'clock in the afternoon, and I found a small meeting in progress at the Marble Arch meeting-ground. The speaker was a religious fanatic whose language was all too familiar to me. After a while he subsided and I stepped forward into the ring. I began to speak about my prison experiences.[5] The crowd grew; no one interrupted. Everybody seemed interested and not unsympathetic. I finished, and a man stepped from the crowd and said: 'Well, people, you have heard this young man's story. He is up against it. I need say no more. You can see him outside the gates.' He conducted me towards the gate and told me to stand there while the crowd came out. It seemed that collections were not permitted inside the Park, but you could invite those who thought your speech worthy of support and desired to contribute to come outside the gates. I took three shillings. [. . .]

In the evening I spoke in Hyde Park once more, going outside the gates again and collecting about one and sixpence. I was interested to find the great MacCutcheon[6] had been listening to me. He came up to me outside the gate and told me that he too was staying at Bruce House. He and I spoke together for many months, taking the chair for each other alternately. Life was not too easy. It took me all my time to raise enough in collections to pay my 'kipp' each night and get something to eat each day. I lived on

---

[5] In 1908 Thompson was sentenced to 12 months' imprisonment for causing wilful malicious damage to public buildings as part of an anti-capitalist protest on behalf of the unemployed.

[6] James Lister MacCutcheon, whom Thompson describes as the leader of the Manchester unemployed.

about fifteen shillings a week, but there was no regularity in the life I had chosen.

Sunday was the best day for meetings. I held three, one at twelve in the forenoon, one at three in the afternoon, and the third at six-thirty in the evening. I took about ten shillings altogether. Had collections been allowed on the spot, I should have taken a great deal more, but London people are not in the habit of running after anyone to give them money, whether it has been earned or not. I certainly earned all I received. Public speaking is hard work. Done under my conditions, it was a labour of loathing, but I persevered. Sooner or later, I told myself, I shall be recognized as an orator of more than common gifts.

I knew that I still had much to learn, but in the rough and tumble of street-corner and public-park speaking one could not help but learn. I spoke nearly every day, and sometimes twice and even three times daily, until the outbreak of war in 1914. On Sundays I always addressed large meetings, each of which lasted an hour. A wet Sunday washed me out and washed my livelihood away. In the winter the struggle was severe. Park crowds were smaller, and those who came had very little to give away.

The first winter that I spent in London saw me without the price of a bed on many occasions. I walked the streets until daybreak, and in the morning washed in the Serpentine. This is not allowed, and I had to keep a look-out for the policeman while I washed. Often I went without food – but I went on speaking. I had to – there was nothing else I could do.

One thing I never thought of doing, and that was to look for work. I would not have minded a good job, but no one ever offered me a good job. My ambition was to become a great orator – to be well paid for speaking. At the same time I was not prepared to speak unless I had full liberty to say what I liked. My ideas were socialistic and anarchistic. I turned out that sort of stuff because, at that time, I believed in it as much as I believed in anything. I have never been a bigot. There is nothing of the zealot in my nature. I inclined, however, more towards revolutionary ideas than to any others. [...]

On Easter Monday, 1911, I was addressing a meeting in the Park, and at the end of my speech I asked if anyone wished to ask any questions. This was a mere formality, as I had no wish to be bothered with questions. Questions break the spell of a meeting and do the speaker no good at collection-time. The crowd becomes so interested in the stupid questions – all questioners are stupid – they would not be questioners if they were not – that they forget all about the speaker's need to live. It was this kind of thing that first made me realize how callous and mean the people are generally who take an interest in economic, social, and political questions.

Naturally I did not welcome a question that came, on this occasion, from a young man in the crowd. I cut him off sharply so that I could get to the gate and collect my wages. The questioner, however, followed me out. I would have dismissed him as civilly as I could, but his appearance and manner were so likeable that I forgave him for asking the question and entered into conversation with him. He was a tall youth about my own age, with fair hair and blue eyes. He had a frank, open countenance with an attractive and friendly manner. He was dressed in rags. We chatted for a few minutes and then parted.

I have met so many people, most of them bores, that ordinarily I am only too anxious to forget fresh acquaintances. The trite remarks, commonplace observations, and the banal and stupid chatter of the thousands of people who have insisted on conversing with me outside the gates of Hyde Park have contributed substantially towards the ruin of my nervous system. It does not pay to be too ruthless with them when one is dependent upon them for a livelihood, but murder has often rattled through my brain while I have been under the harrow of their maddening conversation.

Above all I have always resented their vulgar and insensitive familiarity. I am never safe from molestation by these hollow-headed bores. In the bus, the street, the café, the train, even in the theatre, there is no guarantee that I shall not be set upon. The physical torture of replying to their utterly uninteresting comments upon things quite beyond their mental scope, but upon which they imagine themselves to be authorities, is refined. It is not enough that as a public speaker one must cope with financial insecurity and economic adversity, but one must withstand the bore, the boor, and the blockhead as well.

31
Patrick MacGill, *Children of the Dead End: The Autobiography of a Navvy*

(London: Herbert Jenkins, 1914). x, 305pp.; pp. 213–16.

If unskilled Irish migratory workers in twentieth-century Britain may be said to have anything so lofty as a literary laureate, then Patrick MacGill (1890–1963) has first claim to the title. Born to a desperately poor Donegal family, MacGill was hired out as a farm labourer while still a child and by the age of 15 was 'tatie-hoking' (digging potatoes) in Scotland. He subsequently worked as a navvy, railway platelayer and labourer on the construction of an aluminium smelter at Kinlochleven reservoir, until the favourable reception of his first volume of verse, *Gleanings from a Navvy's Scrapbook* (1910), led to a job with the London *Daily Express*. MacGill's journalistic career proved short-lived, however, and by the time *Children of the Dead End* appeared in March 1914 he was working as a librarian in Windsor Castle, under the supportive tutelage of Canon John Dalton. The book became an instant bestseller, though its critical and commercial success in England contrasted starkly with its hostile reception in culturally conservative Irish quarters, including MacGill's home town of Glenties.[1] Within months, he was serving with the London Irish Rifles in France, an experience he immediately drew upon in verse and fiction, notably in his war trilogy *The Amateur Army* (1915), *The Red Horizon* (1916) and *The Great Push* (1916). Although he continued to write prolifically, MacGill's popularity waned significantly in the post-war years. By the 1930s he had developed multiple sclerosis and was living in Florida with his wife and fellow author, Margaret Gibbons. His death in November 1963, within hours of the assassination of President John F. Kennedy, went unnoticed. Since 1981 Glenties has hosted an annual summer school named in his honour.

Children of the Dead End is the book that more than any other inaugurated the archetype of the poorly educated rural Irish migrant struggling to cope materially and psychologically with the disjunction between the economies and values of a traditional Catholic society and those of a modern, Protestant, industrialised one. Described by

---

[1] In *Heat the Furnace Seven Times More* (1967), discussed below, Patrick McGeown recalls making a literary pilgrimage to Glenties in the early 1950s and finding much local antipathy towards MacGill.

MacGill in his foreword as a tribute to 'the navvy; the life he leads, the dangers he dares, and the death he often dies', the book's vividness of description and emphasis on witness underwrite its credibility and engender a strong spirit of acceptance in the reader. This helps explain why the book has long been valued by historians as an indispensable source for Irish immigration to early twentieth-century Scotland, its status as fictionalised autobiography notwithstanding.[2] From a literary perspective, MacGill's casting of himself as a third-person protagonist, Dermod Flynn, can be viewed as an exemplary attempt by a working-class autodidact to negotiate the processes of authorship while faithfully narrating the truth of his own experience.[3] And while his novelistic imagination aestheticises experience throughout, the fictive elements of the narrative never undermine the text's claim to historical authenticity, which lies in the sociological and psychological precision of MacGill's prose, as illustrated by the following chapter, entitled 'De Profundis'. MacGill's influence on later migrant autobiographers is often overlooked. His testimonial aesthetic and incisive anti-capitalist critique provided imaginative sustenance and inspiration for Dónall Mac Amhlaigh, John B. Keane, Jim Phelan and Patrick McGeown, all of whom cite him as an exemplary pioneer in depicting a way of life that had never previously found expression. His authenticating example strengthened their sense of entitlement to write autobiographically and developed in them a belief in the inherent value of their own life experiences as a subject worthy of record and evaluation.

At that time there were thousands of navvies working at Kinlochleven waterworks. We spoke of waterworks, but only the contractors knew what the work was intended for. We did not know, and we did not care. We never asked questions concerning the ultimate issue of our labours, and we were not supposed to ask questions. If a man throws red muck over a wall to-day and throws it back again to-morrow, what the devil is it to him if he keeps throwing that same muck over the wall for the rest of his life, knowing not why nor wherefore, provided he gets paid sixpence an hour for his labour? There were so many tons of earth to be lifted and thrown somewhere else; we lifted them and threw them somewhere else: so many cubic yards of iron-hard rocks to be blasted and carried away; we blasted and carried them away, but never asked questions and never knew what results we were labouring to bring about. We turned the Highlands into a cinder-heap, and were as wise

---

[2] See Owen Dudley Edwards, 'Patrick MacGill and the making of a historical source: with a handlist of his works', *The Innes Review*, vol. 37, no. 2 (1986), pp. 73–99. Dudley Edwards is among those who posit a direct correlation between author and protagonist: ' "Flynn" is MacGill in his experience growing up in Donegal, being sent out to hire as a child labourer in Tyrone, migrating to agricultural work in Bute, tramping, working as a navvy at the Kinlochleven reservoir, becoming a writer and finding work as a journalist' (p. 74).

[3] For an alternative reading of MacGill's blurring of the line between memory and imagination, see Bryan Giemza, 'The Technique of Sorrow: Patrick MacGill and the American Slave Narrative', *New Hibernia Review/Iris Éireannach Nua*, vol. 7, no. 2 (Summer 2003), pp. 73–87.

at the beginning as at the end of the task. Only when we completed the job, and returned to the town, did we learn from the newspapers that we had been employed on the construction of the biggest aluminium factory in the kingdom. All that we knew was that we had gutted whole mountains and hills in the operations.

We toiled on the face of the mountain, and our provisions came up on wires that stretched from the summit to the depths of the valley below. Hampers of bread, casks of beer, barrels of tinned meat and all manner of parcels followed one another up through the air day and night in endless procession, and looked for all the world like great gawky birds which still managed to fly, though deprived of their wings.

The postman came up amongst us from somewhere every day, bringing letters from Ireland, and he was always accompanied by two policemen armed with batons and revolvers. The greenhorns from Ireland wrote home and received letters now and again, but the rest of us had no friends, or if we had we never wrote to them.

Over an area of two square miles thousands of men laboured, some on the day-shift, some on the night-shift, some engaged on blasting operations, some wheeling muck, and others building dams and hewing rock facings. A sort of rude order prevailed, but apart from the two policemen who accompanied the letter-carrier on his daily rounds no other minion of the law ever came near the place. This allowed the physically strong man to exert considerable influence, and fistic arguments were constantly in progress.

Sometimes a stray clergyman, ornamented with a stainless white collar, had the impudence to visit us and tell us what we should do. These visitors were most amusing, and we enjoyed their exhortations exceedingly. Once I told one of them that if he was more in keeping with the Workman whom he represented, some of the navvies stupider than myself might endure his presence, but that no one took any heed of the apprentice who dressed better than his Divine Master. We usually chased these faddists away, and as they seldom had courage equal to their impudence, they never came near us again.

There was a graveyard in the place, and a few went there from the last shift with the red muck still on their trousers, and their long unshaven beards still on their faces. Maybe they died under a fallen rock or broken derrick jib. Once dead they were buried, and there was an end of them.

Most of the men lifted their sub. every second day, and the amount left over after procuring food was spent in the whisky store or gambling-school. Drunkenness enjoyed open freedom in Kinlochleven. I saw a man stark naked, lying dead drunk for hours on a filthy muck-pile. No one was shocked, no one was amused, and somebody stole the man's clothes. When he became sober he walked around the place clad in a blanket until he procured a pair of trousers from some considerate companion.

I never stole from a mate in Kinlochleven, for it gave me no pleasure to thieve from those who were as poor as myself; but several of my mates had no compunction in relieving me of my necessaries. My three and sixpenny keyless watch was taken from my breast pocket one night when I was asleep, and my only belt disappeared mysteriously a week later. No man in the place save Moleskin Joe ever wore braces. I had only one shirt in my possession, but there were many people in the place who never had a shirt on their backs. Sometimes when the weather was good I washed my shirt, and I lost three, one after the other, when I hung them out to dry. I did not mind that very much, knowing well that it only passed to one of my mates, who maybe needed it more than I did. If I saw one of my missing shirts afterwards I took it from the man who wore it, and if he refused to give it to me, knocked him down and took it by force. Afterwards we bore one another no ill-will. Stealing is rife in shack, on road, and in model, but I have never known one of my kind to have given up a mate to the police. That is one dishonourable crime which no navvy will excuse.

As the days went on, I became more careless of myself, and I seldom washed. I became like my mates, like Moleskin, who was so fit and healthy, and who never washed from one year's end to another. Often in his old tin-pot way he remarked that a man could often be better than his surroundings, but never cleaner. 'A dirty man's the only man who washes,' he often said. When we went to bed at night we hid our clothes under the pillows, and sometimes they were gone in the morning. In the bunk beneath ours slept an Irishman named Ward, and to prevent them passing into the hands of thieves he wore all his clothes when under the blankets. But nevertheless, his boots were unlaced and stolen one night when he was asleep and drunk.

One favourite amusement of ours was the looting of provisions as they came up on the wires to the stores on the mountains. Day and night the hampers of bread and casks of beer were passing over our heads suspended in mid-air on the glistening metal strings. Sometimes the weighty barrels and cases dragged the wires downwards until their burdens rested on the shoulder of some uprising knoll. By night we sallied forth and looted all the provisions on which we could lay our hands. We rifled barrels and cases, took possession of bread, bacon, tea, and sugar, and filled our stomachs cheaply for days afterwards. The tops of fallen casks we staved in, and using our hands as cups drank of the contents until we could hold no more. Sometimes men were sent out to watch the hillocks and see that no one looted the grub and drink. These men were paid double for their work. They deserved double pay, for of their own accord they tilted the barrels and cases from their rests and kept them under their charge until we arrived. Then they helped us to dispose of the contents. Usually the watcher lay dead drunk beside his post in the morning. Of course he got his double pay.

32

Jim Phelan, *The Name's Phelan: The First Part of the Autobiography of Jim Phelan*

(London: Sidgwick & Jackson, 1948). viii, 298pp.; pp. 192–8.

Jim Phelan (1895–1966) spent his childhood years in Inchicore, Dublin, where his wayward personality was evident from an early age. His formal education ended when he was ten, after which he worked for brief periods as a telegram boy, an apprentice blacksmith and a fit-up actor before devoting himself to a life of vagrancy, tramping his way through Ireland, America, France, Scotland and England. In 1923 he was involved in a shooting incident in Liverpool that led to his wrongful conviction for the murder of a post office clerk. Having had his death sentence commuted to penal servitude for life, Phelan spent over 13 years in various English prisons, during which time his desire to become a writer crystallised. From the late 1930s onwards he published prolifically, moving between fiction, scriptwriting and journalism. The twin themes of imprisonment and vagrancy inform his best work, which includes the novels *Lifer* (1938) and *Wagon Wheels* (1951) and the more overtly autobiographical *Jail Journal* (1940) and *We Follow the Roads* (1949). In *The Name's Phelan* he sets out to tell 'the story of how one writer came to be', keeping 'apologetics or evasions' to a minimum. The portrait that emerges is of an archetypal wanderer for whom 'every place is a starting-point'. He begins his autobiography by frankly stating: 'I am a tramp. That is almost all my story. Now I shall write a long and, I hope, an interesting book about the things I have done. But at the end I shall only have amplified the statement in that short line.' Just as MacGill wrote to educate readers with his insider account of navvying, Phelan provides first-hand insights into the subculture of the 'roadster', often with a certain braggadocio, in order to correct 'the slobbering falsities of the sentimentalists', as he puts it in the following excerpt from Chapter 15.

To this day I am proud of the fact that, steering by nothing but instinct and the sky, asking no questions after the first few had shown me that no Londoner knows anything whatever about London, I went straight to the place where the main north-west road forks off.

There were then no motorists' signposts such as one knows to-day. All the others were worse than useless. London is some twenty-four miles across, from north-west to south-east.

No citizen of London knows anything about main roads – why should he? A stranger might walk for a week, or even for a month, through the endless rows of houses, without ever finding an escape from the labyrinth.

By the shortest road, there are thirteen miles of streets between Seven Dials and Barnet, where Watling Street[1] strikes off towards Chester and the north-west. I might have ridden a tram for much of the way – if I had known even one name of a place. Not knowing one, I padded on, with an occasional sniff at a street-crossing, and came before midday to Barnet and Watling Street.

There was a most definite thrill in passing the last house, seeing the green road ahead. This in spite of the fact that I liked London. Roads always look better. I was going to Dublin, and it might have been at the next cross-roads from the way I stepped up that first green mile.

Within the hour I had made friends with a tramp, the talk with whom slowed my gait to a normal padding. This was the first vagrant with whom I had ever talked much, although I had seen dozens in Cork and Marseilles, scores in New Orleans and Waterford. My first venture, with the degenerate on the Southern Pacific, had prejudiced me. This Watling Street man was different.

In the very beginning he attempted to beg cigarettes, then struggled hard for a drink, or even a few coppers, but I met each request with a nonchalant and obvious lie, to the effect that I was penniless and would myself be glad of a little assistance. Thereafter we got on well.

It may be taken as an axiom that no person who gives a tramp anything, however trifling, can hope to be treated with human respect or met on a basis of equality. (As well buy expensive drinks for a hostess in a night-club and then expect her to be friendly, or give one sausage from a string to a prowling dog and hope he will ignore the remainder.)

My road-companion was called Toaster Dick, and at first sight appeared to be about sixty. He wore long hair and beard, had the old-roadster crouch, and behaved in general like an ancient, but after the first few minutes I knew he was a young man. From his talk – of having joined the army early in the Boer War – I reckoned him to be not more than thirty-five.

Toaster and I made friends – as far as tramps do, which meant that we agreed to keep together for a while. The arrangement delighted me because, in a vague way, ever since New Orleans, I had been hoping to know a real tramp. Two others came my way that first morning – I had a worthy trio of masters, but the lesson was brief.

Near a village called Mimms, where a narrow by-lane came in from Elstree, Toaster hung about for a few minutes, without explanation. From his glances

---

[1] Name given to a Roman road running from London through St Albans in Hertfordshire to Wroxeter in Shropshire.

up the lane one would have thought he had an appointment, and that his man was late.

Less than a quarter of an hour after we had arrived, two tramps came down the lane from Elstree. Toaster talked, and I learnt their names – Joe Ockley and Pimple Simmons.

Toaster and they had not met for nine weeks. All three had arrived at the lane-corner within fifteen minutes of one another. Pride was mine, even for being allowed to witness such a meeting.

First I had not wanted to be a genius. Now I was not even sure that I wanted to be a writer.

When the boys had left, down the by-lanes for Enfield and Essex, Toaster suddenly seemed to become weary of me. All our projected double-travelling had gone by the board already. Somehow I had done wrong, or Ockley and Pimple had suspected or feared me, and passed on the feeling, for Toaster made flimsy excuse to turn off on a by-road.

I never saw him again. But I met Joe Ockley many times, wrote a story about him years ago, an article about him years later, and tried to sell a photo-feature based on his life when I met him, twenty-nine years after that first meeting, still walking down Watling Street.

He was an ancient-looking, ragged, whiskered man that first day. Either he is now over a hundred years old, or his whiskers were even better camouflage than Toaster Dick's.

Up the road to St. Albans, after my 'friend' had left, I fell in with another friendly tramp, Irish I believed, although he said he came from Liverpool. We also were to go together up Watling Street, I to join him on the listin-leg after we had done a bit of parson-thumping at a nearby place called Colney.

It sounded far more attractive to me than the dressing-room talk of the fitups, and I know no higher praise.

The parson-thumping, as I had expected, meant scientific fadging at vicarages. Near Colney there were three, all good according to Jemmy Suttle, my new mentor. He went into the first, and emerged in three minutes with a sixpence. After a decent interval I opened the garden gate and went up the path.

Unfortunately I did not know the tramps' first rule – to have a story ready and be prepared to make instant adjustments. When a pleasant-faced woman came to the door I simply goggled. She stared. So did I. She spoke first.

Then and there I learnt my own particular variant of the tramps' first rule, which I here pass on, for latter-day roadsters and for all whom it may concern. It is far better to let the other person tell the story for you. Nearly everyone wants to.

Nowadays I do not tell stories for sixpences. I sell them to film-producers or editors. But the principle is the same. Half a dozen times I have evolved and sold a good film story, a score of times I have polished – and peddled – a feature article, all on the interruptions and emendations of the person I set out to impress.

That day at the vicarage the woman smiled at my awkwardness, put me at my ease, asked if I was hungry, and gave me my sixpence. At the other two vicarages I said little or nothing either.

Jemmy had warned me at the last place not to say I knew any clergyman whatever, anywhere, especially at my home, as 'the bloke puts the pump on then.' I said practically nothing, and got my sixpences.

Coming into St. Albans, Jemmy popped aside twice, at large houses, each time returning with a shilling, each time announcing that the houses were 'no bottle' for me. I did not insist on proof of my incapacity. But I felt hurt just the same. It would have been interesting to try.

We stayed at a lodging-house, where we paid sixpence each and shared a bed after we had eaten our supper in the common kitchen. There were five other tramps staying that night, and one man who was contemptuously dismissed by Suttle as a young mug, with the emphasis on the adjective, although the man was nearing fifty.

Next morning after breakfast, out in the streets of St. Albans, Jemmy said the K.R.R.[2] would be best for me. The depot was away in Hampshire, and I could hammer the leg right up the road, maybe to Brum, as the scream would not be out for more than four days. He would do the Tillery for the same reason, and we could keep together until the scream was ahead.

If it had been Greek, or Gaelic, or even Toulonese French, I might have extracted some sense from the explanation. As it was, I did not understand one word. Wherefore I nodded comprehension, grunted agreement, made wise faces, and started slowly up Watling Street. Jemmy explained that the office was the other way, in the market-place.

Only when we reached the market-place, only when we came to the office itself, the wealth-project made itself clear. Apparently it was a well-practised branch of craft, for Suttle seemed quite at home with the details. We were to join the British Army, take our few days' advance-pay, desert, and go to the next town at once, repeat the process there, and go repeating it up Watling Street until things got too hot for us. That was the listin-leg.

Turning down the nearest lane, with a muttered excuse about finding a lavatory, I hurried away. In roundabout fashion I got back on to Watling Street again.

Then I went fast, up through Hockliffe and Dunstable, to keep ahead of Jemmy and his own particular 'scream.' I was ashamed. Also I was disappointed with Jemmy and with myself. But I could see I had no future on the listin-leg. I had not the necessary courage!

Up the road I met and spoke to many tramps (they averaged one per five miles or thereabouts), but kept away from anything like companionship. The

---

[2] The King's Royal Rifle Corps, a British army regiment, then based in Winchester.

second night up from St. Albans I stayed at Towcester, having covered more than forty miles in the two days.

No 'working' tramp, I found out, would attain one-third of the speed. Logically enough, I suppose. The sportsman passes many rabbit-warrens to reach the place where he is licensed to shoot. The pot-hunter stops, because he is on business, to interview the first rabbits that show.

At Towcester (it is pronounced Toaster, like my ancient-seeming friend's nickname) there were half a dozen tramps in the lodging-house, and I listened eagerly to the technical talk. Besides detailed discussions of territory and prospects, there were also statements of rights, of pre-emption, of free and untrammelled choice as to direction and terrain.

The frankness and freedom, the fearless and unhampered assertion of manly right, would have delighted one of the people who write vagrant verses and romances of the road.

Thus, a flimsy-looking tramp with a cough and a whine said he was going to work the back road from Towcester to Northampton. A bulky man with an under-slung jaw said threateningly that anyone who didn't want their guts kicked out better keep off the Northampton road next morning. Thereafter it was fairly and democratically agreed in amity and comradeship that the bulky man was going to Northampton – first.

Being first was apparently important. Many people will not tolerate two tramps in a day, may even set the dogs on the second. Having read much about the brotherhood of the road, and having seen my moron from Houston, I liked those discussions. The reality was far better at bottom, and far more attractive than the slobbering falsities of the sentimentalists.

Partly because I was not going anywhere, partly because the information that I was going straight on had eliminated me as a possible competitor, partly because I could have knocked out any of the six, I enjoyed those Towcester discussions.

The grey-haired young mug who had been at St. Albans was here again at Towcester, although I had not seen him on the road. He was a pariah.

The tramps ignored him, or treated him with open contempt. His clothes were searched, in the common bedroom, before he was fairly asleep. He did not dare any objections, and was off on the road at dawn.

Like many people, I had taken it for granted that the average tramp was an itinerant out-of-work tradesman or labourer. The writers had misled me rather badly. Because the timid man was the only work-seeker of our company.

All the way up Watling Street I enjoyed myself. (Tramps go up Watling Street: motorists go down it.) I had one lift from Weedon to Cannock in a big furniture-lorry, and one from Stoke-on-Trent almost to Warrington with a cattle-wagon, shortening my journey by more than a week. For the rest I walked, fadged, parson-thumped, and stayed at tramps' doss-houses.

Long before Warrington, no one would have taken me for anything but a tramp. Even a very young sociologist would have hesitated before adding me to the unemployment statistics.

The gait and the outlook of the roadster were mine, and I liked them. Mainly because I thought they were not mine, because I wore them as an amusing disguise, I liked them.

North from the Potteries there were many genuine work-seekers on the road, but they always went past with some shamefaced, awkward, crudely phrased question as to where there was work or whether such and such a place was good for employment. I did not know and could only say so. The regular tramps hardly bothered to say as much.

The work-seeker is always called a young mug, whatever his age, until the day when he abandons hope, becomes a beggar in desperation, turns tramp by chance, learns to live on the road.

Some of them never learn, become loathsome objects of dirt and disease, infesting the tidy roads and destroying a decent tramp's chance of food or coin by revolting and nauseating the housewives.

They make themselves a nuisance to the police in the towns, frighten the children in the villages, dirty the doss-houses, and depress the company at night by croaking their eternal wretched queries about work.

The sociologists think those people are tramps. The tramps hardly admit them to be human. My vote, if I have one, goes to the tramps.

33
Patrick McGeown, *Heat the Furnace Seven Times More*

With an introduction by Asa Briggs (London: Hutchinson, 1967). 192pp.; pp. 15–16; 29–32.

Patrick McGeown was born in 1897 in the industrial Scottish town of Craigneuk to immigrant Armagh parents. As the title of his autobiography suggests, his working life was spent in the steel industry, first in Craigneuk, where his father was a furnaceman, and later in Wigan and the Ancoats district of Manchester. He was also a keen student of WEA courses, which led him to the view that every steelworks should have a library, 'as centrally situated as the work's canteen, and used as frequently'. The documentary realism of his account of the different phases of his working life makes his memoir a valuable source for the social history of twentieth-century steel production, replete with insights into differential pay grades and occupational hierarchies. However, in contrast to Patrick MacGill and Alice Foley, McGeown does not represent industrial toil as a wholly alienating experience; to him, skilled labour can also empower: 'To the first-hand melter there was great satisfaction as he watched the metal stream from his furnace into the waiting ladle. He had an awareness of creation; seven or eight hours previously this surging white-hot liquid had been one hundred tons of solid limestone, steel scrap, and hot iron.'

McGeown's craft pride coexisted with a lifelong literary ambition: 'For me there was no prouder title, nothing I wanted more than to be a writing man.' He eventually realised his ambition by becoming a freelance writer for radio and magazines after his retirement in 1963. In a 1965 *New Statesman* article he characterised himself as a 'wordster' who 'sits at his desk in a quiet room and chases every prize, no matter how humble, with his one-fingered, hammer-stroked typewriting'.[1] Success proved elusive, however, as did stylistic mastery: 'I have a habit of throwing a handful of commas in the air and letting them land where they may.'[2] While chapter titles such as 'The Art in Manual Labouring' and 'Nightshift Moods' signify the centrality of work to McGeown's autobiographical self-identity, he also writes perceptively about his second-generation

---

[1] Patrick McGeown, 'The Wordster', *New Statesman*, 28 May 1965, p. 839.
[2] Ibid., p. 840.

Irish upbringing in turn-of-the-century Scotland in early chapters entitled 'Where I was born' and 'School', from which the following extracts are taken.

There was nothing lovely about Craigneuk. It was, and is, about twelve miles from Glasgow, and a centre of heavy industry.

Steelworks, ironworks, coalmines, are not beautiful but they have their moments. I liked Craigneuk, I thought it was a grand place and I liked the name of it too. I was sure there was a history in it but I never found out. I was sure too that it had been a beautiful place before the advent of slag tips and belching stacks. Even my uncritical eyes could see that.

That was before the Irish and the Poles and the Lithuanians arrived. Most of them penniless and none of them welcomed by the Scots. Only the most broadminded of heavenly beings could have welcomed that lot. I don't know about the Poles and the Lithuanians but the Irish had been coming from the end of the eighteenth century. The first Roman Catholic church was opened in Paisley in 1808, and the first Roman Catholic school was opened in Glasgow in 1817.[3] They were built by the pennies of the Irish immigrants. There were 120,000 Irish born residents in Scotland in 1841, and they were still packing them in, in overcrowded ships from Londonderry and Belfast. The ships *Londonderry* and *Thistle*, both less than 300 tons, often carried 1,700 people at a time. Even in good weather the journey would be uncomfortable. It was very cheap, sometimes as low as sixpence per head, and there was no Avilion at the end of the journey. Most of them landed up in disease-ridden Glasgow slums, where 60 per cent of the population lived in one-roomed homes, and where in 1832 more than 10,000 people died of Asiatic Cholera.

No wonder the Scots didn't think much of the Irish, or their Roman Catholic religion. It was no consolation that many immigrants were not Catholics, but Orangemen. It only added to bloodshed and distress when the rival factions met on St. Patrick's Day and on the 12th July, the celebration of the Battle of the Boyne.

Still they were there, and the Scots had to learn to live with them. They had even to tolerate a lot of inter-marrying. For it wasn't unnatural for a Scots Jeannie to fall in love with an Irish Paddy, even if her Paw and Maw referred to him as, 'That Irish Pig.'

Ah well! The Scots are no' sae bad. No sae bad ata! I liked them fine and I was an Irish Paddy too, and a Catholic to boot. To boot? That rings a bell! By jings it does, as we used to say in Craigneuk long ago. [...]

Craigneuk was just as good a place for a kid to find fun as anywhere else in Scotland. We played football all the year round, we knew no close season and we had never heard tell of cricket; we stole strawberries from the fruit

---

[3] St Mirin's church in Paisley was the first Catholic church to be built in Scotland since the Reformation. A number of Catholic schools were built in Glasgow from 1817 onwards.

farms on the Clydeside; we bathed in the Calder River, and we played tig and hopscotch in the gaslit main street evenings. We stole empty bottles from the Beehive and we sold them back to it to get money to enter the geggies. That was the name for the travelling shows who set up their marquees and stayed as long as it was profitable. The fee was a penny for children and twopence for grown-ups. We patronised the ice cream palaces, they were the best lit, brightest, cleanest shops in the 'Neuk' and entirely run by Italians. It was in one of them that the Cowie Square Wanderers Football Club held their meetings; I was left half and club secretary.

We played on a strip of land divided from the back of the steelworks by a wire fence, and oh the joy of starting a match on a bright crispy, winter day! Our jerseys, when we managed to get some, were red, a compromise; the Irish section wouldn't wear the blue of Scotland, and the Scots wouldn't wear the green of Ireland. We didn't say it outwardly but we were delicately intercepting the implacable bigotry of our parents. A year or two later and it would seep through our systems too, some would adopt the Glasgow Rangers religion and like myself others would be steeped in the Glasgow Celtic religion.

To this day the Glasgow Rangers football club have never signed on a man who is a Roman Catholic. Glasgow Celtic are a trifle more broadminded, if the Protestants are good enough players then the Celts will have them. I remember them signing Billy Hogg, a non-Catholic and an ex-Ranger player. 'Ye kin hiv 'im,' sniffed our neighbour, Sanny Morton. 'He's only a hog anyway, efter this he'll be an Irish pig.'

Being an Irish Pig was something we at St Pats graduated to. While we were there we were promising sucklings, and once out in the world we showed 'em, or tried to. I can't say I tried very much myself, I left it to the spirited ones; myself, I was a shocking coward. The one time I all but broke from my craven spirit, proved me to be the complete coward. Myself and Paddy Murphy were set on by three Scots lads, one tackled the smaller Paddy, and two tackled me. I was anxious to shine in front of young Paddy, he was tough, confident, and rich. His parents ran a grocery store, his pockets were always filled with stolen sweets, and he actually came to school on a bike, the only one among us who could afford one.

I walloped away that day gloriously, and it pleased me even more to take punishment unflinchingly. I was right out of this world, the equal for once of fine tough fellows like young Paddy Murphy. As I slammed away, it encouraged me to hear cries for mercy coming from the other fight, and I told myself that Paddy had torn his opponent in two. I wasn't surprised, for Paddy I believed was terribly tough, come to think of it, so was I, and fit company for heroes. I snatched a moment to look across at the remains of young Murphy's opponent, and to receive my accolade, and maybe a bit of help in my own affair. To my horror it was Paddy who was howling, and the other fellow was doing the murdering.

My spirit crumbled like a handful of crushed biscuits, my opponents pummelled me till they were tired. The other one let go Murphy so they could finish me off. When at last I could scramble up my opponents had gone, and Murphy was still lamenting. He made me so mad that I nearly refused a bar of plain chocolate which he'd pinched from his old man's store.

The Murphy family were the only Irish I knew who had pulled themselves out of the pick and shovel range. Indeed they hadn't travelled far, for the business was teetering on the unsteadfast footing of a spear. I heard my father say so to my mother, only not knowing Shakespeare he put it a different way. For success Mr Murphy needed rid of two things, one was young Paddy who stole half the stock, and the other was Mrs Murphy who gave the other half away. She had a kind heart and as most of the customers had no money and consciences to match, the kind heart ticked while the tick was mounting.

My mother was always a paying customer, and an occasional ready money one after my father was promoted to third-hand melter. More than once Mrs Murphy confided to my mother that she would love young Paddy to study for the cloth. He never did, not her way, but he did have an affinity to cloth for later on he became a traveller in suit lengths and silks. He was a real traveller too, for he ranged the British Isles. His method was to buy cheap material in warehouses, wrap it in a piece of canvas, and then dressed in a blue jersey, reefer jacket, and glazed peak cap, he traded in the Irish clubs and pubs. He was always the sailor newly off ship and giving away bargains in smuggled goods. Some fell for it unknowingly, but others bought knowingly and willingly and with a certain admiration.

Paddy Murphy was only one of many operators in Scotland and Ireland; many of them originated in Crossmaglen, a quiet little place not far from my parents home in Co Armagh. Their activities were celebrated in song, 'Crossmaglen, where there's more rogues than honest men.'

But for the daily experience of jeers, and sometimes stones, as we passed Craigneuk Public School, I could have imagined I was at school in Ireland. Whether we were Ireland born, or first, second, or third generation Irish, we all boys and girls, had names like the map of Ireland. If the Protestant pupils of Craigneuk Public had to be believed, our faces were like the map of Ireland too. Not being brave made me seek allies past the Public school, and that was little trouble. All I did was lay in wait for Tommy McGuinness, Tommy Kelly, Peter Scullion, and Harry McInally. It preserved me physically and morally for there was safety in numbers, and a coward could pass muster in a crowd.

34

Pat O'Mara, *The Autobiography of a Liverpool Irish Slummy*

(London: Martin Hopkinson, 1934). 307pp.; pp. 74–6; 84–9.

Born in a Liverpool slum tenement to a first-generation Irish mother and a third-generation Irish father, Pat O'Mara (1901–1983) grew up in a multiethnic melting-pot, surrounded by 'Negroes, Chinese, Mulattoes, Filipinos, almost every nationality under the sun, most of them boasting white wives and large half-caste families'. His vivid recollection of his abjectly poor childhood reads like an Edwardian version of Frank McCourt's *Angela's Ashes* (1996), complete with violent, alcoholic father, pious mother, doomed infants and serial evictions, though without McCourt's self-pitying sentimentality. O'Mara escaped this brutalised environment by signing up as an ordinary seaman on the eve of the First World War. In 1920 he emigrated to America and eventually settled in Baltimore, where he was working as a taxi-driver at the time his autobiography appeared. The success of his novel, *Taxi Heaven* (1932), encouraged the New York Vanguard Press to publish his picaresque autobiography in 1933; it appeared in Britain a year later. In it, O'Mara portrays himself as an opportunistic survivor, though unlike other working-class accounts of slum life the narrative lacks a political subtext, least of all a socialist critique. As a self-styled 'paradoxical' Irishman, O'Mara is notably more willing than either Tom Barclay or Joseph Keating to acknowledge the composite, indeterminate nature of his cultural identity, which he shows fracturing under the twin pressures of an imperialist English Catholic education and an Irish nationalist upbringing, rendering him unable to identify unequivocally with either country. What we find articulated in the text, therefore, is a hybridised version of belonging in which Irishness is mutually constituted with Britishness. As the following extract shows, however, O'Mara ultimately hierarchises his multiple identities in an analogous manner to Keating, placing primary emphasis upon his Irishness, a self-identification that was underlined by his choice of title for the follow-up volume, *Irish Slummy in America* (1935).

St. Peter's school in Seel Street was, in a way, a new vista opening in my life. Here was an English school filled mainly with Irish-Catholic boys. But the tutors in this school, though all of them were Catholic, had been trained in England and all their teaching smacked of this English training. The Empire and the sacredness of its preservation ran through every text-book like a *liet-motif*. Our navy and the necessity of keeping Britannia ruling the waves is another indelible mark left in my memory – though the reason for this was never satisfactorily explained. Pride in our vast and far-flung colonies and the need for their protection and preservation were emphasized, as was the confidence that in any given crisis the colonies and the motherland stand as one.

The British always won wars – not the English, but the British – giving the impression that we were all more or less brothers under the skin, the Irish, the English, the Welsh and the Scotch. We were the kingpins; and we were always in the right – these are the straight, patriotic impressions that remain. And then came religion – and that was something else again. Oliver Cromwell might have been a hero in Protestant St. Michael's but not in our school. And so, with forthright pastors like Father Toomey, it wasn't long before religion got to race, and from race to definite biases .... The best I can say is that what I derived from my elementary English-Irish schooling was an intense love for the British Empire and an equally intense hatred for England as opposed to Ireland.

Our mothers and fathers, of course, were unequivocal in their atti-tude – destroy England, no less! But we children at school, despite the intense religious atmosphere of the Catholic school, were rather patriotized and Britishized – until we got back to our shacks, where we were sternly Irishized .... The paradox has remained in my make-up for years – the sound of a patriotic Irish air will make me want to get out my shillalah for the old wrongs of Ireland; but the moment the music is over, common sense will warn me to put it back. My mental prejudices, today as an adult, work some-thing like this; ferocious, sacrificial Irish-Catholic (die for Ireland's freedom) first; ferocious sacrificial Britisher second; and patient, wondering dreamer third. This three-way ticket may seem silly to more civilized people, but as long as it is true, open confession, as my poor benighted father used to say, is good for the soul. And what is true of me is true certainly of most slummy Irish-Catholic 'Britishers.'

Among the active members of our gang were Joe Manassi, a belliger-ent, stocky boy of Italian parentage; Harold May, Protestant, very English and quiet; Johnny Mangan, heavy set, Irish, belligerent; Johnny Ford, the same; Henry Roche, wiry, belligerent, Irish but no relation to me; my cousin Bernard Roche, thin, quiet, a true fighter; Frankie Roza, half-caste Protestant Manilla boy, who played the concertina and was the favourite of the gang; Jackie (Quantino) Sanchez, fiery yet amiable Spanish boy, whose mother kept the big Spanish boarding house at the corner of Corn-wallis Street and Park Lane; 'Lepsey' Phillips, Protestant boy – mother, a very belligerent gypsy, and father, Irish – a quick tempered boy; Jackie Oldham, dare-devil and English; Freddie Seegar, comedian, of German-Irish parents, lazy and improvident; and a waif known to us all only as 'Mickey' – an up-country boy who had drifted into Liverpool and slept at the Working Boy's Home. The three Protestant members (Protestant only at the insistence of their parents) attended St. Michael's Protestant school in Pitt Street. This was our 'gang', and our 'corner' was the empty house in White Street at Pitt, opposite Mrs. Mallin's pub, until Aeroplane Joe, the bobby who wouldn't let us play pitch and toss, the war and death broke us up. [...]

Whenever we had money, Ted Heaton's baths in Cornwallis Street, in lieu of the docks, was our favourite spot. Here all the school speed trials were held; here the swimming team to compete with other swimming teams in the Empire was selected. As in the case of the twopence to admit me to the Palais de Luxe, I used somehow to corral twopence (most of the time from Jackie Sanchez) for these baths and stay there as long as my strength held out. It was a dirty place for dirty boys – though not nearly so dirty as the Gore-Street baths in the south end. Sometimes this feeling of dirty water in our mouths and eyes would send us scurrying to the rear of the place where we could steal a surreptitious smoke.

In these impromptu symposiums the subject of conversation was almost invariably our fathers. Mothers were insignificant – it was the daddy that counted. Could he swim? Could he fight? Was he big? What was his history and background?

Joe Manassi would say proudly: 'My daddy's an Italian and he can talk Italian!'

Lepsey, the dissenter, would retort, quietly vicious: 'My mother's a gypsy!'

'Yes, but what's your daddy?'

'He's a gypsy, too – an Irish gypsy!' Everyone would want to laugh, but no one dared, for Lepsey, not realizing the humor of his statement, was there to back it up.

Somebody would ask Roza, 'Frankie, is your father a Nigger?'

And Frankie would reply proudly: 'No, he's a Filipino, and he used to be a cowboy ...'

A question would be asked of Jackie Sanchez whether or not there were cowboys in Spain and Jackie would reply proudly that there were – that Spain wasn't far from the United States and the cowboys often rode over there. Freddie Seegar bragged about the superiority of the Germans as sailors (his deceased father was German) and almost got to blows with Jacko Oldham who averred that the English were the best sailormen; but a few moments later, under the belligerent stares of us Irish risen now in a bloc, he tempered the English down to the 'British'. Mickey wasn't at these swimming symposiums; he had to be out on the look-out for work during the day – his understanding with the Working Boy's Home.

The get-together usually ended with the St. Peter's Catholic gang turning on our three willing-to-be Catholic pals and asking them in bluffing belligerent tone whether or not they were I or O (Irish or Orange; the challenge to strangers on St. Patrick's Day), and although they invariably gave us the desired answer, 'I', we would pick them up and throw them into the pool – religion forgotten.

I got my first taste of actual religious battle strangely enough not on St. Patrick's Day but on the twelfth of July or, as we were raised to call it, 'King Billy's Day', the day on which the Protestant boys sung:

> 'St Paddy was a Bastard,
> St Paddy was a thief,
> And he came to our house
> And stole a lump of meat'.

Instead of confining our efforts to our own neighbourhood this day, Joe Manassi suggested going down toward Netherfield Road to witness the Orangeman's parade and (bettering our elders) to do our bit toward making it a failure. Mickey had just put in an appearance at the corner and, upon hearing the suggestion, vanished – afraid of being ousted from the Working Boy's Home if discovered on such an errand. Harold May, Frankie Roza and Lepsey Phillips were, of course, kept indoors. It was a long way over, but the rest of us made it mostly by swinging on to the tail of tramcars and the back of floats pulled by galloping horses. I think we were all more or less tremu-lous heroes when we got within the enemy's gates and I know by the time we reached the start of the parade (George Wise's Protestant Reformed Church in Netherfield Road) and perceived just what we were up against, we rather repented our daring.

A huge crowd of our worst enemies (the 'O's') with bands and banners carrying inscriptions that made our blood boil, surged around us. Orange everywhere and not a bit of *green*! I had never known there were so many enthusiastic Protestants. I had always been brought up in the belief that Protestantism was a dying cult, and its adherents cowards, easily frightened; but this mob up here, led by that magnificent white horse bearing a little boy dressed as a perfect duplicate of Prince William, didn't look frightened at all. Presently the bands flared up and the horde headed down Netherfield Road; we straggled along, in the rear, fearful lest we be discovered. Down Netherfield Road the procession marched, turning into London Road.

'Are they going to Scotland Road, Joe?' I asked Manassi, fearful and won-dering what awful calamity must occur if they touched this stronghold of the 'I's'.

'I hope they bloody well do!' said Joe grimly, disclosing a brick hidden beneath his coat. 'They'll get "what for" then! I'm going to fling this brick at that bloody kid on the horse!'

But the parade very discreetly kept away from Scotland Road, executing a nice detour at London Road and Lime Street and heading then toward Parliament Street and Knowsley Park. Here we decided to leave them, for so far we had escaped detection and none of us, I think, was brave enough at the moment to continue on into the vastnesses of Protestant Knowsley Park. But just as we were about to escape into Lime Street, the parade stopped. The bands became silent. We pressed forward to see the nature of the trouble and, getting to the front, were astounded to see a little old chip-chopper we all knew from the South End holding her skirts sky high (disclosing a fine pair of green drawers), and shrieking defiantly: 'Here's a "Downey" bird' (Catholic Bishop Downey of Liverpool) as she danced slowly and defiantly backward.[1]

Our enthusiasm was inflamed to such a pitch that we yelled as one, 'Good on yer, missis!' and instantly we were set upon by the Protestant youths in the parade. I never found out how the brave little woman of the green drawers fared, but our gang in its entirety was booted all over the place. I think before the boots stopped kicking they had us all singing with the rest of the stopped parade, 'We are the sons of Billy and to hell with Popery!' But after the parade moved on and we gathered ourselves together, one by one we muttered the old refrain:

'King Billy's mother runs a whorehouse in Hell ….'

I should add, in all fairness, that the Protestant paraders, unlike our crowd on the seventeenth of March, weren't really looking for battle; and if our crowd had only used half so much prudence as they, there wouldn't have been any. One day, however, the opposition did make a serious mistake. Instead of the usual route of march, which went across the Everton valley, they detoured into Shaw Street and past St. Francis Catholic Church where at that moment a very pious congregation of Irish Catholics were witnessing the ordination of three young priests.

The flaunting Protestant banners drew alongside the church at the very moment when the Catholic crowd surged out of it. Bedlam was the result. The little child who impersonated King Billy on his white charger had his head staved in with a brick, falling off the horse bleeding and screaming with pain. As long as it lasted it was a gruesome sight, with the women shrieking and the yell 'Police! Police!' in the air and the poor bobbies being thrown helplessly from one side to the other. Our crowd did itself full justice, especially Jacko Oldham, who wound up with two 'O' boys' shirts under his arm as souvenirs. We all had souvenirs, I think – watches, caps, handkerchiefs and other articles pilfered from fallen foes. The Rose Hill lock-up was overcrowded that night.

---

[1] Kilkenny-born Richard Joseph Downey (1881–1953) was appointed Archbishop of Liverpool in 1928, becoming, at 47, the world's youngest Catholic archbishop.

35
Bill Naughton, *Saintly Billy: A Catholic Boyhood*

(Oxford: Oxford University Press, 1988). 219pp.; pp. 56–9.

Although he is primarily remembered as an English writer, Bill Naughton's (1910–1992) Catholic Irish upbringing forms an important part of his literary sensibility. Naughton was born in Ballyhaunis, County Mayo, to impoverished parents who emigrated to Bolton in 1914. He left school at 14 to work in a local cotton mill and subsequently held a succession of labouring and driving jobs before moving to London in the early 1940s, where he was a wartime conscientious objector. Having long struggled – in an almost classically working-class fashion – to get into print, Naughton had his first short story published in the *London Evening News* in 1943. The success of his debut novel, the autobiographical *A Roof Over Your Head* (1945), gave him the confidence to write full-time, and throughout the 1950s he produced a steady stream of short stories for the magazine market. But it was as a playwright that Naughton made his greatest impact, the trilogy *All in Good Time* (1963), *Alfie* (1963) and *Spring and Port Wine* (1964) establishing him as a shrewd chronicler of northern English working-class life. Naughton continued to write plays and fiction following his move to the Isle of Man in 1968, but his best late work is contained in his autobiographical trilogy, *On the Pig's Back* (1987), *Saintly Billy* (1988) and *Neither Use Nor Ornament* (1995), which is replete with vividly recalled incident and acutely observed social detail.

The desire to dispel pejorative misconceptions lies at the heart of Naughton's aesthetic; he was appalled to discover that 'almost every portrayal of working-class life and people that I read was a travesty. No wonder the different classes had such absurd notions of how one another lived.'[1] This corrective impulse coexists with a retrospective desire to reclaim that which was lost as a result of his childhood removal from the west of Ireland. The first two volumes of the trilogy are particularly compelling exercises in redemptive recollection, wherein Naughton seeks to recover a living continuity with his childhood self by reconfiguring his life-story around his fragmentary memories of being uprooted. This primary event fundamentally conditions his interpretation of his past, so that dislocation is portrayed as initiating the slow erosion of his organic cultural identity. The result is a marked duality of autobiographical vision, whereby

---

[1] Bill Naughton, *On the Pig's Back: An Autobiographical Excursion* (Oxford: Oxford University Press, 1987), p. 34.

Ireland is idealised as an imaginary homeland of utopian self-fulfilment, the antithesis of a self-annihilating England. But as the following extract shows, the forces of anglicisation complicated this duality, causing young Bill to develop a cultural inferiority complex about his Irish heritage, the corollary of which was an envious regard for the perceived self-possession of his English friends. That such conditioning left its imprint on Naughton's imagination is evidenced by his comparative analysis of 'the nature of the Celt and that of the Anglo-Saxon' – terms freighted with racial implications – which confers superiority upon the English and abjection upon the Irish in a manner that echoes the Celticism of Matthew Arnold.

Even as a small boy I was seldom unaware of how vulnerable we Irish were. Although we had a good family sense, which was comforting, we had only a remote feeling of belonging, since we were aliens. That was a feeling I never lost. The attitude towards the Irish in those days, when Ireland was part of Great Britain, and Britain had a vast empire, was different from that of today, although more than a trace of it may remain. The Irish – like many other nations and races – were looked down upon. Nor could one blame the English, since it could hardly be otherwise. At school the huge map of the world would be spread on the blackboard, the vast British Empire marked in red, and Miss Newsham with her long cane would point out the many and various colonies, dependencies, and other possessions, and explain how on the Empire the sun could never set, since it stretched around the globe. I would watch my mates staring agog, as though asking, *'Dominion over palm and pine* – am I an' mi' mum an' dad an' mi Aunt Flo' an' our Sarah Jane included?' Even the Lancashire little-piecer, undersized and underfed, working from the age of thirteen what had customarily been fifty-six hours a week in a cotton-mill – now at last reduced to forty-eight – had somehow been persuaded into considering himself a vital member, or at least a member, of the British Empire. Perhaps he was. At least I, being Irish, would have to admit an inferiority on that score, if on no other; although we were reluctant members of that same empire. Moreover, I found I was drawn to such an English boy; indeed in many ways more than I was drawn to one of my own. I respected and half-feared his cool Englishness. What made him appear superior to me and mine in the first place was that he felt himself so, and I found that a difficult thing to counter, even though it may have been assumed on dubious grounds. The Irish seemed to live in the past and the English always in the present, and that certainly put them ahead. That the Englishman was part of a society more ordered than that of the Irish could not be gainsaid: the English responded to the factory buzzer with a promptness beyond the understanding of the Irish mind, which was quite untrained to punctuality; also they were a people clearly more law-abiding and hard-working, for the Lancashire miner could leave the leisurely Irishman behind.

It was as navvies the Irish came into their own – and this difference seemed to be reflected on their faces. The Irish face – except for those of coal-miners – was ruddy and fresh, set on the broad red neck with the round cleanshaven nape, and it would be simple for anyone to pick out such a one in a crowded English street, especially so since no Irishman ever hurried. The more intelligent Irish face had a lively mobility and friendly expression, quite unlike that of the simian-featured Irishman of English cartoons; even as a small boy I felt offended by this caricature of our people. Yet it was clear that the emotional Irish expression must defer to the stolid English look, and that the swift fluty tones of the Irish lacked the authority of the strong flat English voice. Apart from these and certain racial differences, one further comparison could be made: the Irish face was free of – or possibly had not yet acquired – that certain look which industry stamps upon its subjects. There was no doubt, however, that the countenance which had grown up on familiar terms with machinery, and had acquired that particular concentrated look – a form of sophistication – was the one which would prove superior in a material or worldly sense. The face that told of outdoor labour, of familiarity with the earth, the spade, and the muck fork, must give way to the one acquainted with the spanner. Moreover, a people who have been subject to another nation for centuries need a generation or two to shake off their inadequacies and equal up (if indeed they ever can without the superior nation going down a bit).

Nor was the superiority always of a remote order: the English were a reliable people, the Englishman's word was his bond – allowing the exception of a politician – and, if he promised to see you at the Ram's Head corner at eight o'clock and lend you a pound (or more likely ten shillings), you could bet he would be there, dead on eight, without any of the Irish excuses, and the note safe in his waistcoat pocket. Nor was the Englishman deep, treacherous, or given to feuds or grudges; and, although a peaceful man, never quickly pugnacious, he would seldom duck a fight. Then there would be the calm English ritual of jackets off, and not flung down but folded up carefully, sleeves calmly rolled up, the opponents set facing each other, left fist forward, right hand on guard, and no getting the first blow in, with someone to see fair play, not a move until the call was given; the commands, *Fists only! No feet!* and *Don't hit a man when he's down!* would be followed. (I had soon discovered he might drop his guard, dodge down and grab you by the knees, and flip you on your back in a trice.) Calls of *Play the game!* and *Play the white man!* would be made from the spectators during a fight; calls never heard, I imagine, at an Irish fight. The nature of the Celt and that of the Anglo-Saxon were decidedly different in many respects.

'I've had Irish chaps workin' here for me for years,' I once heard a Bolton farmer say, 'the same family – come over here for the hay they do, an' I hire 'um for the month. You never saw better workers in your life; an' I'll tell you summat, they're not clockwatchers, they're gradely workers – they keep gooin' till the job's done. Now at the end of the month on the Saturday night, when they're being paid off an' ready for gooin' off, it's always been my custom to tak' 'um to the pub an' stand 'um a pint or two. Sometimes they'll get other Irishmen from other farms about droppin' in, an' a nicer crowd o' chaps you never met – that is, until they begin findin' out they're related, an' they shake hands an' start kissin' one another. Then I'm off. For once the Irish start kissin', you can be sure that soon the fists will start – an' they get agate fightin'. Aye, as soon as I see that first kiss I make for the pub door.'

36
Margaret McAloren, 'The Wild Freshness of Morning'

Unpublished typescript. 92pp.; pp. 47–9; 52–3.

Margaret McAloren was born in 1902 to poor Irish Catholic parents in Silvertown, North Woolwich, a place she describes in her unpublished autobiography, written in 1978, as 'not a slum but definitely a working-class district'. Reviewing the first 30 years of her life, she briskly chronicles her experiences of war, work and relationships, as well as the many comings and goings in her 'slap-dash poor Irish home'. The following extract comes from Chapter 4, in which she briefly recollects her involvement with the Gaelic League and her brush with militant Irish nationalism in London in the aftermath of the 1916 Rising. McAloren's early life was dominated by family tragedy: her father died suddenly when she was three, two of her older sisters died within months of each other during the First World War, and four of her brothers succumbed to illness and disease during the 1920s. Her grief was compounded by the loss of her fiancé Harry, who died on her twenty-fifth birthday in 1927. Recalling the death of her brother John on New Year's Day 1929, she pithily remarks: 'Nobody first-footed us – only Death!' Bereavement is therefore the keynote of McAloren's autobiography, which takes its title from Tom Moore's 'I Saw From the Beach' and is written in an animated conversational style that effectively reproduces the cadence of her speaking voice. Yet for all her losses, she never succumbs to self-pity: 'Writing this – and I'm seventy-six now – I wonder how the hell we lived through it all. We just seemed to make the best of what we had. Once somebody said to me that we were a very "tragic" family, which made me indignant: I think we were a very happy family, and losing one after another of them only made the others more precious.'

There was quite a little colony of Irish people in Silvertown, but in my father's days they had not been popular with the factory owners. Keiller's Jam factory, for instance, run mostly by Scottish Presbyterians, had once had notices on the gates when jobs were vacant: 'No Irish need apply'. When the Easter Rising of 1916 took place in Dublin, Irish sympathy and patriotism burst into flame. One must remember that a lot of the older immigrants in Silvertown were not wholly contented with the menial jobs they were confined to. There had been little outlet for their higher aspirations. Together with a few others, Nell, who had learnt a lot of Irish history first-hand from my father, started a branch of the Gaelic League. This was purely cultural, concentrating on music, dancing, folklore, and Irish history, which Nell pushed. Everyone went madly Irish – we even had a class learning Gaelic and I can remember a little of it to this day!

The dancing class was very popular and a set was formed which travelled to different parishes. I was desperate to get into this, but although I could dance I was never chosen – perhaps being small and wearing glasses went against me. I could sing too, but was too shy to perform solo. This reminds me that at school Micky Brush had often been furious with me for closing up like a clam when he called upon me to sing; he'd said it made him sick to think of me having a lovely voice and not using it. Years later when I had mastered this shyness I was singing at a concert in the Tate Institute; Micky met Nell afterwards and told her my singing had moved him to tears. My brothers said they were not surprised – having suffered themselves!

It was during this period of feverish Irish patriotism that I was briefly drawn into the more frightening side of 'the struggle'. Nell had a friend in North Woolwich, Maggie Sullivan, who was not only fanatically pro-Irish but had also recently got engaged to a young man called Jim Hurley who had joined the Irish Volunteers and was caught up in active work with them. One evening there was a knock at our door and as I was the only one at home I answered it, to find Jim Hurley standing on the doorstep looking very thin and bedraggled. He asked to speak to Nell and when I told him she was out he handed me a small wrapped parcel and said it was a box of chocolates which I was to give her when she came in.

When Nell *did* come in I gave the box to her, and she opened it to find it contained not chocolates, but *bullets*! We were shocked and very scared too. It was like planting a bomb on us, we felt. The police were very active going into the homes of Irish people and searching for illegal evidence. One or two men had been arrested and kept in the police station for a day or so. We had visions of Nell being arrested as everyone knew her views – and our family's – on the Irish question.

We thought of all sorts of ways of hiding the bullets but couldn't come up with anything until my friend Nan had a brainwave. I should stress she had no sympathy for the Irish cause, being a Scottish Presbyterian, but she was so close to our family that I had no hesitation in confiding our problem to her. Nan suggested we took the bullets to the cemetery at East Ham and *buried* them in her grandmother's grave – Nan said no one would suspect two young girls visiting a grave. On the Saturday this is what we did, feeling very frightened but also daring and brave. We heard no more about those fateful bullets, so I presume they are there to this day. But since I can't remember whether the grandma buried at East Ham was on Nan's maternal or paternal side I haven't known where to look. Good old Nan – she'd have a fit if she thought I was writing this!

One last detail about the Gaelic League. Nell was made secretary of it and as such she was responsible for arrangements to meet and 'feed' the speakers who were sent to speak to the Silvertown branch. Now and again she brought them home for a cup of tea and a sandwich prior to the meeting. The only ones I particularly remember coming to speak were Dame Maud Gonne McBride and Countess Markievicz.[1] [...]

As the war drew to a close, our lives settled into a familiar routine. Many of our social activities were connected with the church – dances, concerts and so on. I was still very friendly with Nan. We went to the office together and came home together. Occasionally I went to her house for tea, or she came to mine, but only informally. One lasting enthusiasm was the Gaelic League, which was still going strong, with lots of meetings. Nell was still secretary and by now Paddy was chairman. Feelings were particularly strong, I recall, when the IRA prisoners were brought over to England and put in Wormwood Scrubs. Members of all sorts of Irish groups went on silent protest marches up to the prison and stood outside saying the Rosary. I only went once or twice. But I can remember getting out of the train at the terminus in London (probably Liverpool Street) where our own pickets were handing out *bandages* of all things. This scared me sick. We got to the Scrubs and said the Rosary without any interference and were marching quietly back to the station when a riot started. There seemed to be men and boys coming from all sides, wielding sticks and throwing stones.

Nell was hit on the shoulder by a stone, and then someone shouted 'There's a priest down', and most of our section dashed to the rescue of the priest. But these didn't include our Paddy, who hustled Nell, me and his girlfriend Florrie down a side-street and onto a tram. Discretion was certainly the better part of valour on that occasion. We could see cartloads of policemen as we marched, but they gave us no protection when we were attacked – I think they wanted the hooligans to give the Irish a dose of rough medicine. It was all very exciting if one happened to be brave, but bravery was not my forte.

I *did* march in Terence MacSwiney's funeral procession. He was the Lord Mayor of Cork and was arrested for being a rebel and brought to England, where he went on hunger strike in prison, and died (September 1920). His death aroused terrific feeling among the Irish and they arranged a relay silent

---

[1] Maud Gonne MacBride (1866–1953) and Constance Markievicz (1868–1927), leading activists in the political and cultural movements that coalesced into the struggle for Irish independence. Gonne was the inspiration behind many of Yeats's poems. Markievicz became the first woman to be elected to the House of Commons in 1918 but did not take her seat. She was appointed minister for labour in the inaugural Dáil Éireann the following year.

march carrying his body all the way back to Ireland.[2] My boss said if any Irish went to MacSwiney's funeral service they would be sacked. Of course there were only two people in the office that this warning could apply to – Florrie and me – but we went despite it, and strangely enough we *weren't* sacked. I might have been cowardly in some respects, but I would argue with anyone in the office who said anything about the Irish. It was laughable, I suppose. There was little ginger-haired me standing up to hulking blokes: a yapping Irish terrier snapping at English bulldogs. I expect they ribbed me just to have the laugh of seeing me riled.

---

[2] The death of Terence MacSwiney (1879–1920) in Brixton prison after a 74-day hunger strike provoked widespread nationalist anger and mourning at home and abroad. Further evidence of its impact upon Irish nationalist sentiment in Britain can be gleaned from Bill Naughton's account of his father's anguished response to news of MacSwiney's death in *On the Pig's Back*, p. 175.

37
Robert Collis, *The Silver Fleece: An Autobiography*

(London: Thomas Nelson and Sons, 1936). 290pp.; pp. 50–1; 55–9.

Robert Collis (1900–1975) was born in Killiney, County Dublin, to a prosperous solicitor father and a mother who lavished affection on him from infancy, to the detriment of his neglected twin brother John, whose work is featured later in this volume. Collis's schooldays at Rugby coincided with tumultuous events in both Ireland and Europe, the contrasting local reactions to which he succinctly evokes in Part 2 of his autobiography, from which the following extract is taken. He studied medicine at Cambridge and also excelled at rugby, winning seven caps for Ireland during the 1920s. Although he subsequently flourished professionally during his time in various London hospitals, Collis increasingly felt himself to be a 'prisoner of the machine age' in England and hankered after the pastoral landscapes of his youth. *The Silver Fleece* ends with his dream of return coming true. In 1932 he was appointed to the staff of the National Children's Hospital in Dublin, a post that launched him on a path that led to his becoming an internationally renowned paediatrician and a pioneer in the treatment of tuberculosis and cerebral palsy. After the Second World War Collis worked with the Red Cross to rehabilitate Holocaust survivors at Belsen and, with his partner Han Hogerzeil, adopted five liberated children, one of whom, Zoltan Zinn-Collis, published his memoirs in 2006. Collis also wrote two plays, *Marrowbone Lane* (1939) and *The Barrel Organ* (1942), and acted as authorial mentor to the disabled Dublin writer Christy Brown, for whose acclaimed autobiography, *My Left Foot* (1954), he wrote a foreword.

At the age of sixteen one is only half conscious; one does not regard oneself objectively in one's surroundings. Although the events of the Easter holidays had made a profound impression upon my mind and actions, yet when the holidays were over I looked forward eagerly to going back to Rugby, seeing all my friends again, and resuming my place in the House life. After all, my family had all given themselves to the Allied cause; even my father, who was nearly sixty, had spent the previous summer driving an ambulance in the Italian army.

On arriving back at School I was full of the descriptions of the fighting in Dublin, regarding myself as having now first-hand information on modern war. To my surprise I found my popularity had vanished. This was due partly, no doubt, to the fact that this was the cricket term, and the moment for others to be the House heroes; but I soon discovered that the English boys resented my talk, and were inclined to mutter 'bloody rebels' when I spoke of Ireland. Further, that they tended to feel that all Irishmen had some responsibility for the happenings in Ireland, and to regard any refusal on our part to accept such a position as bad form. Soon, however, such thoughts vanished in the routine of school life and the noise of the guns from France, which now began to overshadow our small existences. [...]

At first the war had been merely an exciting game to us, portrayed in the papers by maps with black lines representing the armies, and arrows pointing for direction of attacks; and by visiting lecturers, among whom was a famous author, who explained the strategy of the Allies, always assuring us of victory in six months' time. As he put it:

'Other things being equal, numbers prevail.'

As time went on, however, the conflict became more personal. Many had fathers and brothers at the front; boys we knew began to appear on the casualty lists. Our beloved House tutor said good-bye to us one Sunday afternoon, and was blown to pieces a few days later. Gradually the shadow crept closer. I remember sitting in the House quad during my last year, with two companions, looking up at an aeroplane stunting high above and wondering where we would be that day next year. Both companions were dead before its anniversary was reached.

Memorial services were now a regular feature of school life. Once or twice a term a special service was given in memory of the boys who fell. Their parents were invited, and usually came. The service was quite simple. The names of the fallen were read out and God was asked to take care of them, and a few prayers were offered for them and for victory. Then an address was given, in which the parents were assured that their sons had fallen fighting bravely in the great cause – the war to end war; in defence of smaller and weaker nations, for the honour of England, for God. The preacher would then turn to us and pray God that we also would acquit ourselves with equal valour when the time came.

On one occasion this routine procedure was broken. The preacher, a certain Mr. Simmonds, instead of saying what was expected of him, broke all the rules of the game and actually spoke what he felt. He said that war settled nothing, that it was wrong however you looked at it. He suggested that it was more than probable that somewhere in Germany at that very moment a similar service, attended also by sorrowing mothers and fathers, was being held. He even said that perhaps it was as fine to stand out against the whole foul thing and receive all the calumny of the world, as to die gallantly, like the boys whose deaths we were commemorating that day. Gradually the congregation became restive. Finally a bereaved father got up and stamped out of the School chapel, followed by one or two others.

How dare this chap mention their gallant sons' names in the same breath as Ramsay MacDonald[1] and the other filthy pacifists? I was sitting just below the headmaster; his face became more agitated as the preacher proceeded; but a pulpit is an unassailable rostrum, and he had to sit and bear it to the end.

The sermon raised a storm of protest among the masters who had not gone to the war, and certain of the parents.

After chapel we went back to our Houses discussing the matter in some excitement. On the whole we agreed with the preacher, but considered it rather bad form on his part to have said it at that particular moment. Also, we felt nobody could expect our fathers to understand such a point of view. We being next on the list, so to speak, knew instinctively that most of the war propaganda, such as corpse factories, was false.[2] We were beginning to cease hating the Germans, though our changing attitude made no difference to our future course of action, and all of us automatically went out to fight on reaching the killable age.

Boys ever live in the moment, but at that time we grasped the present utterly and made it our whole; because for us there appeared no gradual attainment of manhood. As soon as we left school the complete responsibility of adult citizenship was to be thrust upon us in the horrible form of a uniform in the army. So our school endeavours were magnified, and we cared more fiercely about our little affairs than any other generation, before or since. I remember one football game which nearly broke our hearts. Rodger, Barber, and I were now the first three forwards in the School Fifteen. It was Barber's and Rodger's last term. We decided, as a fitting end to our companionship, to win the Cock House match. We had a very uneven team, but we beat it into shape by weeks of careful training. We won the first few House matches easily; in the semi-final we met our only real opponents. The match was played on the old ground in the Close, where Rugby Football had first been played. We hung our blazers on the same old elm trees that William Webb Ellis[3] and his companions had hung theirs on, ninety-two years before. We felt the thrill of the game we were about to play, and the aura of all the other matches that had gone before. Now only one thing mattered in our lives; all else, past and future, was forgotten. We went out to win.

It was an heroic encounter; Barber crashed over the line for a try first; then a pass was intercepted and they scored. Then I, who had gone out to play

---

[1] Ramsay MacDonald (1866–1937), who became the first British Labour prime minister in 1924, opposed the First World War, believing that Britain and Germany were equally to blame.

[2] In 1917 false reports began circulating that the German authorities had set up factories for extracting fats from the bodies of soldiers killed in battle.

[3] William Webb Ellis (1806–1872), who attended Rugby School from 1816 to 1825, is popularly credited with having 'invented' rugby in 1823 when he picked up the ball and ran with it during a football game.

wing threequarter, scored a desperate try by the corner flag – handing off three opponents and finally diving over the full back to ground the ball. We appeared to have the game in hand, our spirits rose, our supporters yelled themselves dumb. Then, suddenly, a minute before time, they dropped a goal. It was too late to rally for another effort; the whistle blew a moment later, and we found ourselves beaten by one point.

Spent and speechless with disappointment, Rodger, Barber, and I walked home together, our faces white and drawn with tiredness and misery. Our whole world seemed shattered. The small boys stared at us; nobody dared speak to us. We went back to our studies and sat dumbly looking at the floor, forgetting even to change out of or soaking clothes or to wash.

In a few months Barber was a mangled corpse and Rodger in hospital with shell-shock.

38
Darrell Figgis, *A Chronicle of Jails*

(Dublin: Talbot Press, 1917). 130pp.; pp. 64–9; 74; 79–80.

The nationalist writer and politician Darrell Figgis (1882–1925) was born to an Anglo-Irish family in Rathmines, Dublin, and raised in India. He worked for his uncle's tea brokerage business in London and Calcutta between 1898 and 1910, after which he became an editorial advisor to the publishers Dent & Sons. His first poetry collection, *A Vision of Life* (1909), was quickly followed by his debut novel, *Broken Arcs* (1911), and a critical study of Shakespeare. Figgis's prolific output continued over the next decade, taking in freelance journalism, literary and historical studies, political tracts and more novels, including *The Return of the Hero* (1923), published under the pseudonym 'Michael Ireland'. Figgis's republican activism increased following his return to Ireland in 1913 and, with Erskine Childers, he was instrumental in the purchase and landing of German arms for the Irish Volunteers at Howth in 1914. He later served as honorary secretary to Sinn Féin and was a member of the first Dáil Éireann, chairing the committee that drafted the Irish Constitution of 1922. Figgis committed suicide in Bloomsbury, London in October 1925, within days of the death of his partner Rita North and less than a year after his wife Millie took her own life.

A Chronicle of Jails records Figgis's harsh experiences of internment in Irish and English prisons following his arrest in May 1916 as part of a military crackdown. Although the text is incomplete – ellipses mark the British censor's deletions, as in the extract below – the book reads as a testament of both political and psychological assertion in which the resilient hero marshals the resources of memory, intellect and imagination to combat a penal system designed to reduce him 'to the utter blankness that is its ideal'. Though rarely considered as such, *A Chronicle of Jails* belongs to the extensive subgenre of Irish nationalist prison memoir that ranges from John Mitchel's *Jail Journal* (1854) to Danny Morrison's *Then The Walls Came Down: A Prison Journal* (1999). Irish political prisoners' accounts of their English incarceration form a substantial part of this literary substrand, which includes landmark texts such as Jeremiah O'Donovan Rossa's *Irish Rebels in English Prisons* (1882) and Brendan Behan's *Borstal Boy* (1958), as well as lesser-known works such as Colm Ó Gaora's *Mise* (*Myself*, 1943). Figgis's lapidary, reflexive style makes *A Chronicle of Jails* a superior example of its type, a text in which the author's searing critique of British rule in Ireland and vivid portrayal of prison hardships are leavened by a desolate lyricism and droll irony: 'It was extraordinary how soon one's hip-bones hardened to the floor, and the simplicity of toilet was a great boon to anyone who had found dressing and undressing labyrinths of inconvenience.' Yet it is a work that stands somewhat apart from this tradition, Oscar Wilde's 'The Ballad of Reading Gaol', that *A Chronicle of Jails* most strongly echoes in its emphasis on the dehumanising effects of incarceration. It is entirely appropriate, then, that Figgis's short spell in Reading should bring Wilde's words powerfully to mind in the closing chapters.

At the North Wall we were put on board a cattle boat. The cattle were herded at one end of the pens, we were being herded at the other end of the pens. When it came to my turn to be penned I was surprised to hear myself accosted by the Embarkation Officer:

'I'm B——, you know.'

'Certainly', I replied; 'we meet again.' But I had not the dimmest notion who he was.

'I hope to be in Castlebar soon,' he said. 'I haven't been back since I went out.'

'Is that so?' I said. 'I was in Castlebar a fortnight ago. I was stopping at the jail.'

He laughed, and turned to P. J. D.,[1] who stood beside me as we awaited our turn to be penned. His manner was frank and pleasant and not at all constrained, although his penning of us was quite efficiently done. I informed him that I was not well, and asked if certain accommodation could not be found slightly more efficient than a cattle pen packed with my fellows. He promised to see what he could do, and went off. When he had gone, P. J. D. informed me that he had been a Volunteer when I was in command of the country, and had since gained some distinction in the European War. Presently he returned, and conveyed some of us to a room in the forecastle, where we had seats on which we could stretch ourselves.

When we arrived in England, however, we struck quite another atmosphere. Inquisitive crowds gathered about us who lost no opportunity of displaying their enmity and hostility. German prisoners of war might have aroused an equal curiosity, but they could not have an equal enmity. Clearly and sharply we stood out, whether we gathered on railway platforms or were marched through streets, as nation against nation, with an unbridgeable hatred between us. Any attempt on our part to meet taunt with taunt was at ....; and so we were compelled to stand as the mark of contumely and the target of contempt. To be sure, that only stiffened us, and we held ourselves high and unflinchingly before the crowds. Nevertheless, there was

---

[1] Patrick J. Doris, joint founder of *The Mayo News* with his brother William in 1892. William Doris was Irish Party MP for Mayo West from 1910 until 1918, during which time his support for John Redmond's war policy alienated Patrick, who held his brother personally responsible for his internment after the 1916 Rising.

a sickening in most of us, for Ireland was behind us and we were utterly in the stranger's power.

I had lived some years in England, and had formed many good friendships. Unlike many of my companions, England and the English were no strange things to me. Yet I came then into something utterly strange, foreign, and hostile. I could not more strangely have been led captive among the mountains of the moon, so icy was this world and such leagues apart from that which I had known.

Everything was coloured by that relation. One looked on England with new eyes, and old thoughts became startling new discoveries. Stafford lay for the most part steeped in slumber as we were marched through its streets in the morning, accompanied by a small, inquisitive crowd. It looked incredibly sleek and prosperous beside our Irish towns. The villas were sleek and comfortable; the roads were sleek and neat; the very grass beside the canal looked sleek as though nurtured with the centuries. Everything had an air of being well fed and well groomed, and quite consciously proud of the fact that it was part of a prosperous whole, where no invader's foot had trampled, where no spoliation had dared to efface the moss that had gathered for centuries on the gables, or to rough the smooth lawns. The villas might be the latest examples of modernity, yet that was the air they suggested, for they became part of something that was smooth and sleek. How different to our Irish towns, that look as though they – not the people in them, but they themselves – live a precarious day-to-day existence. Each suggests the history of their nation. One has grown sleek with prosperity, and smooth and round with the large air of the conqueror, with shores that have never known invasion. The other has been hunted from end to end by rapacious conquest; the forests that were its pride burnt away the better to root out its people; the people hunted until they lost the instinct to build for themselves permanent abodes, and, more latterly, rack-rented till they stealthily hid any small savings and kept middens before their doors, until a show of poverty from being a disguise became a habit; rising against the conqueror in a series of revolts foredoomed to failure, but triumphant in what they spoke of – a spirit still unbroken; stricken to earth again by soldiery that marched through the land; and harnessed by a network of legislative acts that intended to inhibit industry and commerce with the nations of the earth, and that succeeded in their intention. And yet there was no question of a choice between the two. For with one individuality had become smoothened away, the wheel having come full circle; with the other individuality was sharp and keen, angular it might be, but alive for the future.

H. P.[2] and I were speaking of these things when we arrived at Stafford Jail. It was about six o'clock in the morning as we were marched through the gates

---

[2] Herbert Moore Pim (1883–1950), Belfast-born author who converted to Catholicism in 1910.

and lined up outside the prison. The building looked gloomy and forbidding as it frowned down on us with its hundreds of barred windows. It had lately been used as a detention barracks; that is to say, as a prison for soldiers, the major part of the population of England having donned khaki but not having doffed their sins therewith. Therefore, it was staffed by military, who received us from our escort and marched us up the great building to the cells that had been allotted us. And once again I heard the key grate behind me. [...]

All that I had feared in Castlebar now returned upon me; yet, curiously, not so keenly, not so sharply. Already there had been a dulling of consciousness, a blunting of the susceptibilities. During the early morning we were examined medically and then bathed in antiseptic. We needed it; herded on the dusty floors of Richmond Barracks we had collected what was to be collected, and had, as a Tyrone lad put it, 'grazed our cattle through-other'; and the doctor nodded gravely over his inspection, like one who thought, 'Well, this is the Irish nation: report has not spoken untruly of them.' Then we were taken back to our cells. During the afternoon we were taken out for a quarter of an hour's exercise in silence round one of the yards at the back of the prison, and solemnly informed that if any attempt to communicate with one another were detected we would be removed to special punishment cells and fed on bread and water for a week. Back to our cells then until the following afternoon. [...]

At five came tea, which was a repetition of breakfast; and then set in the hours we most dreaded. The staff went home at five, and silence settled down over the prison – a silence that was not broken till five the next morning. Now and then as the night watchman passed in his padded shoes I would hear the spy-hole slot being moved aside and would know that an eye was looking in upon me. Then the slot fell back again. The eye had passed on to the next cell. But all the time the silence was profound.

The lengthening day, with the altered hour, gave light till ten at night. That is to say, the customary twilight of the cell did not change to profound gloom and then to darkness till after that hour. That made the case worse, for one would not take refuge in sleep. It would be hard to say how many times I counted the number of bolts that studded the door, how many times I counted the number of bricks in each wall, how many times I measured the number of feet from end to end of the cell, from side to side, and from corner to corner. This was one's occupation for twenty-three hours out of the twenty-four, save for the time given to sleep, until one fell back on bitter blank staring ahead.

Sometimes, as though to make the silence still more oppressive, I heard one of the other prisoners somewhere down the prison break into song. Then a harsh voice would loudly call on him to be quiet; and silence would be supreme again. Already on my first day I had established friendly relations with my corporal. He was, I discovered, a London Irishman, and he happened to be more easily quickened to interest on that account. I asked him once what the other men did with their time, when he spied in upon them, thinking to find comfort for my hours in a more intelligent knowledge of the life that was silently proceeding around me.

'Most of them just sit on their stools and stare at the wall. It's horrible to see them. Lots of them are crying – some that you wouldn't think of. And a lot of them are praying, always praying. And that's worse, for things are not as bad as that. It makes me feel bad to see them.'

I thought of Dame Quickly with her, 'Now I, to comfort him, bid him a' should not think of God; I hoped there was no need to trouble himself with any such thoughts yet,' and smiled.[3] But I wished I had not asked him any question.

Yet, strangely enough, the thing that I had feared with such horror in its coming at Castlebar did not quicken in me such fear now that it had settled upon me. The process had, as most processes do, brought its own rather ghastly relief. In Castlebar I had been keen and sensitive; my mind had been quick to speed ahead and anticipate the approaching evil; and that, if painful, was a preferable estate to this dead inertia, when the mind seemed hardly to have any existence in the body. .... and I cannot wonder at it; for often one would spring to one's feet and march up and down the cell in a mental excitement that was almost unendurable. Such times, when they came, came intolerably, for they came with diminishing frequency; but the usual state was inertia. There was something of learned patience about it; something of a reserve that waited its day; but deeper set than these things was the blankness of being that it was the first duty of the whole system to achieve.

I tried, for instance, to bring before me the faces of those whom I knew, and to imagine what they might be doing as I thought of them. I sought, thus, to give myself a life in the life that others were living; but could I think of those lives, could I bring their faces before me? It was not that they fled me. The mind simply would not rise to the effort. I tried to surrender myself to problems of thought that had fascinated me in the past, and to problems of being into which all life's meaning had to be crowded. But at most the wheel only spun round, never gripping the metal; and more often the wheel refused to move. The life within the cell was significantly told by the card outside: the name was turned to the wall, and only a number was turned to view. Prison cells are not dwellings, they are sepulchres.

So the days passed, one by one, while the summer rolled by outside. Even the will to fight seemed lost.

---

[3] Lines spoken by Mistress Quickly on the death of Falstaff in *Henry V*, II. iii.

39

Elizabeth Hamilton, *An Irish Childhood*

Illustrated by Norah McGuinness (London: Chatto & Windus, 1963). 212pp.; pp. 74–7; 199–202.

Elizabeth Hamilton was born into a landed Protestant Wicklow family in 1906. Her early years were dominated by two pivotal events that shaped both her life and her narrative recapitulation of it. While she was still young, her father resigned his commission in the British army to take up dairy farming, but when the enterprise failed he was persuaded to sell Mount John, the family's Georgian mansion, and emigrate to Florida. The move proved disastrous, forcing the family to return within six months, not to Ireland but to England, where her father rejoined his regiment. For Elizabeth, the loss of Mount John and the leaving of Ireland represented an abrupt expulsion from a childhood idyll that she transmutes in her writings into an emblem of permanent exile: 'I was banished from Eden. An angel with a flaming sword was barring the way. That was how it seemed to me. And, in a sense, I suppose, from that day on I was trying to find my way back.'[1] The biblical imagery here hints at the second formative turning-point in Hamilton's life: her conversion to Catholicism in her early twenties, while studying at London University. In a late work, *I Stay in the Church* (1973), she re-evaluates the reasons for her apostasy, seeing it as an act of parental rebellion rather than a repudiation of her Protestant past: 'Buried among other motives, as I now see it, was a desire for retaliation. Through the years I had not wholly forgiven my parents for having left our home in Ireland: my mother for having made the suggestion, my father for having fallen in with it.'[2]

In her autobiography proper Hamilton recalls her childhood in the full awareness that 'The past must always be unreal, in that, like a dream, it has gone beyond recovery.' This sense of irretrievable loss has an analogue in the author's chronic homelessness, which was exacerbated by her family's peripatetic progress through wartime England, impressionistically described in the extract below. Her rootlessness is also a function of a deeper dislocation, a vestigial sense of outsiderness traceable to the paradoxical cultural position of the Anglo-Irish in independent Ireland. Sequestered in a state of

---

[1] Elizabeth Hamilton, *I Stay in the Church* (London: Vision Press, 1973), p. 18.
[2] Ibid., p. 26.

hyphenated stasis, the traditions of this community had all but withered by the time *An Irish Childhood* was published. These aspects inevitably call to mind the ambiguous affiliations of Elizabeth Bowen, yet in contrast to her, Hamilton refuses to base her claims to belonging on genealogical pedigree or patrilineal descent – a measure, perhaps, of her desire for a different kind of autobiographical self-authorisation, one that stresses the contingency of all definitions of self and other.

I do not think that my father had any personal vanity, but like others of his generation and background he had family pride. He was proud of the Hamilton motto – *qualis ab incepto*: as from the beginning; the crest depicting the demi-antelope holding in its paws the bloody heart of Raplock; and the tradition that forebears of his descended from Charlemagne had fought in the army of William the Conqueror at the battle of Hastings. He knew all the ramifications of his pedigree – where precisely each member of the family belonged. James, Hans, Rowan, Archibald, William, Charles, Claude, Frederick, James. Names that repeated themselves from one generation to the next flittered about my ears.

Only a few of these were more to me than names. James Hamilton of Sheepshill, my great-great-great-grandfather, had thirty-six children. An earlier James, the first Hamilton to settle in Ireland, was a boon companion, so the story goes, of King James VI of Scotland. When the two had drunk their fill the King would say: 'Snuff the candles, Jamie', and Jamie retort: 'Snuff 'em yourself.' This James, while acting as a spy in Dublin on behalf of the King, opened a Free Latin school in Great Ship Street to hide his activities. He became one of the original Fellows of Trinity and tutor to James Ussher afterwards Archbishop of Armagh.[3] Later he went north where he devastated the country and helped in forcibly establishing the reformed religion. In this way he acquired tracts of land, including the castle of Killyleagh, which is described on an old map as being so vast that 'the smallness of Rome would not contain it'. In recognition of his services he was created Viscount Clandeboye in the year 1622.

I have inherited little of my father's family pride. There is no place for it in the world we know today. Nor does nationality mean much to me. I care for persons for their own sake regardless of country or political background. I am at home with Spaniards in Spain, Norwegians in Norway, in Israel with Jews, but no less so with Israel's minority of Arabs or the Arabs in Jordan. I am conscious of no colour prejudice; in company with Bernard Shaw I think that a dark skin can sometimes be preferable to a pink one. Possibly I find it easier than some to adapt myself to different peoples because I am to some extent rootless, used, once the first seven years in Ireland had ended, to going now here, now there; to digging myself in, so to speak, only to find it is time to

---

[3] James Ussher (1581–1656), Church of Ireland archbishop and clerical scholar, was one of the first students to enter Trinity College following its foundation in 1592.

move. I feel with all displaced persons – the homeless, refugees, Mary fleeing into Egypt with her husband and her Child; and with travellers – the Magi journeying to Bethlehem:

> *Just the worst time of the year*
> *For a journey, and such a long journey;*
> *The ways deep and the weather sharp,*
> *The very dead of winter.*[4]

To be Anglo-Irish is not conducive to a sense of stability, in that to belong to two countries is to belong that much the less to each. It means, in the republic of Eire, to be to some degree an outsider – the spectator of a regime in which as a citizen of Britain one has no part; in England, to be at a distance from – not wholly identified with – one's fellows; to be conscious – and proud, too – of one's Irish origins; quick to take up the challenge for Ireland; resentful perhaps of that faintly patronizing tone the English can adopt regarding any people other than themselves.

Yet this two-fold allegiance makes it the easier to adapt oneself to change. Although the thought of a journey (or of anything in the nature of an upheaval) disposes me to a sense of apprehension, yet the initial step taken, I welcome each fresh scene, circumstance, encounter. Some feel that to be ill in a country other than one's own is a particular misfortune. I have not found this to be so. On the contrary the difficulty of communicating one's needs, instead of proving a barrier, served only to make those about me the more solicitous and myself the more aware of the bond, transcending language, that unites human beings – no matter what their race – provided they be of good will. The ancients did well to believe that Zeus, the father of the gods, watched over travellers with a special care. To show kindness to the stranger appears to be an instinct proper to man. A stranger in a strange land, we say as in compassion. The deeper one's roots the more strange the land of another must seem. The Jews wept by the waters of Babylon, remembering Sion. For those whose roots are less deep or whose loyalty is divided it is easier to settle afresh – so that a strange land begins soon to lose its strangeness. [...]

The War Office accepted my father's offer of service. But to his chagrin he was not, as he had hoped and long continued to hope, sent to France, to the front. London. Liverpool. The Isle of Man. Preston. Bury. Manchester. London. Now here, now there, now somewhere else. Furnished rooms on the sea front at Douglas, Isle of Man – an aspidistra in a window that in wild weather was lashed with spray. More furnished rooms in a street reaching back from the sea. A furnished house rented by the month. Another.

---

[4] Lines from T. S. Eliot's 'Journey of the Magi', written after his conversion to Anglicanism in 1927.

And another. In Preston an hotel poised above the railway: trucks shunting, engines clanking, trains thundering through the night – sparks showering upon the darkness. In Bury, uncarpeted rooms in an hotel that was being taken over by troops. Then a commercial hotel furnished in heavy Victorian style. Then rooms on the Tottington Road – a view of factory chimneys, the clatter of clogs on cobbles, women wearing black shawls. Manchester: rooms in Moss Lane in a gaunt house lit by flaring gas-jets; in Victoria Park a house overlooking an infirmary where wounded soldiers, wearing hospital blue suits and scarlet ties, hung out of windows or sat on the steps. In London, a private hotel in Lancaster Gate: old ladies, a French baron, his elegant daughter, an Armenian with manicured hands and shining black eyes. So it went on.

In the Isle of Man I had gone to a day school, but this came to an end when we moved to England. The precariousness and day-to-day uncertainty of life made for excitement, a sense of adventure. But it also made me feel at the mercy of circumstances over which I had no control. To compensate I developed a craving for independence, a determination to strike out on my own. In Manchester a remark let fall by my mother about White Slave traffic and the consequent danger of a child going out alone in a city made me only the more resolved to evade what seemed to me an exaggerated solicitude. Seizing the first opportunity that presented itself I slipped out into the winter dusk, and once out went further than I had intended, my imagination fired by the mystery of the dark streets, the crowds and the shop windows, eventually attaching myself to a queue waiting outside a grocer's to buy margarine – supposing my mother would be delighted, at this time of scant rations, with my purchase. I was nonplussed on my return to find her too distraught with anxiety at my absence to care.

At Bury I made friends with a barmaid at the commercial hotel; I used to sit by her, on a high stool behind the counter – entranced by the smoke-laden atmosphere, the roar of voices, the clink of glasses, the variety and colours of the drinks. On her half-day, when she changed her dress of tight-fitting black satin for a claret-coloured coat and skirt with a toque to match, we used to set off on some expedition on the top of a rattling, whining tram – to Rochdale or Bolton or Oldham or to a terminus on the town's edge from which we walked over a treeless countryside of stone walls and bleak stone villages.

I was corresponding, too, with an elderly naturalist who had befriended me at Preston, receiving from him closely-written pages illustrated in the margins with diagrams and drawings of flowers, plants, frogs, butterflies and beetles – as well as presents that included *Just So Stories*, Faber's *Book of Insects*, *The Call of the Wild*, Aesop's *Fables* and a translation of *Les Fables de La Fontaine*. At Lancaster Gate I played chess with the Armenian. Because we were both excitable the game sometimes ended in disorder; on one occasion he tipped the board over, scattering the pieces on to the floor.

I wanted freedom, yet without knowing it I wanted order – so that I made no protest when in the spring following the armistice, as my eleventh birthday was approaching, it was arranged for me to go to a school in South London; first, while my parents were living in furnished rooms nearby, as a day pupil; later, when they moved out of London, as a boarder. It is a tribute to the school that, having come to it with no idea of life in a community and with enormous gaps in the knowledge that might reasonably be expected from a child of that age, I was for the greater part of the six years I spent there not merely resigned or content but happy. I had been at the Isle of Man school long enough to know the exhilaration that comes of having one's wits pitted against those of others – long enough to be tantalized – but not bored – by the glossy maps in an atlas, the faces of the Plantagenets and the Stuarts looking out from Gardiner's History of England, the antics of a Latin verb leaping down a page. When I had been taken away from the school a curtain had dropped. Now it had lifted.

40

Louis MacNeice, *The Strings Are False: An Unfinished Autobiography*

Edited and with a preface by E. R. Dodds (London: Faber & Faber, 1965). 288pp.; pp. 76–9.

The 'two-fold allegiance' that shadowed Elizabeth Hamilton was also a defining element in the life and imagination of Louis MacNeice (1907–1963). The cry heard in the following extract from his autobiography – 'Oh this division of allegiance!' – reverberates throughout much of his work. MacNeice's poetic vision has long been recognised as double-edged, his creativity sourced in a displacement that was 'pre-natal'.[1] Born in Belfast and raised in Carrickfergus, where his father, a Church of Ireland bishop, ministered, MacNeice's unhappy childhood led him to mythologise the west of Ireland, where his parents came from, as his 'true' home. Yet he was never more than a visitor in the west, despite his rapturous response to the Connacht landscape. Nor did he ever seriously contemplate settling there. Education, career and artistic milieu anchored him in England, where he lived from the age of ten, first as a student at Sherborne, Marlborough and Oxford, then as a university lecturer in Birmingham and London in the 1930s, and finally as a London-based writer-producer for the BBC from 1941 until his death. Yet England was never fully home to MacNeice. London retained its foreignness, even after 20 years of residence, whereas Dublin was ever familiar, despite his conviction that the city 'will not / Have me, alive or dead'.[2] His uneasy sense of in-betweenness is memorably encapsulated in a line from a 1948 letter to his friend Eric Dodds, himself an uprooted Ulsterman: 'I wish one could either *live* in Ireland or *feel oneself* in England.'[3]

A deeper homelessness is suggested by MacNeice's description of himself as 'a mere nomad who has lost his tent' in the opening paragraph of *The Strings Are False*. The book reads as an extended meditation on the feasibility of realising an intellectually

---

[1] Louis MacNeice, 'Carrick Revisited', *Collected Poems*, ed. Peter MacDonald (London: Faber & Faber, 2007), p. 262.

[2] Ibid., p. 179.

[3] Quoted in Jon Stallworthy, *Louis MacNeice* (London: Faber & Faber, 1995), p. 342. Original emphasis.

coherent self: 'I am 33 years old and what can I have been doing that I am still in a muddle?' Fittingly for a writer in whom the desire to move on, to metamorphose, ran deep, the early chapters were written on board the ship that took him back to England in late 1940, after a year in America.[4] MacNeice was willingly returning both to a country at war and to a place that had long functioned as a testing-ground for the possibilities of selfhood. In childhood, England presented itself to him as a laboratory of self-improvisation where intractable Irish realities might be transcended. Thus, in 1917 young Louis departed for preparatory school in Sherborne, eager 'to be rid of my family and start making good'. Here he is two years later, freshly aware of the impossibility of the task, having just been reacquainted with his Down's syndrome brother Willie during a holiday in Carrickfergus. MacNeice's sombre reflections on this inadmissable family trauma – 'When he [Willie] left in a fortnight to return to his Institution I felt a great relief but a guilt that more than balanced it. And the bloom, I felt, had gone off the Dorset hills. And the boys at Sherborne seemed suddenly terribly young; I had learned their language but they could not learn mine, could never breathe my darkness' – provide a haunting counterpoint to his evocation of the fleeting joys of adolescence in what follows.

But Sherborne was gay enough once I went back to it. There was a new master from Oxford, a Mr. Charles, who arrived to teach us English, History and Geography. He told us we need not bother with History and Geography; all that really mattered was Keats. He was tall and slim, with small features and a mouth that could sneer, he wore a grey check suit with a grey check shirt and a grey check tie and grey check socks, and he left little islands of scent behind him in classroom and garden. He filled his room with a bust of Dante and Keats's death-mask, and wrote Greek verses on the wall which we thought were his own composition. Cricket, he said, was a classical game, an art, but rugby football was barbarous.

For some time we thought that being taught by Mr. Charles was a picnic, he flattered us by denouncing Philistia and aligning us with him against it. It was our first taste of aesthetic snobbery and was sweet enough in the mouth; poor Mr. Cameron was out of it. Then one day Mr. Charles said to a boy in class: 'Have you ever heard of Mazzini?' and the boy said, 'No and I don't want to.' Mr. Charles, who had been born in Italy, flared into a rage that dwarfed Mr. Cameron's. 'Damn you,' he said, 'little middle-class brats.' It was all a mistake, he saw now, trying to assist us to culture, pearls before swine. He left the room in a tantrum, banging the door, and we were too appalled to enjoy the rest of the hour's idleness.

He had a worse tantrum later. He had offered a prize for an English essay – to be done in our own time and the entries voluntary – on some subject like the Poetic Function of the Imagination. The eldest among us were thirteen and none of us understood the title but Mr. Charles seemed very keen on it, was

---

[4] Ibid., p. 286.

always giving us hints, and a few of us – many weeks after the competition had been announced – were about to begin an assault on the Imagination when Mr. Charles suddenly in class asked us which of us were entering. No one was brave enough to hold up his hand. Mr. Charles went white and tense; this, he said, was the end. He had done all he could to no purpose. Very well, in future he would meet us on our level. Savagely he tore a quire of foolscap into quarters, threw them at our heads. 'Spell,' said Mr. Charles, spitting the words like a machine-gun, 'spell. It is all you are good for. Spell erysipelas, symmetry, asyndeton.'

Mr. Charles by these outbursts put himself in the same category as the others, was no longer an exception to the rule that masters do not belong. We had been fools to try to accept him; masters are always outsiders. But it did not matter so very much; we went on with our collecting of stamps, butterflies, fossils, our catalogues of brands of car and motor-cycle, our mimicries and private jokes, our paper aeroplanes and trove from Sunday walks – an old sheep's skull, the corpse of a stoat, a bunch of cowslips. Things and statistics and names are more important to boys of twelve than friendship with any master.

Inspired by Mr. Charles I had read Malory's *Morte d'Arthur*, sitting in a windowseat and reading with such concentration that my hair stuck to the paint of the woodwork. The book was very long but by no means too long for me; I revelled in the reiteration of incident; to go from joust to joust and count how many knights Sir Tristram or Sir Pelleas unseated was as exciting as reading the County Cricket batting averages. My friends and I found a table in an old summerhouse and became the knights ourselves, drawing lots for the leading names. On Sundays we rode about the country on branches of trees, each with an ashplant for a sword, and tried to use the Malory diction. It was my last open make-believe before my adolescence, after which time, like everyone else, I lived half the time in fantasy, but craftily, deceiving both others and myself. This adult make-believe is something we have foolishly ignored. Teddy Bock[5] is always with us, and in the epoch of Hitler – Siegfried Redivivus – it is not only a mistake but a disaster to ignore those underground motives which cause both art and war. Economic factors? Yes, but they aren't the whole story. Man is essentially weak and he wants power; essentially lonely, he creates familiar daemons, Impossible Shes, and bonds – of race or creed – where no bonds are. He cannot live by bread or Marx alone; he must always be after the Grail.

Together with the *Morte d'Arthur* I studied astronomy which combined the excitement of collecting with the glamour of Church. I would read about the nebulas and the stars that had gone black, and that was like organ music;

---

[5] A character in MacNeice's private childhood mythology, whom he describes in his autobiography as 'my oracle, my familiar and my general consolation'.

and I would learn by heart the distances of the stars and the diameters of the planets, and that was like Sir Pelleas or Hobbs. Then when the night came I would go out collecting, and this was made attractively difficult at school by our early hours and in Ireland by the cloudy sky – you might just pick up a star here or there in a rift. In January 1921 I found myself wonderfully alone in an empty carriage in a rocking train in the night between Waterloo and Sherborne. Stars on each side me; I ran from side to side of the carriage checking the constellations as the train changed its direction. Bagfuls and bucketfuls of stars; I could open my mouth to the night and drink them.

In my last two terms at Sherborne I took things easy, for I had got an entrance scholarship to Marlborough College and felt that this interim was only marking time. When I told Mr. Powys[6] there were seven hundred and fifty boys at Marlborough he said he hoped I would keep my head above water. I was a little alarmed at this remark, decided that at Marlborough I would behave quite differently; no more buffoonery. At Sherborne I had become established as an eccentric and that gets awfully boring.

On the Twelfth of July Powys came into my dormitory and said: 'What is all this they do in your country today? Isn't it all mumbo-jumbo?' Remembering my father and Home Rule and the bony elbows of Miss Craig and the black file of mill-girls and the wickedness of Carson and the dull dank days between sodden haycocks and foghorns, I said Yes it was. And I felt uplifted. To be speaking man to man to Powys and giving the lie to the Red Hand of Ulster was power, was freedom, meant I was nearly grown up. King William is dead and his white horse with him, and Miss Craig will never put her knuckles in my ears again. But Powys went out of the dormitory and Mr. Cameron came in, his underlip jutting and his eyes enraged. 'What were you saying to Mr. Powys?' Oh this division of allegiance! That the Twelfth of July was mumbo-jumbo was true, and my father thought so too, but the moment Mr. Cameron appeared I felt rather guilty and cheap. Because I had been showing off to Powys and because Mr. Cameron being after all Irish I felt I had betrayed him.

Before I left, Mr. Powys gave me a sex-talk, putting it very delicately, working up from butterflies to birds. I could not make head or tail of it and when he said, 'You know what part of the body I mean?' I said, 'No, I don't.' So Powys began again with a joke about a baby wetting its bed, and that put me off the whole business because I was very prudish. I felt a chill in my bones and a weight on my stomach, and when I got back to dormitory I was silent and thought about it. But decided it was best not to think about it.

---

[6] Littleton Powys (1874–1955), headmaster of Sherborne, was a member of the famous literary family that included the novelist John Cowper (1872–1963). MacNeice's biographer suggests that Littleton may have been 'an idealized father-figure' to young Louis. See Stallworthy, *Louis MacNeice*, p. 60.

Once a week we used to go and shoot in a miniature rifle range. The entrance was at the far end and the path which ran along outside the range had a border of snapdragons. They were very gay in that last summer, opening their mouths and snapping, the name reminded me of the raisins burning in the brandy and the harsh reports of the shots inside the wall counterpointed them oddly, both colour and noise were vital. If only one could live the life of the senses and have no problems, no need to keep one's head above water! But even the senses had their problems – there was always that baby in the bed.

That September, before I went to Marlborough, my family took me to Anglesey and we attended a church service in Welsh. Religion in Welsh seemed more primeval and in the pew behind was a woman suckling her baby. Her breast was round and white and, though I did not like the noise of the baby sucking, I was not disgusted. It was talking about these things that was disgusting but the things themselves seemed all right. They sang the Gloria in Welsh and I thought what fun – always moving on, Sherborne to Marlborough, sandstone to flint, Glory be and Glory be and the world is there for the having.

41
Kevin FitzGerald, *With O'Leary in the Grave*

With an introduction by Philip Mason (Salisbury: Michael Russell, 1986). 175pp.; pp. 103–6.

Born in London to a well-to-do family of Irish descent, Kevin FitzGerald (1902–1993) grew up in Radlett, Hertfordshire, where his father owned land and property. His autobiography covers the first three decades of his life, beginning with a detailed recollection of his middle-class Catholic upbringing and English public school education, and ending with an account of his experiences as a farm labourer in Western Canada in the 1920s. FitzGerald explains that his decision to emigrate was provoked by a row with his father, who is memorably portrayed as a man of Dickensian eccentricity, given to haggling over the price of restaurant meals and publicly berating complete strangers for their perceived shortcomings. In 1919 this formidable patriarch purchased a large estate in County Tipperary for his son, who had by then decided upon a career in farming. FitzGerald's memories of his time on the farm are among his most treasured. Amplifying the note of wistful nostalgia suggested by the book's Yeatsian title, he reflects: 'I never found anything to beat the pleasure of ploughing with a pair of horses, on a fine October day in a vanished Ireland.' When the War of Independence made life in Tipperary untenable, FitzGerald was sent to study agriculture at Seale Hayne College in Newton Abbot, Devonshire. In the following extract he describes his first, fractious encounter with the college principal, Lieutenant Colonel D. R. Edwardes-Ker, which took place in the summer of 1921 against a backdrop of intense political activity that was the prelude to the Anglo-Irish Treaty negotiations of the autumn. As FitzGerald presents it, this larger political conflict was played out in miniature during a testy battle of wills.

The first meeting of the Seale Hayne Union Club took place about three weeks after the beginning of term. On that hot summer night in 1921 we assembled in the Refectory to form a Union Club. We were, the Principal said, as he took the chair, to elect a President and a Committee. We would become responsible for the 'tone' of the College, all its internal affairs as they affected us as students, and would put forward recommendations and suggestions to himself and through him to the Board of Governors. We elected a President and an Editor for a magazine. The Principal departed and a general discussion began about what we thought the College should be like.

Someone said something about the food. Someone else said it was appalling, dogs would flinch from it. I asked what could be done. The Chairman said he was prepared to lodge 'the general feeling of the meeting' with the Principal. I asked what was the good of that. The Principal would say that he would look into it, would have a word with the Steward, who no doubt would have a word with the chef. I said that a better idea occurred to me. At the 'meat tea' next evening, as the servants came in with plates of disgusting sausage meat, we should sit in silence until all were served and then, on signal from our Chairman, rise and hurl the contents of our plates – not, mark you, the plates – at the Steward as he stood smirking by the doors to the kitchen. He would, I suggested, look pretty ridiculous standing there covered with sausage meat in front of the staff at High Table. He would be unharmed, and we would have made our point in a way which could not be ignored. There was laughter and some cheering, but it was decided to leave matters to the Chairman. It was all rather fun and rather enjoyable and we broke up affably and went to our bedrooms.

The following day I was asked if I would make it convenient to call upon the Principal in his office. I think I rather expected to be asked my opinion on one or two practical matters. His secretary told me to go in, and there I was on the first of the many office 'mats' on which I was to find myself as I fought my way through life.

Edwardes-Ker was a tall, immensely handsome man and he smiled upon me. I smiled back. I am even now constantly smiling at men holding concealed knives which they are about to drive into me.

'FitzGerald,' he began, 'you are Irish, I think.' I had not yet grasped that this is the typically British beginning to particular forms of insult. 'You are Irish, I think' is a useful all-round opening for 'You are dirty; dishonest; seem to have acquired some unpleasant habits; are a Catholic, militant Protestant, red revolutionary', or anything else which the speaker dislikes. When I answered the Principal that, yes, I was Irish, he went on: 'You are also, I gather, a dangerous Bolshevik.' This seemed a trifle extreme and I said of course I wasn't, and why was he saying that. I was very polite, using the word 'sir' a lot, and feeling a bit worried. He was stern and unyielding. 'My information is that you made a highly charged inflammatory speech at the Union last night, suggesting, nay, urging, an attack on our most excellent Steward and endeavouring to create here the kind of atmosphere which this country is now putting down with absolute finality in the country from which you have just come.'

I said it was not like that at all. That I hadn't just come from Ireland, although my father owned land there. I had come from Lambeth where I had been working in a garage. 'Where you have clearly picked up some very dangerous ideas,' he said. He went on to say that he understood that I had received my education at the most exclusive Catholic School in the world,[1] that surely the schoolmate of the Duke of Norfolk, the Lord Dormer, the Viscount Southwell, the de Traffords, the Scropes, all the old English Catholic families, was not trying to import into this peaceful Devonshire enclave the kind of regime which had destroyed the Romanoffs, produced Rasputin, created a bloodbath in Eastern Europe. I began to see that I was going to be sacked. I stammered out something about thinking I was making a cheerful speech about nothing very much, that people had laughed, that no one had actually done anything. 'FitzGerald,' he said, 'you are that detestable and dangerous animal, a silver-tongued rogue and agitator. There is to be a short meeting of Governors within the hour, prior to their Annual Luncheon; the First Annual Luncheon, indeed. I have decided that you will have an opportunity to state your case before them. If they think as I do you will have to leave us, FitzGerald. That is all.'

I hung about for the rest of the morning until just before lunch when I was 'called in'. There they all were, filling the Principal's office. One of them became a lord, one lived in a castle, one was President of the South Devon Herd Book Society; they all looked grand and intimidating. The Principal introduced me and they began to ask questions, beginning of course with: 'Colonel Edwardes-Ker says you are Irish.' There I stood, hands behind my back, in the attitude of that boy in blue velvet who was being asked when he last saw his father. The inquisition went on until suddenly a stout lady intervened. 'Mr Principal and gentlemen,' she said, 'we are making ourselves ridiculous. It is perfectly obvious to me that this handsome [that's what she said] this handsome young Irishman is a gentleman, with the habits of one, and with an extremely amusing face. I wish I had heard his speech; I feel I should have been won over, and have thrown my luncheon today at our Steward. I suggest that we ask Mr FitzGerald to go away and return to his studies. Let us caution him of course, and remind him that life here is a grim and serious business into which no comic relief must be allowed to enter.'

Everyone laughed, and I was told to go. I was saved only by Miss Calmady Hamlyn,[2] a famous breeder of Dartmoor ponies, long dead I suppose, but never forgotten by me. I only saw her once more over the years. She was walking across the quadrangle after a meeting and our paths crossed. I bowed, and she smiled: 'Ah, the Bolshevik,' she said, laughed at me, and went her way. I wish her well, wherever she may be.

---

[1] FitzGerald was educated at the prestigious Catholic London Oratory School.
[2] Sylvia Calmady-Hamlyn was honorary secretary of the Dartmoor Pony Society for over 30 years.

42
Sean O'Casey, *Rose and Crown*

(London: Macmillan, 1952). 306pp.; pp. 1–5.

Sean O'Casey (1880–1964) was at once a compulsive and a hesitant self-portraitist. Six volumes of autobiography, written over a period of 25 years and published between 1939 and 1954, testify to a protracted obsession with textual self-definition. Yet in his written comments on these works he was reluctant to use the term 'autobiography', preferring instead synonyms such as 'reveries' and 'biographical sketches'.[1] Such semantic scepticism points to the experimental nature of O'Casey's autobiographical writings, further signified by his use of third-person narration and a protean protagonist who is variously 'Johnny Casside', 'Irish Jack', 'Sean O'Cathasaigh' and, finally, 'Sean O'Casey'. Being disquieting and provocative was, of course, part of the playwright's mission in life. His celebrated Dublin trilogy – *The Shadow of a Gunman* (1923), *Juno and the Paycock* (1924) and *The Plough and the Stars* (1926) – was inspired by his fierce and often fractious involvement with the enmeshed politics of Irish language revival, trade unionism, socialism and nationalism, which began with his joining the Gaelic League in 1906. The Dublin premier of the *Plough* outraged nationalist audiences in February 1926 and within weeks O'Casey had departed for London to attend a performance of *Juno* and collect the Hawthornden Prize. Although he fully intended to return, his exile became permanent after his next play, *The Silver Tassie*, was rejected by Yeats and the Abbey Theatre in 1928.[2] In 1938 O'Casey moved to Totnes in Devon with his actress wife Eileen and family. Sixteen years later they relocated to Torquay, where he died in September 1964.

Like many creative migrants, O'Casey's physical separation from Ireland acted as a catalyst for narrative self-interpretation. As early as August 1926 he wrote to his publisher: 'I have thought of writing a book reminiscent of my experiences'; over two decades later he was still to be found 'with a pen in one hand and a spy-glass in the

---

[1] Michael Kenneally, *Portraying the Self: Sean O'Casey and the Art of Autobiography* (Gerrards Cross: Colin Smythe, 1988), p. 237, n.6.

[2] Christopher Murray, *Sean O'Casey: Writer at Work, A Biography* (Dublin: Gill and Macmillan, 2004), pp. 183 ff.

other – to take an odd look at Eirinn through'.[3] O'Casey went further than most in adjusting the autobiographical lens to suit his aesthetic ends, however. His primary concern, as Michael Kenneally observes, 'is not with the palpable events which might constitute historical truth, but with their impact on the shaping consciousness of the protagonist'.[4] His eschewal of the autobiographical 'I' in favour of a series of personae is the stylistic expression of O'Casey's awareness of the impossibility of penning down in words an ultimately unknowable self. The gulf between narrator and protagonist further underscores the dynamic nature of personal identity, while also accentuating the extent to which the time and place of writing conditions the configuration and evaluation of the past. Thus, in the following extract from the opening chapter of *Rose and Crown* – a volume written between 1947 and 1951 – the omniscient narrative viewpoint complements the perceived objectification and commodification of the newly notorious 'slum dramatist' on his arrival in London in March 1926.

Here he was now, planting a foot for the first time on the pavement of London; planting it firmly, with a confident air and a fluttering heart. Sliding with the hiss of steam and the throb of pistons into the heart of the

> Great flower that opens but at night,
> Great city of the midnight sun,
> Whose day begins when day is done.

A London apprentice now. Listen!

> Oranges and lemons, say the bells of St. Clement's.
> When will you pay me? say the bells at Old Bailey.
> When I grow rich, say the bells at Shoreditch.

How different was the view now from that of the lovely coast of Wales, lacing the land's edge from Holyhead to Chester. Coming within the grip of the city, he had been wondering through miles of the journey at the dismal wretchedness of the houses, apparently trotting away from him as the train ambled to the end of its journey; trotting away from him so that he mightn't fully see the abject royalty of their miserable appearance. The train had run through a long, drab gauntlet of houses, some of them fat with filth. The magnificent, wealthy city of London, with her gilded Mayor and red-robed Aldermen, was entered through long kennels of struggling poverty and disordered want. Sisters to the houses he had so often seen, slinky with

---

[3] Cited in Ronald F. Ayling, 'The Origin and Evolution of a Dublin Epic', in Robert G. Lowery (ed.), *Essays on Sean O'Casey's Autobiographies* (London: Macmillan, 1981), pp. 4, 28.
[4] Kenneally, *Portraying the Self*, p. 143.

shame, in the shabbiest streets of Dublin. There were the lacerated walls, the windows impudent with dirt, the poor, shrinking clothing, reluctant to be washed, hanging from poles thrust through the windows, fixed to the sills. Just like the hidden parts of Dublin. 'Faith, her privates we. One didn't land in London through a lane of roses.

Euston! Alight here as many Irish had done before him; a short visit so often extended to take the emigrant's rest of life. England; Sasana! Euston; a sprawling untidy place, dim and dark; tormented with many sounds – the clatter of trucks, the patter of hurrying, fussy feet; babble and squeak of passengers not sure of the right train or the proper platform; the sibilant hiss of steam; the sturdy smell of smoke; the soothing, sickly scent of oil; porters hurrying, guards sauntering amid the rustle of paper and magazine, bought by people who would never read the half of them; women sitting semi-alert on benches, waiting for the hands of a big clock to tell them when to move; streams of men, women, and children, dropping from the train that had just stopped, pouring along under the grimy roof like an underground river towards an open sluice-gate, to divide into rivulets and trickles, spreading fanwise to different parts of the mammoth city. Each one an individual, a soul-body; something separate from each so like itself, conceit concealing that each one is a simulacrum of the other;

> Albert Johnson is my nayem,
> England is my nation;
> London is my dwelling-place,
> And heaven my destination.

Heaven! Meanwhile, we must be satisfied with the smoke and the grime of Euston. 'Seen at night, or through a mist, Euston Station is one of the most impressive sights in London', said Aubrey Beardsley. Well, seen by night, or through a mist, there may be many things appearing impressive, be it either man or dog or eunuch; and the picturer of his own horrible delusions added, 'Euston Station has made it unnecessary to visit Egypt'. The slimy, fruitful Nile, sun, sand, date-palm, and bedouin – none are needed. Pharaoh porters about here.[5]

To Sean, who stared at the building before he hid himself away in a taxi, the entrance looked surlily bewildered, as if it had been set down in the wrong place, as indeed it had, for ancient Egyptian architecture does not wed itself with English life. Though it forced itself into the appearance of a temple, here was no shrine at which to pray for a safe journey from one place to another.

---

[5] Aubrey Beardsley (1872–1898), the avant-garde illustrator, was eulogising Euston's Great Arch, completed in 1837 and demolished in 1962 against a chorus of opposition.

The ponderous pillars holding up its tremendous back looked like a monster's heavy feet standing in a jungle clearance, the whole brute staring in front of itself, not knowing which way to turn.

There was James B. Fagan[6] hurrying towards him, having caught sight of the red muffler encircling Sean's neck, the insignia Sean had written to say would reveal his advent to London. Sean's play had been transferred from the Royalty to the Fortune, a little theatre directly opposite the towering, bully-like Royal Theatre in Drury Lane – Falstaff and the little page.[7] The play was to open itself out in the new theatre two nights from now, and Sean was to be kept hidden till then so that familiarity with others should not mar the appearance of the slum dramatist on the first night in the Fortune; enhancing publicity by standing on the stage, grinning, bowing, and saying a few sweet words to the applauding audience that had filled the house for the first performance.

Embedded in a taxi, he was bowled off to the Kenilworth Hotel, Bloomsbury; hustled up in a lift to his room, while Fagan waited below, like a warder, till Sean had freshened himself with a wash, and was ready for Fagan to take him off silently. He was to be kept like a peril in an oyster till the first night of the play had passed into time that neither he nor Fagan would ever touch again. After a light meal in Fagan's flat in Great Russell Street, Sean was again embedded into a taxi, and taken, like a prisoner out for an hour's amusement, to the Duke of York's Theatre to see Jean Forbes-Robertson[8] playing in Chekhov's *Uncle Vanya*. The theatre he was in was no different from the big ones of Dublin. That was all he learned from this outing. Things were so different with him now, so new, so far from what he had been used to; his future was so uncertain, his mind so buoyant with jostling thoughts; and he was hushed so deeply back to the rear of the box, with Mary Grey[9] and James Fagan in front of him, that to this day he cannot remember a single thing about the play, the acting, or the production. The one memory remaining is the name of the play and the name of the leading actress, and these were fixed in his mind by the lovely coloured lights of red, yellow, and white, flashing over the entrance of the theatre, telling out her name and the name of the Russian play she acted in. The first London play he had seen, he hadn't seen at all. A long wait in the box when the play was over to ensure that the crowd had gone, in fear anyone among it should have recognised Sean, and

---

[6] James Bernard Fagan (1873–1933), Belfast-born actor, theatre manager and playwright, who staged the London premier of the *Plough* at the Fortune Theatre in May 1926. Fagan was O'Casey's minder during his first few months in the city.

[7] *Juno* transferred from the Royalty Theatre, where it had its London premier on 16 November 1925, to the Fortune on 8 March 1926.

[8] Actress daughter of the famous Shakespearian actor and theatre manager Sir Johnston Forbes-Robertson (1853–1937).

[9] The stage name of James Fagan's second wife Ada Bevan, whom he married in 1914.

have shouted out the hot news that O'Casey was here. Then a quick retreat into a taxi again, and so to bed.[10]

He was to be shown off, a new oddity, an odd wonder; a guttersnipe among the trimly educated and the richly clad; the slum dramatist, who, in the midst of a great darkness, had seen a greater light. Fagan was constantly pulling Sean away from his own thoughts, trying to listen to the part of England speaking to him, trying to see the part of England passing him by. He was pulled here, pulled there; brought, bowing, before young men and women, before elderly men, before anyone who could write about him in the daily papers and in the weekly journals, so keeping the romance of his arrival in London before the people in order that the beautiful sign of House Full should garnish the front of the theatre nightly.

He was photographed getting into a taxi and getting out of one; photographed in the theatre, and in the flat where he lived; photographed talking to policemen; brought face to face with those whose pencils could dash down a swift impression to appear fresh and full-blown in some paper the following day, or in some periodical at the end of the week; some, grinning and ghastly, showing themselves in a paper on the Lord's day. Coriolanus O'Casside hurried here and there by Menenius Fagan, to show himself, to say what a good fellow he was. He was tired of it before it had well begun. Very boring, for Sean in his heart didn't care a damn what anyone thought of him. Once, when a photographer handed him a huge, green, cardboard shamrock, telling him to fix it in his coat, and look gay, Sean let loose on him; and James Fagan, going white, heard for the first time the savage and profane vernacular of the Dublin navvy.

---

[10] An example of O'Casey's punning style. Fagan's play, *And So to Bed*, was staged at the Queen's Theatre in 1926.

43

Rearden Conner, *A Plain Tale from the Bogs*

(London: John Miles, 1937). 256pp.; pp. 217–23; 226–7.

Dublin-born Patrick Rearden Conner (1907–1991) was the only child of a Royal Irish Constabulary policeman, a fact which led to him being bullied at school and socially ostracised during his adolescent years in a city convulsed by political turmoil. The first part of his autobiography forms an absorbing record of the insurrectionary drama being played out on the streets of post-1916 Dublin and Cork, where he was sent to be educated, and his changing responses to it, responses that were deeply coloured by his estrangement from a father who was hostile to his son's literary ambitions. Disillusioned by the suffocating conservatism of post-revolutionary Irish society, Conner emigrated to London in the mid-1920s, where he endured periods of unemployment, homelessness and depression before finding regular work as a landscape gardener. All the while, the urge to write persisted, as the following extract from his autobiography attests. The success of his debut novel, *Shake Hands With the Devil* (1933), a melodrama set during the War of Independence, was the turning point that launched him on a writing career that quickly became prolific: Conner published a further five novels in the 1930s alone, as well as *A Plain Tale from the Bogs*. Outspoken and forthright, the book is both a document of artistic development and a self-portrait of an outsider's struggle to assert himself creatively in the face of poverty, social prejudice and a predilection for existential despair. Having charted his circuitous route to literary success, Connor offers a critical overview of social and cultural trends in 1930s Britain in the closing chapters, and concludes with a forceful left-wing critique of the anaesthesising effects of a 'sugary' commercialised culture, which he sees as stifling individualist thought and collective action in equal parts.

Life proceeds almost to a pattern. Nineteen twenty-nine, 'thirty, and 'thirty-one are 'boom' years for me. The suburb around us grows under our very eyes. I am kept busier than any bee all through the winter months, laying out or helping to lay out gardens. Throughout the spring and summer months I have little time to spare of an evening. But then comes a pause. The suburb is reaching its boundaries. There are only a few more houses to be built. The 'boom' is at an end. [...]

During the 'boom' period, although labouring very hard, I found time to read the works of contemporary authors from the local Boots' library.[1] I have still with me the desire to write, sometimes even stronger than ever. In slow stages I scribble off a novel about suburban life in London. I buy a rebuilt typewriter on the pay-by-the-month system. The old game starts afresh. The MS. is sent off, and comes bouncing back again and again like a large rubber ball in a spell of catch-as-catch-can. I dash off short stories, tales of detection and adventure. They are seeds that fall on rock. My wife points out that I never say, '*If* this comes back from So-and-So I'll send it to So-and-so,' but always '*When* this comes back ——'.

Yet, I do not lose hope. I am a pessimist by training, if not by nature. I have found so often the sneer behind the smile, the sting in the smooth phrase, that my belief in the goodness of Man is badly shaken. But I am unable to bring my pessimism to my writing. It colours it; but it does not prevent me from going on and on with it in the hope of eventual success.

The world around us changes. Its hectic pace is slowing down. Short skirts, showing knees and legs that sometimes charmed and often disillusioned men, have passed away. 'Talkies' have come to the cinemas. 'Sonny Boy' has washed its saccharine waves over our world. 'The Wedding of the Painted Doll' becomes as significant as 'Alexander's Rag-time Band'. Errand boys go around whistling 'If I had a talking picture of you-ou——!' or 'Just like in a story-book——'.

The age of film 'musicals' has replaced the age of film 'epics'. Paul White-man[2] begins to mean more than D. W. Griffith.[3] Hollywood is ruling our world at last, giving its inhabitants new manners, a new mode and code of life, even a new accent. Young girls cast aside their personalities and change their spots as rapidly as any chameleon. They are Clara Bows one week, Greta Garbos the next, Janet Gaynors another week. The menace of 'crooning' creeps into our lives. This is the dawn of the Romantic Age. We have been told over and over again that there aint no sense in sittin' on the fence all by ourselves in the moonlight.

Six-wheeled buses are on the streets of London. On the Underground trains sliding automatic doors have replaced the old cage doors at which a guard used to stand. Long escalators in the stations make country cousins giggle nervously. Marble-walled palaces, with jazz music poured out by gaily-clad bandsmen, raise their elaborate outlines in the name of Food at Popular Prices. Cinemas become super cinemas. Film critics are on the verge of

---

[1] Boots' Booklovers' Library was founded by the retail chemist Jesse Boot (1850–1931) in the 1890s as part of his company's expansion and diversification.

[2] Paul Whiteman (1890–1967), popular American orchestral leader of the 1920s.

[3] D. W. Griffith (1875–1948), pioneering American film director.

hysteria through trying to think up adjectives in praise of the mammoth productions of Hollywood magnates. London takes on a more garish note, a more strident voice. The 'cat's whisker' retires before the onslaught of the loud speaker. The name of J. L. Baird[4] is being spoken of in households as that of the man who has the 'mad' idea of one day showing us the Derby on a screen while it is being run miles away. Greater London shows signs of becoming a menace. The 'flat' craze takes hold, and huge blocks of them are built.

In fiction the day of Michael Arlen[5] is over. Evelyn Waugh has ridiculed without mercy the Bright Young and Not-so-Young Things. Edgar Wallace has his pulse on the wrist of the nation. The war novels come with a rush, and ebb out like a tide. The Richard Aldingtons and the Sarah Salts tinge the printed page with mild cynicism. Mr. James Douglas[6] takes up the cudgels on behalf of morality in fiction. The word 'gigolo' begins to mean something to the general public, and the younger novelists make merry with it in no uncertain manner. But this little wave of cynicism cannot stem the flow of romanticism that gushes out from the 'talkies'. The world wants to believe that every night is as 'blue as your eyes are blue' and that romance can be found on every 'bench in the park'.

I have a deeper worry than the inability to crash the walls of the literary Jericho. The winter ahead of me stretches bleak and barren. The foreman tells me frankly that there is no work for us in sight. No contract job has been secured. The world that seemed so safe and firm rocks like a raft under my feet once more.

But again I am lucky. I am picked as one of a gang that is to clear a wood for building purposes. A road has been cut through this wood. Houses are to spring up on both sides of the road. The trees will have to be cleared back to a good depth to give room for gardens at the fronts and backs of the houses.

We arrive in the wood one morning with saws, spades, ropes, and mattocks. I assume that we are to fell the trees with a cross-cut. The man in charge tells me that we are to dig out the trees, so that no root will remain to impede the men who lay out the gardens or to send up sucker shoots when the lawns are laid. I look at the tall stout elms with their widespread branches and think that the man has a slate loose somewhere. But I realise very soon that he is saner than myself.

One of us climbs each tree and ties a heavy rope to a stout branch just above the fork. Then three of us start digging a trench around the tree, some feet out from the trunk, as men do when root-pruning fruit trees. The first thin roots we meet are chopped away with a hatchet. We dig on and come to thicker roots. These are cut with an axe. Now we are down to our knees,

---

[4] John Logie Baird (1888–1946), inventor of television.
[5] Michael Arlen (1895–1956), Bulgarian-born novelist, author of *The Green Hat* (1924).
[6] James Douglas (1867–1940), journalist, novelist and *Daily Express* editor during the 1920s.

finding stouter roots. We clear the clay away from them and use a handsaw to cut through them, removing the complete section so that the trench is clear. Down, down, we go, up to our hips, then to our waists. The roots here are very thick. The section cut out to the width of the trench is a long log of black soapy wood, useless for burning, curiously fleshy, yet tougher than any leather. These thick roots are severed with a special flexible short cross-cut. [...]

In this manner I help to dig out four elm trees a day. We work in groups of three. The job lasts until Spring. I realise now that I am as a man re-born. This is certainly the hardest job that I have ever been called upon to do. At times the cold is bitter when rain and wind grip us in the clayey trenches. Warm hands and warm feet are out of the question. Yet, I am not unhappy. There is no bitterness in my heart, no abuse of my lot. I accept my fate. I am not dissatisfied with it, because I know that I am fortunate to secure this work. I have seen the most intense and unuttered suffering brought on by lack of work among those more deserving of it than I.

My heart may ache when the fine elms are knocked flat to make way for brick boxes. But a job is a job, and I have to lay my thanks at the feet of Progress. Our spades ply vigorously. Behind us the cross-cuts of our mates hum merrily as the long trunks are sawn into transportable sections. Great bonfires devour the brushwood. Many a man goes home in the evening with a few logs from the end of a branch in a sack, or tied up with rope under his arm. Door-to-door timber hawkers are attracted to the scene like wasps to a pot of jam. We have to keep a sharp eye out in case they 'pinch' the wood when we are having our midday meal. We sell them logs at so much a hundred. They split these generously-proportioned logs into two and make about three hundred per cent profit, because they sell a hundred of the thin logs at a higher price than they paid to our foreman for a hundred of the fat logs.

As Spring comes we listen often to the mating songs of birds in the wood that stretches away behind us. For minutes on end every man stands still, drinking in the liquid song of a blackbird. Early in the morning as we approach the wood I am conscious of a hush, as though the trees and birds know that we are coming to desolate this paradise. The frost thaws, and long drops hang like jewels on the branches. On frosty evenings the sky is blood red. One early evening we stand watching an airplane making its way slowly across the crimson background. Every man stands silent, gripped by the spectacle of the plume of smoke trailing out from the darkened plane against the black-red sky. [. . .]

Now something of the aloofness of the earth I dig seeps into me. I move through the outer world between home and work as though in a dream. Around my ears flows the sugary 'theme song' music. But I do not let it enter my mind. Literary critics gush in print about this or that 'masterpiece'. But I pass them by on the library shelves. I have emerged from the stage when 'life' seems the presentation by some woman of five hundred pages of love and renunciation. I am unable to believe any more that realism means describing how a man shaves or gets into bed with a person of the opposite sex, or of the same sex. The 'marvellous picture' of a proletarian in So-and-So's new book is constantly blurred for me by the image of an old man I have seen shivering with exposure while his urine ran down his legs from his weak bladder.

But it seems that life in books has to have a capital 'L'. What I have seen of it is only life itself, the small 'l' unromantic form of existence. In this new age we must not be unromantic. We must romanticise everybody, the domestic servant, the East Ender, the workless tramp, the prostitute, the miner. It is dangerous to look too closely around us in case we see the poverty so near at hand. In Wales, in the North, or even in the East End, it is at a safe distance. But it is not pleasant to think that it lurks over there on that estate of Council houses within a mile or two of our most exclusive suburbs.

I think often of evenings that I will take pen and paper and write all this down, that I will fashion it into a novel to illustrate the hopelessness, the bitterness of the lot of far too many. The young among the poor may turn to sex, to love, to the cinema, for escape from the drabness of life. In this way they win happiness for a time. But they are fighting a fierce battle, living hand to mouth all the time. Illness is there round the corner, with 'short time' and 'slack time' ahead of it. Middle age creeps quickly into old age. It is not of the young that I think, but of the look in the eyes of the ageing and of the old. This look I cannot keep from haunting me.

An old man shoulders his spade at the end of our day's work and says in a tone that has no trace of bitterness in it, no trace of sadness, 'Never mind, Paddy mate! That's another day nearer the grave!'

44
Michael Stapleton, *The Threshold*

(London: Hutchinson, 1958). 272pp.; pp. 48–51; 58.

Michael Stapleton (1923–1994) was born in Dungarvan, County Waterford. When he was four, his family moved to Hackney in north London, where he was educated. He left school in his early teens to become a butcher's boy and later served as a merchant seaman during the Second World War. After the war he worked as an actor for a short time before swapping the theatre for a career in publishing. He worked as a proof-reader with Oxford University Press in the 1950s and later became a commissioning editor with the Hamlyn Group. Stapleton's abiding love of opera inspired a short book on the Sadler's Wells Opera in 1954. This brought him to the attention of Edith Sitwell, who encouraged him to write his autobiography, which became one of the first titles to be published by New Authors, an imprint launched by the Hutchinson Group in 1957. The stated aim of this new publishing venture was to reconcile 'the frustrations of the new writer who has something of importance to say' with 'the harsh economic climate of publishing as it is today'. As if to reassure hesitant readers, *The Threshold* is prefaced by a selection of approbatory comments from critics who read the work when it was still in manuscript. Special praise is reserved for Stapleton's social realism, particularly the documentary accuracy of his account of swapping 'a classless Waterford existence for the revoltingly petty class consciousness of N. E. London; one facet of despair for another'. At the heart of this narrative of transition is a richly evocative account of an extended, carefree holiday the author spent with his mother and brother in Waterford in the early 1930s. As this extract makes clear, this visit grew ever more paradisiacal in retrospect, partly because this was to be the last time that Stapleton would see Ireland and partly because 'home' would gradually lose its Edenic lustre over time.

I can't remember when it was that I ceased to regard Ireland as my home. I suppose it must have been when I ceased to think of anywhere as my home; when I was full of a longing to break the loose threads that still held me and seek my identity in the wide world. By then the place where I lived had ceased to be home, it was merely the place where I ate, slept and to which circumstance confined me. It was no place to which I loved to come when I was weary, it was the only place there was. But at the age of seven, Ireland was home. It was where I was born, where my mother was born, and where our hearts were. Ireland was where we would all return and stay, if we could. In Ireland were wide horizons and immense skies, not one stifling city that had no end. Ireland was the beautiful country the English had dishonoured and whose sons had died for her; where the songs were sung of a Celtic golden age, and a sadder age much nearer to us. Ireland was home.

On that morning we hurried on deck to look at Ireland, but in the early morning light there was little to see. Just the docks, a ship or two, and a little distance away the train we were to board. But how different, once aboard!

It coughed and snorted its way through Wicklow, through a land as fair as anyone could have hoped for. The sun was shining, the air like crystal, and everything as green and spectacular as we convinced ourselves we remembered it. Mammy watched us, smiling. What was she thinking, I wonder. Was she as glad to be home as we? I remember that she looked very happy, and I like to think she was.

We were met at Dungarvan by my father's father. He was, of course, my grandfather, but we were later to meet my mother's mother who was my grandmother. They were in no way related, which I couldn't understand, so I always thought of them afterwards in separate terms. We, the grandchildren, were fussed over to a degree which quite overwhelmed us. All the people we met during the short walk to my grandfather's house carried on in the most extravagant fashion.

'Here's Jack's wife, come home for a while,' he would say, 'and these are two of my grandchildren.'

'Are they now? Sure they're fine children, Mrs Stapleton. What are ye'r names?'

'Michael,' I said, politely. 'Richard,' said Dick, politely.

There would be a great gust of indulgent laughter.

'Sure ye'r oul' English children, I'm thinking. Do ye go to school over there?'

'Yes. I'm in Miss Poole's class and Mick's in Miss Ives's.'

Dick always seemed to have this information ready before me.

'Are ye good? Or do they belt ye, the teachers? What d'ye learn? Can ye read?'

At this point Mammy would tell them that I could read when I was five and that Dick was nearly as good now. That I had made my first Holy Communion and had won a prize last year. That Dick was Miss Poole's favourite and he had a poem he learned all by himself and had to recite everywhere he went ....

Dungarvan enchanted us, for it was a town from which you could see right into the hills beyond. The sea lay just behind and ahead of us stretched miles and miles of fields and green hills.

It was a short journey to my grandfather's house, but he found time, on the way, to buy us enormous swanks of sweets. My mother was staggered at the quantity:

'Don't be eating them all yourselves, now. Keep some for Joe and Dick.'

The mention of my cousins reminded me that our journey wasn't over yet; we still had a long ride ahead of us in a pony and trap which Mick Ryan would bring to the house some time in the afternoon. He was my Aunt Maggie's husband and that made him, as far as I was concerned, my uncle.

In the early afternoon I heard a horse stop outside. My mother fairly ran to the pavement and I saw her embrace a dark-haired, serious-looking man at the door. I ran out with Dick, and were once more shown to someone. Mick Ryan gazed down at us and said:

'They turned out fine, Mary. Ye did right, taking them away.'

Then he took his arm from her shoulder and bent down to look more closely.

'Dick's just like you, Mary, and Mick's the image of Michael. Wait till Mamah sees him – she'll have a real turn.'

He put an arm round each of us and lifted us into the air, a wide smile lighting his face. I put my arms round his neck and laughed into his thick black hair, while my mother looked on, smiling with happiness.

There was a meal waiting for him, and while he ate questions flew back and forth. I gathered that a visit to Dungarvan was something Mick couldn't afford to make very often once the spring had begun, and apart from the questions that rained on my mother, there were many more that Mick and my grandfather had to ask each other.

Every so often Mick would look straight at me and his dark features would break into a smile. I would smile back, then laugh, in a mixture of pleasure and embarrassment. My grandfather noticed this.

'Ye can look, sure,' he said, 'I saw it meself, the minute he got off the train.'

'He's the image of him. When Michael was that age he had the same round face, and when he was a man you'd never remember it, with the fine bones in his cheeks that he had, and the lines at his eyes where he'd always be laughin' ....'

'When he was a man.' My grandfather broke in with a deep sigh. 'He hadn't much chance to be a man, the poor divil. He was ready, thank God for it. Some of the poor sheevras didn't have a chance to see the priest even.'

My mother tried to intervene.

'Whisht, now. What'll ye have the kids thinking?'

Mick sat back from the table and beckoned me over to him. He pulled me between his knees and said:

'Michael was your mother's brother. He was a fine man, God rest him, and if ye're half the boy he was ye won't turn out so bad. The Black-and-Tans got him, after Mass on Easter Sunday morning. They called you Michael after him and you're the same as him, every bit o' ye.'

I was fascinated by this dark handsome man. I knew about the Black-and-Tans; they were evil Englishmen who murdered decent Irishmen because they wanted their country back. I had heard my mother sing the songs that were left from that time of grief and glory and I was to hear much more about it while we stayed in Ireland.

At three o'clock we piled into the trap and set off on the long ride to Cappagh. The journey was enchantment – never was there so much to see and exclaim about. As we left Dungarvan and proceeded into the country, a vista unfolded such as we had never dreamed existed. It was, in spite of our deep consciousness of being Irish, completely new to our eyes, this country in which we were born and extolled whenever we could. We had been babies when we left; it had faded from our memories as though we had never travelled this self-same road on our way to England. It was a glorious day in mid-April and we could see for miles. To our right the soft, undulating Waterford countryside rolled on to the sea, and to our left the land rose gently to the high hills that bordered Tipperary. [...]

I remember those days in Ireland as the happiest in my life. My mother had decided before we left London that it wouldn't be worth sending us to school, feeling sure that a new way of teaching for a period of a few months would do us more harm than good. So we were completely carefree, enjoying a procession of glorious days on which I look back as a life's treasure.

45
John Neary, *Memories of the Long Distance Kiddies*

(Australia: Tony Ross, n.d. [1994]). 66pp.; pp. 47–52.

John Neary (1910–2003) was born near Swinford in County Mayo and raised on a small farm which, in his own words, provided 'very little future and limited subsistence'. The eldest of five children, he was groomed for emigration from an early age and in 1926 he duly departed for the Skipton hiring fare, where his life as a 'long distance kiddy'– a colloquial term for a notoriously nomadic and individualistic breed of spalpeen[1] – began. After a year of itinerant labouring, Neary found regular employment in a beet-processing factory in Selby, Yorkshire. He returned to Mayo in 1932 but soon re-emigrated to Selby, only to be confronted by economic recession and redundancy. Neary's subsequent attempts to find work in London and the south-east are the subject of the following excerpt from his short autobiography, in which he records his memories of his childhood, emigration and working life up to the point when he became a part-time fire officer in London during the Second World War. Although, as a navvy autobiography, *Memories of the Long Distance Kiddies* stands at the opposite end of the literary spectrum to *Children of the Dead End* – Neary has little of MacGill's linguistic flair, authorial self-consciousness or polemical brio – it does contain many useful historical insights into the inner workings of navvy culture in 1930s England. Through it, we can trace some of the changing social codes, attitudes and work practices that link MacGill's Edwardian labourers to Mac Amhlaigh's post-war tunnellers.

Soon after my return to England the sugar factory was forced to close its gates because of the depression and, like thousands of others, I was now redundant. All roads, it seemed, led south, to London. Known as the First City of the Empire, London was beginning to show signs of expansion. Overcrowding was at last being addressed and surrounding areas were being redeveloped

---

[1] See Ultan Cowley, *The Men Who Built Britain: A History of the Irish Navvy* (Dublin: Wolfhound Press, 2001), ch. 4.

to cater for the ever increasing population. New railways were built, new tunnels were dug, whole new suburbs were being built.

This type of work, though unknown to many of us transient Irishmen, became the most plentiful. I was persuaded to join the ranks of the hard men as they dug and blasted their wages out of the suburbs.

It was a cold March day when my companion and I made our way through the Essex countryside to the market town of Brentwood. A new railway, complete with station, was being built. As we neared the new site, my companion hopped into a ditch, covered his shoes with dirt and mud, removed his tie, replaced it with a large handkerchief, pulled his cap to a jaunty angle and, with a wink, swaggered into the site just like an old-time navvy. I, on the other hand, had committed the cardinal sin of being too well dressed. My neat navy blue suit, collar, tie and smart grey trilby hat were not at all suited to the conditions.

A team of some fifty young men, mostly Irish, were digging and carrying in mud and grime. Although it was a cold day, many of the men had removed their shirts and were building up a real sweat. The pace they worked at was fast and furious. A sign on a nearby shed stated 'NO PASSENGERS' and, from what I saw, it was taken very seriously!

We tried to make contact with the foreman, known as the kiddie or slasher. He was a big man, standing well over six feet, wearing the trademarks of his profession – a red handkerchief around his neck, corduroy trousers gaitered below the knees and the heavy donkey jacket. His pipe was well anchored in his gaiter. Each time we approached him, he walked away, shouting the odd 'dig deep you lot' or 'dig hard or you go!' My mate, dressed similarly to the slasher, moved in amongst the diggers and, after a few well-chosen words, was given a job. Now, it was my turn.

The slasher heard my request, looked at my neat appearance, reached down for his pipe and told me to come back when I was properly dressed! There was a group of men sitting in a nearby field. They sat on newspapers to protect them from the damp ground. I asked the slasher who they were and was told that they were also waiting for a job. They would sleep in the field so that they would be on the site at first light next morning in the hope of finding a vacancy. Knowing that I stood no chance of getting work here, I moved on.

I reached the market town of Romford and made enquiries of work in the building trade. I was directed to 'The Pig' – a pub in the market place, well known for what I had in mind, call for a beer and ask for 'Big Mac'. This I did and, upon meeting Mac and buying a considerable number of liquid refreshments served up in pint pots, I was given a job in South Croydon. Arriving at the town I discovered that there was no place for me to stay, so I took to the fields again!

Next morning, Mac arrived and said I'd got my medal for being a hard man for sleeping out in the open, however, this job would be finished today but, if I ever wanted another job he could be found in 'The Pig' and don't forget to bring the rake! The rake was a slang term for a generous call in a pub, which meant the same as saying 'no rake – no job!' I was learning a lot of hard lessons the hard way in order to become a truly hard man in a hard profession.

Not for me the crawling around the pubs to get a job, not for me the buying of beer to satisfy the thirst of an employer and his hangers-on. I had heard that a whole new town was being built by Costain, a large building contractor. I decided to go straight to the top! I got an interview with one of the Costain directors, a Mr Bond, at the company headquarters in London. I was given a job immediately! It was to operate a large sand and ballast pit. My task was to supply the raw materials for enough concrete to build a thousand houses!

I was able to observe the many Irishmen who came from all over England in search of work. Some were big and bronzed, used to heavy outdoor work. These men became the labour backbone of many a building contractor.

A great force of job hunters descended on the quiet village of Dagenham, set in the Essex countryside near the River Thames just east of London. This rural haven was to be turned into the biggest housing development in the world. Henry Ford built a car plant. Many other companies were to later set up their factories along the river.

From the depressed northern towns they came; one man I knew travelled all the way from Newcastle on a bicycle! A large number came down from Scotland; Ireland sent people over by the boatload! Armies of miners from the now deserted coalfields of Wales arrived seeking a living. Some made good, a great many didn't. Those seeking jobs soon outgrew the work available. Rural Essex soon became filled with homeless job hunters living off limited charity. [...]

Meanwhile, the giant Ford foundry continued to be the biggest single employer. The work was hot and hard where only the strong survived. The molten metal was poured into moulds and men had to take out the cast parts. The heat was intense, the smoke so dense that it was almost impossible to see who you were working next to. The acrid fumes made it difficult to breath.

The 'uniform' in the foundry consisted of scanty clothing, leather gaiters to protect the lower legs, clogs or stout shoes with gaiters to protect the feet, a cloth over the mouth against the fumes and goggles for eye protection. Even with the protection of these bits and pieces, body burns were very common. When the men tried to clear their throats, their spittle was black with dust that had filtered through their masks. These foundry workers became unrecognisable due to the grime and soot which became ingrained into their skin.

About 65% of the supervisors in the foundry were Irish, many of them coming originally from the mother plant in County Cork. Although most of them were good Catholics and regular churchgoers, the language they used in the work-place was extremely coarse and discipline went far beyond that stated in company rules.

As in the case of the building workers, where you drank often determined if, where and how you worked. The Irish supervisors, like the building site foremen, often treated those in their charge little better than animals. During my time in Fords, I had one brush with a supervisor. I was discussing a problem with him when he was called away. He told me to wait where I stood. Being in the aisle of a busy thoroughfare, I moved back about eighteen inches so that I would not block any movement down the aisle. On his return, the supervisor suspended me for disobeying an order.

I refused to be bullied and sought justice from higher up. Through the corridors of power I went in search of someone in authority. I stated my case to the head of company employment and was immediately reinstated. The supervisor was disciplined instead. A new chapter had been opened for the likes of me and confidence of a fair deal was made public in that great company.

These bullies who got the jobs as supervisors and foremen were known collectively as Culshies, though truly meaning men from a small town in County Mayo.[2] They descended on the Essex countryside in search of their own crocks of gold. These were the true hard men. They were all fluent in the Gaelic, and had a turn of phrase that would turn up the toes of a saint! They also had the well-earned reputation of getting the job done. Here were the diggers and the blasters that were reshaping the surrounds of London. Here were the tunnellers, the road builders, the bridge builders, every one of them as hard as nails. Here were the men who fried up their morning bacon and eggs on their shovels over an open fire, and whose doctor came in a pint glass.

The Culshies preferred their own company and rarely mixed with the other workers. They had their own form of bush telegraph through the doss houses and the pubs. They could be picked out of a crowd by the way they dressed. Usually clad in moleskin trousers with gaiters, hob-nailed boots, the heavy donkey jackets and the red neckerchiefs knotted with the special pincher's or navvy's knot. The Culshies were, indeed, the elite of the building sites. I've seen what happens when they arrive at a site with their stock of food and billy can strapped to their waist belts. On approaching the site foreman, they were given the nod and told 'In the morning' – then the foreman would sack an equivalent number of site workers to make room for the new arrivals! It was understood that, on these large sites, the Culshies were always to be considered above the others because of their reputations.

It could almost be guaranteed that where a building site foreman was found, there you'd find a Culshie. They were also known as the men with the shout! This was because of the vast amounts of foul language and abuse they threw

---

[2] The mildly derogatory term 'culchie', which reputedly derives from the Mayo town of Kiltimagh, refers to a person from rural Ireland.

at the men under their ruthless control. It was not uncommon for a group of men to be given the job of digging holes and being told that the last to finish would be sacked, or that they would all be sacked if the Culshie couldn't see the steam rising off their backs within ten minutes of their labour! Hard men indeed! [...]

Death among the hard men was something special. As a mark of respect, all work ceased on the funeral day of a workmate. It was usual for a goodly sum of money to be collected for his dependents and the local pub was expected to put on a bit of a 'do' for the departed. It was a day of very heavy drinking which ended with the ganger man and five others hoping to carry the coffin at shoulder height on the last steps of the internment.

One local resident, on seeing such a procession, asked the ganger man why so much alcohol, style and expense accompanied these events for just a lowly building labourer. The quick reply was that they looked after their own and what little alcohol they had was merely to get them from the boardroom to the bedroom and on to the building site!

However, alcohol did play a large part in the lives of the Irish building worker. Most days usually ended in the bar of one pub or another to wash away the tiredness of a hard day's toil. Sometimes it turned into a celebration lasting well into the night. [...]

The sands of time were running out for many of the old-timers. The days of sleeping in rail wagons and hedgerows are now long gone. The image of the Irish navvy in his donkey jacket and hobnailed boots has changed. The new generation of the hard men are now solid members of the community with families of their own living in the homes that they helped build, their children attending the schools and churches they helped pay for.

I am proud to be part of them and what they stand for and will always remember the white sign – 'NO PASSENGERS' – they were the Culshies, God be with them!

46
Matt McGinn, 'Autobiography'

From: *McGinn of the Calton: The Life and Works of Matt McGinn 1928–1977*, with a foreword by Jimmie Macgregor and an introduction by Janette McGinn (Glasgow: Glasgow District Libraries, 1987). 203pp.; pp. 21–6.

Matt McGinn (1928–1977) describes himself in his autobiography as 'a Scottish Irish mongrel', being one of nine children born to Glaswegian parents of Irish descent. Although his formal schooling ended at the age of 12, he won a scholarship to Ruskin College, Oxford, in the late 1950s and gained a diploma in economics and political science. He subsequently trained as a teacher and spent three years in a Glasgow school before becoming a full-time folk singer and performer, using music as a means of attacking poverty, bigotry and social injustice. McGinn's career as folk activist spanned 15 years, during which time he wrote a large number of protest songs and humorous folk ballads about Glaswegian working-class culture. His commitment to revolutionary socialism made him a staunch supporter of workers' control of industry and a tireless fund-raiser for various left-wing causes. Following his death in a fire in his Glasgow home, some of his ashes were scattered on the grave of the revolutionary socialist John MacLean. In 1987 a celebratory volume of his work appeared, entitled *McGinn of the Calton*. It featured several of his best-known songs, together with excerpts from his untitled autobiography, in which he recalls his impoverished upbringing, his trade union activism and his involvement in the 1960s folk revival. The following extract is taken from the opening section, 'The Gallowgate Calypso'.

'The three coldest things in the world,' my father said on one occasion, 'are a dog's nose, a man's knees and a woman's arse.'

But on the last account he personally could not have had much to complain about. My mother bore him nine children of which I was the eighth, delivered on The Midwife Special on the Seventeenth of January nineteen twenty eight if we are to believe the birth certificate, and I know of no valid reason for disbelieving the record of the Registrar.

'Oh Mrs McGinn, he's got a lucky cap,' said the nurse and proceeded to take the unbroken caul and place it carefully around a saucer. She had just taken away the last lucky thing I was about to have about my face to leave it on the mantlepiece to await the arrival of a sailor. Superstition had it that these cauls could act as charms at sea and that the seaman who had a lucky cap in his possession would never come to any harm. Mine was to prove an exception.

A sailor, Tommy MacCallum, who lived in the Gallowgate heard about this lucky cap, came knocking on the door, paid a sixpence for this piece of unbroken skin, tucked it in an empty shoe polish tin, went off to sea and was drowned three days later.

First memories I suppose have got to be shockers of some kind and mine are of an elder brother then fifteen years old being taken off to the Infirmary with rheumatic fever in an ambulance, and then of his remains being brought home to a very very sad house indeed, to lie for three days before the set-in kitchen bed on trestles. I was three.

We were brought up Catholics and that in Glasgow also meant Celtic supporters and there were plenty of objects and ornaments about the house to indicate to any stranger who came our way what we were at a glance, like holy water fonts, scapulars, pictures of the Sacred Heart and the Virgin and tea plates with pictures of the Celtic team on them.

Our house was a room and kitchen on the ground floor of number eight Ross Street in the Calton district of Glasgow. From both windows we had a magnificent view of a five-horse stable and looming above it the Ham Curer's with, as often as not, the thick black smoke belching from its windows to decorate the other buildings around.

Against these obstacles my mother in common with the majority of neighbours fought a constant battle to keep the house and ourselves spotless. With scrubbing brushes and flycatchers she managed.

The street, with no more than a hundred yards of it, was more like a village, there being in that tiny stretch two pubs and a sweetie shop, a joiner's and a blacksmith's shop, a garage and a Unitarian church which really had no right to be there because there wasn't a Unitarian in the street; there was a gasfitter and plumber's, a sausage casings manufacturer's and a zoo, no less, which still left room for a high class florist, a bookshop, the five-horse stable, a grocer's, the back end of a foundry and a Women's Model Lodging House; and there were five hundred of us living in one-, two- and three-roomed houses in three-storey tenements.

The walls of those tenements had a story to tell. The story of births, marriages and deaths, or, as my mother called them, hatches, matches and despatches. As children we played in that street at 'Shops' and 'Release the Box' and 'Kick the Can' and cards and rounders and boxing and singing and peever and moshie and kicking doors after we'd tied them with string to some other neighbours' door and at guesses and at all kinds of races and we had to be good runners from the police who haunted the street.

Then too there were the sights around the pubs and the model lodging house where the Bad Men came from afar to look for the Bad Women of the

'Model', sights which I tried to recapture in one of my songs, 'The Gallowgate Calypso'.

The names of the policemen in the song were genuine. 'Eat the Moose' who was one of the very few reasonable policemen who came around the area was so called after he had confided to a local shopkeeper that while in the trenches in France 'Ah ate a moose' and John the B, who was severely beaten up in the area on one occasion, was so called because he was a proper one.

We had a picture of Canon O'Reilly in the house. It hung beside the mantle-piece, commanding as proud a place as that of the Blessed Virgin, of Christ bleeding on the Cross or even that of the Celtic Team in full colours which graced an ornamental plate beside the set-in bed.

Canon O'Reilly, although before my time, was a legend in the Gallowgate. A legend of a walking stick and a canon's hat bursting upon the youths and young men in the area and bashing them physically in an unholy effort to break up coin tossing and card schools and games of football which were favourite pastimes.

He would lash out regardless of the religion of his victims, safe in the knowledge that most of them had been baptised Catholics. He was fortified in the wisdom that no one would hit him back if only because there were stories credited as true by the local Catholics that such and such a man had a bad leg simply because he had tried to kick a priest, the crippled limb being an immediately inflicted Act of God! One poor man's arm was permanently stationed parallel with his shoulder because the Lord (so it was said) had not been at all pleased by his attempt to take a punch at one of the clergy.

These Acts of God were speculative, but there was no speculation regarding the violent sorties of Canon O'Reilly into the closes and backcourts of Ross Street, Kent Street, Bain Street, the Gallowgate and Well Street.

Irish accents were rare, most of the populace speaking with the Glasgow Glottal Stop, but the names left no doubt as to the genealogical origin of the Dochertys, Donnellys, Reillys, Connollys or the Quinns.

I was a firm believer in the religion of my forebears, or at least the more recent among them; the more recent among them because those further back – before the legendary Saint Patrick – were pagans and heathens and indeed appear to have been as content with these beliefs as their successors became with theirs. It is worthy of recall that there was an Irish race long before there was any such thing as Christianity.

Then, too, I remember Saint Patrick's day when everyone around wore shamrocks and when, with the half-day holiday we were given, we would go over in droves to Dovehill School and throw other kinds of rocks at the pupils there.

It was impossible also to be unaware of the feverish atmosphere around the Twelfth of July when the Dorises who lived next door would go out in the middle of the night with a pot of paint and brushes and decorate the well at Charlotte Street a proud shade of green and then use the same paint on the red circles of the barber's pole. Then Mrs Makem in the Ham Pend would throw a pail of excrement over her third-storey window at the Orange Walk as it stomped up the Gallowgate. I knew also that there were Protestant hymns which I had heard the Salvation Army women sing of a Sunday in the Ross Street Home for Females. But I did not really know what all this Protestantism was about, apart from the fact that –

> We'll hang John Knox on the barren rocks,
> With the Sash his father wore!

At the age of five I was severely disappointed and kicked up quite a riot because I could not go to the Protestant school which my pal Colin McConnell was already attending in the Great Dovehill, but had to go to the Catholic School, Saint Alphonsus, in Greendyke Street along with Charlie Logan with whom I had just fallen out over a piece of rope he claimed was his and I claimed was mine because I had seen it first. But I soon got into the religious thing and didn't even use sweary words. When Charlie would sing on our walks down the Glasgow Green:

> Please keep off the grass and let the ladies pass
> Here comes the parkie sliding on his arse,

I would sing bumbaleerie.

I still did not swear, even when we were being taught the catechism, like my older brother Gus had done. Gus was just getting on for seven when the teacher started preparing the class for their First Holy Communion which involved learning the catechism:

'Who made you?'

'God made me.'

'Why did God make you?'

'God made me to love him and serve him in this world and be happy with him in the next.'

'What is God?'

'God is a supreme spirit.'

It was a truly magnificent method of teaching. You did not have to use up too much mental energy in things like thinking. Here you were not only given the question; you were also given the answers and in the exact words.

So the priest was coming round one day to examine the class and see that they had all learned their catechism by heart, and the teacher had allocated all the questions to her pupils to be answered parrot fashion and Gus, who was sitting second from the door in the front row had been given the second question. In the priest came and the stupid teacher, forgetting that the boy to whom she had given the first question had just asked with his hand up, permission to 'Leave the room', told the priest to start with the front row from the door. The priest asked Gus, 'Who made you?' 'Please Father,' said Gus standing, 'God didnae make me. God made the boy that's away for a shite.' Needless to say, with this the catechism examination had to halt. Gus was given the belt and my mother was sent for. 'He never learned that language in ma hoose,' said my maw.

I made my First Holy Communion firmly believing in the righteousness of religion and of the Catholic faith in particular. This belief I kept until the age of sixteen when I became as I have remained since a firm atheist with nonetheless a respect for other people's religious leanings. For although I find it almost incredible to see anyone believing that there could be someone with an almighty power in his hands who could allow sickness, famine and war, I nonetheless know that I did in fact believe it for a time so I know such belief is possible in others.

47
Peter Donnelly, *The Yellow Rock*

(London: Eyre & Spottiswoode, 1950). 216pp.; pp. 117–21.

'If it is ungrateful to regret one's birthplace, then I must be counted ungrateful; for in a life mercifully free from complaints I have this complaint, that I was born out of Ireland.' So writes Peter Donnelly (1914–1998) in the opening chapter of his autobiography. The birthplace in question was Barrow-in-Furness in Cumbria, to where Donnelly's parents emigrated from south Armagh in the early 1900s. He himself studied for the priesthood at Ushaw College in Durham between 1928 and 1935 but left before being ordained. Returning to Barrow, he found work as a storekeeper in the local steelworks but increasingly felt that writing was his true vocation, 'the work around which my life revolved'. Donnelly's literary ambitions remained unrealised by the time *The Yellow Rock* appeared, however; indeed, the book is in part the testimony of a frustrated writer *manque* whose deepest desire is 'to write one poem that will make men gasp to read it'. Donnelly moved to Limerick in the 1950s and spent the remainder of his working life with the Shannon Free Airport Development Company. He continued to write poetry and plays but published very little in his lifetime, certainly nothing as accomplished as *The Yellow Rock*. In it he artfully interweaves the story of his journey from seminary to steelworks with an empathetic account of the culture and beliefs of his fellow workers, whose subjugation by industrial capitalism he deplores throughout. Like Bill Naughton, Donnelly uses his autobiography to challenge stereotypical perceptions and caricatured portrayals of working-class people by emphasising the diverse particularity and flawed human complexity of actual workers. He is also sensitive to the plight of the many 'broken or stranded Irishmen' who passed through his parents' house in Barrow, one of whom, Mick Rush, he retrieves from anonymity in the following vignette, which condenses much social history into an elegiac tribute.

Death must for ever be a mournful phenomenon, for as it is an occasion of sorrow when an emigrant departs from his friends to a far-off country, how much more poignant is the sorrow when he removes into eternity. In Ireland when anyone was leaving for America the celebration before his departure was called an American wake. Let the guests be as roysterous and merry as they would, still the gaiety had an undercurrent of sadness. Even though we believe in the immortality of the soul, which should make us rejoice at death, this life is pleasant and desirable; and there are but few of us who so much retrieve what Adam lost that they long to die. At best, we prepare ourselves to meet the dissolution when it comes, but do not pray to hasten it. Life is sweet. We are loath to leave it, and it saddens us to see our friends go from it.

But the sadness of death as it is experienced by a Christian is different from sadness for the same cause experienced by a pagan. The one looks on death not as an end but as a beginning, and cries out of the depths of uneasiness about his own worth, protesting that his soul has hoped in God, and clamouring for His abundant mercy; the other ennobles his despair and sings a sad song for Heliodora. After these there remain many who, belonging neither to one category nor the other, have a sentimental regret for death, a horror of it, a morbid interest in it. They gather round a funeral house in excited groups to stare at the coffin. They count the mourners and the cabs in the procession. They observe the wreaths and flowers and comment on them, for the panoply of death attracts them as violence does when it is reported in the Sunday papers. When death comes in their own houses, they hasten to remove the body. It is not that they have considered the Christian teaching of everlasting life and rejected it for a noble alternative. They do not face the fact of death to integrate it with their lives, but when it forces its attention on them they regard it with uneasy, doubting indifference. They are inclined to believe that there is nothing beyond the grave; at the same time they are inclined to believe that there is immortality, because they have not escaped completely from the Christian tradition, and because even they are puzzled in the will by that 'dread of something after death, the undiscovered country.'[1] So they stare at coffins, then hurry off to other business for distraction, as you might turn your collar up on a raw night to keep the wind away.

The saddest and most impressive funeral which I attended was that of Mick Rush. There were only four of us there, including old Dan, and we collected the body from a slab in the workhouse mortuary. The burial of Mick Rush affected me very deeply and left an impression of loneliness which constantly intrudes upon me.

Mick was an Irishman who had come to Barrow as a young man and had not been back again to Ireland. He lived all his life in lodgings and never had a home. He used to come to our house frequently, sometimes to borrow a shilling for a drink, sometimes to pay it back again. We loved him when we were children in spite of the fact that it was impossible to cadge pennies from him, since he had so few and we knew before asking that he would answer, 'Where would I get it? Sure I haven't the price of a pig's waistcoat.' A pig's waistcoat, according to Mick, was value for twopence halfpenny. He was a

---

[1] Words spoken by the Prince in *Hamlet*, III, i.

big, strong man with a rough moustache. He was never elegantly dressed, but always neatly, which was, perhaps, attributable as much to his landlady's attention as his own desire, though he was careful of his person. Except on pay night, he never had any sum of money; in spite of my mother's exhortations and appeals to him to lay something by in the fat days to help him over the lean ones, he refused to save money, for he believed that 'a penny after my day will be lost money.'

He had never any settled occupation, but worked wherever there was hard work – at the docks, in the ironworks, in foundries, with navvy contractors. He seemed always to be in search of work, either unemployed or about to become unemployed. His reason for borrowing was that 'the bit of a job I had is finished'; his surety was the rumour that a deal boat was coming into the docks, or an ore boat or a china-clay boat. If there was no work in Barrow he would walk to Kendal, or up into Cumberland to find a farmer who would employ him.

There was no one belonging to him in Barrow, and it was so long since he had heard of them that he believed all his kin in Ireland were dead. When a cancer began in his mouth he was taken to the workhouse infirmary, and died there. My mother went to visit him; I went with three others to bury him.

Some time later I had to spend rather more than a week in London, and I had my first experience of living in lodgings. I was told that because accommodation was so scarce in London, I was lucky to have a room booked for me before my arrival. But as I walked down the long streets of houses with painted pillars in front of the doors – mottled pillars, black pillars, black doors, and bits of shining brass – I felt threatened and deserted.

I knocked at a black door and was greeted by a young, blowzy straw-haired doll with a baby in her arms and another tagging on to her skirt. She left me at the door. A moment later an old doll arrived in a dressing-gown, with her thin hair streeling down her face, dishevelled and apologising. She had lumbago, she told me, and would I excuse her appearance because she was just after a bath. She begged me also to forgive the state of the house, for that was due to the lumbago.

The house was bare and repugnant, upside down, through-other, dusty, littered with odds and ends, lacking in any comfort, and obviously worked upon in occasional places by eager but inexpert hands. There were dabs of black paint everywhere, painted lines which were intended to be straight, but had wandered. Down in the kitchen, which was a basement room, I was given my supper – tea and bread-and-butter. Damned bad tea from a thick chipped cup, with the young doll and the old one taking turns at nursing the child and trying to quieten him. There were napkins strung across the fireplace; a basin of water was on a chair in front of the fire; clothes were piled on the other chairs. There was green lino on the floor; on the lino dirt and rubbish.

I escaped to my room. As I climbed the stairs the figures of other lodgers flitted past me with kettles and jugs in their hands on the way to the bathroom for water. In my room there was a little black iron bed with bedclothes too small for it, shrinking, as if it were ashamed to be seen, into the corner. There was a rickety chair, a washstand without water, a big window without curtain which looked upon the chimney-pots of South-West London and dirty grey bricks.

As I sat there looking at the chimneys and considering my fortune, I began to know the desolation of spirit which must have weighed always on men like Mick Rush, in places where no one knew them nor cared who they were. God rest him.

48

J. S. Collis, *An Irishman's England*

(London: Cassell, 1937). 228pp.; pp. 45–9.

John Stewart Collis's (1900–1984) memories of his Dublin childhood differed markedly from those of his twin brother Robert, author of *The Silver Fleece*. Whereas the latter was showered with maternal devotion, John was shunned by his mother from the moment of his birth. So deep was his unhappiness that he admits in *Bound Upon a Course* (1971) to having no adult memory of his life before the age of nine. After Rugby and Balliol College, Oxford – to which he said he gained entry by cheating at Latin – Collis entered theological college in 1923 but left after one term. Two years later he published a critically well-received study of Shaw but was unable to repeat this success with subsequent works. By the time he came to write *An Irishman's England* Collis was married with two children and eking out a precarious living from freelance journalism and part-time teaching in London. The early 1940s marked a turning-point in his career, however. Periods spent as a farm labourer in Sussex and Dorset led to the publication of two books, *While Following the Plough* (1946) and *Down to Earth* (1947), which were acclaimed for their blend of scientific curiosity, philosophical gravitas and poetic vision. Though he later published respected biographies of, among others, Strindberg and Tolstoy, it was these two works – published in a single volume, *The Worm Forgives the Plough*, in 1973 – that brought Collis belated recognition as a precursor of the ecological movement, and led A. N. Wilson to eulogise him as 'a man who combined the irony of Shaw, the eye of Kilvert and the vigour of Cobbett'.[1]

An Irishman's England is Collis's impressionistic subjective survey of English culture and society since the end of the First World War, written in a spirit of critical admiration from the perspective of an outsider inside, one with a personal investment in the country that he had made his home. The narrative at once gestures towards and shies away from autobiography; the lens of personal experience dominates but the self-reflective element is subdued. In his preface Collis explains: 'An Irishman educated in England can neither pose as a foreign observer nor pontificate as a detached outsider. But he has this advantage, that while having experienced England as thoroughly as an Englishman, he is able to record his impressions with an unEnglish bias.'

---

[1] A. N. Wilson, 'John Stewart Collis', *The Spectator*, 10 March 1984, p. 13.

As this statement suggests, the author's attempt to comprehend the 'extravagance and eccentricity of the English' is fundamentally conditioned by his experience of doubleness, new landscapes and social customs being continually calibrated in relation to those left behind in Ireland. Collis found the idiosyncrasies of London and Londoners especially captivating, as the following excerpt attests.

I once met a man walking up Charing Cross Road accompanied by a small elephant. There was a certain element of incongruity in this spectacle, one might even call it surprising. But what surprised me more than the elephant and its companion was the minimum of attention which they attracted. To say that no one took any notice of them would be an understatement. A good many passers-by turned round and stared, while some stopped and gazed after the pair. But they created little comment and no stir.

The most delightful thing about London is that nobody minds what anyone does or says – within the bounds of morality. There is an individual freedom about the place which fittingly symbolizes the English spirit. Barrie[2] is held to have said that the chief thing about London is that you can eat a bun in the street without drawing attention to yourself. You need not wear a hat. No garb is laughed at: a man clothed in the flowing robes of a Franciscan Friar with long hair down his neck will occasion as little surprise as a parrot perched on someone's shoulder – while during a heatwave there is such an extremity of unconventionality as to scandalize many foreigners who do not understand the effect which a few days' continuous sunshine has upon English people. Anyone may talk to himself aloud without notice: indeed, the number of persons who smile and chat to themselves alone as they walk through the streets makes up for their reserve when they get together.

On the other hand, a welcome is given to anyone who wishes to draw a crowd. Street-entertainers, some of whom perform nothing more elaborate than the tearing across of a telephone directory, can gather the most patient and good-natured audiences. Prophets who wish to give their message in the street easily find a following. The pavement artist has his best chance here. And at the same time the incongruous and crushing comment in the spectacle of able-bodied men selling fluffy, jumping toys on the kerbs of the rich pavements, makes no one pause.

When the image of London rises before me all these things form part of it. But one thing more than these – the street singers. In many districts I have seen and heard musicians and singers banding together with so much dignity and power of expression that their very act has been a triumph and has raised up my heart even at the moment when it was most cast down. I call to mind especially one band of Welsh miners who had taken up their position in the full and noisy Holborn quarter. As I passed one day I saw them marching

---

[2] J. M. Barrie (1860–1937), Scottish playwright and novelist.

slowly onwards singing. At first their voices were drowned by the traffic. Then they rose above the roar. Their song conquered the clamour. They climbed above it in a swelling chorus. I could not see them now, for they got mixed up with the crowd at the other side of the street, but I still heard their voices. With triumphant irony, these men who had been thrown aside by society, neglected and betrayed, were singing with a power and beauty that raised them high above the corruption and the wrong!

However, neither this nor anything else disturbs or surprises the Londoner. Even when Nature refuses an elementary office and the next day does not dawn and night follows the night, he still goes about his business as if all were in order. The mere fact that there is darkness when there should be light does not derange his equanimity. Indeed, he enjoys it. I enjoy it myself, I confess. This happens when the famous London fog forms above the city instead of in it. It is a rather rare occurrence, but it holds the attention. A lid of fog too thick to be penetrated by the light of the sun is laid over the town about the height of a church spire from the streets. Thus at ten o'clock in the morning it is as dark as at ten o'clock in the evening. The lights are lit and everyone carries on in a city of continuous night.

But when this lid descends to the streets, then even the Londoner finds life difficult. I have never seen one of those fogs when it is said that 'you cannot see your hand in front of you.' It is sufficiently intriguing when you cannot see across the road. Strange things happen. You alight from a car to look for the kerb – the car disappears and you cannot find it again. A lamp, far away like a light-house in the sky, next second strikes against you. A moving cliff hung with lights, suddenly shaped from the insubstantial mist like an act of creation on the First Day, collides against your own trembling barque. You have re-entered, it seems, an earlier period in the earth's history, and may even have become a wanderer in the Immense Inane.

The reader must consult heavier volumes than this to find out the scientific cause of these fogs – whether due entirely to the smoke or to changes of temperature in the moist atmosphere. As I feel pretty sure that smoke has less to do with it than natural causes, I dare say it will remain one of the characteristics of London. I hope so. For the same cause is probably responsible for the hazy blue light, the gauzy veil of blue through which one walks in the dusk. I would call that the most movingly lovely thing in the world. It melts the mind. I always miss it when I go away from London. I do not forget the innumerable blues of the Celtic scene, I know what it is to be cut off from those visionary roads and high paradises that are lost in that light. But this blue is not inferior. It joins God and Man, refusing the immeasurable melancholy of manless beauty. When, in the Bloomsbury Squares, I see hanging in that blue, interwoven with that gauze, light as air, substantial as rock, the little balls on the plane-tree's tracery – when I see them scriptured in the dusk of the cold winter sky – then I know that London has claimed me for her own.

49

Nesca A. Robb, *An Ulsterwoman in England, 1924–1941*

(Cambridge: Cambridge University Press, 1942). viii, 175pp.; pp. 156–9; 161–4.

Historian and literary scholar Nesca Adeline Robb (1905–1976) is perhaps best known for her two-volume biography of William of Orange published in the 1960s. She was born to a well-to-do Belfast Protestant family and educated at Oxford, which awarded her a doctorate in 1932. She subsequently taught in Cambridge and London until 1940, when she became an advisory officer for the Women's Employment Federation. It was during this time that Robb wrote an impressionistic and highly literate account of her experiences in England, graphically evoking the 'strange, marooned kind of life' that war had engendered, while also bringing a supple intelligence and Christian humanist perspective to bear on such topics as the rise of fascism and the role of universities in the reconstruction of post-war Britain. Robb's work for the Federation also made her keenly aware of women's lack of fair employment rights and opportunities, imbuing her narrative with a note of feminist protest. In her foreword she explains that the book 'has something of the character of a long, rambling letter to the people at home', while also being 'a tribute of deep, if not wholly uncritical, affection for the country in which I have now spent many years of my life'. This duality of emphasis and perspective reflects the complex set of identities that her narrative negotiates. Although her succinct self-description suggests an unequivocal Britishness – 'I was born a little Unionist; bred royalist and loyalist from the start' – Robb also acknowledges an affinity for Ireland and a 'sense of kinship with the rest of its inhabitants'. Migration further complicated her affiliations. Despite being looked upon as an Irish outsider by many English people, she was powerfully drawn to their fortitude and 'sovereign assurance', and discovered in wartime London a sense of belonging which was 'akin to the small and homogeneous community of my childhood'. Writing in May 1941, Robb's vivid evocation of the vicissitudes of daily life in the capital incorporates perceptive and at times remarkably lucid reflections on the wider cultural and psychological effects of a conflict that was still unfolding.[1]

---

[1] For an analysis of the contrasting perspectives of a younger woman from a similar background, see Colin Pooley, 'From Londonderry to London: Identity and Sense of

A winter less rigorous, but more prolonged than the last, has resolved itself into a cold and tardy spring; and I find myself looking back over the world-wide panorama of the war, and over the small, disjointed fragments of it that have found their way into this book. The last months of the old year and the early ones of the new have brought so swift a rush of events that we are all a little stunned by its impetuousness. For the time being the war has surged away from us, though there is no knowing for how long our respite will last. Europe lies pinioned, since the sad, heroic end of the campaign in Greece; beyond it, in Africa and Asia, battle is joined again, and we have had great victories and sharp reverses. The vicissitudes of our world are certainly absorbing to follow, if terrible to endure. The days rise full of new menace and new uncertainty, but also not without new hope. We are still in a pretty pickle, but when one looks back on the past twelve months the wonder is not that we should have so much still to contend with, but that we are here at all and reasonably lively and pugnacious at that. Life is grim in its larger aspects and sometimes drab in its details, but it has a shilling-shockerness about it that makes it still faintly unreal. It is only a few days since Rudolf Hess landed in Scotland,[2] if not exactly like manna from heaven at least with some points of affinity between him and the beings who are first reputed to have made the descent. What the import of his coming may be is still in doubt: its sensational quality is beyond question. After this, imagination will no longer boggle at anything.

Against such a background of tragedy and melodrama, of giant treacheries and giant heroism, one's private history, with its work and recreations, its small personal and domestic concerns, seems almost ludicrously common-place. What should such fellows as I do, crawling between heaven and earth? – writing this book, trudging home from the First Aid Post in the wind-lashed small hours of a winter day or between moon-set and dawn of a May morning? One's immediate world is still fairly normal, but the war colours and overshadows everything in it, like the sinister darkness of an eclipse spread over the earth. Sometimes, too, one walks into the conflict in the oddest ways, as I did, one foggy day in January, when I carried on a business interview to machine-gun obbligato, among the battered and crater-pitted fastnesses of the Charing Cross Road; and later drove up a Piccadilly which the damp mist and the thunder of a persistent barrage had almost emp-tied of people. London now, after long intervals of quiet, punctuated by a few savage raids, shows obvious marks of tribulation. Many of the 'sights' are gone irretrievably; and of those that remain there are few without a scar. Still

---

Place for a Protestant Northern Irish Woman in the 1930s', in MacRaild (ed.), *The Great Famine and Beyond*, pp. 189–213.

[2] Hitler's deputy Rudolf Hess (1894–1987) parachuted into Scotland on the night of 10 May 1941 in an apparent attempt to negotiate an Anglo-German détente.

work and life go on; and there is surprisingly much of the old gay London; theatres and concerts; pleasant clothes in the shops; pleasant, if restricted, meals in the restaurants. Spring has brought out the flower barrows heaped with tulips and narcissi, and has softened the stark ugliness of destruction. The Park, with its delicate trees and grazing sheep, lies like an expanse of cool water beneath charred shells of buildings in Park Lane and Bayswater Road. Near my house two long files of pink double cherries, now in full bloom, and looking like fluffy Renaissance angels against the blue of the May sky, screen the bare ground where those five neighbours of ours were killed last September. The city has never known more violent or abounding contrasts of beauty and horror, heroism and absurdity; or stranger minglings of pathos and comedy. [...]

Other cities have suffered these things too, my own among them. As we sailed down the Lough[3] in August 1939 I wondered if I should see it again, and my heart misgave me. Now, whatever my own fate may be, I know that I shall never again see it as it was. Still it is better in this war to be battered with London than to be unscathed with Paris and Rome. Even when I have grieved most over what has happened in Ulster there has been some comfort in that thought. Besides, if England is not now faced, on her Western approaches, with an Ireland in enemy hands; and if Catholic Eire is not under Nazi domination, I think they owe something of their immunity to those unaccommodating Ulster people. If we win the battle of the Atlantic, the world will owe them something too. For the fact that Britain can dispose of some sea and air bases in Ireland, and can hold some forces there against a possible invasion of Eire, may well alter the course of the war. As for what permanent effect *this* war will have on the incredible island time alone will show. So many hopes and prophecies have already shipwrecked there that I will not add to them. I would only drop a word of warning to those – I have met a number of them – who think that the Irish question is solved because fire brigades from Eire gave their help in the air-raids on the North.[4] We have all been deeply thankful for that help, and we would do as much any day for the people of Eire if they stood in need of it; but that is quite a different thing from changing one's allegiance. [...]

Of England itself what can I say? Any generalization can at best be only a 'near miss'. My own experience covers only a very limited field; yet it would be strange if no difference were perceptible between the England of to-day and the country as it was even a year ago, let alone when I knew it first.

---

[3] Belfast Lough.

[4] On the night of 15 April 1941 nearly 900 people were killed when Luftwaffe bombs fell on Belfast. The following day, 13 brigades of fire engines and ambulances were dispatched from Dublin, following a request for assistance from John MacDermott, the minister of public security at Stormont.

One characteristic is at any rate still evident. English pride, like English cloth and English leather, wears well. It has had a few rude shocks and is in consequence a good deal less unthinking than it used to be, but I doubt if a morbid humility will ever be the national weakness. 'An Englishman ne'er wants his own good word', said Defoe, in a shrewd satire on his fellow-countrymen, as apt to-day as when it was written in 1698.[5] We have all met the newspaper article beginning: 'It is not the English way to boast', and all know this opening gambit as the accepted introduction to an eloquent 'write up'. This immense *National* self-confidence, whose strength and weakness have been so startlingly displayed in recent history, can be quite independent of personal conceit. The individual Englishman may be either complacent or humble about himself, but to the general proposition that one Englishman is equal to any three foreigners his whole subconscious being assents, whatever his conscious mind may say; and the belief helps to make him so heedless of warnings and so doughty in battle. In the middle of last autumn, someone who could never be accused of personal complacency told me with an air of final conviction, 'I don't see that Germany has a chance'; and only the other day, after the fall of Crete, an unknown lady said to me: 'We're wonderful people.' They really are. Sometimes their sovereign assurance in so grave a pass alarms me. It makes me wonder what new blow is to be hurled against it, what volcano they have now chosen to picnic on in their leisured way. I make fun of them, but I am not really in a joking mood. The situation is altogether too serious and too complicated; and their over-confidence has so repeatedly been their deadliest foe. I often wish they believed rather more in God and in the Devil – and rather less in themselves.

Yet can I pay them any higher compliment than to say that after two years of war spent among them, I feel more hope for this country, and even for mankind, than I did for years before the war broke out? What more can I, or anyone, say of their courage, which has won even the grudging praise of enemies not given to generosity? These years have revealed plenty of sloth and greed and of the most appalling incompetence and muddle-headedness in our midst; but they have also proved that though darkness is over the earth, the things that make men great are still alive. It may sound strange, but I think I should have felt much more at home if I had arrived for the first time in this warring England, rather than in the bewildered and bewildering society of the twenties. Here is something more akin to the small and homogeneous community of my childhood, with its basis of faith and its atmosphere of social ease, preserving, among all its faults, some of the fellowship of the Church and the loyalties of the clan. It had been ready to fight passionately – wrong-headedly if you like – for an idea; and there was a vigour about what it did and thought and felt that was intensely stimulating to live with, even if

---

[5] Line from 'The True-Born Englishman' by Daniel Defoe, first published in 1701.

it sometimes expressed itself in narrow and repellent forms. In its own way it had a grasp of fundamentals. To-day a common danger has given the English people a feeling of solidarity and common purpose greater than anything they have had for years past. I would not of course suggest that the whole body politic has been galvanized. A good deal of the national effort still moves to the slow strains of the departmental minuet rather than to the trumps of war. Large-scale muddling is still too often evident. There are plenty of people who even now have very little idea that there is a war on. Yet, though many have suffered, it is also true that many have gained things that their peace-time life denied them. The urgencies of war have given back to the individual a lost sense of his own significance, even while he sinks his individuality in the general effort. Of late years life has often held few prospects; it has often meant work that gives little satisfaction to hand or brain or, worse still, no work at all. It has witnessed the growth of huge populations who inhabit a limbo between town and country, and lack the sense of belonging to any real community, rural or civic. People have tended to feel at once isolated and hemmed in, and to suspect that they are spending their time and labour on matters of very doubtful value. Now the day's work has acquired the dignity of vital service, the isolated units have become part of larger groups and something essential – purpose and fellowship – have been restored to them.

50
Mauyen Keane, *Hello, Is It All Over?*

(Dublin: Ababúna, 1984). 80pp.; pp. 17–22.

Mauyen Keane's short autobiography is centred around her experiences of work, war and romance in Jersey and Germany during the late 1930s and 1940s. The narrative begins with her account of her journey from Athenry in Galway, where she was born in 1917, to St Helier in Jersey to begin her nurses' training in the autumn of 1936. She remained on the island for the next seven years, during which time she endured the privations of the German occupation that began in July 1940. The following excerpt casts light on the contrasting responses of Jersey-based Irish doctors and nurses to the prospect of imminent invasion in the spring of 1940, and the kinds of personal and professional dilemmas they faced. Keane's account of the occupation itself is notable for the way in which it humanises the Nazi troops and illuminates the disconcerting emotional intimacies produced by the enforced proximity of islanders and invaders. This empathetic portrait of the enemy is itself conditioned by the life-changing events it describes: the author's falling in love with a German soldier and her dramatic journey across war-torn Europe in the spring of 1943 to join him in Jena. When formal permission to marry was refused on the grounds that the bride had a 'slightly Jewish' appearance, the couple married in secret and concealed their relationship for the remainder of the war. In 1947 they were allowed to leave Germany and immediately travelled to Ireland, their homecoming providing an appropriately happy ending to a suspenseful narrative of transgressive wartime romance.

At the end of May, panic struck the island and chaos followed in its wake. The bailiff of Jersey had just announced the occupation of Paris by the Germans. He added that the invasion of the Channel Islands was imminent and might only be a matter of days. Loudspeakers blared out, advising the people to remain calm, that free passage to the mainland would be available for as long as possible. People were asked to form queues taking only necessities with them.

Inside the hospital, doctors, nurses and porters were rushing here and there. All of Matron's staff seemed to be queueing up outside her office to pick up their diplomas or references. Others went straight over to the hotel to pack, not even bothering to do that. I remember entering the office and seeing Matron's face as she signed papers for her staff, pausing every now and then as she wrote to look up with pleading eyes, desperately hoping that at least some of us would stay.

The familiar voice of our lecturer, Mr Haliwell, was heard over the loud-speaker. He was calling all the nurses to the committee room which also acted as a lecture room. Matron's pen dropped from her hand with relief and we all followed her to hear what Mr Haliwell had to say.

We found him standing beside the skeleton, his usual position. How wonderful it would be I thought if this were just another ordinary day. The sun shone in on his troubled face, and his proud Englishman's voice began to tremble as he addressed us:

'Nurses, I have decided to send my wife and children to the mainland and I advise those of you who have ties there to leave. I know you will depart with the dignity befitting your profession. This is a very grave time for all of us and we have no way of knowing how long we may be under German rule. Prisoners we will be, of course, but naturally those of you who volunteer to stay will be most welcome. Let me assure you that you will be needed.'

Silently, we filed out of the room as though we'd been given tranquilizers but outside, chaos still reigned. Everywhere we went we heard words like, 'Go, go now, while you still can, no one will be safe!', and 'The Germans are brutes, they're uncivilized, they'll kill us all!'

Running with a crowd down the hospital avenue towards the big gates, I could see nurses coming out of the home clutching small suitcases. I sat on the steps wondering what I should do. What would my parents think of me if I stayed? But I had already made up my mind. Nurses shuffled past in a hurry, looking back and asking, 'What are you doing, Keane? Why aren't you packing?'

One nurse in particular, from County Cavan, stopped and stared at me in amazement. 'Come home, you fool, come home!' She pulled at my cape, tearing it in her excitement. Josie and Kate shook me out of my stupor. They were from Northern Ireland and had also decided to stay. We were joined by Joan from Tipperary and all four of us clasped hands in silence and smiled, like four children lost in a wood and meeting up at the same time in mutual support. A Jersey sister was later to christen us 'The Four Musketeers'.

We went straight on to all the wards and the welcome we received made us feel very happy in our professions as nurses. 'We thought you'd left us all high and dry!,' one of them exclaimed with a big beam on his face.

As we rushed from ward to ward we were welcomed by a grateful Mr Haliwell and the medical officer, both of whom were unable to conceal their relief and delight. The Dublin doctor, Bill Henderson, came rushing up to congratulate us; he himself was on his way back to Mother Ireland, he said. We gave him our addresses and he promised to let our people know that we were staying on. The doctor from Northern Ireland had decided to remain and he too rejoiced in the news that we weren't leaving. Two of the English sisters stayed as did the Jersey nurses, of course.

We gathered together over a cup of tea and discussed the fairest method of distributing our skeleton staff. This time we were all as one, sisters, junior nurses: now that the war had begun for us, our military regulations were quickly forgotten. We were like one big family.

I had to make a fleeting visit to Brendan and Dorothy. They weren't leaving the island but Brendan had tried to persuade me to return home while I still could, as boats were available for another day or two. But nothing or nobody could make me change my mind now. I always wondered what the real reason was for my 'stubbornness' in insisting on staying behind. Was it my professional need to help? Or sheer youthful curiosity and the spirit of adventure?

Two days passed and trickles of people were still putting out to sea in the last few boats. The last plane had flown out and the airport had closed down. We heard that the very last boat was due to leave. Then all communications to England were finally broken off. We were alone. My musketeer friends and I went down to the harbour to watch the boat sail out. The gangway was up and the passengers waved to us. They must have surely felt that they were bidding us a last farewell. It was all like a dream. We stood there on the deserted harbour in silence, watching the boat recede, ever so slowly, out over the curve of the sea. It was gone. 'Ah well, we volunteered, didn't we?,' said Joan, and we hurried back together in the direction of the hospital.

If work can be described as a therapy for sadness, then we certainly had more than our share of it. I remember sitting on the steps of the hospital one sunny day, snatching a few moments rest with Anne, a Jersey nurse. There was no official off-duty and we never left the grounds. The stillness in the street opposite us and the eerie silence of that bright day in June 1940 was quite unforgettable. How would they invade us?, we asked each other, and when?

There were times we wished they would hurry up about it and get their blasted invasion over and done with and leave us to concentrate on our work. Tension and anxiety became unbearable. The days went by. Still no sound from the notorious Luftwaffe. Were they really brutes? Would they ship us off to God knows where, as rumour had it? Matron, instead of her usual morning and evenings rounds, was now always seen walking through the wards calmly and with a watchful eye, checking that her nurses weren't exhausting themselves.

One night, as we were resting, still in uniform, we were startled by the roar of low flying planes. We jumped up and rushed over to the hospital but could only hear the terrifying drone of the planes fading away into the distance. It was 4.00 am. We decided to stay on duty. The Matron arrived early and told us to take it easy and see the film at the local cinema to get our minds off the work and the terrible anticipation of war. The cinema was called The Opera House and only afternoon performances were shown since the crisis began.

Joan and I looked forward to the break and hoped we'd be able to concentrate on the film which, ironically enough, was called 'Vigil In The Night', about a nurse. But even if we had been able to pay attention to the story-line, we were destined not to see it through to the end: mid-way through, the whole house shook with a loud bang like an explosion. Rushing to the exit was no problem because there were so few people in the cinema, and there was no panic. Then we saw that a German boat had entered the harbour and had been fired upon by a band of local militia. The Germans had dropped a bomb from the aircraft escorting the boat. Machine-gun fire had been directed at the locals standing by.

Twenty-two patients were admitted to the hospital and trips to the operating theatre continued throughout the night. Brendan and other doctors came in to help, though not many doctors were left in Jersey at this time.

Of the twenty-two, eleven patients survived.

As we worked away on that June evening, leaflets were dropped by low-flying Luftwaffe aircraft with the orders: 'This is the German Wehrmacht. We are coming in. Place a white flag on your highest peak. Surrender and no-one will be hurt.'

The surgical wards were now busier than ever. I was in charge of day duty and Josie, my Northern Irish friend, was on nights. One morning I came in early on duty and noticed that something very unusual had happened in the wards. Instead of the usual first reading of the reports to me, Josie related the tidings of the night. Around midnight she was startled by the sound of soldiers' boots on the stone corridor. A German doctor, accompanied by a very young soldier, greeted her with a click of heels and an outstretched hand. He spoke very little English and, with the aid of a dictionary, told her that the soldier was to be admitted with suspected appendicitis. She tried to tell him that there was no room in the hospital but then he did a round of the four wards and found a bed inside the door of one of them. Here in this small ward lay the victims of the German machine-gunning. I went over to the ward and saw the young German lying there, screened off from the others, unable to understand a single word we were saying. He couldn't have been more than nineteen years of age; at this moment in time, his parents didn't know whether he was alive or dead. He was indeed the first of many German patients I was to treat, and as I continued on my morning round, I was met by hostile glances and bitter reproaches. 'Why was the enemy being treated?,' I was questioned time and again. I reminded them that the nursing of the sick knew no national boundaries, but they insisted that he was the enemy and should be treated as such. I assured them that I would try to have him removed to another ward, but I had no time to carry out this promise. The doctor of the night before had arrived with an interpreter, a German who had been a resident of the island. With a low bow and clicking of heels, the middle-aged doctor introduced himself. After examining his patient, he said that he would like to remain on a little longer for observation. Then Matron was summoned. That's when things began to get a bit dramatic. Having lost all her composure, she looked completely upset as she awaited her orders through the interpreter. All the wounded natives of the island in the ward had to be transferred to another ward. They put me in charge and gave me the task of recruiting other nurses as there were to be more admissions. The unfortunate wounded were now in a crowded ward. Matron, shocked and shaken, visibly trying to collect herself, reminded the doctor that there was an acute shortage of trained staff, that she needed me and could she not arrange to let him have junior nurses instead? The answer was a firm No. The doctor bowed and clicked and simply added, 'It is the war, *gnädige Frau.'*

The Matron looked at me, her arms folded in helpless resignation, and left the ward.

51
Seán MacStiofáin, *Memoirs of a Revolutionary*

(London: Gordon Cremonesi, 1975). x, 372pp.; pp. 18–22.

Seán MacStiofáin (1928–2001) was born John Stephenson in Leytonstone, east London, and raised in Islington. In 1945 he was conscripted into the RAF and posted to Jamaica, where his first-hand experience of the iniquities of the British colonial system confirmed him in his anti-imperial views. On his return to London MacStiofáin immersed himself in Irish culture, although it was not until 1950 that he first visited Ireland, by which time he had formed an IRA unit in London. In 1953 he was sentenced to eight years' imprisonment for his part in a foiled raid on a military base in Essex. He moved to Cork after his release in 1959 and was appointed director of intelligence of the IRA seven years later. MacStiofáin opposed the drift towards Marxism within republicanism during the 1960s and was one of the leaders of the militarist faction that became the Provisional IRA in 1970. Following his arrest and imprisonment for IRA membership in November 1972, he went on hunger strike in Mountjoy prison. His abandonment of his strike after 57 days led to him being ousted from the leadership in 1973, after which his involvement in republican politics effectively ended. He spent the remainder of his life living and working in Navan, County Meath.

As one of the first republican memoirs to be published during the 'Troubles', MacStiofáin's autobiography serves several purposes. It is primarily an apologia for the author's particular brand of separatist republicanism, in which he explains the development of his political philosophy and gives a detailed account of the inner workings of the republican movement in Ireland and England from the 1950s to the early 1970s. The book's corrective agenda is commensurate with its self-justificatory nature. MacStiofáin is keen throughout to counter media misrepresentations of the motives of the Provisionals and to expose examples of 'black' propaganda against the Northern republican community. As such, *Memoirs of a Revolutionary* can be read as a function of the propaganda war between the British political establishment and the Irish republican movement that was a crucial counterpart to the military conflict.[1] In the following excerpt MacStiofáin outlines the childhood origins of his consciousness

---

[1] See David Miller, *Don't Mention the War: Northern Ireland, Propaganda and the Media* (London: Pluto Press, 1994).

of being Irish and his corresponding desire to strengthen his identification with the politics and culture of the country. In view of the formative role his mother, who died in 1939, played in cultivating his sense of identity, it is worth noting that her own assertion of Irishness was later found to have rested on a single Irish grandmother, which meant that her son's implacable identification with Ireland was based on a lone great-grandparent.[2]

When I was very young, not more than seven, my mother had said to me, 'I'm Irish, therefore you're Irish. You're half Irish, anyway. Don't forget it.'

I never did. This is the incident to which I attribute the fact that, in spite of having been born and brought up in England, I never considered myself anything but Irish. And it was by no means the only time she reminded me of her Irish connections. I can distinctly remember her greeting Irish people in London on two or three occasions.

'Hello,' she would say to them, 'I'm from Belfast. Where are you from?' Then they would talk about Ireland. There were some Irish connections on my father's side too, but he was vague about them and they certainly meant nothing to him.

Some months after my mother died I remember walking with my father in Islington when he met an associate of his and they stopped to talk in the street. It was a warm summer's day and we were standing by some steps that led down from the pavement to the roadway. My mother was mentioned, and then Ireland came into their conversation. My father turned and pointed to me and said to the other man, 'Well, *he's* fifty per cent Irish.'

The IRA bombing campaign in England was under way, and that may have been why their talk turned in this direction. At any rate, I can clearly recall a number of similar references to my mother or myself when my father was with some of his friends or relatives. They had the effect of first arousing my curiosity about the Irish people, then leading me to seek them out and gradually develop a feeling of being at one with them.

The fact that wartime Britain drew hundreds of thousands of workers and recruits from Ireland never seemed to count when the South was condemned for its neutrality. I had already come across this in the factory, when some of the men were telling each other what ought to be done with De Valera and the rest of the Irish race.

'Hold on,' I said. 'My mother was Irish.'

'So what?' one of them said. '*You're* not. What the bloody hell has it got to do with you?'

I was very lucky not to get a hiding from them on that and several other occasions. The general opinion was that a damn cheeky kid who had the

---

[2] Sean Swan, 'MacStiofáin, Sean (1928–2001)', *Oxford Dictionary of National Biography*, online edition, Oxford University Press, Jan. 2005 [http://www.oxforddnb.com/view/article/75880, accessed 5 Sept. 2007].

fantastic good fortune to be born in England had no right to argue when they spoke of Irish people in this way.

The foreman plumber, whose name was Clark, liked to provoke such clashes when we knocked off for dinner. While we were working on a house in Chelsea, I discovered that he had been with the British troops who had tried to hold down Cork under martial law in the 1920s, and that he felt quite smug about it.

'It's a pity the IRA didn't get you,' I told him once when I got fed up with his master-race wisecracks.

I was staggered by the vehement prejudices of labourers, bricklayers, plumbers and others around me. They usually wouldn't say anything in the presence of people they knew to be Irish. That was why their reactions were so often surprise and anger when I put them right about where I stood. Since those experiences, I have come to believe that there is an inherent anti-Irish feeling in most English people. There is plenty of evidence that such a feeling has existed for centuries. Possibly they, and especially the working class, are unwitting victims of the propaganda and the cruel caricatures of their Irish neighbours instigated by British governments and editors since the seventeenth century. Much of this propaganda can only be described as racialist, and so much of it is still on file to be read by anybody with two eyes in his head that the point is not worth arguing. The image of the Irish as a lazy, good-for-nothing and untrustworthy race has always been accompanied by the harshest oppression, which is a familiar combination in colonial history. Over such a long period, perhaps it is not surprising that so many ordinary and otherwise decent English working people have been brainwashed into accepting it. At any rate, I experienced it for myself as soon as my political ears opened as a young workman in the early 1940s, and for more than a decade afterwards.

One of the great drawbacks for anybody who wanted to learn more about Ireland was the lack of an Irish cultural centre in London. I knew nowhere I could go to find a good Irish library, nor did the men I met at work. But the Islington and Holloway public libraries turned out to have a reasonable selection on their shelves labelled *Ireland*. I built up a small collection by hunting through the secondhand bookshops in the Charing Cross Road and the open-air barrows in Farringdon Road. I studied my way through a stack of works, beginning with a good general history of Ireland. When I was nearly sixteen I carefully read a history of Sinn Féin. And somewhere or other I managed to dig up some pamphlets on James Connolly.[3] They were heavy going for me at the time, with no one to guide or tutor me, but I read and

---

[3] James Connolly (1868–1916), socialist and trade union organiser. He was commandant of the Irish Citizen Army, a socialist militia set up to defend picketing workers' rights in 1913. In 1916 he joined the IRB and was executed for his part in the Easter Rising.

reread them until bit by bit I could make out both the national and the social shapes of the Irish revolutionary philosophy. They seemed to point to one simple fact anybody could understand. None of the risings and revolutionary movements in Ireland had to do with any single leader seeking power for himself. All had the same objectives – justice and freedom.

Needless to say, I came across some weird and useless books as well. I remember one very peculiar volume called *Ireland: An Enemy of the Allies*.[4] It was a black-propaganda job, but the effect it produced on me was the opposite of what the author intended. That book opened my eyes to how officially inspired British methods were being employed in the attempt to discredit Ireland. Oddly enough, its last line provided me with the first phrase I ever knew in Irish – a most unlikely one, as it turned out: 'A Dhia saor Eire agus Almáin' – God save Ireland and Germany. According to the propagandist, it was supposed to be a greeting, though I never heard anyone use it then or since. The second part of the phrase didn't fit my sentiments at all, but 'A Dhia saor Eire' did.

I made several visits back to Warwickshire to see Stan and Gladys Hall.[5] We were glad to meet each other, but they seemed disturbed at the way my ideas were developing. When I tried to explain them once, Stan said, 'But your mother was born in *Northern* Ireland, and that's ours. So therefore you're British.' Much as I liked them both, that was something I would never accept.

The radio brought Ireland a little closer to me. The signal wasn't very strong but it was better after dark. From 1942 to 1944 I got the Radio Eireann programme after 10:30 almost every night, and I wouldn't go to bed until it closed down with the *Soldier's Song* about half an hour later.[6]

I went to Irish dances. There were lively ones in a hall near Goodge Street underground station in the Tottenham Court Road. I liked listening to céilí music and watching the sets, but the main thing was being among the people and getting to know them. I would sit there drawing them out in conversation. Sometimes we would be interrupted by a fight breaking out in the hall between men who had had too much to drink.

'Ah, don't bother yourself about Ireland,' was the advice I got from a few. 'There's nothing there. If there was, we wouldn't be over here.' Cynical remarks like that puzzled me at first, until I understood the British stranglehold on the Irish economy and how you could never get real growth and employment while the profits streamed out of the country.

---

[4] *Ireland: An Enemy of the Allies?* (1919) by Rodolphe Escouflaire, originally published in French in 1918.

[5] MacStiofáin spent almost two years with this couple when he was evacuated from London during the early part of the war.

[6] 'The Soldier's Song' ('Amhrán na bhFiann') was composed in 1907 by Peadar Kearney (1883–1942), a maternal uncle of Brendan Behan, and Patrick Heeney (d. 1911). It was adopted as the national anthem of the Irish Free State in 1926.

I still had a circle of Irish friends in London from my schooldays, and I went on making more. A family from the Irish midlands lived in Finsbury. One of the boys was a year or two older than I was, and his brother was older still, but the three of us got on exceptionally well. I was a regular visitor at their house, and it was there I first saw old IRA medals. They had been issued by the Free State to a relative of the family. I read the Irish newspapers they received with deep interest. The ambition to live in Ireland was beginning to form. Feeling as I did, the logical thing was to move there sooner or later. I didn't want to spend the rest of my life in England.

Early in 1944 my feelings suddenly came to a head. There was a surge of speculation in the British press that the 'neutral' territory of the twenty-six counties would shortly be occupied. My younger friend in Finsbury and I decided on a scheme for getting back to Ireland if that happened. There we would join the Southern army and fight.

Having got that far with our plan, I asked some of our London Irish pals if they were willing to come with us. Their reactions killed certain illusions of mine. They said they had been born in London and their parents had been earning their living in England most of their lives. If there was an invasion, or any clash between England and Ireland, their own loyalties and sympathies would be with the English.

The invasion threat passed. Though I remained friendly for some time after that with the lads who had refused to join us, my association with them gradually ended. Our lives had begun to head in quite different directions.

52
Dónal Foley, *Three Villages: An Autobiography*

(Dublin: Egotist Press, 1977). 100pp.; pp. 52–6.

At the time of his early death in 1981, Dónal Foley was one of Ireland's most popular journalists, widely known for his weekly satirical column in the *Irish Times*, 'Man Bites Dog', selections of which were published annually in book form. Born in the Ring Gaeltacht in County Waterford in 1922, he worked as a postman, labourer and railwayman before emigrating in 1944 to London, where he began his journalistic career, working first for the Irish News Agency and then the *Irish Press*. In his autobiography he reveals that one of his first reporting assignments was to cover the London funeral of the writer James Stephens in 1950, at which there were less than a dozen mourners, among them the publisher and future British prime minister, Harold Macmillan. Foley joined the London office of the *Irish Times* in 1955 and moved to Dublin eight years later to become the paper's news editor. He was appointed deputy editor in 1977, the same year in which he published *Three Villages*, the latter part of which is given over to a chronicle of his emigrant years. As a reluctant economic migrant, in flight from unemployment, penury and poor prospects at home, Foley is typical of many of those who left rural Ireland in the 1940s for the urban centres of Britain. His comparison of the emigrant ship to 'a travelling Irish town, moving slowly and darkly across the water' in the following excerpt graphically evokes the scale of this exodus, and it is clear that the emotions and experiences he describes – the pain of separation, the unfocused anger at having to leave, the bewilderment of the new, the cleaving to 'the comradeship of adversity' – were shared by many of his fellow travellers. In later chapters Foley provides a brief, impressionistic portrait of emigrant Irish culture in post-war London, mischievously noting such details as the ubiquity of the national emblem on St Patrick's Day: 'In London, even the prostitutes wear their shamrock with pride, many of them perfectly entitled to do so having impeccable racial qualifications.'

That day in September 1944 when I kissed Mother goodbye, I did so with a very heavy heart. My absence from Ireland, I vowed that day would be of short duration. It was not to be like that. Indeed, it was fully twenty odd years before I was enabled to return to Ireland. It was really another lifetime.

The usual crowd of unemployed men were standing in an aimless group at the street corner and they wished me good luck almost nonchalantly. It was not an unusual event in those days when every Irish village was being stripped of its young, as was Ireland herself. We were 'going, going, going, from the valleys and the hills,' as Parnell's sister Fanny wrote of another generation a hundred years before.[1]

I was luckier than most. At least I had a case, albeit a cardboard one, in contrast to many of my fellow emigrants who carried their few belongings tied in a newspaper. I had a pair of shoes, a reasonable coat (a Lord have mercy, as we used to call clothes inherited from dead relatives). My brother-in-law had died a little time previously. The other emigrants that day were, in the main, poorly dressed. A ragged, penniless army with nothing but their health and strength to hurry them on their way. No mean attributes, mind you, on those dark days when Britain needed the workers to carry the hod and make bombs. [...]

The station at Waterford as I left was crowded with young women and men with white anxious faces and parents looking even more anxious still. The young people, like myself were mostly in their twenties, all waiting to catch the 3.45 train to Dublin and emigration. Most of the men were travelling on Wimpey's vouchers en route to the building sites of England, power stations, munitions factories, roads and bomb damaged areas.[2] Big strong men, pale and unsure, taking up their first jobs, all of them fleeing from the demoralisation of unemployment, and ready to send money home to the helpless ones still left. I was seen off by Jim 'Black' Norris, so known because of the jet colour of his hair. A few months later he was killed as a rear gunner with the R.A.F. over Germany. He was our finest corner forward as a hurler.

The train to Dublin was packed with people from Waterford, county and city. At Kilkenny the platform was crowded with young people, the mothers clinging on to them loath to let them go and anxious to get the last seconds of their companionship. So it was at all little stations, until finally Kingsbridge. This was neutral Ireland. It was a silent, expectant train. Tongues sometimes unloosed slightly apprehensively about what was in store. The story of Ireland since black '47. The Globe Hotel in Talbot Street was the Mecca of the building workers. It was there they were given their destination and their work permits. I was going to London to work on the railway and didn't have to stay in the Globe. Instead I stayed in the respectable suburb of Mount Merrion Avenue with my sister Sheila and got my first glance of suburban Dublin. It was then growing fast. We all met up later on and discovered on board a ship ironically named 'Hibernia' that we were all to do work

---

[1] A quotation not from Fanny Parnell but from 'The Passing of the Gael' by Ethna Carbery (1866–1902). The poem opens with the line: 'They are going, going, going from the valleys and the hills'.

[2] Ultan Cowley observes that the British construction firm Wimpey 'employed so many Irish labourers in the postwar era that their name became a witty acronym for "We Import More Paddies Every Year"' (*The Men Who Built Britain*, p. 11).

for the British Ministry of Labour which was described on our work permits as work of 'National Importance'.

The Irish government of the day, of which Mr. de Valera was Taoiseach, had made an agreement with the British Ministry of Labour which shipped us into exile. We had to notify our place of residence in Britain, report to the police every week, leave the country when requested to do so by the British Home Secretary. Unquestionably an odd form of neutrality, but it did ensure that our country was not continually bombed by the Germans, although, there were some strange errors when the Germans bombed the North Strand in Dublin, and made a direct hit on a lonely farm house in Mount Leinster.[3] One of de Valera's great acts of statesmanship and charity was the occasion he sent the Dublin Fire Brigade to Belfast, when that city was burning as a result of German bombers. It seems even at this remove a more important act than that much talked about a cup of tea Mr. Sean Lemass, the Irish Taoiseach, enjoyed with Mr. Terence O'Neill, the Northern Ireland Prime Minister, very many years later.[4] There was more charity and concern involved in sending the Fire Brigade to Belfast.[5]

The British Railways ship on which we travelled was like a travelling Irish town, moving slowly and darkly across the water. Only the voices of the people, the shouts of command of the sailors and constant gurgling of the channel disturbed the eerie silence of that night. All the lights were blacked out, the first grim reminder that we were travelling to a country at war.

Down in the bar of the ship hundreds thronged round the serving hatch and the inadequate counters looking for drink. In the corridors and on the benches men and women tried to sleep and occasionally one saw mothers pushing bottles on unwilling babies. In one corner a group of Mayo men argued about Irish neutrality. An Englishman who tried to keep his side up was told to go back to his own country, which seemed to be just what the little man had in mind.

For myself, I was totally confused. I did not want to leave Ireland at all. Indeed, I still did not believe I was doing so. This was a nightmare adventure in which I was involved with all these strange people and strange faces. Inside me a resentment was building up against I knew not what. Why should I have to go and leave all those others at home in comfort? I would soon go back, I told myself.

---

[3] German bombs fell on the North Strand area of Dublin on 30 May 1941, killing 34 people and injuring several hundred. The German government later apologised for the incident, describing it as a mistake.

[4] Terence O'Neill (1914–1990) hosted the historic visit of Seán Lemass (1899–1971) to Stormont on 14 January 1965. The two premiers met again in Dublin the following month.

[5] See note 4 in the excerpt from Nesca Robb above (number 49).

In the darkness a young clear singing Cork voice pierced the silence like a rapier: 'Boys like Barry are not cowards ... British soldiers tortured Barry just because he would not tell.'[6] A primitive feeling of fellowship with that young defiant voice welled up in my breast. The song was taken up by hundreds and when our ship landed at Holyhead, that strange chorus filled the dark air. The Customs officials and the soldiers looked on impassive, unaware of our sentiments, even if they did mean nothing. They checked our passports, went through our luggage, for what it was and sent us on our way.

We shuffled off the boat, a long dark crocodile of people, walking as it were into the unknown except for those among us who had known the horrors of Camden Town, Kilburn, Birmingham, Glasgow, Coventry, Leeds, Reading and Slough before now. Horrors, yes, but warm with consolations too. The welcoming pubs, the weekly wage packet and the comradeship of adversity. The muted lights showed us the general direction of the train for London and as we shuffled a dread sound, which we were later to know well as the air raid siren, reminded us that the German bombers were in the vicinity. The real meaning of those sirens only came home to me some weeks later when two Irish girls who served behind a bar were blown to their deaths.

That night we were conscious only of the sharp wind, the dark and the dreariness of Holyhead, surely the unfriendliest spot during those years in the whole world. The train stopped at Crewe first, a dark jungle of a junction with only the hissing of the steam trains, and the incomprehensible shoutings of the porters to be heard. Cups of tea could be got if one were quick and adventurous enough to dash across two platforms. I sat tight, afraid I would get lost if I ventured away from the London train. Stations with hissing trains have always had the effect of filling me with panic, and that night was no exception. Suddenly, an authoritative cockney voice could be heard above the din. 'All chinge.' We obeyed and piled urgently on to the dark forbidding platform, clinging to our bits of luggage. In a short while the first glimmerings of grey dawn were beginning to show.

Crewe looked even worse in the half light than in the stygian darkness. Women pushed laden barrows, and were continually blowing whistles. It was another reminder that Britain was at war and that women were doing the jobs normally done by men. The tearoom advertised bacon and eggs. The egg seemed to be a dark coloured black platter with a foul taste, and the rasher a slice of spam of similar hue. I protested that both tasted badly, but the young girl in charge, a smiling Wicklow girl, saw that I was an innocent. 'There will be no more fresh Irish eggs for a while', she said gaily. She explained to me that the bacon was spam from America and the eggs made of powder. 'You'll

---

[6] Lyrics from a republican ballad commemorating the execution of IRA man Kevin Barry, who was hanged on 1 November 1920, aged 18, a week after the death of Terence MacSwiney in Brixton prison.

get used to it' she said, 'and even like it.' The tea was good and the bread better than we had had at home. There was a three hours unexplained wait before we eventually boarded the train for London. We seemed to be coming into London for hours. A back door view of that great city, the washing hanging out and the women cleaning the windows. We were tired, hungry and a little frightened. I had to get to Broad Street, which is in the heart of the City proper.

There is a special confusing urgency about early morning London. The people seem to be filled with a dogged determination to get somewhere fast. The heart of the City could be described as sound, even if the body was falling apart. I had never experienced a big city before, at peace or at war. Even to this day I tend to lose my way constantly in the city of Dublin. An English friend whom I had volunteered to take from Westmoreland Street to the Wicklow Hotel got lost with me, and later sent me a map of Dublin.

Euston Station that morning seemed to be stretching itself from its slumber. People setting up their wares. Unaccustomed noise of machinery everywhere. Another scream from an air raid and the reason was all too plain. A small object like a plane was careering across the London sky, a small plane shooting out in front. 'It's all right, the engine is still going well', said a reassuring voice, a veteran of the doodle bugs, those terrible last fling weapons of Hitler. A group of us watched it in awesome fascination as it sped across the morning sky, until the engine stopped and it shot down into some unsuspecting London suburb. [...]

That night I met my sister Cait in Mooney's Irish House in the Strand, then the longest bar in London. We clung to each other before leaving and cried profusely. She to make her way to New Eltham where she was a nurse and me to a vague address in Victoria, which I found after hours of feeling my way in the darkness. My landlady was a kindly Waterford woman, so it wasn't a bad start. I had a room to myself with a view of a tiny garden, a good bed and it was only a few minutes walk to Victoria Underground. Never was warmth and sleep so welcome, and that night there were no sirens to send us to the air raid shelter, which was a part of every house. I was a real emigrant now.

53

Elaine Crowley, *Technical Virgins*

(Dublin: Lilliput Press, 1998). 196pp.; pp. 137–40.

Elaine Crowley was born in the Liberties area of Dublin in 1927 to a Brighton-born father and an Irish mother. Her father's death from tuberculosis in 1942 exacerbated the family's economic plight and brought closer the prospect of emigration. She eventually left Ireland at the end of the Second World War and joined the Auxiliary Territorial Service (ATS) – a branch of the British army staffed entirely by women – which took her to a base near Chester in Cheshire, where she met the Welshman she would later marry. After periods spent in Germany and Egypt, the couple settled in Port Talbot in Wales to raise a family of six. It wasn't until Crowley was in her fifties that she acted upon a long-held literary interest by joining a writers' group in Swansea. This proved to be the stimulus she needed to produce her first novel, *Dreams of Other Days* (1984), a family saga set in Famine Ireland. Its commercial success led to a further seven romantic novels published over 20 years, together with two volumes of autobiography, *Cowslips and Chainies* (1996), which recreates her Dublin childhood, and *Technical Virgins*, Crowley's account of her ATS years in the late 1940s. In chronicling her transformation from naïve Catholic teenager into streetwise young woman, Crowley offers a version of emigration from de Valera's Ireland which, by accentuating the triumph of agency and adaptation over anguish and nostalgia, contrasts markedly with that of many male autobiographers of the same period. Far from being a living hell, England was for Crowley a place of joyful liberation, a 'land of Tír na nÓg', as she memorably phrases it in the following excerpt. And so in place of the tearful backward look we have here a clear-eyed repudiation of 1940s Ireland from a young woman's perspective, a compelling reminder that the country did not automatically become a landscape of loss in the mind of every post-war migrant.

One evening Katy, Breda, Sylvia and I were talking. They were doing most of it. My mind was miles away. Imagining how I'd be received by my father's people. The fuss my grandfather would make of me. I would be staying with my aunt in Brighton. She had, according to my father, the same beautiful hair as her mother. She'd talk to me about her mother. About my father. Remember incidents from their childhood. The holidays they had spent in Horsham. She'd make him seem alive again.

Katy's voice broke in on my meanderings. 'Did you hear what I was saying?' she asked.

'Bits,' I replied. 'Tell me again.'

'I was just saying how this time next year we'll all be gone.'

'Gone where?'

'Home. Edinburgh, Ireland, Southampton. Wherever we decide to settle. Demobbed. Out of the forces.'

Not me. She had mentioned Dublin. But Katy couldn't have meant me. It seemed only yesterday I had joined up. This doubt must have showed on my face. For Katy asked, 'What year did you join up in?'

'1945.'

'Next year's '47. You'll have served your time. You didn't think it'd last for ever? You didn't want it to, did you?'

Oh, but I did. Forever and ever. My paradise. My haven where no one got seriously ill. No one died. No one talked of death. Where everyone was young. My land of Tír na nÓg.

Where I watched the seasons change. Spring resurrect the trees. Deck them in green buds. Cover the branches in leaves. Hang pussy willows from them. Set horse chestnuts ablaze with pink and white candles. Litter the woods with bluebells and primroses. Hear the cuckoo. Wild flowers in abundance. Lacy-headed cow parsley. I was learning to identify flowering weeds. Such names: Dusky Cranesbill, Shepherd's Purse, Lady's Slipper, Nipplewort.

Later on rowan berries. Prickly podded sweet chestnut nested in their fleshy white wombs. Scarlet, white-spotted toadstools. Like pictures in a storybook. And the golden, yellow, russet leaves in my place of the trees. And the sky. The endless sky. On clear nights filled with stars and the face of the man in the moon. And when it snowed it stayed white as it had fallen. Lay on the branches of trees. Covered the cricket field, the ground each side of the slope down to the cookhouse. No, I didn't want to leave, didn't want to go home, back to a factory treading a machine. I wanted to stay. Stay where grown-up girls played games. Bathed six times a day if they wanted to. Had six pairs of knickers, unglamorous though they might be. Where white sheets and towels were laundered once a week.

I was devastated. How had time flown so quickly? Why hadn't I been aware that it had? Because I had been so happy. Every moment filled with pleasure. Pleasure I was constantly aware of. Surrounded by attractive, adoring men. Aware that I had blossomed. Being in love. Being loved in return.

No mother prying, preaching, probing. I couldn't go back. Not to a factory. To compulsory mass. Chapels where you paid your entrance. A penny for the body where the poor sat. Almost all in shabby clothes. Some in dirty ones. Watch the lice weave in and out of their hair. Farting men who'd drunk too much the previous night, the smell of their foul wind wafting around mixed with burning grease of candles, incense and the sour breath from stomachs fasting from the night before so they could receive Communion. While in the threepenny and sixpenny places sat powdered women swathed in sealskin and musquash. Men in pressed suits, clean shirts, collars and ties and their children in camel's-hair coats, brown velour hats and polished shoes.

And the priest's voice droning on and on to his captive audience.

No, I didn't want any of that. Nor the dancehalls. Stand waiting for the men who had been viewing you like cattle in a market. Their numbers swelling when the public houses closed. Nudging each other. And, when their courage was up, crossing the divide in your direction, you hoped. Though often it was the girl next to you they asked up. I wanted none of it. I'd sign on for another two years.

'You're mad,' said Katy when I announced my decision. 'Everything'll change. Me and Breda gone. All the gorgeous men as well. The camp'll fill up with National Service blokes. Kids just out of school and twerps of Officer Cadets that you can't date anyway. Only ones left will be the regulars. And they're either ancient or married. The girls coming in now are different. You can see that already. Young kids, seventeen and eighteen.'

'But what'll I do if I don't sign on?'

'Go to Glasgow. Steve's there. Get work as a telephonist.'

'Where would I live?'

'Oh, for God's sake! Lots of places. Lodgings. A bedsit. You won't be the only one living alone. There'll be thousands out there.'

I had never had to find a job. I was landed into the one I had. I'd never lived on my own. I'd be afraid. Always I'd shared with other people. You felt safe. Irritated by coughs, by snores. But secure in the presence of others.

Sylvia said, 'Katy, you're forgetting the full-time PT course. She'll have to sign on, otherwise that's off.'

'Why would it be off?' I asked, more startled by the prospect of not achieving my ambition than returning to Ireland.

'Not worth the cost,' Sylvia explained, 'if in six months you'll be gone.'

The next day I signed on for a further two years.

54
John B. Keane, *Self-Portrait*

(Dublin: Mercier Press, 1964). 106pp.; pp. 31–5.

The subdued resentment that Dónal Foley harbours towards an Irish government that could permit the continuing haemorrhage of emigration swells to an angry shout in the work of John B. Keane (1928–2002). Born and raised in Listowel, County Kerry, Keane spent just over two years in England in the early 1950s, long enough for him to become acquainted with the heartbreak, degradation and discrimination experienced by many of the 1950s generation of unskilled migrants. After the success of his first play, *Sive* (1959), he turned his outraged gaze upon the causes and consequences of the depopulation of rural Ireland in the plays *Many Young of Men of Twenty* (1961) and *Hut 42* (1962), both of which castigate the hypocrisy and indifference of politicians towards the fact of mass emigration. In *Self-Portrait* Keane writes of his own experiences, addressing the reader in an intimate, confessional voice that often seethes with emotion, as in the following excerpt, in which he seeks to jolt the would-be emigrant out of any lingering sense of complacency.

It was firmly in my head for some time to emigrate to America, and it was probably the hopelessness of my position with regard to marriage that was most responsible for my leaving Ireland.

So, on the 6th of January, 1952, I set out to make my fortune.

I chose England. It was nearer for one thing, and many of my friends were already settled down there. I decided to apply beforehand to Boots Chemists for a position. It was better, my father said, to have something waiting over – 'something that will keep the bite in your mouth, anyway!' he said. I said goodbye to Mary. It was a tearful one, but I would be home in the summertime for a holiday, a long wait between dates, however.

In Dublin I met Eamonn.[1] He was with Radio Eireann then. It was to be some time before he had his disastrous clash with the Minister for Posts and Telegraphs. We celebrated the beginning of my exile in true style. We started

---

[1] Eamonn Keane (1925–1990), well-known Irish actor and broadcaster.

at three o'clock in the Tower Bar at the corner of Henry Street and O'Connell Street and I made the eight o'clock boat with only minutes to spare.

I was more than slightly intoxicated but not even that could dispel the gloom which I felt at leaving home for the first time. I remember, as I walked up the gangplank, I heard Eamonn shouting after me. 'Write!' he yelled. 'Write something every day…Write…Write…' His voice tailed off. There were hundreds of other good-byes.

When I boarded the train at Listowel that morning it seemed as if everyone was leaving. It was the same at every railway station along the way. Dun Laoghaire, for the first time, was a heartbreaking experience – the goodbyes to husbands going back after Christmas, chubby-faced boys and girls leaving home for the first time, bewilderment written all over them, hard-faced old-stagers who never let on but who felt it the worst of all because they knew only too well what lay before them.

It was a cold night, with high seas as they say. Conditions were shocking – that is for second-class passengers, or, if you like, the steerage-type exile, which breed constituted the great majority of my fellow-travellers.

In my hip-pocket I had a naggin of Irish whiskey. It was a poor consolation, a parting gift from Eamonn whose last words were still ringing in my ears. Maybe if I stuck to writing it might eventually get me back to Ireland.

I joined forces with a pale-faced, red-haired woman whose name was Nora. She was the mother of five children and she was trying to look after the five on that draughty deck. She was on her way to join her husband in London. After two years of separation, neither could tolerate it. He was lucky to find a two-roomed flat at four pounds a week in the suburbs of London. […]

All around us as we left Dun Laoghaire, there was drunkenness. The younger men were drunk – not violently so but tragically so, as I was, to forget the dreadful loneliness of having to leave home. Underneath it all was the heartbreaking, frightful anguish of separation. It would be a waste of time for me to launch into a description of what went on. A person has to be part of it to feel it. The whole scene reminded me of the early Christian martyrs going out to face the terrors of the arena. Laugh if you like, but there was an unbelievable spirit of fraternity, a kind of brotherhood, a communal feeling of tragedy which embraced us all.

It is no laughing matter to those who took part in the pilgrimage.

Everybody was helping somebody else. A few rough diamonds came to the assistance of Nora and took charge of the five children. They looked after their every want till morning. One man of about fifty, a time-scarred buck-navvy, insisted on changing a nappy. It was just a formality. He wasn't embarrassed and nobody took any notice. It would have been a real tragedy if somebody did. Of all the things I've ever felt or seen, nothing ever so moved or affected me as the sight of these men and women being torn away from home. If you want to laugh, now is your chance. Laugh loud and high and you'll be heard by some lonely old couple whose loved ones are lost forever.

Recently in Dun Laoghaire, in hotels and loungebars where I have been accorded some attention by the proprietors and others of consequence from the neighbourhood, I was tempted to elaborate on the theme of departure from the pier when I was asked if I liked Dun Laoghaire or if it was my first visit.

It wasn't!

They wouldn't have felt or understood the anguish of perpetual departure. For them Dun Laoghaire was a soft bed, good fires and excellent reception from cross-channel telly. For us, as it was then, it was the brink of hell and don't think I use the word hell lightly! If there is an artist in this country – a real artist who wants to capture the truth for eternity on his canvases – my advice to him is to go to the North Wall, to Dun Laoghaire, to Rosslare or to Cork. Watch the faces, and, unless you're a heartless inhuman moron, you'll feel something and your conscience will begin to bother you. I have been accused on several occasions of highlighting the problem of emigration and of evading the issue of a solution. The solution is – don't go! Stay at home. We are your people and this is your country.

We – the ones at home – are responsible for you.

A country is like a parent. It must provide for its children, so stay at home, and when the urge which is part of the heritage of the Irish race takes hold of you, plant your feet firmly on your own soil and don't go. I have heard England referred to as the land of cups of cha, the land of jellied eels, etc. All this is most derogatory. At least the English are a race who look after their own. They conquered the world to provide for younger sons.

It is all right if you're English, or that way inclined, but to me, and to millions of others, it means banishment.

Don't go! Don't panic! This is our country. That's all you have to remember.

Another thing the uninitiated second-class exile will long remember is the contempt of elusive stewards and channel officers for our type of cargo. It is never expressed in words – they wouldn't dare (we'd break their necks if they did!) – but it is written over their faces: contempt, scorn and disinterestedness. The tourist is fawned over and spoiled, but they can't wait to deposit the departing Paddy on the other side.

How different it is all coming back for the annual holiday: the melodeons and fiddles and the sing-songs, the exuberant boys and the friendly girls, the attentiveness of the grasping stewards and the cheerful quips flung at the generous Paddies who cannot spend it quickly enough. Back again then when the short holiday is over.

55

Dónall Mac Amhlaigh, *An Irish Navvy: The Diary of an Exile*

With a preface by Valentin Iremonger (London: Routledge & Kegan Paul, 1964). ix, 182pp.; pp. 175–82. Translated by Valentin Iremonger from *Dialann Deoraí* (Dublin: An Clóchomhar Tta, 1960).

John B. Keane's view of emigration as a profoundly deleterious social phenomenon which is inimical to the integrity of nation, community and the self is loudly echoed by Dónall Mac Amhlaigh (1926–1989) in *An Irish Navvy*, a work that powerfully registers the bitterness and sorrow of a 'lost' post-war generation of Irish migrants. Mac Amhlaigh tallies with dismay the symptoms of cultural dissolution, only occasionally finding consolation in the restorative thought of an Irish Catholic diaspora that has forged a 'spiritual empire' from the privations of exile. Born in Galway and educated in Kilkenny, Mac Amhlaigh worked at a variety of low-paid jobs before joining the Irish-speaking regiment of the Irish army in 1947. Four years later he emigrated to Northampton, joining the throngs of migrant labourers fuelling the post-war British construction boom. From the late 1950s until his death in 1989 he combined the roles of full-time labourer and part-time writer, producing nine books in Irish as well as a wealth of journalism in both Irish and English. While his semi-autobiographical novels won him a substantial readership, it is his *journal intime* that has assumed iconic status as the *locus classicus* of the Irish migrant working-class experience in 1950s Britain.

Loosely structured around a series of diary entries dating from the author's arrival in England in March 1951 to Easter 1957, by which time he was a fully-fledged navvy, the narrative vividly records the tribal milieu and *mentalité* of transient economic migrants, from the melancholic gaiety of their social gatherings to their gauche and often rough-tongued interactions with the host population. While Mac Amhlaigh later expressed dissatisfaction with the text's lack of polish, it is the very artlessness of the work that gives it its distinctive appeal. The bluff immediacy of the language makes the reader feel that he or she is eavesdropping on intimate, unguarded thoughts and impressions that reveal more about the diarist than he might wish. Certainly, the book shows how emigration reinforced Mac Amhlaigh's sense of cultural separatism, the key markers of which were Catholicism and the Irish language. He wore his faith proudly – many of his entries were made on Church feast days – and was happiest when in the company of Gaelic-speaking Connemara men, who embodied his austere ideal of virile, 'authentic' Irishness. Return visits to Ireland renewed his devotionalism and reactivated his longing to remain there permanently, as the following excerpt from a chapter entitled 'An Exile's Homesickness' demonstrates. The year is 1957.

Good Friday. I always feel very guilty on this day and I'm always glad when it's over. There's a great difference between Good Friday at home and Good Friday here.

To the English, it's only the beginning of the holiday, a day on which you eat hot-cross buns; and they work on that day so that they can have Easter Tuesday off. Some of the Irish are just as bad and they think nothing of going out drinking and celebrating that night. Well, it wasn't like that for the old people who would have nothing to eat but a bit of dry bread or to drink but a drop of black tea throughout the whole day and who would spend most of the time saying the Rosary.

First thing in the morning, I felt I wanted to get home. Some of the lads were talking of going to Dublin for Easter and I began to think of doing the same. Like Raftery[1] long ago, I had no peace until I gave in to my urge.

When I got home from work, I gave myself a good scrubbing, put on my Sunday suit, took three spare collars and a toothbrush, stuck a razor in my pocket and made my way to the station. I was as excited as a child as I thought of the trip particularly as I had started out quite spontaneously. I was amazed at how many were making their way home.

As usual, I slept most of the way from Rugby onwards. I never can stay awake with the noise of the wheels and the swaying of the train on the rails. As we crossed Conway Bridge, the noise woke me up but I fell asleep again; and when I woke up again, I saw the sea stretched out like a mirror under the moonlight.

I got a great kick out of going through the Customs shed at Dun Laoire in the morning with nothing whatsoever to declare. I had a good breakfast in that café that is directly opposite Westland Row Station. You have to be impressed with the waitresses in the restaurants in Dublin – they're so chatty and contented in themselves unlike their counterparts in England. When I finished, I moved off down town to have a look at the place. Isn't it maddening that I know more about London than I know about Ireland's first city?

For instance, I wouldn't know where in Dublin to look for the kind of company I frequent over there – that is, if there is any equivalent. Here in Dublin, there are Irish of all kinds – rich, poor, intelligent and ignorant – but in England, for the most part, there is only one kind of Irishman and that is the worker. If you live long enough over there, you begin to think that all the Irish are working-class – which, of course, is not true.

---

[1] A native of County Mayo, Anthony Raftery (1779–1835) was a blind poet who spent most of his life wandering the Galway and Mayo countryside, composing poems and songs on contemporary themes.

I bought an Easter Lily[2] on the Bridge and walked slowly up O'Connell Street. I bought a copy of *Inniu* and of *Aiseiri*[3] in Eason's and took them in with me to the Tower Bar. I knocked back two pints very pleasantly while I listened to the chat all around me. The atmosphere in the pubs here is marvellous compared with those over the way. There's a depth and a vigour in the talk you hear; and the odd time you get women present, they're not screaming and roaring like the English women. In Dublin pubs, you'd know that the drink and the conversation were the most important things; but in England, the drink is only an excuse for playing cribbage and darts. May our lovely Irish pubs last forever!

The two things I noticed most here in Dublin were the prettiness of the women and the poverty of many of the people. If you had nothing else to remind you that you were in Ireland, the women's faces would confirm the fact for you. Irish women facially, don't resemble the women of any other country, I think. High cheek-bones, freckles, grey-blue eyes and black curly hair are what you notice most about the women in this city. And it's amazing how many girls have those characteristics when you recall how much Danish and English blood has been here for so many centuries.

Alas, the other matter, the poverty is as noticeable here. You'd be hard put to count how many people passed you by in old, worn clothes. Most of them are in threadbare overcoats and their shoes are badly worn down. You don't see people like that in England at all nowadays; and, in themselves, they epitomise the bad way in which Ireland finds herself.

Two hours it took on the diesel to Kilkenny. On my way home from the station, I dropped into Stephen Brennan's for a drink. Stephen nearly had a fit when he saw me coming in.

'Oh, by God,' he cried, 'I thought you were gone!'

'Gone where?' I asked him.

'Over the way,' he said.

'Well, I've come back,' I answered.

'Well, by the honey, England must be a great country,' he marvelled as he pulled me a pint. They'll all be talking now about the great earnings in England that enable people to come home again after a bare seven weeks.

My father and mother got a right start when I walked in the door on them. The old lady started cooking straight away and the old man was tremendously

---

[2] Emblem worn by some Irish nationalists at Easter to commemorate those who died in the cause of independence.

[3] *Inniu* ('Today') was an Irish-language newspaper published weekly between 1943 and 1984; *Aiséirí* ('Resurrection'), a monthly periodical which ran from 1944 to 1975. Ciarán Ó Nualláin, brother of the novelist Flann O'Brien, was the first editor of *Aiséirí*, which espoused a very right-wing politics initially. See Clair Wills, *That Neutral Island: A Cultural History of Ireland During the Second World War* (London: Faber & Faber, 2007), pp. 364–9.

bucked up. Thank God, the weather is great and looks like continuing. It's nice to see the active young boys playing among themselves out on the grass – a sure sign that the country is not beaten yet. If things improve gradually and if everyone can earn a decent living, we'll have to have plenty of people to enjoy what comfort will be going!

I went to Confession in the Abbey; it was like Heaven inside there were so many candles burning and flowers decorating the altar. Ireland is the most Catholic country in the world; you can be sure of that.

Easter Sunday. A lovely morning, thanks be to God. To Mass early in the Black Abbey with my mother. The people are lovely and happy here together, greeting each other kindly coming from Mass. It's only an ignorant man that would say life is better over the way, despite the money you can earn.

I met my father after eleven o'clock Mass and we walked down town. A group of cyclists from Dublin came down Patrick Street and stopped for a rest on the Parade. They were happy, loud-voiced, amused by the country people but for all that full of harmless fun. There was a good crowd already there as we made our way into Larry's. Larry and the lads were amazed to see me coming back so soon.

I ate a fine Irish dinner: bacon, cabbage, roast and boiled potatoes with a nice sweet to follow. I was the only one of the family present. Kevin is in Daventry, Noel in Hampshire, Brian in Sussex and Dympna, our only sister, in London. It's the same story in many houses here and, indeed, all over Ireland.

I got out the bike after dinner and went out the Callan road to have a look at the countryside. Spring is in full sway here while it's only the beginning across the water. The little peaks of Tullaroan were on my right hand side, Mount Leinster and the other mountains on my left, all standing out clearly against the background of the sky and directly in front of me, the majestic mass of Sleivenamon, unchanged from the time of Finn MacCool.[4] Round these parts lived Humphrey O'Sullivan, the diarist.[5] He left us an accurate and lively account of the lives of the people here and the doings of his time.

Humphrey always lamented the oppression of the Irish by the English; but in this lovely countryside, the Irish are in command now – those of them that are left. The Irish language has taken itself away from these rich lands – across the Corrib and into the bleak lands of Erris and the islands off the west coast. One man and his few cattle live here where, in O'Sullivan's time, twenty people lived – Irishmen speaking Irish. What could have been better – to give a good livelihood to the people when they were here so that they would have

---

[4] Celebrated hero of Irish mythology and leader of the Fianna warriors.

[5] Killarney-born Humphrey O'Sullivan (1780–1838) was the author of the first known diary in Irish, which records his activities during the 1827–35 period. He ran a shop in Callan, County Kilkenny, close to where Mac Amhlaigh's family lived.

self-respect and treasure their national language, or to try to bring Irish back from the grave so that it can be on Irish lips again?

Gloomy thoughts, and this is Easter, the time of hope and courage; and all I have is two more days before I have to get back into that tunnel at Rugby. To hell with them for thoughts! [...]

I didn't bother taking a drink tonight. I walked home at my ease enjoying the healthy night air. I stood at the gate looking up at the stars. It's the same sky that will be over me when I get back to Northampton in a couple of days time – but I feel more natural with it here.

I'm really lucky so far as the weather is concerned anyhow. Today is altogether beautiful and I don't remember when I felt so well.

Myself and the old lad mooched off down town before eleven. People were walking around at their ease and the girls looked lovely in their summer dresses. The amount of lovely women that are in this town! Times I think it might be nice to settle down and marry one of them. For a man like myself that has reached the age of thirty, it's not at all too soon to be thinking of the like. Indeed, I suppose a lot of us would do it if we could stay at home but what's the good of talking about that? I've often said that it's a good thing to stay in the place in which you were born and where the seven generations before you lived. You'd feel you belonged to the place, that your roots were there, so to speak, instead of feeling like visitors as we do in England. If there was work to be had here, there's not a town in Ireland could compare with it, for they're a generous light-hearted people, the Cats.[6] [...]

Tuesday, 23.4.1957. A bit cool today. My father and I spent a couple of hours in Larry's before dinner. There weren't many there; the holiday is over. I savoured the atmosphere of the place to the full: a peaceful quietude and the steady tick-tock of the old-fashioned clock above the bottles on the top shelf, the heavy-sweet smell of the porter and the low voices of the men talking quietly as if they did not wish to break the silence. Larry shook hands with me as I was leaving and wished me a good journey.

I found the time trying while I was hanging around waiting to leave the house. The old lady was very sad even though many's the time before I had gone away. Will anyone ever get used to parting?

Two hours on the train to Dublin. I had a good short holiday and I shouldn't be unhappy. But after all, I envy the cattle lying on the green grass of Ireland gazing cow-like at the C.I.E. carriages riding by.[7] But even the cattle are trundled across too, like the Paddies and Brigids of Ireland.

Coming into Dun Laoire, I saw men in white clothes playing cricket and, somehow I felt annoyed. A young man and his girl were walking by

---

[6] A nickname for the Kilkenny hurling team.

[7] Córas Iompair Éireann, the state-owned Irish national rail and road transport system.

themselves down below us in the golden evening sunlight. It's well for you, my friend, that every day you arise can be spent round about this place.

The White Boat is laden down with people. Most of them, I fancy, like myself, returning after Easter. I can see, too, that others are going across for the first time. On my right, there is a little group from Connemara talking in Irish. If I live at all, surely that's Horse Flaherty down below! If it is, we'll have great sport in no time!

Doesn't Dun Laoire look beautiful with the mountains behind it? The quay is lined with little sailing boats, and wooden rowing boats. The wealthy own them, those who can stay behind here.

And then, without warning, she drifts from the quay. Wasn't I the inattentive one that I didn't see them getting ready? I can sense the old feeling in my stomach that I get each time I leave Irish soil, but it won't last long. I'm getting used to it now.

The Wicklow mountains are on the right, merging into the darkness of the night. Do their colours change, I wonder, like the Twelve Pins.[8] The sun has gone down now but there are faint golden rays in the west still. For a minute, I have a vision of Lough Corrib and again I get that sensation in my stomach.

Somewhere around me a man is singing the 'Rose of Tralee.' Someone else yarns.

We're a great people, surely.

---

[8] A mountain range in County Galway.

56

Richard Power, *Apple on the Treetop*

(Dublin: Poolbeg, 1980). 200pp.; pp. 196–200. Translated by Victor Power from *Úll i mBarr an Ghéagáin* (Dublin: Sáirséal agus Dill Teoranta, 1958).

Dublin-born Richard Power (1928–1970) was a bilingual novelist and short story writer whose best-known work, *The Hungry Grass* (1969), is a novel dealing with the last days of a parish priest in rural Ireland. Eleven years earlier Power published *Úll i mBárr an Ghéagáin*, an autobiographical work in which he recalls the periods he spent living on the Aran Islands, where he studied Irish, and in Birmingham, where he worked as a navvy and manual labourer during the mid-1950s, before moving to Iowa. Translated into English by his brother Victor, the book's last five chapters provide a rare autobiographical insight into Irish emigrant culture in post-war Birmingham. In recording his impressions of the Irish men and women he encounters in the boarding houses, pubs and dancehalls of the city, Power is troubled by 'the restless, unsettling way of life that they engaged in, without any definite goal, without household, without authority, without having to answer to their family, to the state, to anyone at all'. Yet their seizing of the personal and social freedoms offered by emigration makes him question his own preconceptions about the privations of exile and the consolations of nostalgia: 'Could it be that my own memories were already eroding so that they'd be consistent with the unreality I'd carry about with me from now on?' The final chapter, reproduced below, shows the narrator leaving Birmingham by train and finding himself eavesdropping on a subdued, tragicomic mini-drama which, as Power configures it, has the unity, momentum and compressed lyricism of a short story. Indeed, the chapter's diminuendo mood and mimetic power are reminiscent of Sean O'Faolain's 'A Broken World' (1937), his Joyce-inspired attempt to write a chapter in the moral history of his country, which is also set in a train compartment. It may not be too fanciful to read Power's sharply observed vignette, with its deep and steady sympathy for a hapless victim of circumstance, as an instalment in the moral history of his compatriots who had lost their country.

The months slipped past. Spring arrived, the sap of life rising in the trees, and the city of Birmingham became more hideous by the day. I hated the fresh-green evenings getting longer and the plain streets becoming even more unattractive.

One cold night in February, I said goodbye to Cóilín and Mike and my other friends. Frost rimmed the shovels that day, ice sheeted the water puddles and stiffened sand so that you needed a pick to loosen it. The east wind blasted across the desolate fields. It gave me a great relief to throw aside the shovel with the arrival of night.

The same cold wind blustered through the streets of the city as I hastened to the railway station. There were only a few people standing in the streets, flayed by the sharp cold outside the cinemas. Half the workers had gone home, and the other half were already clocked in for the night's shift. It was the daily turning of the tide.

It was a wasteland, this black city under the glacial street lamps, a moonscape where you could hear the constant throbbing of machinery, with never a let-up. In a way I was sorry to leave it. There was a curious vitality about it. In the pubs, as I passed, lights were gleaming, the clash of glasses; high-pitched conversation, the warmth of fellowship. It was the same animation that infused the lives of the expatriate Irish who lived here, drinking, working, eating, condemned to relentless proximity to one another. And although this galloping dissipation of life attracted me, it was not what I was seeking.

There were two others in the carriage along with me. A black man in the corner, quiet, perceptive, curiously observing the people who walked past on the platform. Next to him an Englishman read a newspaper, his face set against conversation for the rest of the journey. Just as the train was pulling out, the guard entered, gripping a drunk.

'Sit down there,' said the guard testily. He was from Wales. 'I'll tell you when we reach the station.'

'The second shtop,' said the drunk, as he tried to put his luggage up on the rack. 'The second shtop.'

'Here, give it to me,' groaned the guard, and hurled overhead the old fibre suitcase, fastened with rough twine. 'Didn't I say I'd call you.'

'The second shtop,' repeated the drunk, holding up two fingers as a reminder. He was Irish. 'The second shtop . . . .'

'Sit down and shut up,' ordered the guard, going out.

He sat down. He gazed about him, yawning. The train tootled a whistle and began to glide. He stretched out his arms and sat next to me. He farted. The Englishman glared at him and turned over the page of his newspaper.

'Where are you heading for?' asked the black man.

'The second shtop,' replied the Irishman.

'But where is that?' asked the black man, laughing.

'The second shtop, I tell you. Is it looking for fight you are?'

'Ah, sit down, brother,' said the black man evenly.

He was twice as brawny as the next man. He laughed quietly.

'I'm a working man and you're a working man. Why are you looking for fight?'

'Matter a damn. The second shtop, I tell you.'

'All right, brother. The second stop. Whatever you say.'

That was the end of the conversation. The drunk fell asleep. The English-man worked through the newspaper, one page after another.

I had nothing to say but began to doze in the corner.

The black man looked around at all of us, a faint smile playing on his lips.

The train halted for the first time. The drunk woke up. He got up, startled, and grabbed his bag.

'This isn't the second stop,' said the black man. 'Sit down, brother.'

'I will not. This is the second shtop.'

'Sit down,' I said, 'the guard didn't come yet.'

'He didn't musha,' said the Irishman. 'You're Irish? You're right. The guard didn't come in yet.' He sat down. He yawned several times on the way to the second station. He lifted his feet onto the seat. He continued to stare at his boots and then, all of a sudden, began to take them off. He was barefooted by the time we drew into the second station.

'Aren't you going to get out?' I asked.

'The guard didn't come in yet,' he said.

'But this is the second stop.'

'Naw. This is the first shtop. The guard knows.' He opened his bag and began to poke about in it. He took out a bottle of stout and offered it to me. 'You're Irish! Drink up!'

I refused and said that it was already time for him to leave.

The Englishman peered over the top of his newspaper and spoke for the first time.

'This is your station. Get out.'

'I won't. My Irish friend here said that the guard didn't come in yet. Drink up, my friend.'

'This is your station, I tell you,' said the Englishman.

'What the hell do you know about it? Drink up, old pal.'

'Now listen here....' The Englishman became enraged. He put his paper aside. The black man was looking at both of us, laughing to himself. Just as the Englishman began to talk, the train shunted forward.

'Now,' said the Irishman, 'wasn't I right?'

The Englishman continued to lecture him for a while but the Irishman paid no attention. He began to yawn and fall asleep.

He was awakened as we drew into the third station. The servant boy came to the carriage and gave him a poke.

'Out with you,' he ordered. 'Weren't you supposed to get out at the last station?'

'Now,' declared the Englishman, 'wasn't I right? I told you repeatedly....'

'You were wrong, then, mister. Matter a damn to me about the station. Aren't they all the same? I tell you, wasn't....'

'Get out,' said the servant. 'Here, take your bag....'

'Take your time, take your time ....' He was searching for his boot on the floor. He put one boot on and then crouched under the seat to look for the other one.

'Hurry up,' said the Englishman irritably.

The servant boy gave him another nudge. He nearly fell out onto the platform. I found his boot and threw it out the window after him. He bent down to pick it up. The train took off.

I looked back at him. He was standing on the platform, alone, boot in hand, looking after us. Beside him on the platform was the old, ruptured fibre suitcase, the small rope fastened about it to keep his clothes inside. There was nobody else on the platform but himself. It was midnight. I failed to decipher the name of the station and the lights disappearing out of sight behind us.

I shut the window. The Englishman was reading his paper again as if to say everything was as it had been and all was in order. The same mocking smile was on the lips of the black man. He caught my eye and laughed. 'That was a strange scene,' he said.

But I didn't laugh. A sudden sad feeling came over me. I had seen a form, a tragic shadow of my race, appear before my eyes.

57

John Boyle, *Galloway Street: Growing Up Irish in Scotland*

(London: Doubleday, 2001). xi, 224pp.; pp. 14–19.

John Boyle was born in Paisley in 1941 to poor Catholic parents from the west of Ireland. He left Scotland at 19 to pursue a teaching career that took him to various European countries and then to America, where he changed careers and made his name as a commercial voice-over artist. In his foreword to *Galloway Street* Boyle traces the book's origins to his visit to Achill Island in County Mayo for the funeral of his aunt in the winter of 1993. Boyle spent several months on the island as a child and his return activated deeply charged memories that disrupted his adult composure and crystallised his desire 'to rediscover – truthfully, without embroidery – the boy I had been'. This need to reconnect with an earlier, truer self was heightened by feelings of spiritual enervation brought on by 'years of expatriate drift' and impending crises in his personal life: 'I was no longer sure what my true voice was.' Calling forth the voice of his ten-year-old self is therefore central to the book's autobiographical impulse. Boyle explains that it led him to abandon his attempt to write the memoir in two distinct voices in favour of a style that ventriloquises his long-vanished Paisley accent and idiom. The narrative is more than a recreation of a childhood past, therefore; it is also an attempt by the author to re-member his fractured identity by reinstating the erased voice of his boyhood self, a voice that repeatedly mocks the 'middle-aged raconteur' Boyle feels he has become. So in contrast to the hierarchised ordering of identities fashioned by earlier Irish-descended autobiographers such as Joseph Keating and Pat O'Mara, Boyle frames his second-generation Irishness in dialogical and contrapuntal terms, presenting it as an ongoing conversation between warring selves. That voice itself is thematised as part of the narrator's interrogative encounter with his former self is borne out by the following excerpt, taken from a section dated 1947, which reveals the narrator's sensitivity to different accents, vocal registers and forms of pronunciation.

The only visitors we get in Galloway Street are relations, except when Mrs Higgins on our landing or one of the Deveneys from down the stairs comes to the door for the lend of a cup of milk or sugar or to change a shilling for the meter. But they're not real visitors so they don't count. Most of our relations are not real relations either, though my mammy says it comes to the same thing.

Aren't they Irish, God help us, no more than ourselves?

There's my Uncle John who's my daddy's real brother though you'd never think it to look at him, a big man with buck teeth who's got a cushy job up in Riccartsbar Asylum. He tells us great yarns about the loonies and the daft antics they get up to and he likes to sing old Irish songs especially when he has a whisky in him. *Hallo Patsy Fagan you're the apple of my eye*, he sings, or *I met her in the garden where the praities grow.*

The funny thing is, my Uncle John's got a terrible stutter. Hallo Ma-Mick, he says to my daddy when he comes in, and Hallo Ma-Maggie to my mammy. But he never stutters when he's singing. Maybe that's why he likes singing so much.

The grownups all tap their feet and clap and say, Good on ye, John! He sings 'The Homes of Donegal' and they start wiping their eyes. He sings 'The Mountains of Mourne Sweep Down to the Sea'. He sings till they start taking wee fly keeks at the clock and saying The Lord save us, is that the time already?

My Uncle John lives in the prefabs with old Jimmy Bradley and Missis Bradley. They're not his real mammy and daddy but that's another story, my mammy says. I still have to call them Uncle Jimmy and Auntie Bradley.

My Uncle John is big and stout and tall, six foot four, he says. My daddy looks dead wee and skinny beside him.

I'm five foot eight, he says and he always straightens himself up when he says it. Same heighth as yer mammy.

Heighth. That's how he says it.

But anybody can see she's a bit taller, even when she's only wearing slippers on her feet.

My daddy's mammy died in Donegal when the two boys were still wee weans and my grandpa Boyle couldn't bring them up on his own and it was fixed up that one of them was to be adopted by the Bradleys in Scotland. So they took John, the eldest, and left wee Mick behind in Donegal with his old man.

An' a hard life Ah had of it too, he's always telling us. Out of school by the time I was twelve and up at six every morning to help the old man in the field.

Ah well, it's too bad about ye, man dear, says my mammy. But would ye be up to them Bradleys? How well they took the big healthy one?

I get the feeling she doesn't like the Bradleys that much.

One time she hints that my Uncle John is only my daddy's half-brother though it seems to me it should be the other way round. But when I ask her about it all she says is, Never you mind.

It's a mystery.

And then there's my Auntie Margaret who's not really my auntie, just my mammy's second cousin from Achill. She's a nicelooking lady with a lovely smile and a comfy chest and her married name is Mrs Young. Her man is Jimmy Young but he never comes near us because he's a Protestant.

Barney Molloy is a big dark man from Donegal with a wee tash on his lip who's a labourer like my daddy and sometimes they work together digging roads and building houses. He never takes a drink, only a cup of tea with plenty sugar, and he never says much.

Ah but he thinks a lot, the same Barney, my mammy says.

No flies on Barney, believe you me.

His wife is Mrs Molloy and she's a wee skinny woman with a pale face and coalblack eyes with dark rings round them. She just sits there and stares and never a word out of her.

Nobody ever says her first name, even Barney calls her Mrs Molloy.

Most of the time the visitors just turn up on our doorstep. I don't think we're ever expecting them because my mammy always flies into a panic when she hears them chapping the door.

Quick, she hisses at us. Pick up the papers, quick, hurry up. Put them toys and things out of sight. Oh Jesus Mary and Joseph look at the state of this house.

The way she says it you'd think she's nearly greetin'. We all have to rush about picking up wee bits of paper and fluff off the carpet and cramming clothes and toys into the drawers.

Then it's Well, is one o' ye going to open that door, or what's the matter wit' ye at all? Are ye sleepin' or what?

She says this in her normal voice, out loud so the visitors will hear her. Hoping they'll think it was just us weans that forgot to open the door.

Well hallo, she says when the door is open at last, and they're standing there on the landing in their good visiting clothes.

Come in, come in. Ye're welcome. The house is upside down, but come in anyway, take your coats off, sit yerselves down.

Arra don't be silly, they say. Sure the house is grand.

They all sit round the fire with cups of tea and buns or biscuits and talk about Home.

Home means Ireland. My mammy even calls it that when she's sitting there at our own fireside.

I had a letter from Home last week, she'll say, or Have you any news from Home?

She's always hoping for news of Poor Pat that I've never seen. My mammy's got three sisters, my auntie Bridget, Mary and Annie and Poor Pat is their brother who went missing years ago. Nobody knows where he is, or if he's alive or dead, but there's always rumours about him. Some say he's in America, doing well for himself, running a big public house. Or he's down in England somewhere, on the building sites.

I have a notion he's on the ships, Old Jimmy Bradley was saying one time. Sailing the seas, that's where he'll be.

That's my favourite. I like to think of my mysterious Uncle Pat on the deck of a big ship, in his seaman's gansey, staring at the far horizon. I've only got three uncles and it's a bit sad that there's one I've never seen, so I'm hoping he comes home one day.

Wherever home is.

If Ireland is Home, I wonder, what about this place? What about Galloway Street and Scotland? Do they not count?

When I ask my mammy she only laughs.

Ah it's just a habit, *ahashki*. Force of habit, as the one said.

But Scotland's hame noo, intit?

Yes, it is. Paisley. Paisley, Scotland. That's my home now.

She says it as if she's testing to see what it sounds like. But it makes no difference. Home means Achill.

To hear them talking Achill is a great place and so is Donegal where my daddy grew up. Barney Molloy comes from there as well. There's fairies and ghosts in Ireland, and haunted houses and banshees. The banshee is my favourite.

The name makes me think of the ghosts you get in the *Beano* and the *Dandy*, a white sheet shaped like a head and shoulders with empty eyes and a long floaty tail, and nothing inside only an evil spirit. When the banshee is seen near somebody's house, you know that person is going to die. Sometimes you don't even see the banshee, you only hear it moaning and howling in the night.

The one that tells us about the banshee is Old Jimmy Bradley. He used to be a nightwatchman on the railways. I picture him sitting up all night staring into the dark with just a wee fire for company. That's probably how he knows.

But whether you see it or whether you hear it, says Old Jimmy Bradley, taking his pipe out of his mouth, damn the bit of difference does it make for it means you're a dead man, and that's as sure as I'm sitting here tonight.

He sits there nodding heavy and slow with his hands on his knees and the women make the sign of the Cross and mutter The Lord bless us and save us and keep us from harm and for a while you'd swear the heat had gone out of the fire. Everybody goes dead quiet and I wonder if they're all like me, thinking about the banshee out there in the dark, hovering, waiting.

58
John Healy, *The Grass Arena: An Autobiography*

With an introduction by Colin MacCabe (London: Faber & Faber, 1988). xiv, 194pp.; pp. 6–11.

John Healy was born in Kentish Town in 1943 to poor parents who emigrated from the west of Ireland in the 1930s. In the opening paragraphs of his acclaimed autobiography he describes, in spare, transparent prose, the severe beatings he received from his father as a child. These traumatic scenes form the overture to a life-story dominated by savage violence and brutality, as Healy chronicles his years of alcoholic vagrancy on the streets of London during the 1960s and 1970s. Although later chapters record his emergence from this hellish world through his therapeutic obsession with the game of chess, the kernel of the book's narrative power lies in its graphic evocation of the bleak misanthropy of the 'grass arena', Healy's term for the network of inner-city London parks inhabited by winos, prostitutes and petty criminals. His refusal to sensationalise, sentimentalise or polemicise his experiences adds to the text's visceral impact. In the early chapters of the book Healy recalls the periods he spent living with his relations in Sligo. His representation of these visits as idyllic respites from an increasingly turbulent London existence invokes a familiar version of Irish pastoral in which intimate contact with landscape and community engenders a sense of healing belonging. Healy's 'return to roots' was far from a wholly happy experience, however, as the following excerpt from Chapter 2 shows. His distressed response to an animal castration activates a residual anglophobia in his Sligo friends, which is the flipside of the racial hostility Healy encounters back in Kentish Town. Thus, like many so-called 'plastic Paddies', the young narrator finds himself trapped in a doubly 'inauthentic' position, unable to lay full claim to an unequivocal Irish or English identity.

There's a sort of calmness that seems to come out of the grass and the ditches and the mossy banks. Lonely mists that suddenly spread over the fields give an old feeling, cosy and warm. Always a lot of work to be done everywhere. The bogs are very ancient. The people, especially the women with their delicate skin, soft as the misty climate, give the warmest welcome to friend and stranger alike. Each time I returned these feelings became stronger. It was nice to be on a farm: the world is contained within it. Animals, relations, the weekly jaunt to church or the shop; things to occupy the days ... Of course, I didn't experience any difference there between myself and the people around me, everybody was friendly, everybody knew me. I did not have to prove anything.

Leaving Ireland was always a wrench. Each time an aunt would be sent with instructions to bring me back to London. I'd manage to avoid this at first by being near hysterical every time the matter was mentioned. They'd return without me. Then sterner methods would be employed. I would be dragged kicking and screaming up the hill and on to the back road to catch the once-a-day bus for town, in tears all the way back to London. Later on an aunt would only have to arrive at the farm and I'd run away or hide on the day we were supposed to leave. They had to devise ever more tricks and traps to entice me to go with them, so by the time I realized the trick it would be too late! The journey itself was not without fears for me. It was the waiting that worried me most. It seemed I was always waiting; I waited and watched the luggage. My aunts would go off and sometimes not return for an hour, one time it was three – running out of money in Dublin they left me looking after luggage while they went off to another aunt's house (a fifty-mile journey or so) to borrow some more.

From the age of two I would be brought over to Ireland from time to time and left with my grandmother and her sons and daughters. She had altogether three boys and eleven girls, including my mother. My first recollection of Ireland was when I was about four years old – playing in green fields, surrounded by animals, loved by my uncles, grandmother, grandfather and especially by young aunties, who seemed to be Love itself. No matter what I did my uncles would not punish me. [...]

After I'd been staying with my grandmother for some months, the authorities said I'd have to attend school. So one fine morning my granny packed some sandwiches for me and I headed off towards the gate by the sand road, where it was arranged that the Coyle boys would take me to school. There were four of them, three older than myself; the youngest, Sean, was about my age but a lot bigger. We set off along the road. None of us wore any shoes. None of the kids wore shoes in the summer months, saving them for winter as money was scarce. One of the lessons consisted of learning to speak Gaelic. I could not understand it at all. What use was the Irish language to me? So I never tried. Then Miss Barnes, our old Infants' teacher, asked me to stand up and read some Gaelic words to the rest of the class. I just stood there. 'Come out here,' she said. 'You're as thick as Conner's ass.' She walloped me with a ruler – not too hard so I didn't really mind. Besides, I liked the place.

One Saturday everyone seemed very busy on my uncle's farm. My uncles and grandfather rounded up two young bullocks and tied them by their heads to the posts in the cowhouse. It seemed funny to be milking at that time of the day – round noon – so I watched them. They tied ropes around the animals' back legs, and pulled them tight up to the front stalls so they could not kick back. Everybody was talking as if something different was going to happen, when a tall man came down the lane on a bike. Getting off his bike, he shook hands with everybody, then bent down and made a big fuss of me. They all went into the cowhouse. The tall man pulled a package from his coat pocket and took out a cut-throat razor like my grandfather used to shave with . . . Suddenly he bent down behind the nearest bullock and catching what seemed to be his privates, he ran the razor slowly down the bullock's long ball bag. The bullock did not seem to notice. He did it again and the bag split open. I could see red and white meat inside; the blood started flowing out; the bullock was lifting his back legs with pain and trying to kick out, but was held tight by the ropes. I got scared. I felt shy, but mostly I got very angry. I could not see why they should do such a terrible thing, the most evil thing I had ever seen. I was so confused that I could not speak. My uncle told me to go and get a jam jar of Jeyes' fluid from my granny. I did not move, I would not go, I would not help them hurt this bullock any more. My uncle put his arm round me but I started screaming at them for cutting the calf. They said it had to be done or he would ruin the cows. Did I want the cows to be ruined? 'No.' Then they said they had to do it. 'No,' I screamed. They said he would not only ruin *our* cows but would jump over the ditch into Casey's land and ruin his cows. My grandfather came back with the jar of Jeyes' fluid and Mr Farrel shoved the jar up between the calf's legs and rinsed it round. They untied him and drove him out. He tried to run but his back legs were too stiff after what they'd taken out of him and he staggered along in a giddy sort of way. I went away into the house crying. My granny gave me some sweets and sat me by the fire.

After a while the men came in. I was still mad at them and would not speak to them. My uncle put his hands round me and picked me up. Kidding me to make me laugh, he said, 'Shall we take one out of little Johnny?' I knew they were only fooling but I would not look at him or at any of them. I could not see how the bullocks would ruin the cows. They were all friends in the fields. I had seen them playing together, and the bullock would put his two front feet up on to the cow's back and try to get a piggy-back off her. What harm had he ever done?

We used to finish school at 3 p.m. in the summer, and as well as the Coyles, the Farrel kids used to walk our way. Two boys older than me and a girl called Mary. One day coming home from school I found out that the Farrel kids' father was the man who had cut our calves. I kept quiet until we reached the county crossroads, then I started screaming at them: 'Your father is a pig . . . he cut our calves!'

The Farrel boys started laughing and tried to make me shut up but I went on. So they picked up stones and started throwing them at me, shouting, 'You English cur! Go back to England!' The row had arisen. I went for one of the boys. We punched each other in the face. Then Mary and her brother went for me, but the Coyle boys pulled them off, separating us, warning the Farrels to keep going on in front quick-like. They kept shouting back, 'You English black and tan swine!' I kept shouting that their father, mother and all belonging to them were evil calf cutters. After this I refused to attend school. So my uncle asked if I would go if he took me in the horse and trap. I said I would if he made the horse gallop past the Farrels. And that's how I went to school for a few weeks. But me and the Farrels were always fighting, and the others started siding with them, saying, 'Go back to England, John Bull.'

'Calf cutters!' I'd shout back. Then we'd start throwing stones at each other. Fair Play to the Coyle boys, they'd always take my part.

After a while it got out of hand and I refused to go to school at all or be near the Farrels. So I was taken back to England. [...]

I'd go down to the corner to play. Some of the older boys would start putting on an Irish accent and take the mickey out of me. One guy, Ronnie, would never let up; he was about five years older than me and twice my size; no chance. He could not lose. All his mouthy family were behind him too. I was playing with his brother and a few other kids one day when he came up.

'Top of the morning to you, Paddy,' he said.

All the happiness went out of me but I pretended to smile. 'What you laughing at, you Irish cunt?'

'Nothing,' I said.

'You better not be laughing at me, you cunt,' and grabbing me by the collar he kneed me in the bollocks. I went down holding my privates, tears coming out of my eyes, but I was not crying.

Some of the kids laughed and his young brother said, 'Leave him, Ron, he's not laughing at you.'

'He'd better not be.'

I got off the ground but did not go – he'd not hit me again that day. Besides, I had nowhere else to play.

59
George O'Brien, *Out of Our Minds*

(Belfast: Blackstaff Press, 1994). 200pp.; pp. 11–14.

George O'Brien was born in 1945 in Lismore, County Waterford where, because of his mother's death and his father's absence, he was raised by 'three parents': grandmother, aunt and uncle. After a short time working in Dublin in the early 1960s, he moved to England and took a BA degree from Ruskin College, Oxford, and a PhD from Warwick University, where he lectured in English from 1976 to 1980. Since 1984 he has taught at Georgetown University in Washington, DC. *The Village of Longing*, the first of his three highly literate volumes of autobiography, was published to critical acclaim in 1987. *Dancehall Days* followed in 1988 and *Out of Our Minds* six years later. Collectively, these works recreate, in richly allusive and self-reflexive prose, the author's journey from cloistered childhood to expansive early adulthood, a journey that reads as a protracted prospecting for a secure sense of home and belonging. In *Out of Our Minds* O'Brien creatively adapts the dominant discourse of post-war migration found in the autobiographies of Keane, Mac Amhlaigh and others by delineating a decentred autobiographical persona for which exile acts as a metonym. Writing out of a peculiar, depleted subjectivity, he presents emigration as an opportunity for further self-improvisation rather than a threat to the integrity of self and the fealty to origins. Already unhoused at home, O'Brien displays little of the embittered homesickness of other migrant memoirists. On the contrary, 'sliding from one self to another seemed part of the swing of things' to a narrator so enmeshed in contingency that he can contemplate his lack of exceptionalism with cool detachment: 'There was no visible me. I'd happened a million times before in all those lads and lassies from all those Lismores, all those suitcases hauled through Euston secured with binder twine, all those unavailing Pioneer pins and scapulars and miraculous medals, all gone for good and nothing to show for it.' So rather than purporting to write about an 'I' that is unified, self-sufficient and knowable, O'Brien's trilogy skilfully enacts the quest of an inadequate, threadbare self for a voice shorn of cliché and convention.

The shortest way to Lambeth was via Kilburn High Road. That was where the Emerald Staff Agency was, fount of life. I'd seen its ads in the *Irish Independent* when I was sacked in Dublin and in dire need of agency. Getting the looking for work done for me seemed a brilliant, ultramodern, totally non-Irish idea.

The very thought converted dislocation and disorientation into fantasies of self-sufficiency and ready money – all from just a rub of the Emerald green! And any minute now, this best-foot-forward day, I'd make fantasy come true.

I didn't trust London buses, though. Apart from their cocknified, vowel-swallowing destinations – Hammersmith Bdwy, Wandsworth Bdg – they often indicated they were bound for different places even when they had the same number and the same direction. They were streetcars named desire, for their ports of call were all seduction and their route numbers mighty high. When my geographical sea-legs were less rubbery we'd rove out together. Me and London. Me and the new life. The good life.

Meanwhile, I stuck to the supposedly foolproof tube. But here it had fetched me up at Kilburn Park, with neither sight nor light to be seen of Emerald, famed emblem of remuneration and of ease. I had to walk. That was fine, at first. I enjoyed imagining myself free. From newsagents' racks the *Kilkenny People* and the *Connaught Tribune*, the *Anglo-Celt*, the *Kerryman* waved to me, limp semaphores. Cork crooning and the West's flat vowels floated towards me during lulls in traffic. I gave them a deaf ear. If that lad ducking into the Fox and Grapes, gumboots, split and dried plaster holding together caubeen and gansey, turned out to be Kip Tobin of Botany, or Andy Ahearne of Church Lane, Lismore, I'd have jumped on a bus to avoid him. He could have even been my Uncle George himself, who years before had vanished into England. I would have run without a second thought to his disappearing act, wanting only that he leave me to mine. Transported beyond the let-down that was Ireland, I could at last reject the roles that had failed me there. Now I could begin. With nothing, as nothing. Agency would fill my vacancy. My mind was a blank cheque.

By Quex Road I wondered why I couldn't smell the ocean. I'd been walking all morning, but still no beacon of green did me beguile. Pangs of smallness, tiredness, began to play on me. Passers-by were making the sign of the cross. Quex Road, where the chapel was! There my pal in boarding school, Johnny, prayed with his people. They were from Kilmallock. They had a flat nearby: Salisbury Road. John had a father and a mother. Brothers. John brought back pictures. His brothers looked big and strong. One worked in the underground, the other in a bank. Now they had a house, lived together. A family.

I stood at the traffic lights. The light was green. I couldn't cross. I felt unwanted, erased, disembodied. It was kind of numbing, a kind of clouding over. London and I dissolved into a dream that somebody (maybe even me) had then forgot. Fitter by far for me a visit to the Blessed Sacrament. Leave the cash nexus, foreign ways. Confess, repent, amend. God will provide. But I could no more go down that road than I could use the phonebox opposite, reverse the charges and ring home. I had no reason to believe anyone would answer me. I went into an ABC for a coffee. A black woman with a faraway look created steam, made change, said, 'Thank you.' The thing in the cup tasted like an idiot child of Horlicks, but warmed me. The woman was humming though her eyes were sad. I dreamt of a rosy-cheeked, roly-poly countrywoman at the Emerald door, calling to me gaily, 'Wisha, come in; you must be famished. Would you down a pullet? I've the kettle on.'

It was a glass door that met me, at the head of thinly carpeted stairs above a confectioner–tobacconist's, and a girl with a jet-black crow's nest of a beehive hairdo. Could she help me? 'Please' came into what I said a lot, and I smiled till my face felt tortured. 'Fenkew,' the girl kept replying, variously pitching the second syllable. She'd see what she could do. I took a seat. She gave me a form, and teetered off on her stilettos to quell a screaming kettle.

The form impressed me. Up to now the blanks had all occurred when least expected, unofficially, in the family, in Dublin's lack of promise. These London blanks, so simple by comparison, seemed to say I was expected. Somebody like me, anyhow. I felt encouraged. Age: nineteen. Name: Seoirse, styling himself George. Should I put that? I gnawed the end of the Biro, gazing blankly at the certainty of things, the grey filing cabinets, dull flooring, the shriek of colour from the apple-green telephone, the *Mirror* folded by the Royal typewriter, the box of Guards. Education? Roaring priests and stinking cabbage. Futile Irish, steady Latin. The confessional of state exams. Gold Flake. Radio Luxembourg. And in my experience nothing worked. Not I, fired twice. Not family, who offered no alternative to the boat and recollection. Not father, who'd remarried, as I thought, rather than take me to himself in fabulous Dublin, where I'd never feel loneliness or longing any more.

There was no room for any of that. There wouldn't be enough room in a book for it. Miss Emerald would hardly want my life story. And I certainly didn't want it. For me, the fresh start, the clean sheet, the new leaf. Name, rank, serial number, and nothing but. Being someone else was all I could think of. I had no idea that fleeing only kept alive what was left behind.

'This way, please, Fenkew.'

60
Bob Geldof with Paul Vallely,
Is That It?

(London: Sidgwick & Jackson, 1986). 352pp.; pp. 59–61.

The colloquial title of Bob Geldof's (b.1954) autobiography neatly captures the sense of chronic self-deficiency that frames the author's account of his transformation from 'juvenile Marxist' into internationally famous rock musician and sainted philanthropist. The book begins with a prologue that shows the subject frozen in the spotlight of a spectacular, epoch-defining event: the Live Aid concert at Wembley Stadium on 13 July 1985. Geldof remembers the moment as one of clarifying self-fulfillment. Prior to this, 'Things felt good or bad, but never complete'; now he had 'absolute certainty' and 'utter clarity of purpose'. Or had he? As in so many Irish autobiographies, the dream of definitive self-completion materialises as dissonant experience. The narrative ends with Geldof pondering the existential resonances of a teenager's throwaway remark at the end of the Philadelphia leg of Live Aid: 'Is that it?' And so the Godot-like waiting for 'something else – something unspecific' goes on. These companion scenes bookend the story of Geldof's bleak Dublin childhood and adolescence, and his subsequent attempts to redeem 'a sickeningly futile and chaotic life' through music and performance. Like *Out of Our Minds*, *Is That It?* portrays emigration as a spur to self-reinvention. Leaving is embraced as liberation rather than lamented as betrayal. In this excerpt, the insistent 'beep beep' of the Apollo spaceship's low-frequency radio transmission acts as a potent symbol of both the new possibilities that were then opening up and the global reach of Geldof's future fame.

When I left school I ran out of the front gates, and didn't look back once. I embraced whatever lay ahead with trepidation, but with an overwhelming feeling of release. I tried to return once for a TV show and then I could only go twenty yards inside the gate before I was filled with loathing and anxiety, and retreated. But in order to remember and be accurate here, I returned recently and felt an unbelievable sadness for the ghost of the boy in the fog-filled corridors. It was not self-pity, it was more as if I had held hands with someone else, someone who lived a long time ago and who had no connection to the man who stood in the high-windowed dormitories and the fresh-painted chapel. It was hard then to accept that every moment of the past makes its contribution to the present.

I had no hopes when I left, no ambitions, no clue as to what I should do. Even if I'd got my exams, I would have refused to contemplate university. I'd had my fill of academia. Besides, students to me were pretentious wankers who wore Kenneth More-type scarves, dabbled in silly politics and joined earnest clubs. I could see no value in having a degree: it didn't seem to brighten the prospects of anyone I knew. Despite my father's insistent chanting of the benefits of a further three years in school, I was off.

Off meant England. England had given me my first sense of real liberty when I was fifteen and I had gone to Lincolnshire and worked there in a factory. We stayed in houses owned by Italian or Pakistani families who slept three or four to a room in order to make some extra money from these rowdy Irish kids who came over every summer and worked long night shifts, six days a week. The factory produced tinned peas – sweet, stinking peas in numberless profusion and they put £32 a week into our hands, which was OK money in those days. Now I was back again for the third year running. I had lied about my age originally to enable me to work nights and thus double my income. Now I was seventeen, and I had to be consistent and pretend to be twenty-one. This took a lot of sorting out later when I collected dole and the social services had me registered as four years older. It was a boring job, sorting peas on the conveyor belt. You would fall into a trance, occasionally flicking a blackened pea off the line. Chlorine stung your eyes and dried your mouth and nose. Your ears were assaulted by the constant clatter of empty cans rattling down the runners on to the hoppers, then on to loading racks to be boiled. When we got bored, we turned a can sideways on the runners and the line would stack up behind the overturned tin until it ran back and jammed the machines. We'd hang around until the fitter came to fix it.

It was mind-numbing. I had jeans with two holes on the cheeks of my arse. I was very thin, my jeans were tight, and I wore red underpants. I don't know if this was why I nearly got raped. I was threatened with a crowbar and pushed against a can feed-line behind the hoppers. I was shouting and fighting, but the noise obscured my terror. He was a big man and I was ineffectual against his swinging crowbar. He grabbed my crotch. I tried to kick him. He put the crowbar against my throat. I scratched his face and put my fingers in his nose and my thumbs in his eyes. One of his mates came looking for him, called some other people and pulled him off. They began to beat the hell out of him. I got in one really good kick.

We'd buy trendy clothes at Harry Fenton's and wear them at the weekend in Peterborough. We thought we were cool. In fact, we were green. The green dye never washed off your face and hands and your hair stank of brine, sugar, dye, mint and chlorine. We were usually drunk on scrumpy at sixpence a pint. We would lurch, puking, up the road carrying Doyle, or Cully, or myself. Once we got locked out. Doyle climbed up on the spiked metal fence and began scaling the drainpipe. Somehow he reached the top and was forcing open the window when he fell back, missing the spikes by inches. He picked himself up and we pressed the doorbell continuously. The Italian landlord yelled, 'Fuck off, Irish peegs.' We began to insult his fat son Bruno at which he opened the door, charging at us. We ran past him, shut the door and ran upstairs to the room. He never threw us out. In fact, he never mentioned it again.

I was caught in bed with a girl by her Polish parents. Her father was a flight sergeant in the RAF. He was a big man. It is a funny thing being caught – the girl is always called a slut and a whore by the mother and you can just hear as you disappear out the front door the strangled sob, 'How could you do this to us?' The father is usually speechless and slightly confused and a little embarrassed. I was a coward and it was a cliché. I grabbed my trousers and shoes and shirt as soon as the mother came into the room and screamed. The father was just behind her. It was a ground-floor room with a window to the garden which was open in the summer night. I went through it. The following day, to my horror, I received an invitation to tea. Maybe they thought I was going to marry her. I went. Mother and father were very polite and not too inquisitive. No one brought up the night before and as I left her mother gave me a parcel. I opened it when I returned to my digs. Inside were my socks, underpants and jumper, freshly laundered and pressed.

This year I was surprised to get the job again. The year before, when a vast consignment of peas arrived to be canned as 'Petits pois' for a famous upmarket store, we had been prominent in organizing a strike. The peas were in fact the same as the ones that went into the factory's ordinary cans, but it was a prestige order and who was going to tell the difference? The strike was timed for when there was a danger of the entire batch rotting and was an attempt to gain equal pay for the casual workers – us – and the permanent staff. We worked the same hours, did the same jobs, we wanted the same money. Foley rang up some papers and filed a story. We negotiated, and the peas began to rot. Within two days we'd won. It was thrilling, we were beholden to no one. I thought we were justified and therefore any risk was acceptable.

Now it was July 1969. I wasn't going back to school. Whatever money I was going to get was going to have to last a while. Still, as I stood out on the loading bay in the early hours of the morning and looked up at the moon huge in the sky, the factory quiet behind and the transistor loud on the packing cases beside me, I listened to the disembodied voice another planet away and I thought of the time ten years earlier when I'd stood open-mouthed with my family, staring wide-eyed at the sky, trying hard to find the sputnik. The intervening years had been spent in a state of panic and confusion. My mother was dead, my schooldays had finished but at least now I had some freedom. No longer would I have to go back to that house, no longer endure the ennui, the pretence, the emptiness. I had hated being a teenager, I longed to be twenty. Now life could begin. The sixties were dying and I was delighted. I listened with genuine wonderment to the awkward platitudes of the man on the moon. I considered I hadn't come very far, but then neither had mankind. Neil Armstrong[1] was saying 'Beep, beep' up there.

---

[1] American astronaut Neil Armstrong (b.1930) became the first person to set foot on the moon on 20 July 1969.

61

John Walsh, *The Falling Angels: An Irish Romance*

(London: Flamingo, 1999). 282pp.; pp. 218–22.

John Walsh's witty, urbane memoir is the most sustained autobiographical exploration of the cultural and emotional dualities of the second-generation Irish experience in post-1960s Britain, as seen from a middle-class, metropolitan perspective. Written in the aftermath of his mother's death, and as such an oblique elegy for her, Walsh's self-reflexive text anatomises the 'constant switchback' of his relationship with Ireland and England across four decades. Born in Battersea in 1953 to a father who was 'too Irish to be happy in England' and a mother 'too English to be happy anywhere else', Walsh grew up in a state of intercultural suspension, caught in an 'endless falling between sense and sensibility, between south London and the west of Ireland'. From this he developed a romantic desire for rootedness in an ancestral homeland made mythic by received memories, songs and stories. The various phases of his quest to realise this desire are powerfully evoked, culminating in the narrator's attempt to authorise a version of diasporic belonging that would exceed the 'essences of Englishness and Irishness' and reconfigure home as a genuinely hybrid space.[1] The following excerpt is taken from Chapter 13, 'Parting of the Ways', in which Walsh dramatises the inter-generational faultlines opened up by the 'Troubles' and the kinds of dilemmas they created for the 'English-Irish' in 1970s London. Walsh's account of his father's indignant reaction to the word 'immigrant' is particularly instructive in that it precipitates a deftly rendered moment of diasporic dissonance between first-generation father and second-generation son in which a mutual othering takes place, the son racialising the father as an undesirable alien, the father regarding the son as a xenophobic native.

Since the Troubles had re-started in 1969, things had become increasingly sticky and unpleasant for all Irish people living in England. With each new atrocity of shootings, kneecapping and revenge demolition, with the entry of the words 'Provos' and 'sectarian' and 'Bogside' and 'three-minute warning'

---

[1] For a fuller analysis of Walsh's memoir, see Liam Harte, '"Somewhere Beyond England and Ireland": Narratives of "Home" in Second-Generation Irish Autobiography', *Irish Studies Review*, vol. 11, no. 3 (2003), pp. 293–305.

and 'Shankhill' into common currency, the abrupt arrival of bombings on English land and the territory we ourselves walked – Oxford Street, the City, even Lavender Hill police station (where a famous IRA bombing was carried out, overseen by Special Branch helicopters, across the road from where I used to borrow library books), with every new reminder of Ireland's ancient wounds at English hands, and her long, unforgiving culture of reprisal, the English-Irish came in for troubles of their own.

No matter how faithfully they might report the IRA's campaign, the newspapers seemed determined to consider domesticated exiles from Cork or Waterford to be just as implicated in the violence as if they'd come straight from Sinn Fein HQ. A century after *Punch* cartoonists routinely pictured the Irish as thick, ape-jawed, stove-hatted and blunderbuss-carrying seditionaries, the papers ran cartoons featuring my parents' countrymen (and, as far as I was concerned, my own) as maddened, blood-lusting, implacable bombers, all staring eyes and (for some reason) sharp teeth. Jak[2] in the London *Evening Standard* was a special offender. But then the *Standard* seemed to nurse a special animus against the London Irish. Several of its regular columnists in the seventies, such as Angela Ince and Lord Arran, regularly wondered aloud about the dark side of the Irish character that could find expression in acts of senseless public mayhem.

The issue of repatriation, too, reared its head at this time: following his 'rivers of blood' speech about the influx of black Britons, Enoch Powell came to suggest that other 'immigrants' besmirching British soil, the ones with green passports, might be helped on their way home by government intervention at some future date.[3] I remember my father gripping the *Standard*, the evening paper that he'd read so faithfully over the years, and taking in the news that his English neighbours would be happy to see him get the hell back where he came from.

'Immigrants,' he said, as if the word had been 'criminals'. '*Immigrants.* The bloody nerve of it. After everything Ireland's done for England. Didn't the Irish fight for them in two world wars?' (Technically this wasn't strictly accurate, since the Irish Republic declared itself neutral in the Second World War, but large numbers of Irish joined up, wore British uniform and died as a result.) 'And didn't the Irish build half the buildings of London, and half

---

[2] Pseudonym of Raymond Jackson (1927–1997), political cartoonist of the *Evening Standard* from 1966 until his death. One of his most controversial cartoons, which depicts the Irish as psychopathic bloodthirsty monsters, appeared in the *Standard* in October 1982 and prompted the Labour-controlled Greater London Council to withdraw its advertising from the newspaper in protest.

[3] On 20 April 1968 Enoch Powell MP (1912–1998) made a speech in Birmingham in which he predicted widespread social unrest unless measures were taken to stop mass immigration into Britain. In it he quoted from Virgil: 'Like the Roman, I seem to see the River Tiber foaming with much blood.' Powell also advocated a policy of voluntary repatriation for migrants, especially those from Asia and Africa.

the ships that sailed out of Liverpool? ... and where in God's name would English hospitals be without Irish nurses, and who built bridges all over the British Empire, if it wasn't feckin' Irish engineers ...?'

He paused, red-faced. A super-orbital vein stood out an inch on his hot forehead. I had rarely seen him so angry. And as I looked at him, I was aware of him looking at me, regarding him. What was he seeing? An Englishman regarding an Irish immigrant? His own son, with the studiedly English voice and manner was suddenly one of the throng of British people who had decided they didn't want to have their uncouth Celtic neighbour around any longer. My father was suddenly transformed in front of me, from an exile (about which you could sing any number of sentimental oh-for-my-little-homestead-in-Leitrim melodies) into an immigrant (about which you couldn't sing anything, except perhaps a glum chorus of 'Deportees'). He hated it. He was the local Battersea GP, for Christ's sake. He was a man of stature and learning, held in respect by his patients, by the community of the sick, not some dubious alien who had arrived in the cargo area of a long-haul truck. Immigrant indeed.

It wasn't even that his sympathies went in the direction the *Evening Standard* assumed they would. Or did they? My father, born in 1916, grew up a natural Republican. His family had had encounters with the Black and Tan enforcers during the Troubles of 1922 ('the absolute scum and vermin of the lowest English prisons, that's who they sent over to keep the peace'). His people had learned the arts of silence and saying nothing, of keeping alert for traitors and informers and people who wanted to know your business, of combining a seeming passivity with sudden bursts of passionate, implacable, do-or-die patriotism. They had learned to define themselves by opposition, and by a kind of Homeric sullenness in the face of tyranny. And they had passed it straight into my father's genes. He had no sympathy for the IRA. He was as appalled as our London neighbours when the news arrived, week after week in the seventies, of letter bombs and pub explosions and detonated flesh. But he had a strong attachment to the *old* IRA, the freedom fighters in the hills, the IRA of *Shake Hands With the Devil* and Sean O'Faolain's stories, and 'Come Out You Black and Tans', the IRA of Moran in John McGahern's *Amongst Women*. I doubt if my father had ever knowingly met a genuine IRA man in his pre-London life; but he had a patriot's admiration for the type.

And now? He steered clear of voicing any opinion, most of the time. Whatever he thought, he said nothing. If the conversation at home turned to Ulster or the IRA, he would look grim yet knowing, an expression that became standard on London-Irish faces in those years. Talking about personalities offered a way round uttering statements of approval or dismay: it was easier to mock the Reverend Ian Paisley than to talk about Freda, the daughter of my mother's Sligo friend Margaret, who had got picked up by the Garda as a member of a Provisional cell in Dublin, because one might then have to voice some opinion about the daughter's sympathies or commitment, or about the value of arresting her.

In my father's dining room and my mother's kitchen, the London Irish subtly evaded the subject of Irish terrorism; it went beyond diplomacy; it was a thing of murmurs and tiny wisps of agreement, like an old-boy network. It was discreet, fastidious, muted. It was unbelievably *British* – or at any rate, a complicated complicity of both British and Irish reserve.

Only once did the murmuring get any louder. It was when Mountbatten died.[4] I remember going into the living room to get a book, and finding my father, his friend Eddie from Wicklow, and the local curate sitting in a suddenly tight silence. My father grunted. 'You have a point, there,' he was saying, whatever the point had been.

'They simply had it comin',' Eddie from Wicklow said, evidently for the second time. 'You cannot say they weren't warned.'

Another silence fell.

'Well, they'll learn their lesson eventually, I'd say,' said the priest.

I stopped in the doorway as it dawned on me what they were discussing. 'Are you talking about Mountbatten?' I asked.

'Go on, John, hop it,' said my father. 'This doesn't concern you.'

'You were talking about the English Royal Family being taught a lesson, were you?' I asked in amazement. 'You don't mean you think they deserved it, do you?

'This has nothing – '

'That they were asking for it?' I interrupted my father. 'Is that what you're saying? You think Lord Mountbatten deserved to be blown up because he's an English Royal?'

'John –'

'How can you say that? How can you say anyone deserves to die because the IRA decide they're a good representative of the enemy?'

'What the IRA said about the bombing,' said the curate, 'was that they wanted to tear the sentimental heart out of England. And by God that's what they did.' He nodded. He stopped just short of saying, 'and fair play to them'.

What could I say? None of these men thought it was right to kill. But they were faced with an absolute division of loyalties to which I had no access. The rest of the conversation is a confused recollection of raised voices, somebody saying there was a war on but I didn't realise it, and my father frowning at me because I wasn't showing respect to a man of the cloth.

It was not a pleasant encounter. Their conversation was only possible because they were all in private agreement; they didn't want to be part of a debate. They weren't sure they liked what had been done. They were really sorry about the two children. But they couldn't condemn the grandeur of the gesture.

---

[4] On 27 August 1979 Lord Louis Mountbatten was killed by an IRA bomb on his yacht in Mullaghmore harbour, County Sligo. His grandson and a local boy also died in the blast.

62

William Trevor, 'Blockley, Gloucestershire'

From: *Excursions in the Real World* (London: Hutchinson, 1993). xv, 201pp.; pp. 94–8.

Now in his eighth decade, William Trevor has been widely feted as one of the finest novelists and short story writers of his generation. Born William Trevor Cox in Mitchelstown, County Cork in 1928, his Protestant unbringing in various provincial towns – his bank-manager father changed posts regularly – placed him at an oblique angle to the dominant Catholic nationalist culture of independent Ireland, an obliquity which he found imaginatively stimulating. As he explains in his introduction to *Excursions in the Real World*: 'I was fortunate that my accident of birth actually placed me on the edge of things. I was born into a minority that all my life has seemed in danger of withering away.' A similar preference for the unobtrusive periphery characterises his authorial stance as an Irish writer in England, where he relishes the feeling of being 'beyond the pale' and specialises in narrative perspectives that blend irony with empathy. Trevor left Ireland for the first time in 1951 with the intention of financing his journey to Paris and Salzburg by working as a potato-picker in Cheshire.[1] And so it was that this urbane anatomist of blighted lives, whose work is often read alongside that of Elizabeth Bowen within the long tradition of Irish Big House fiction, briefly became a spalpeen in the mould of MacGill and MacGowan. Trevor has lived in England ever since, first in London and latterly in Devon, though he is seldom absent from Ireland in his imagination.

Excursions in the Real World, a collection of 29 occasional essays, is the closest Trevor has come to writing an autobiography. In it, he applies his coolly affectionate gaze to his experiences of living in, and between, Ireland and England. Many of the essays, including the one reproduced here, are studied exercises in self-effacement that show the author to be a 'cagey autobiographer who proceeds by indirection, gives us hints and guesses rather than apologia, and vanishes into his narrative just when we think we are about to pin him down'.[2] The book also showcases Trevor's profound affinity for places and the people they 'encase'. Here, it is the enduring, 'undramatic' ordinariness

---

[1] William Trevor, 'A clearer vision of Ireland', *The Guardian*, 23 April 1992, p. 25.

[2] Douglas Archibald, 'Introduction'. William Trevor Special Issue. *Colby Quarterly*, vol 38, no. 3 (September 2002), p. 276.

of a certain landscape that acts as a guarantor of an essential, ordered Englishness, which Trevor remembers and reveres from a distance. The pastoral radiance of this Cotswold scene strikes him with religious force, impelling him towards an amplified, affirmatory climax that recalls Philip Larkin's beatific evocation of 'unfenced existence' in 'Here'.[3]

When I think of landscape which is special I find myself back in the County Cork of my childhood. But as a child in Youghal and Skibbereen – poor little towns in those days – I wondered about England: there was a Royal Family, Henry Hall on the wireless, important weddings in the *Daily Sketch*. England spelt elegance, and style and graciousness. It had a capital city so huge that I was assured it would stretch all the way from Skibbereen to Cork City. Occasionally a G.B. car went by, always gleaming, grey or black. If it stopped by the roadside a picnic would take place, a special little kettle placed on a primus stove, sponge cake brought in a tin box from Surrey. Accents were polished, ladies kindly smiled. One of them gave me a fig-roll once.

There was a board-game we played, long before Monopoly. It had to do with train journeys up and down England, all of them beginning at railway stations that had a magic ring: Paddington, Victoria, Waterloo, King's Cross. 'Gloucestershire?' my father said. 'It's a county. Like County Cork or County Clare.' If you were lucky with your dice you might hurry away by G.W.R. to Gloucestershire, while others were stuck en route to Huddersfield or Belper. I imagined a leafy place, nice for picnics, threads of gold among the green. It spread itself out like a tapestry in my mind: nothing was ruined there, no burnt-out houses or smashed castles, no brambles growing through rusty baronial gates as we had in County Cork. The Duke of Gloucester would never have permitted that.

Many years later, when I was in my early twenties but still had not once left Ireland, I came a little closer to Gloucestershire, told about it by the girl I was to marry: about the Slaughters and the Swells, and Adlestrop and Evenlode, in particular about the village of Blockley. That Cotswold world began in marvellous, onion-domed Sezincote, one of Gloucestershire's stately homes which in 1939 briefly became a haven from German bombs. Afterwards there was a cottage in Blockley itself: Little Manor, a bit overgrown these days, opposite the smart new restaurant that has put the village on the gastronomic map.

For being told about this part of England made me want to visit it, and returning now, I find my childhood vision of an orderly dukedom shattered yet again: it's the hard years of war that come rushing back on a warm July afternoon. Cycling to the grammar school in Chipping Campden, taking the wet batteries to be charged, that's where Miss Tavender lived, that's cruel

---

[3] Philip Larkin, 'Here', *Collected Poems*, ed. Anthony Thwaite (East Saint Kilda and London: The Marvell Press and Faber & Faber, 2003), p. 80.

Fish Hill where you pushed your bike for a mile. The three great houses – Northwick Park and Batsford as well as Sezincote – cannot be as once they were, nor is Sleepy Hollow nor Donkey Lane. And Rock Cottage, where that doubtful prophetess Joanna Southcott spent the last ten years of her life, has been burnt down. But leeks still thrive in the garden that was Sergeant Wall's, and Rose of Sharon in old Mrs Whale's. A pear-tree still decorates a façade in St George's Terrace, the house called Rodneys is still the smartest. Irises and lacy delphiniums prosper, valerian sprouts from the cracks in soft brown walls. Old-fashioned roses are everywhere.

In wartime Blockley there were Italian prisoners of war, laughing while they mended the roads. American soldiers eyed the solitary wives and gave a party for their children, real paste in the sandwiches. 'Aluminium for the war effort!' these same children cried from door to door, taking it in turn to push the pram. They came away with broken saucepans, and between his dozes on a sunny step the village fat boy watched and was amused. He watched as drowsily when the bull ran madly down the long main street, and again when Mrs Jones was dragged the length of it by her husband, unexpectedly home on leave. He watched while villagers brought Mr French a single egg so that he could bake them a cake in Half Crown Cottage. He listened without pleasure while Mr Lunn consoled himself with Bach, or roused himself to warn against the churchyard in the black-out, his thin voice telling of its restless dead.

Blockley nestles, as Broad Campden does, and Shipston-on-Stour. The wolds encase them: lazy undulations, fields guarded by trim stone walls. Patches of sheep whiten the hilly sward, poppies blaze through a field of rye. In the July sunshine the roadside verges are a yard high, yellowing cow-parsley sprinkled with crane's-bill and campion. Elder fills the hedgerows.

In Stow-on-the-Wold you pass down an ancient passage to the Gents, and the hard black oak of door-frames seems tougher than the ubiquitous stone. Above hotels and pubs the wrought-iron signs are motionless on a tranquil afternoon. 'The real McCoy!' an American cyclist proclaims, pausing in one town or another, it doesn't matter which. Tea-rooms are full of shortbread and Bendicks' chocolate mint crisps, part of the scenery.

Domestic pastoral: the Cotswold scene is that, the stone of houses is the stone of the wolds, and Cotswold faces are part of nature too. At dusk, old women in summer dresses make the journey through their village to look at someone else's flowers. At dawn, unshaven itinerants move dourly through the fields from one farm to the next. With passing years, these small conventions remain, even if Northwick Park has become a business school and Blockley's silk mills are bijou residences now. The Gloucestershire voice hasn't altered much, either: on market day in Moreton-in-Marsh it's matter-of-fact and firm, without the lilt that sweetens it further west. Like the countryside it speaks for, its tones are undramatic, as if constantly aware that life owes much to sheep, that least theatrical of animals. While landscape and buildings merge, nobody who lives here is likely to forget that the riches and good sense of wool merchants created the Cotswolds.

When I walk in England I walk in Dartmoor or Derbyshire. I like the English seaside out of season, Budleigh Salterton and Sidmouth and Lyme Regis. But best of all in England there's Gloucestershire to visit and to stroll through, while pheasants rise elegantly from its parklands and rivers modestly make their way. No matter how remote or silent a wood may be there's always a road or a person within reach: I think of Tennyson when I walk in Gloucestershire, the way that runs through the field, two lovers lately wed, an abbot on an ambling pad. I think as well of old Mrs Whale in her lifetime and Sergeant Wall in his, of Albert the footman at Sezincote, Miss Tavender a schoolmistress, and Joanna Southcott. Blockley Brass Band still performs, weather permitting; there are outings to distant Ramsgate. 'Dubious Dog Contest' the sign outside the British Legion hall announces, and I imagine the pink tongues panting on a Saturday afternoon, setters and spaniels that aren't quite the thing, terriers that should have been Dalmatians. The children of the children who ate the American soldiers' paste sandwiches self-consciously tug the leashes. The sun has brought the hollyhocks out.

The countryside is the setting, but people come first: in spite of disturbance and change it is that that continues, and returning now I feel my childhood instinct was not far wrong. In this warm July, or in their wartime years, in snow or sun, the wolds are unique; and their towns and villages perfectly complement them. Crowded with hastening tourists, all three retain their essence: England is unstifled here.

63
Desmond Hogan, 'Catford'

From: *The Edge of the City: A Scrapbook 1976–91* (London: Faber & Faber, 1993). x, 193pp.; pp. 61–4.

Excursions in the Real World ends with the author taking soundings between two realms: the intimations of timelessness inspired by the Tipperary landscape and the 'ephemeral, mortal' reality of Hickey's bakery. This hovering between shadow and substance calls to mind the narrative pose of Desmond Hogan, whose displaced angle of vision further underlines his literary kinship with Trevor. Born in Ballinasloe, County Galway in 1950, Hogan is the embodiment of the solitary nomadic artist. 'I can't call anything home. I just cling to what is remote', he told Robert McCrum in 2004, and many of his characters exhibit a similar restiveness.[1] Of the many unremarkable departures in his five novels and five short story collections published between 1976 and 2005, journeys to Britain are the most common. No other writer of his generation attends to the 'purgatorial world' of the indigent Irish in England with such empathetic insight. Hogan's exiles bridge the temporal and socio-economic gap between MacGill's brutalised navvies and the savvy, middle-class migrants of Joseph O'Connor's early fiction. Ultimately, however, he seems less interested in the experiential dimensions of emigration than in England's symbolic significance as the place where a particular version of Irishness ruptures and unravels. If, as has been suggested, early twentieth-century London was the crucible in which the elements of modern Ireland were distilled,[2] then Hogan's stories show how the city later became a repository for the nation's troubling, unassimilable excess. A line from 'The Sojourner', set in 1970s Shepherd's Bush, brilliantly registers the disjunction between hoary romantic ideal and hidden social reality: 'Irish country and western singers roared out with increasing desperation and one sensed behind the songs about Kerry and Cavan, mothers and luxuriant shamrock, the foetus of an unborn child urging its way from the womb of a girl over for a quick abortion.'[3]

---

[1] Robert McCrum, 'The vanishing man', *The Observer Review*, 14 November 2004, p. 1.
[2] Declan Kiberd, *Inventing Ireland*, pp. 99–100.
[3] Desmond Hogan, *Larks' Eggs: New and Selected Stories* (Dublin: Lilliput Press, 2005), p. 86.

As 'a scrapbook, a diary, a journey', *The Edge of the City* is a collage of Hogan's global travels that inscribes 'a pattern of moving on, always moving on', like the gypsies of his Ballinasloe childhood. At times, he seems utterly cleansed of origins; in other moments, he hankers after felt routes back to a lost Eden: 'I want to find again the after-glow of a performance in a marquee on the fair-green, to return to the eighteen-year-old, to shield him now against all that is going to lash at him. My country, a journey.' *The Edge of the City* also reveals an imagination subtly attuned to the symptoms of human history and the convolutions of memory. Each new location confronts the migrant with his embeddedness in history, just as each new experience redeems a shard of memory, as evidenced by this piece in which Hogan, with a characteristic mixture of intimacy and exclusion, impressionistically evokes his time in the east London suburb of Catford.

It was Bert who wove my life into secret Catford. Bert is a retired photographer who lives up the road from me in a grove of early-nineteenth-century houses off the South Circular. I first saw my potential flat in May 1982, forget-me-nots running up to the french windows. After years of peregrination from room to room in London I hoped it would be my flat. As it turned out I was lucky and on a dank day that autumn I carried my belongings through those french windows. Outside, in the mornings, a ninety-year-old woman would merrily sweep leaves, string upon string of jewels around her neck. My landlady would scurry down the steps in black, off to conduct an atheist funeral. She is a kind of atheist prelate. But the road beyond the grove seemed grey and drab and depleted of life save for the oddity of a woman crossing it in wartime padded shoulders, save for the shop at the corner where two old ladies in blue overalls would preside in the semi-dark behind wartime corsets, waiting for customers to enter this oblique scene. My cat, Eamon, started visiting Bert and I followed him. On my first visit Bert showed me the Rye jug which was made for him on his birth, vines climbing the jug. I began going for walks with Bert. From the top of Blythe Hill behind the grove he pointed out One Tree Hill where Elizabeth I picnicked: in the same spot, with a wave of his hand, he indicated a Roman road where it was suddenly manifest on Blythe Hill against the dramatics of the sky, a road which leads from New Cross to Lewes. Cap on his head he led me to a point on Catford Hill where you can slip through a gap in the wall and immediately the scene is uplifting and you can take an idyllic walk by the river Ravensbourne to Bellingham. Long Meadow Walk it is called. Bert has lots of ancient books and in my presence he opened one on a page about Thomas Dermody. Thomas Dermody was an Irish poet who fought in the Napoleonic wars, lived in Perry Slough on the opposite side of the South Circular, and drank himself to death at an early age. The verses Lady Byron composed in his memory were her introduction to Lord Byron.

> Degraded genius! o'er the untimely grave
> In which the tumults of thy breast were stilled.

On my bicycle I cycled to Dermody's stately tomb in the grounds of St Mary's in Lewisham. The bicycle became of paramount importance in Catford and its environs. On it I made a few trips to a travellers' encampment on the outskirts of Catford. In one of the caravans I was shown books of recent wedding photographs, matchstick barrel-caravans. A travelling lady told me how she'd won a beauty competition at the Puck Fair in Killorglin, in 1955. Many of the children were born in England but they make frequent visits to Ireland, for the erection of a headstone on a grandmother's grave for instance, and they have pony races on disused patches of motorway beyond Woolwich. One little boy sang a Joe Dolan song for me, 'Julie', in such a way that it sounded like a ballad from the Napoleonic wars.

History seemed to come into everything. The barber at the top of Stanstead Road who has recently retired would talk as he cut your hair of his apprentice days in a barber's shop by the sea in Ramsgate. A boy clipping the whiskers of old men. Occasionally a punk girl entered while he reminisced. No, she had to come back on Saturday. His Polish partner was the one who cut the hair of punk girls. The Horniman Museum with its esoteric exhibitions, its flotsam of stuffed chimpanzees, has a patch of ground opposite which is still considered scourged, once the burial ground for plague victims.

To free myself of history I cycle through the flocks of gulls, of starlings in Ladywell Fields.

Talk in Catford can be savage and subterranean. The effigy of a black cat over the entrance to Catford shopping centre distracts you from the fact that Catford is called after a medieval burgher, John de Cateforde. A grey place, the old will always lament the beauty of buildings like the Eros or Gaumont cinemas long turned into office blocks. Anecdote abounds in the streets. As I passed a garage in Brockley once an old lady told me that when she was a child it was a slaughterhouse called Wellbeloved's and one day she saw a goose fly out if it and hide under a tram so that the tram was halted for the day because they couldn't get the goose out from underneath. Pubs are cited because they had Dick Turpin to visit – the Two Brewers on Catford Hill, the Brockley Jack. The Fox and Firkin where I drink scrumpy has a notice banning kissograms and makes its own beer in the back. On Mondays, Wednesdays and Saturdays the best talk goes to Catford Greyhound Stadium where, among the cries of 'Come on, Number Six', you hear the conversations of Irish travellers, the interchanges of modern highwaymen.

I followed Bert one night down Carholme Road to St George's Hall where we watched a performance of *A Letter to the General* by the St George's Players, the tableau of an old nun at the end who sits by lamplight, everybody in the mission safely departed with her help, and she waiting for the hordes. The audience that night was one of ladies in raffish-looking tea-cosy hats, of men in impeccable suits, very often tie pins on the sculpted curvature of their bellies. They are the kind of people who these days eagerly anticipate the opening of the Mander-Mitchenson theatrical collection at Place House in Beckenham Place Park, the most interesting collection of theatrical memorabilia in the country which has moved from the Mitchenson-Mander home in Sydenham. The applause at the end of the play was tumultuous, especially for the old nun. I'd seen *A Letter to the General* once before. In the town hall, Ballinasloe, County Galway, when I was a child.

It's for reasons like this that the grey of Catford and its outreaches has been illumined for me in the last six years, a carefully orchestrated ikon at the end of an amateur performance: on Deptford High Street, suddenly among the goatfish and the jackfish, as you pass on your bicycle, the face of an Irish travelling woman who won the beauty competition at the Puck Fair in Killorglin in 1955.

List of Primary Works

In addition to referencing the editions of works from which excerpts are taken, I provide details of other, usually later, editions below, though this list is not exhaustive. Many of these later editions are facsimile reprints of the original books and some are still in print. The place of publication is the same as that of the original unless otherwise stated.

Barclay, Tom. *Memoirs and Medleys: The Autobiography of a Bottle-Washer* (Leicester: Edgar Backus, 1934; Coalville: Coalville Publishing, 1995, with an introduction by David Nash).

Binns, John. *Recollections of the Life of John Binns: twenty-nine years in Europe and fifty-three in the United States* (Philadelphia: Parry and Macmillan, 1854; Montana: Kessinger Publishing, 2007).

Blake, Jim. *Jim Blake's Tour from Clonave to London* (Dublin: M. H. Gill, 1867).

Bowen, Elizabeth. *Pictures and Conversations* (London: Allen Lane, 1975).

Boyle, John. *Galloway Street: Growing Up Irish in Scotland* (London: Doubleday, 2001).

Burn, James Dawson. *The Autobiography of a Beggar Boy* (London: William Tweedie, 1855; Europa Publications, 1978, edited with an introduction by David Vincent).

Cobbe, Frances Power. *The Life of Frances Power Cobbe* (London: Richard Bentley, 1894), 2 vols.

Collis, J. S. *An Irishman's England* (London: Cassell, 1937).

Collis, Robert. *The Silver Fleece: An Autobiography* (London: Thomas Nelson and Sons, 1936).

Conner, Rearden. *A Plain Tale from the Bogs* (London: John Miles, 1937).

Crowe, Robert. *The Reminiscences of Robert Crowe, the Octogenerian Tailor* (New York: n.p., n.d. [1902]).

Crowley, Elaine. *Technical Virgins* (Dublin: Lilliput Press, 1998).

Davys, Mary. *The Works of Mrs Davys: Consisting of plays, novels, poems, and familiar letters. Several of which never before publish'd. In two volumes* (London: H. Woodfall, 1725).

Denvir, John. *The Life Story of an Old Rebel* (Dublin: Sealy, Bryers & Walker, 1910; Shannon: Irish University Press, 1972, with an introduction by Leon Ó Broin).

Donnelly, Peter. *The Yellow Rock* (London: Eyre & Spottiswoode, 1950).

E., J. 'Life of an Irish Tailor, Written by Himself'. *The Commonwealth*, 18 April 1857.

Fagg, Michael. *The Life and Adventures of a Limb of the Law* (London: A. Hancock, 1836).

Fahy, Francis. 'Ireland in London – Reminiscences', National Library of Ireland, MS 11431. Published edn: Clare Hutton (ed.), 'Francis Fahy's "Ireland in London – Reminiscences" (1921)', in Wayne K. Chapman and Warwick Gould (eds), *Yeats's Collaborations. Yeats Annual No. 15: A Special Number* (Basingstoke: Palgrave Macmillan, 2002), pp. 233–80.

Figgis, Darrell. *A Chronicle of Jails* (Dublin: Talbot Press, 1917).

FitzGerald, Kevin. *With O'Leary in the Grave* (Salisbury: Michael Russell, 1986).

Foley, Alice. *A Bolton Childhood* (Manchester: Manchester University Extra-Mural Department, 1973).

Foley, Dónal. *Three Villages: An Autobiography* (Dublin: Egotist Press, 1977).

Gallagher, Patrick. *My Story* (Dungloe: Templecrone Co-operative Society, n.d. [1945], revd. edn; London: Jonathan Cape, 1939, with an introduction by Peadar O'Donnell).

Geldof, Bob, with Paul Vallely. *Is That It?* (London: Sidgwick & Jackson, 1986; Penguin, 1986; Pan Macmillan, 2005).

Hamilton, Elizabeth. *An Irish Childhood* (London: Chatto & Windus, 1963).

Hamish, Maureen. *Adventures of an Irish Girl at Home and Abroad* (Dublin: J. K. Mitchell, 1906).

Hammond, William. *Recollections of William Hammond, A Glasgow Hand-Loom Weaver* (Glasgow: 'Citizen' Press, 1904).

Hampson, Walter. 'Reminiscences of "Casey"'. *Forward*, 28 March – 31 October 1931 (24 October excepted).

Healy, John. *The Grass Arena: An Autobiography* (London: Faber & Faber, 1988; Kingpin, 2007; Penguin New Classics, 2008).

Hogan, Desmond. *The Edge of the City: A Scrapbook 1976–91* (London: Faber & Faber, 1993).

Jowitt, Jane. *Memoirs of Jane Jowitt, the Poor Poetess, Aged 74 Years, Written by Herself* (Sheffield: J. Pearce, 1844).

Keane, John B. *Self-Portrait* (Dublin: Mercier Press, 1964).

Keane, Mauyen. *Hello, Is It All Over?* (Dublin: Ababúna, 1984).

Keating, Joseph. *My Struggle for Life* (London: Simpkin, Marshall, Hamilton & Kent, 1916; Dublin: University College Dublin Press, 2005, with an introduction by Paul O'Leary).

McAloren, Margaret. 'The Wild Freshness of Morning'. Unpublished typescript.

Mac Amhlaigh, Dónall. *An Irish Navvy: The Diary of an Exile* (London: Routledge & Kegan Paul, 1964; Cork: Collins Press, 2003).

McCarthy, Justin. *The Story of an Irishman* (London: Chatto & Windus, 1904).

McGeown, Patrick. *Heat the Furnace Seven Times More* (London: Hutchinson, 1967).

MacGill, Patrick. *Children of the Dead End: The Autobiography of a Navvy* (London: Herbert Jenkins, 1914; Caliban Books, 1985, with an introduction by John Burnett; Edinburgh: Birlinn, 2005).

McGinn, Matt. *McGinn of the Calton: The Life and Works of Matt McGinn 1928–1977* (Glasgow: Glasgow District Libraries, 1987).

MacGowan, Michael. *The Hard Road to Klondike* (London: Routledge & Kegan Paul, 1962; Cork: Collins Press, 2003).

MacNeice, Louis. *The Strings Are False: An Unfinished Autobiography* (London: Faber & Faber, 1965).

MacStiofáin, Seán. *Memoirs of a Revolutionary* (London: Gordon Cremonesi, 1975).

Mangan, Owen Peter. 'Memoir', Northern Irish Public Record Office, T/3258/53/1.

Mullin, James. *The Story of a Toiler's Life* (Dublin and London: Maunsel & Roberts, 1921; Dublin: University College Dublin Press, 2000, with an introduction by Patrick Maume).

Naughton, Bill. *Saintly Billy: A Catholic Boyhood* (Oxford: Oxford University Press, 1988).

Neary, John. *Memories of the Long Distance Kiddies* (Australia: Tony Ross, n.d. [1994]).

O'Brien, George. *Out of Our Minds* (Belfast: Blackstaff Press, 1994).

O'Casey, Sean. *Rose and Crown* (London: Macmillan, 1952; included in *Mirror in my House*, 1956, 2 vols and *Autobiographies*, 1963, 2 vols).

O'Mara, Pat. *The Autobiography of a Liverpool Irish Slummy* (London: Martin Hopkinson, 1934; New York: Vanguard Press, 1933; as *The Autobiography of a Liverpool Slummy*, Liverpool: Bluecoat Press, n.d. [2007], with an introduction by Colin Wilkinson).

O'Neill, Ellen. *Extraordinary Confessions of a Female Pickpocket* (Preston: J. Drummond, 1850).

O'Neill, John. 'Fifty Years' Experience of an Irish Shoemaker in London'. *St Crispin: A Magazine for the Leather Trades*, May 1869 – February 1870.

Phelan, Jim. *The Name's Phelan: The First Part of the Autobiography of Jim Phelan* (London: Sidgwick & Jackson, 1948; Belfast: Blackstaff, 1993).

Pilkington, Laetitia. *Memoirs of Mrs Laetitia Pilkington, Wife to the Reverend Mr Matthew Pilkington, Written by Herself* (Dublin: Printed for the Author, 1748, vol. 2; London: George Routledge & Sons, 1928, with an introduction by Iris Barry; Athens: University of Georgia Press, 1997, 2 vols, edited with an introduction by A. C. Elias, Jr.)

Power, Richard. *Apple on the Treetop* (Dublin: Poolbeg, 1980).

Robb, Nesca A. *An Ulsterwoman in England, 1924–1941* (Cambridge: Cambridge University Press, 1942).

Smithson, Annie M. P. *Myself – and Others: An Autobiography* (Dublin: Talbot Press, 1944).

Stapleton, Michael. *The Threshold* (London: Hutchinson, 1958).

Sweeney, John. *At Scotland Yard: Being the Experiences during Twenty-Seven Years' Service of John Sweeney*, ed. Francis Richards (London: Grant Richards, 1904).

Thompson, Bonar. *Hyde Park Orator* (London: Jarrolds, 1934).

Trevor, William. *Excursions in the Real World* (London: Hutchinson, 1993; Penguin, 1994).

Walsh, John. *The Falling Angels: An Irish Romance* (London: Flamingo, 1999).

Yeats, William Butler. *Reveries over Childhood and Youth* (New York: Macmillan, 1916; revd. edn included in *Autobiographies*, 1955).

Select Bibliography

Anderson, Benedict. *Imagined Communities: Reflections on the Origin and Spread of Nationalism* (London: Verso, 1991).

Anthias, Floya. 'Evaluating "Diaspora": Beyond Ethnicity?', *Sociology*, vol. 32, no. 3 (1998), pp. 557–80.

Archibald, Douglas. 'Introduction'. William Trevor Special Issue. *Colby Quarterly*, vol. 38, no. 3 (September 2002), pp. 269–79.

Armitstead, Claire. 'My Life as a Story', *The Guardian Review*, 27 January 2001, p. 5.

Arnold, Matthew. *On The Study of Celtic Literature* (London: Smith, Elder, 1867).

Ayling, Ronald F. 'The Origin and Evolution of a Dublin Epic', in Robert G. Lowery (ed.), *Essays on Sean O'Casey's Autobiographies* (Basingstoke: Macmillan, 1981), pp. 1–34.

Boland, Eavan. *Collected Poems* (Manchester: Carcanet Press, 1995).

Bowden, Martha F. 'Mary Davys: self-presentation and the woman writer's reputation in the early eighteenth century', *Women's Writing*, vol. 3, no. 1 (1996), pp. 17–33.

——. 'Silences, Contradictions, and the Urge to Fiction: Reflections on Writing about Mary Davys', *Studies in the Literary Imagination*, vol. 36, no. 2 (Fall 2003), pp. 127–47.

Bowen, Elizabeth. 'Autobiography', in *Afterthought: Pieces about Writing* (London: Longmans, Green, 1962), pp. 199–204.

Brah, Avtar. *Cartographies of Diaspora: Contesting Identities* (London: Routledge, 1996).

Bruner, Jerome. 'The Autobiographical Process', in Robert Folkenflik (ed.), *The Culture of Autobiography* (California: Stanford University Press, 1993), pp. 38–56.

Burnett, John (ed.). *Destiny Obscure: Autobiographies of Childhood, Education and Family from the 1820s to the 1920s* (London: Routledge, 1994).

Burnett, John, Mayall, David and Vincent, David (eds). *The Autobiography of the Working Class: An Annotated Critical Bibliography*, 3 volumes (Brighton: Harvester, 1984–89).

Campbell, Sean. 'Beyond "Plastic Paddy": A Re-examination of the Second-Generation Irish in England', in Donald M. MacRaild (ed.), *The Great Famine and Beyond: Irish Migrants in Britain in the Nineteenth and Twentieth Centuries* (Dublin: Irish Academic Press, 2000), pp. 266–88.

Canavan, Bernard. 'Story-tellers and writers: Irish identity in emigrant labourers' autobiographies, 1870–1970', in Patrick O'Sullivan (ed.), *The Irish World Wide: The Creative Migrant* (Leicester: Leicester University Press, 1994), pp. 154–69.

Corcoran, Neil. *Elizabeth Bowen: The Enforced Return* (Oxford: Oxford University Press, 2004).

Cowley, Ultan. *The Men Who Built Britain: A History of the Irish Navvy* (Dublin: Wolfhound Press, 2001).

Cullen, Fintan. 'Erskine Nicol', in Jane Turner (ed.), *The Dictionary of Art* (London: Macmillan, 1996), vol. 23, pp. 106–07.

Dekker, Thomas. *The Second Part of The Honest Whore* (London: Elizabeth All-de, for Nathaniel Butter, 1630).

Doody, Margaret Anne. 'Swift Among the Women', *The Yearbook of English Studies*, vol. 18 (1988), pp. 68–92.

Dudley Edwards, Owen. 'Patrick MacGill and the making of a historical source: With a handlist of his works', *The Innes Review*, vol. 37, no. 2 (1986), pp. 73–99.

Eakin, Paul John. *Touching the World: Reference in Autobiography* (Princeton, NJ: Princeton University Press, 1992).

Ellmann, Maud. *Elizabeth Bowen: The Shadow Across the Page* (Edinburgh: Edinburgh University Press, 2003).

Felski, Rita. *Beyond Feminist Aesthetics: Feminist Literature and Social Change* (Cambridge, MA: Harvard University Press, 1989).

Fitzpatrick, David. '"A peculiar tramping people": The Irish in Britain, 1801–70', in W. E. Vaughan (ed.), *A New History of Ireland, Volume 5: Ireland Under the Union, I (1801–70)* (Oxford: Clarendon Press, 1989), pp. 623–60.

Foot, Michael. *Debts of Honour* (London: Davis Poynter, 1980).

Foster, R. F. *Paddy and Mr Punch: Connections in Irish and English History* (London: Penguin, 1995).

——. *W. B. Yeats: A Life. Volume 1: The Apprentice Mage* (Oxford: Oxford University Press, 1997).

——. *The Irish Story: Telling Tales and Making it Up in Ireland* (London: Allen Lane, 2001).

Giemza, Bryan. 'The Technique of Sorrow: Patrick MacGill and the American Slave Narrative', *New Hibernia Review/Iris Éireannach Nua*, vol. 7, no. 2 (Summer 2003), pp. 73–87.

Gramsci, Antonio. 'Justification of Autobiography (i)', in David Forgacs and Geoffrey Nowell-Smith (eds), *Selections from Cultural Writings* (London: Lawrence & Wishart, 1985), p. 132.

Gray, Nigel (ed.). *Writers Talking* (London: Caliban Books, 1989).

Greacen, Robert. *The Sash My Father Wore: An Autobiography* (Edinburgh: Mainstream, 1997).

Greenslade, Liam. 'The Blackbird Calls in Grief: Colonialism, Health and Identity Among Irish Immigrants in Britain', in Jim Mac Laughlin (ed.), *Location and Dislocation in Contemporary Irish Society: Emigration and Irish Identities* (Cork: Cork University Press, 2001), pp. 36–60.

Gusdorf, George. 'Conditions and Limits of Autobiography', trans. James Olney, in James Olney (ed.), *Autobiography: Essays Theoretical and Critical* (Princeton, NJ: Princeton University Press, 1980), pp. 28–48.

Hackett, Nan. *XIX Century British Working-Class Autobiographies: An Annotated Bibliography* (New York: AMS, 1985).

——. 'A Different Form of "Self": Narrative Style in British Nineteenth-Century Working-Class Autobiography', *Biography*, vol. 12, no. 3 (1989), pp. 208–26.

Hamilton, Elizabeth. *I Stay in the Church* (London: Vision Press, 1973).

Harris, Ruth-Ann M. *The Nearest Place That Wasn't Ireland: Early Nineteenth-Century Irish Labour Migration* (Ames, IO: Iowa State University Press, 1994).

Harte, Liam. '"Somewhere Beyond England and Ireland": Narratives of "Home" in Second-Generation Irish Autobiography', *Irish Studies Review*, vol. 11, no. 3 (2003), pp. 293–305.

Hartigan, Maureen and Hickman, Mary J. (eds). *The History of the Irish in Britain: A Bibliography* (London: Irish in Britain History Centre, 1986).

Hogan, Desmond. *Larks' Eggs: New and Selected Stories* (Dublin, Lilliput Press, 2005).

Hooper, Glenn (ed.). *The Tourist's Gaze: Travellers to Ireland 1800–2000* (Cork: Cork University Press, 2001).

Hutton, Clare (ed.). 'Francis Fahy's "Ireland in London – Reminiscences" (1921)', in Wayne K. Chapman and Warwick Gould (eds), *Yeats's Collaborations. Yeats Annual No. 15: A Special Number* (Basingstoke: Palgrave Macmillan, 2002), pp. 233–80.

Kenneally, Michael. *Portraying the Self: Sean O'Casey and the Art of Autobiography* (Gerrards Cross: Colin Smythe, 1988).

Kenny, Kevin. 'Diaspora and Comparison: The Global Irish as a Case Study', *Journal of American History*, vol. 90, no. 1 (June 2003), pp. 134–62.

Kiberd, Declan. *Inventing Ireland: The Literature of the Modern Nation* (London: Jonathan Cape, 1995).

Kilfeather, Siobhán. 'Beyond the Pale: Sexual Identity and National Identity in Early Irish Fiction', *Critical Matrix*, vol. 2, no. 4 (1986), pp. 1–31.

Lee, J. J. *Ireland 1912–1985. Politics and Society* (Cambridge: Cambridge University Press, 1989).

Mac Amhlaigh, Dónall. 'Documenting the fifties', *Irish Studies in Britain*, no. 14 (Spring/Summer 1989), pp. 7–13.

McCrum, Robert. 'The vanishing man', *The Observer Review*, 14 November 2004, p. 1.

McGeown, Patrick. 'The Wordster', *New Statesman*, 28 May 1965, pp. 839–40.

MacRaild, Donald M. *Irish Migrants in Modern Britain, 1750–1922* (Basingstoke: Macmillan, 1999).

Matthews, William. *British Autobiographies: An Annotated Bibliography of British Autobiographies Published or Written Before 1951* (Berkeley and Los Angeles: University of California Press, 1955).

Maume, Patrick. 'James Mullin, the Poor Scholar: A Self-made Man from Carleton's Country', *Irish Studies Review*, vol. 7, no. 1 (1999), pp. 29–39.

Miller, David. *Don't Mention the War: Northern Ireland, Propaganda and the Media* (London: Pluto Press, 1994).

Miskell, Louise. '"The heroic Irish doctor?": Irish immigrants in the medical profession in nineteenth-century Wales', in Oonagh Walsh (ed.), *Ireland Abroad: Politics and Professions in the Nineteenth Century* (Dublin: Four Courts Press, 2003), pp. 82–94.

Moran, Gerard. '"A Passage to Britain": Seasonal Migration and Social Change in the West of Ireland, 1870–1890', *Saothar*, vol. 13 (1988), pp. 22–31.

Murphy, James H. 'Between Drawing-Room and Barricade: The Autobiographies and Nationalist Fictions of Justin McCarthy', in Bruce Stewart (ed.), *Hearts and Minds: Irish Culture and Society under the Act of Union* (Gerrards Cross: Colin Smythe: 2002), pp. 111–20.

Murray, Christopher. *Sean O'Casey: Writer at Work, A Biography* (Dublin: Gill & Macmillan, 2004).

Murray, Tony. 'Curious streets: Diaspora, displacement and transgression in Desmond Hogan's London Irish narratives', *Irish Studies Review*, vol. 14, no. 2 (2006), pp. 239–53.

Naughton, Bill. *On the Pig's Back: An Autobiographical Excursion* (Oxford: Oxford University Press, 1987).

O'Connor, Frank. *My Father's Son* (Syracuse, NY: Syracuse University Press, 1999).

O'Connor, Joseph. 'Introduction', in Dermot Bolger (ed.), *Ireland in Exile* (Dublin: New Island, 1993), pp. 11–18.

O'Day, Alan. 'Varieties of anti-Irish behaviour in Britain, 1846–1922', in Panikos Panayi (ed.), *Racial Violence in Britain, 1840–1950* (Leicester: Leicester University Press, 1993), pp. 26–43.

Ó Háinle, Cathal. 'Aspects of Autobiography in Modern Irish', in Ronald Black, William Gillies and Roibeard Ó Maolalaigh (eds), *Celtic Connections: Proceedings of the 10th International Congress of Celtic Studies* (East Linton: Tuckwell Press, 1999), pp. 360–76.

O'Leary, Paul. *Immigration and Integration: The Irish in Wales, 1798–1922* (Cardiff: University of Wales Press, 2000).

——. 'Introduction' to *My Struggle for Life* by Joseph Keating (Dublin: University College Dublin Press, 2005), pp. ix–xxx.

Pooley, Colin. 'From Londonderry to London: Identity and Sense of Place for a Protestant Northern Irish Woman in the 1930s', in MacRaild (ed.), *The Great Famine and Beyond*, pp. 189–213.

Poovey, Mary. 'Curing the "Social Body" in 1832: James Phillips Kay and the Irish in Manchester', *Gender & History*, vol. 5, no. 2 (Summer 1993), pp. 196–211.

Porter, Bernard. *Plots and Paranoia: A History of Political Espionage in Britain 1790–1988* (London: Routledge, 1992).

Priestley, J. B. *An English Journey* (London: William Heinemann in association with Victor Gollancz, 1934).

Rooney, Brendan. 'The Irish Exhibition at Olympia, 1888', *Irish Architectural and Decorative Studies*, vol. 1 (1998), pp. 101–19.

Rose, Jonathan. *The Intellectual Life of the British Working Classes* (London: Yale University Press, 2001).

Ryan, Mark. *Fenian Memories* (Dublin: M. H. Gill, 1945).

Smith, Sidonie. 'Construing Truths in Lying Mouths: Truthtelling in Women's Autobiography', *Studies in the Literary Imagination*, vol. 23, no. 2 (1990), pp. 145–63.

Stallworthy, Jon. *Louis MacNeice* (London: Faber & Faber, 1995).

Swan, Sean. 'MacStiofáin, Sean (1928–2001)', *Oxford Dictionary of National Biography*, online edition, Oxford University Press, Jan. 2005 [http://www.oxforddnb.com/view/article/75880, accessed 5 Sept. 2007].

Swift, Roger (ed.). *Irish Migrants in Britain, 1815–1914: A Documentary History* (Cork: Cork University Press, 2002).

——. 'Heroes or Villains?: The Irish, Crime and Disorder in Victorian England', *Albion*, vol. 29, no. 3 (1998), pp. 399–421.

——. 'Thomas Carlyle, Chartism, and the Irish in Early Victorian England', *Victorian Literature and Culture*, vol. 29, no. 1 (2001), pp. 67–83.

Thompson, Lynda M. *The 'Scandalous Memoirists': Constantia Phillips, Laetitia Pilkington and the Shame of 'Public Fame'* (Manchester: Manchester University Press, 2000).

Townend, Paul. '"No Imperial Privilege": Justin McCarthy, Home Rule, and Empire', *Éire-Ireland*, vol. 42, nos. 1 and 2 (Spring/Summer 2007), pp. 201–28.

Trevor, William. 'A clearer vision of Ireland', *The Guardian*, 23 April 1992, p. 25.

Walsh, Oonagh. '"Her Irish Heritage": Annie M. P. Smithson and Auto/Biography', *Études Irlandaises*, vol. 23, no. 1 (1998), pp. 27–42.

Walter, Bronwen. *Outsiders Inside: Whiteness, place and Irish women* (London: Routledge, 2001).

Wills, Clair. *That Neutral Island: A Cultural History of Ireland During the Second World War* (London: Faber & Faber, 2007).

Wilson, A. N. 'John Stewart Collis', *The Spectator*, 10 March 1984, p. 13.

Wright, David G. *Yeats's Myth of Self: A Study of the Autobiographical Prose* (Dublin: Gill & Macmillan, 1987).

Index